CHARLES DE FOUCAULD

JEAN-JACQUES ANTIER

CHARLES DE FOUCAULD

SECOND EDITION

With an Introduction by
DAVID PINAULT

Translated by Julia Shirek Smith

IGNATIUS PRESS   SAN FRANCISCO

Originally published under the title
Charles de Foucauld
by Jacques Antier
Copyright © 1997 Editions Perrin

Cover photograph:
Fr. Charles de Foucauld in Morocco
© Harlingue-Viollet, Paris

Cover design by Roxanne Mei Lum

ISBN 978-1-62164-515-3 (PB)
ISBN 978-1-64229-224-4 (eBook)

Library of Congress Control Number: 2021948172
Printed in the United States of America ∞

For Prior Christian de Chergé.

For Brothers

Luc Dochier,
Christophe Lebreton,
Bruno Lemarchand,
Michel Fleury,
Célestin Ringeard,
and Paul Favre-Miville,
Cistercian monks of Notre-Dame de l'Atlas in Tibhirine (Algeria).

On May 21, 1996, they gave their lives, as had Charles de Foucauld
in Tamanrasset in 1916, because they believed in love and freedom.
They have found Love and Freedom.
They dwell in the light.

"And I shall be able, if it pleases God, to gaze deep into the eyes of the
Father and contemplate with him his children of Islam as he sees them—
radiant with the glory of Christ, the fruit of his Passion, and invested with
the gift of the Spirit, whose secret joy will always be in establishing communion and restoring similarities, while playing with the differences."

— Spiritual testament of Father de Chergé

CONTENTS

INTRODUCTION

Charles de Foucauld:
A Much-Needed Martyr for Our Time

BY DAVID PINAULT

Blessed Charles de Foucauld—intrepid witness to the Christian faith; hermit, missionary, and martyr—has been in the news just lately. In May 2020, Pope Francis validated the second of two miracles attributed to Foucauld's intercession, thereby clearing the way for his eventual canonization.[1] (Pope Benedict XVI had approved Foucauld's beatification in 2005.)

But his pending sainthood has generated some controversy.[2] Critics complain that Foucauld was no simple Gospel preacher, that he was a colonialist, a tool of imperialism, a French patriot who secretly helped his nation's military while leading souls to Christ. To judge from the indignation with which such complaints are delivered, one might think long-suppressed scandals have just been revealed. But there's no secret here. Foucauld himself would have cheerfully accepted the labels "patriotic" and "colonialist" (though he challenged French authorities for their own shortcomings in colonial policy).

Of much greater interest, to me, is that, although he died more than a century ago, Foucauld faced—and overcame—spiritual obstacles akin to those that Christians face in this 21st century of ours. I think that he provides us something precious now largely lost to sight.

A simple sketch of his life can help us appreciate the guidance he still offers us today.

Born in Strasbourg in 1858, Charles de Foucauld was raised in a devout Catholic family with a distinguished history of service to the Faith. His ancestors included a Crusader slain on an Egyptian battlefield, fighting alongside Saint Louis; a courtier who supported Joan of Arc in her struggle to free France from English rule during the Hundred Years' War; and a bishop who was killed for his faith during the revolutionary Terror of 1792.

But the young Foucauld came of age during much different secularist, post-Darwin times. Roiling France were new currents all too recognizable in our own day: "scientific" atheism; materialist agnosticism; and a skepti-

---

[1] Hannah Brockhaus, "Pope Francis Will Name Charles de Foucauld a Saint," Catholic News Agency, May 27, 2020.
[2] Claire Lesegretain, "Historians Troubled by Upcoming Canonization of Charles de Foucauld," La Croix International, July 13, 2020.

cism about traditional social structures, coupled with a mistrust of the Church and her hierarchy. Foucauld's schoolteachers did little to help; in later years he remembered them, ruefully, as "impartial" and unable to mount a cogent defense of Catholicism against the anti-religious sentiments then so prevalent throughout Europe. "Young people need to be taught," he remarked in later years, "not by those who are impartial, but by believing, saintly souls" (p. 31, below).

As a cavalry cadet at the renowned military academy of Saint-Cyr, Foucauld acquired a reputation as a ladies' man, bonbon connoisseur, and party-hearty hedonist. The classroom and the parade-ground drill both bored him. Mood-swings and melancholy had him in their grip.

The first step in what he later remembered as his "reversion" to Christianity was taken in response to a declaration of jihad in French Algeria. A *marabout* (dervish preacher) named Bou Amama had proclaimed a "holy war" against foreign unbelievers there. Foucauld's regiment was dispatched to North Africa for combat duty, and here—to his own surprise—his life began to acquire purpose, a focus. He loved the stimulus of danger and risk. The discipline of desert treks and wind-swept patrols steadied his errant thoughts. He learned to care for the soldiers under his command. (At one oasis-stop his men had nothing to drink but well-water that tasted of mud and salt. He earned their thanks by passing round a generous bottle of rum he kept tucked in his saddlebag.)

And there was Africa itself—dunes glimpsed at dawn; gazelles in a silent sandscape; horizons arching up to the vast vault of the sky. "A drunkenness that has nothing to do with alcohol," was how Foucauld's colleague Hubert Lyautey put it, "an intoxication of sun, light, and bliss" (p. 60, below). For Foucauld, these sensations amounted to glimmering hints of the Transcendent. Such things appealed to the aesthete in him (as they did to the many painter-pilgrims of the Orientalist school of art).

But with the jihad suppressed, he soon found army life again too dull. Yet he had no desire to leave Africa. He resigned from the military and became an explorer. He chose the sultanate of Morocco as his realm of activity.

At that time, in 1882, Morocco's sultan controlled only a sprinkling of cities in the north. The country was quasi-anarchic and largely lawless; outsiders of any kind—especially *Ifranj* (Christians from dreaded Europe)— were fair game for roadside plunder. Foucauld proposed for himself a solo reconnaissance trip, a surreptitious surveying and mapping of every site and path he found—a project dismissed as foolhardy by his friends.

But they gave him good advice: *To survive such a venture, go incognito, present yourself as someone innocuous, non-threatening.* Perhaps as an Arab peddler? *No, such a disguise would fail. . . .* Foucauld decided to travel as an itinerant Russian Jewish rabbi: unarmed, educated, second-class in status yet nonetheless tolerated as a *dhimmi* (a non-Muslim "person of the Book", despised but allowed to retain his identity as a member of an Abrahamic tradition).

To prepare himself, Foucauld spent many months at the public library in French Algiers. There he studied Hebrew and Arabic and sought out travelers with knowledge of the "realm" he had chosen to explore—geographers, historians, soldiers. There too he befriended a Moroccan Jewish merchant, Mardochee Abi Serour, who agreed to be his companion and guide.

For nearly a year, the two traversed Morocco on foot. Foucauld's notes detail the difficulties. Miserable campsites one night; sumptuous hospitality the next. Robbery at the hands of supposed bodyguards; extortion, threats of exposure, threats of death. For a certain kind of man, life lived at risk means a life lived in full; and Foucauld liked it. He found himself meeting with two types of men—those who would betray him, or knife him, for a fistful of francs; and those who would risk their own lives for his—as several did—out of friendship. He never forgot how intensely such an existence could be felt.

The result of these travels was a much-admired book, *Reconnaissance au Maroc*, which brought him admission to the world-renowned Geographical Society of Paris, and a gold medal awarded by the Society in recognition of his efforts. His future as a celebrity explorer seemed assured.

Yet his time in North Africa had earned him something more precious than gold medals. Jean-Jacques Antier (author of the book you have before you now) quotes from a letter Foucauld sent to a friend in which he sums up his own evaluation of his travels: "Islam has produced in me a profound upheaval. Observing this faith and these souls living with God as a continual presence has allowed me to glimpse something greater and more true than worldly occupations" (p. 93, below). In the end, Islam itself did not draw him; but it opened to him a Reality larger than the day-to-day.

Antier ponders Foucauld's writings from this moment in his life (and one of the many strengths of this biography is Antier's extensive use of Foucauld's correspondence), summarizing the young wanderer's spiritual condition: "Who could quench his thirst for the absolute, which felt to him like a deepening void, a chasm, a summons?" (p. 85, below). This "summons" led the be-medaled voyager back to Christianity.

My own Arabic and Islamic studies have led me—a lifelong Catholic— to a strong sympathy with Charles de Foucauld. Living in Muslim societies has helped deepen my own self-understanding and strong sense of identity as a Catholic Christian. (Sitting in tea-shops, being quizzed by Muslim friends on the Crucifixion and the Trinity, led me to reflect deeply on doctrines I might easily have taken for granted.) And my study of the Koranic Jesus (who is honored in Islam as one of Allah's prophets) has sharpened my appreciation for the Jesus known to Christians through the Bible.

The Koran denies that Jesus is divine or the "Son of God". It denies that He ever died on the Cross or rose from the dead. Moreover, the Koranic Christ shows little emotion and is never portrayed as suffering in any way. Whereas, the Christ in whom I put my faith is the God-made-Man who has chosen to become vulnerable. He chose to experience fully the sufferings that afflict all caught up in the human condition. And these sufferings are fully part of His eternal existence, as attested by the post-Resurrection scars on His risen body, and by His status as "the Lamb slain from the foundation of the world" (Rev 13:8).

In Foucauld's case, his experience with Islam not only renewed his commitment to Catholicism but also awakened a sense of spiritual vocation. These changes led to his ordination as a priest and his life's mission as a witness to Christianity in the land of his earlier military exploits: French Algeria.

The Algeria in which Foucauld labored was a land of predatory tribalism and slave-raids. Antier sums up the situation: "The people of the north, Arab and Tuareg, considered the south with its blacks their traditional preserve of slaves" (p. 183, below). France had abolished slavery after its conquest of the region, but French authority never extended far beyond the military outposts scattered sparsely in the vast Sahara. To maintain alliances with local tribes, colonial officials sometimes chose to overlook incidents of tribal violence and enslavement. Foucauld, as a believer in France's "civilizing mission" in its colonies, criticized the French government whenever it fell short of its own ideals, especially the imperative for the abolishment of slavery in Algeria. He himself ransomed slaves and helped provide employment for them as freedmen.

Such actions illustrate Foucauld's approach to missionary endeavors. He could have rested snug and secure in a Christian parish in Algiers, within sight of the Mediterranean. Instead he chose to make his home in the impoverished deep south, in the village called Tamanrasset, far from any French military base. Rather than preach the Gospel or exhort the villagers to convert to Christianity, he preferred to live among them as a neighbor and friend. This meant helping them with what they needed most in their daily lives: food, water, shelter, and protection against slave-traders from the north.

Foucauld's priestly ministry encompassed not only native Algerians but also members of the Légion Étrangère who garrisoned the region's military fortresses. Whenever he visited the Foreign Legion headquarters at Beni Abbès, near the Algerian-Moroccan frontier, he said Mass for the soldiers on duty at the fort. (The congregation sometimes included local Muslim onlookers who were drawn by his manifest holiness; they called him "the Christian marabout.")

Foucauld biographer Michel Carrouges evokes these worship rituals: "Each morning, very early, before dawn, he would celebrate Mass in the absolute silence of the desert. 'Anyone who's never attended one of his Masses,' recalled an old soldier who used to act as server at the liturgy, 'has no idea what a Mass can be. Whenever he [Father Foucauld] pronounced the *Domine non sum dignus* ["Lord, I am not worthy"], it was with such intensity that people felt like breaking into tears along with him.' " [3]

This "intensity" is related to a key element of Foucauld's inner spiritual life: his devotion to the Real Presence of Christ in the Blessed Sacrament. Wherever he resided, in his wandering ministry, whether in Tamanrasset or at some Foreign Legion outpost, he kept a solitary nighttime vigil in a mudbrick chapel, praying before a small monstrance set upon the altar. The sense of divine intimacy he felt is evident in a meditation he jotted in one of his notebooks: "My Father, my Beloved; you who are there, a few feet from me, under the appearance of the Host, you are the Supreme Beauty. All created beauty, all beauty of Nature, the beauty of the sunset, of the sea lying like a mirror beneath the blue sky . . . the beauty of a rare soul reflected in a beautiful face, all these beauties are but the palest reflection of yours, my God." [4]

The life Foucauld chose for himself was hard. Mistrust and lack of understanding, theft, and threats of ambush: such things assailed him as he worked to gain the confidence of local populations. Worse were the occasional midnight assaults by what he called "unbearable thoughts" from within, a writhing remorse for his past sins. "All that sustained him," Antier tells us, were "the celebration of the Eucharist and the adoration of the Blessed Sacrament exposed." This is what nourished Foucauld, kept him going. A visitor recalled his daily ritual: "kneeling before the Blessed Sacrament, adoring, pleading, thanking, atoning" (see pp. 248, 252, below).

Despite his self-imposed discipline of service to others, this missionary-monk was very much a hermit by temperament. Whenever possible, he chose to sleep in his chapel at the conclusion of his nighttime vigil, curled up at the base of the altar, before the tabernacle—"like a dog," as he himself wrote in one of his letters, "at the feet of his master" (p. 188, below). Frequently solitary in his prayer-life, yes, but by no means alone: for he felt Christ's radiant love in the sacramental Presence.

[3] Michel Carrouges, *Charles de Foucauld: Explorateur Mystique* (Paris: Les Éditions du Cerf, 1954), p. 170.
[4] Robert Ellsberg, ed., *Charles de Foucauld: Writings* (Maryknoll, N.Y.: Orbis Books, 1999), pp. 107-8.

After he died (murdered by jihadists in a raid on his Tamanrasset hermit-age in December 1916), French officers who came upon the death-scene days later discovered that the monstrance containing the consecrated Host was lying on the ground where it had been flung by the attackers, near the spot where Foucauld had knelt so often to keep company with his Friend.

I thought of this man—ex-soldier, ex-bon vivant, fervent servant of God—as I read about a letter sent to the bishops in September 2020 by Cardinal Robert Sarah, prefect of the Congregation for Divine Worship and the Sacraments. The Cardinal acknowledged that the Covid-19 pan-demic had generated a need for televised and online forms of worship but also stated that remote on-screen liturgies were no substitute for personal attendance at Mass and the in-person reception of the consecrated Body and Blood of Christ. "As soon as is possible," the Cardinal declared, "we must return to the Eucharist . . . with an increased desire to meet the Lord, to be with Him, to receive Him, and to bring Him to our brothers and sisters." [5] I'm sure Foucauld would have concurred. His life and good works were made possible by his devotion to the Real Presence.

This, then, is the twofold legacy left us by the hermit-priest of Taman-rasset: *love of God*, manifested in worship of the Eucharistic Christ; and *love of country*, expressed in service to his nation and to everyone with whom his nation came in contact. Personal piety and patriotism—in our age of ready pleasures and distractions, such things have fallen out of fashion. But given the many challenges we face in our day, we need to rediscover those sure sources of spiritual strength. Father Charles de Foucauld can show us the way.

[5] Cardinal Sarah, "Let Us Return to the Eucharist with Joy" (Sept. 14, 2020).

PREFACE

"So you'll be doing yet another Foucauld?" asked the Canadian Little Brother of Jesus I had run into at the Cistercian guesthouse in La Coudre. His pleasant smile belied any nasty innuendo; he was totally incapable of malice.

I replied with the childlike thoughtlessness that has always governed my life: "It's not to write yet another Foucauld, it's to add yet another plus to what we know of Foucauld."

To justify myself further, I continued: "Besides, I was asked to do it."

His smile grew broader, and he said emphatically: "Well, then, on with it!"

With that liberating remark, I suddenly felt filled with the strength I had been lacking. I threw myself into the "sources", into archives and books, as if diving into the ocean.

Very soon, I had sunk. Charles de Foucauld left some seven thousand letters and more than twelve thousand pages of writings, sacred and profane, few of them intended for publication, which did not help matters. As I was about to succumb beneath this documentation, I received a life raft in the form of a sentence from Father Peyriguère, Father de Foucauld's first disciple: "His life is more he himself than what he said and wrote." It was a flash of light.

The real work started. Arduous and full of pitfalls, underbrush, and platitudes. The most difficult task lay in toppling, respectfully, the conventional, brightly painted statuary wrought by the purveyors of religious imagery, who had done the same thing with Thérèse Martin and other "servants of God" in the name of edifying the masses. That done, only one conclusion could be reached: his life remained a mystery, since the witnesses who had actually known and understood him wrote little or nothing on Foucauld.

Then, from beneath the clichés surfaced the freshness, the simplicity, and the intensity of Brother Charles' Christianity. Through a life whose ups and downs could have come out of a novel, there flowed an inexhaustible spring, like the miraculous one sometimes seen in the starkest desert after long and patient digging.

And suddenly the unchanging jewel of faith began to shine like a beacon.

Being a man of faith myself—of little faith, to use the words of Jesus— and a man of doubt, also, and of contradictions, an inept but impassioned observer of the spiritual evolution of our time, I have tried to understand what, for me, distinguishes most clearly Charles Foucauld's life: faith, faith in God. A subject that seems to me all the more important in an age in which skepticism corrodes, churches are emptying, religious vocations are growing rare, promises are no longer kept, and only a small minority of faithful seek the sacraments. At the same time, a disturbing religious fundamentalism is on the increase worldwide, fostering intolerance and hate; an anguished cry for God (but which one?) is being heard; and our society, weakened by the lack of moral guidelines that—along with faith—once gave organized religion its stability, is anxiously examining itself and seeking the how and why of our miserable little planet.

Why did the adolescent Charles de Foucauld lose his faith in spite of living in a right-thinking milieu, where he had the benefit of the finest educators, notably the Jesuits? Why and how did he return to the faith so dramatically at the age of twenty-eight? Why did he persevere until his tragic death at fifty-eight, although his life was a failure on the human level and on the apostolic level? These are the things I have tried to understand.

And, along the way, I have tried to understand, too, why the Catholic Church has not yet beatified this figure. Indeed, his uniqueness makes him unclassifiable, yet he shows that devotion to the "heroic virtues" which Dominican theologian Yves Congar associates with Saint Thérèse of Lisieux, when he mentions "the beacons lit by God on the threshold of the atomic century".

Brother Charles' apparent contradictions probably distress those intellectuals whose passion is order and logic; similarly, his asceticism terrifies the ordinary Christian in an era when the supermarket is worshipped just as the peoples of Israel once worshipped the golden calf.

And what if Charles de Foucauld was a kind of mutant, a member of a very rare species, taking *to the letter* the message that an unknown God sent us two thousand years ago through his Son? To the letter: Is that possible? But if so, then the wish of Henri Bergson, a near convert, would come true: "If only we knew for certain that God existed and that he loved us, we would dance with joy." And we would take to the letter the message of his Son, whose key word is love.

Dance with joy, that is what Marthe Robin also expected to do when she arrived in "heaven", when she "saw God", at last!

Charles de Foucauld encountered God already here on earth, under the vaulted ceiling of Saint-Augustin and deep in the Sahara. "Indescribably happy to be an insignificant bearer of fruit, a tiny spring flowing underground", writes Georges Bordonove. Foucauld loved God without reserve, to the point of saying: "He who loves wishes to imitate; that is the secret of my life." So he was faithful to Christ until death. And now I shall attempt to tell the story of that faith; for there exists here on earth no adventure more beautiful than that of giving oneself to Love, unreservedly and irrevocably.

NB All conversations in the text are based on authentic documents (correspondence, sacred and profane writings), a list of which can be found at the end of the book.

ACKNOWLEDGMENTS

I wish to thank the following for their kind assistance:

The family of Charles de Foucauld: Count and Countess Charles de Foucauld, Madame Charles de Blic, the Marquis de Forbin, Anne de Collongue.

General Michel de Suremain, president of Amitiés Charles de Foucauld, and Clotilde de Foucauld, vice-president.

Bishop Maurice Bouvier, postulator for the cause of beatification, and Bishop Pasquale Macchi.

The father abbot, Dom Pierre-Marie Fayolle, and Dom Claudius Valour, both from Notre-Dame-des-Neiges. Mother Prioress Ines-Mary from the headquarters of the Little Sisters of Jesus in Rome, Sister Annie and Sister Annette de Jésus. The Little Brothers Sylvain (Canada) and Antoine (Tamanrasset). Sister Marie-Claire.

France's national library; the city libraries of Cannes and Le Cannet. The library of the Cistercians at La Coudre.

My publisher, François-Xavier de Vivie, who initiated this project; his successor, Xavier de Bartillat; Christiane Fabretti, Isabelle Chanteur, Thérèse-Marie Mahé, Cécile d'Humières, and Patrick Mérienne.

Henri-Louis Roche, head of the Paris publishing house Nouvelle Cité; he deserves great credit for publishing Charles de Foucauld's religious writings in their entirety, along with his notebooks, a total of sixteen volumes, with an introduction by Bishop Jacqueline; Monsieur Roche has allowed me to quote from these works. I also thank the following publishers: Plon, Le Seuil, Grasset, DDB, Le Cerf, SOS, Arthaud, and Éditions du Chalet.

My colleagues Jean-François Six, Marguerite Castillon du Perron, and Hugues Didier. Philosopher Jean Guitton.

Yvette Antier, and my nephew Bertrand Lépinoy, of the "Charles de Foucauld" class, at the École de Cavalerie de Saumur, 1978.

For illustrations, we thank the Foucauld, Blic, and Forbin families, the Little Sisters of Jesus in Rome, the Abbaye Notre-Dame-des-Neiges, *Cahiers de Charles de Foucauld*, and Transacphot in Cannes.

J-J. A.

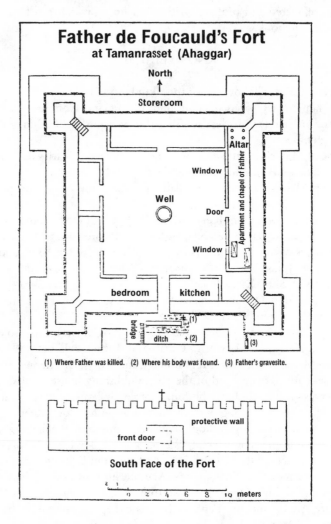

Father de Foucauld's Fort
at Tamanrasset (Ahaggar)

North

Storeroom

Altar

Apartment and chapel of Father

Window

Well

Door

Window

bedroom

kitchen

bridge

ditch

+ (1)

+ (2)

(3)

(1) Where Father was killed.   (2) Where his body was found.   (3) Father's gravesite.

protective wall

front door

South Face of the Fort

0   2   4   6   8   10 meters

Sketch of Father de Foucauld's fort in Tamanrasset, by Second Lieutenant Béjot of the Touat Company, published by R. de Segonzac in *Bulletin de l'Afrique française*, 1918.

I

Tortured Childhood

Brother Charles awakened. He was in total darkness. The alarm clock had not yet rung. The hermit shifted his old body aching with rheumatism and sat up on the sheepskin covering the sand. He shivered in his long white tunic. Winter nights were always cool in Tamanrasset, 4,640 feet above sea level. Through the doorway of his room, Brother Charles saw the stars twinkling, and the familiar sight turned him toward contemplation and a state of pure joy.

The strident sound of the alarm snatched him from his thoughts. 3:30 A.M. Groping, his hand searched the ground for the metallic object. Once the awful signal had been shut off, blessed silence reigned again. Brother Charles could have stayed nestled there for hours, at the feet of the Beloved, contemplating the inner light that filled him.

He rose from the bed, fastened a leather belt around his waist, slipped sandals onto his bare feet, and lit the little paraffin candle stuck to his desk, a table built from packing cases.

The meager light of men replaced the inner light, a painful snuffing out, an agonizing recall to humanity. This was no longer eternity, but December 1, 1916, in Tamanrasset, a less than prosperous farming community where fifty or so poor blacks struggled along under the constant threat from *rezzous* (organized bands of pillagers). And he, Charles de Foucauld, born in Strasbourg, September 15, 1858, was poorest of them all.

The bedroom-office in the fort (not yet known as "the *bordj*") was long and narrow, six by thirty feet, with walls of straw and mud. Papers cluttered the table that served as a desk. Along one wall, boards held a hundred or more books, a treasure trove. Two rickety chairs attempted to stand upright in the sand.

Brother Charles stepped out in the courtyard to perform his ablutions. Thick walls, sixteen feet high, enclosed the forty-five-square-foot area. The light of the stars fell on this austere courtyard, whose only feature was the well in the center. Brother Charles walked to the well and raised its protective cover, a board lined with sheet metal. He took the iron bucket, lowered it thirty feet on the rope, and brought up fresh, pure water for washing his face and lips.

As happened every morning, when he faced the harsh reality of the world, his only certainty was failure: he remained alone. Despite his efforts, no companion, no brother had joined him in this isolated spot, Algeria's Ahaggar Massif deep in the desert of the Sahara. No one had wished to share the joy of abandonment in the Lord. For fifteen years no reply had come to his voice crying out in the desert. He had failed. And that was as it should be.

From this bitter experience arose a certain delight that stemmed from his identification with the Beloved, he too forsaken by the Father and by man, rejected by his own, and nailed to the cross of the rebellious slave. Jesus of Nazareth! He, Brother Charles, formerly Viscount de Foucauld, ex-officer of the French Army, had been completely free to choose. His choice: *abjection* through loving. The abjection, poverty, and failure that were a daily part of his miserable earthly life did not count in comparison with the mystical union joining him to the Whole. And therein lay the daily paradox of his strange, impassioned existence.

Brother Charles took a handkerchief from his pocket and dried his face and beard. He was short (about five feet, four inches), balding, and fifty-eight years old, although his wrinkled, worn face made him look seventy. He hid his skinny body under a wretched tunic of frayed white cotton. Poorly shaven, with no concern for elegance, almost toothless, with a scanty gray beard and mustache hastily trimmed with no mirror, hooked nose, face ravaged by excessive asceticism, he might have inspired pity had it not been for the light in his brown eyes. His gaze was sharp and penetrating, expressive and gentle at the same time. He had the face of an ascetic, which was illuminated at times by an inner light, a supernatural understanding, and an infinite kindness.

He returned to the bedroom-office, took the candle, and headed to the rear of the room, where he lifted the curtain closing off the area. The light revealed the world's most wretched chapel, a few square feet between four walls plastered with mud, a floor of bare sand, and no seats. In the back, against a wall, the altar, a single board on four stakes stuck in the sand. On the altar, the wooden tabernacle, which contained the "Holy Store", the consecrated Host, Body of Christ.

His dazzled look came to rest on the wall behind the altar, where on a canvas held up by nails, the Christ he had painted was fixing him with a solemn stare, which seemed to say: "It is not for nothing that I have loved you."

Brother Charles knelt on the sand, and his fervent voice rose in the night:

> Heavenly splendor
> Light born of light

Before the creation of the universe
You shone in the darkness.

After Matins and Lauds, which he recited in Latin, Brother Charles opened a small cupboard holding liturgical paraphernalia and set out the objects for Mass. He donned his vestments and climbed to the altar, just as if it had been the master altar of the church of Saint-Augustin in Paris or even Notre-Dame Cathedral. His face was radiant. He murmured:

"*Introibo ad altare Dei*. . . . I shall approach the altar of God, the God who gladdened my youth."

Again, the great breath of the Holy Spirit uplifted him. He surrendered to it.

When Mass was over, Brother Charles curled up on the sand at the foot of the altar, his mind elsewhere. He let himself be carried away and floated freely on an ocean of light. It was not yet 5 A.M. Night remained over Tamanrasset.

An hour later, he rose again. The night was still pitch-dark, and the candle was out. He lit another and went to the kitchen, a small room, six by nine, near the entrance to the *bordj*. There he would prepare his *frustulum*.[1]

In the cupboard he found a goatskin filled with soured goat's milk and poured some into a metal bowl. He added an equal amount of coarse-ground wheat flour, stirring it in with a wooden spoon. The cold mixture did not thicken. But Charles' thoughts were elsewhere. He put the bowl on his work table, pushing aside a pile of papers covered with strange writing, neither Latin nor Arabic, but Tamasheq.

He said the blessing and slowly began to eat. Having almost no teeth, he did not even chew the revolting, sourish mixture. He swallowed mechanically, washing down his food with sips of the coffee he had heated in the courtyard by burning a few wood scraps.

The *frustulum* and a little housekeeping had not taken more than twenty minutes, leaving forty before "work" began at dawn, 6 A.M. Brother Charles returned to the chapel for the next monastic offices, Prime and Terce. The psalms, the hymns, how beautiful! Once again, he was filled with joy.

Love of the Father
Love of the Son,
Spirit of life, breath of God,
With your presence fill my heart,
Abide in me, life and light.

---

[1] From *frustum*: snack, bite to eat, light meal.

The offices led naturally into meditation, which, for Brother Charles, could have only one name: Imitation.

Imitation. Had he lived up to the ideal he set for himself in 1886, shortly after his lightning-swift conversion in the church of Saint-Augustin in Paris: to imitate the hidden life of Christ in Nazareth? He knelt on the sand, again taking his place as a watcher at the foot of the altar. Images crowded his mind. Not of Christ's childhood: this time, his own was being shown him. He tried to resist, to come back to the only model. A gentle voice inside him whispered: "Let it happen, little Charles."

He then surrendered to the images, to the little creature he had been. A child unlike others.

Whenever he plunged deep into his past, he would try to see his mother's face: a pale face, gentle and sad, framed by dark hair cut sensibly short and parted in the center. A black dress with a voluminous hoop skirt, in the Second Empire style. Her gentle, melancholy voice rang in his tortured heart. She was not really pretty, but the boy found her melancholy look appealing. Highborn, Élisabeth Beaudet de Morlet had some commoners in her background, including a Joseph Mennet made rich by the French Revolution. At the late age of twenty-six, she had married a man of thirty-five. Something mysterious clouded her life, as if Élisabeth, by all signs destined to be happy, was anticipating the misfortunes that were to strike. Rich, virtuous, extremely religious, she would glide dolefully through the household, convinced that life was but one long ordeal intended to make one worthy of heaven.

Viscount Édouard de Foucauld, an assistant inspector of forestry in Strasbourg, found his work uninspiring. A man with a strong face and heavy build, he had been a handsome blond fellow, charming and good-humored, when he married Élisabeth (for love) in 1855. An attraction of opposites. Élisabeth was introverted and modest, melancholy and tender. Édouard, outgoing, had frittered away his youth, drunken parties with his well-bred friends taking precedence over work.

Little education, no money. But yes, it was indeed a marriage of love. Élisabeth's father, Colonel de Morlet, could offer no objections to the young viscount's aristocratic references, which went deep into French history: Bertrand de Foucauld, crusader, fallen while defending Saint Louis at El Mansûra; Gabriel de Foucauld, assigned by François II to serve as the king's proxy for the marriage to Queen Mary Stuart; Jean III de Foucauld, governor of Périgord, viscount of Limoges, friend of Henri IV.

Édouard, however, came from the younger branch of the family, which the Revolution had ruined. That is why Charles' forebears had ended up in

Alsace, where they took on poorly paid, albeit respectable, employment as foresters. The family was generally Orléanist, the party affording an expedient compromise between royalty and republican liberalism.

Édouard and Élisabeth's first child died at an early age. A bad omen. Then Charles was born, on September 15, 1858, at 3, Place de Broglie, Strasbourg, in the house where Rouget de Lisle had first sung the "Marseillaise". Marie came along three years later, a pretty little girl, from the start delicate and anxious. Meanwhile, the father had been named to a post at Wissembourg.

Then everything fell apart. For inexplicable reasons, Édouard, who had grown fat, underwent a sudden personality change. The man who had once been so outgoing became gloomy, sinking into a depression that meant that he could no longer work. The atmosphere in the house became unbearable, and the poor man left his family in 1863; he was taken in by his sister Inès Moitessier, who lived on rue d'Anjou in Paris. The renowned psychiatrist Dr. Blanche could do no more than diagnose the illness, an irreversible and incurable malady that was dragging Édouard little by little into the abyss of nonexistence. Dejected, melancholy, raving but not violent, soon he was unable to recognize his loved ones. The same year, grief over his son's condition resulted in the death of Viscount Armand de Foucauld.

Élisabeth still loved her husband. During a visit to Paris, she rashly gave herself to him one last time, hoping to stem his drift into madness. Three months later, while staying with her father in Strasbourg, she died at age thirty-four, after a miscarriage; in reality, she had been carried off by despair.

Édouard, in Paris, followed her to the grave five months later. Next was the poor man's mother, at sixty-four the victim of a heart attack. Édouard's two children had been entrusted to her, and one day she took them for a walk in the country near her village, Mirecourt, in Lorraine. As she pushed Mimi, the little sister, in her cart, with Charles running along behind, a herd of angry cows rushed toward them. They managed to move aside in time, but suddenly the grandmother collapsed. Her heart had given out from fright.

This incredible series of family disasters greatly affected the two children. Mimi, at three, was aware only that her father, mother, and paternal grandparents were gone forever. Charles, at six, did not react violently over the deaths of his loved ones. Quite soon, he began to wonder about the God who had so cruelly affected their lives. Yet his mother had been intensely religious. Hers was not a conventional piety. She had loved that mysterious being who is never seen: God; she had loved him wholeheartedly. She had given Charles a small altar, and he had been learning to pray before it. During vacations in Saverne, they would pick armfuls of flowers

together and place them at the foot of calvaries. All that was finished
forever. Why?

Brother Charles rose. A cock crowed in the distance. It was growing lighter
over Tamanrasset; the marvelous stars were beginning to fade. A new day
was dawning. Friday, December 1, 1916. A Friday consecrated to the Sacred
Heart of Jesus, to whom he had dedicated his life. He gave thanks to God
and implored him to sustain him in his trials, the worst of which was
memory.

Élisabeth's sixty-eight-year-old father took in the orphans, and a family
council named him guardian. Colonel de Morlet was an eminent figure,
quite learned, a graduate of Paris' prestigious École Polytechnique, and a
brilliant officer. Prior to his retirement in 1856, he had been in charge of
Strasbourg's fortifications. He and his first wife, Élisabeth, who died in 1850,
were the parents of one child, Charles' mother. His daughter's death left the
colonel inconsolable. He had no children by his second wife, Amélie de
Latouche, whom he had married in 1852. The elderly couple lived in a
single-family house, on rue des Échasses in Strasbourg. The colonel adored
his two grandchildren, whom he indulged excessively to make them forget
the family tragedy.

Charles kept his grief inside; meanwhile the family dreaded that he
might inherit his father's terrible malady. All seemed to be going well. A
good student at the Saint-Arbogast diocesan school, the boy appeared
studious and hardworking, energetic. But at times he would burst out in
violent, inexplicable tantrums, a way of externalizing his silent, repressed
pain. Four years went by. His introverted, meditative personality took shape.
He liked to be alone; he was becoming withdrawn. The Saint-Arbogast
institution closed, and, in 1868, he began his secondary-school studies at the
Strasbourg lycée. He was bright, but poor health kept him from attending
classes regularly.

Younger than most of his classmates and yet more mature, Charles was
unable to fit in. He had no friends, and because he put a minimum of
effort into his schoolwork—just enough not to vex his grandfather—teachers lost interest in the chubby, polite boy who did not hide his boredom in
the classroom. One of his teachers would comment apropos of Charles:
"Bright and studious, he gave no inkling whatsoever of the impassioned,
impulsive character he was to reveal later." [2]

[2] Quoted by J.-F. Six, *Itinéraire spirituel de Charles de Foucauld* (Seuil, 1958), 17.

In the summer of 1868, there suddenly appeared a shining figure who would brighten the scene for Charles. He was ten, she was eighteen; her name was Marie Moitessier. He met this cousin at Louye, the Moitessier château in the Eure region, where he had been invited to spend two months of vacation. Louye was a sumptuous, imposing dwelling surrounded by superb grounds.

Marie was the younger daughter of an unusual couple. Sigismond Moitessier, a rich Parisian banker with a fortune made from importing American tobacco, had married Inès de Foucauld, Charles' aunt. She was the sister with whom his father had taken refuge after depression struck. Bright, determined, beautiful—Ingres painted her twice—Inès hosted a salon at the family home in Paris at 42, rue d'Anjou. The Moitessiers spent summers at Louye.

Inès had befriended Charles. Very generous, she felt responsible for this nephew stricken by misfortune. A perfectionist and rather authoritarian, she hoped to make of him "someone worthwhile". Young Charles would gaze at her, fascinated. If Inès represented for him the ideal mother he had lost, gentle Marie, eight years older than Charles, seemed to him infinitely more approachable. She became like a second mother.

Marie was a brunette with jade-colored eyes. Although short, she carried herself with an inborn nobility. She could be modest, imperious or tender, reserved or bold, according to the situation. She did not really have her mother's good looks, but her grace and her penetrating gaze made her attractive. A bright and curious young woman, she was fond of nature and music. Most significant, she was a contemplative soul, who hid under apparent shyness a will of iron and a perfectionism that marked her as Inès' daughter.

In the company of these two very different women in this château where servants abounded and cabinet ministers came to call, Charles finally felt at peace. He was enjoying himself in a feminine world. With Marie and her sister, Catherine, the two girls duly chaperoned by their governess, Mlle Kiener, he would listen as the latter recounted the pious history of Abbot de Rancé, whose grave was in nearby Mortagne, at the famous Trappist monastery of Soligny. Rancé, a converted freethinker, had finished his life in asceticism and had reformed the Cistercian order.

Later, Charles would recall "the Moitessier family, object of passionate attachment in my early years". For him, the Moitessiers always stood for the beautiful and the good, virtue and wealth, a contradictory combination. But he did not find putting wealth and faith side by side offensive; lovely Inès was sincere and generous. Her faith was real. She gave unstintingly. And so did her daughter Marie.

How does one explain the mutual attraction that was to bind together a little ten-year-old boy and a young woman of eighteen? She became both sister and mother, with an added element, something more disturbing. "She moved him and charmed him", writes Marguerite Castillon du Perron, who provides the best analysis of the complex feelings involved. "In her company he had a blissful feeling he had never before experienced. He admired her and fed on what she was thinking. He observed her and followed her everywhere. She could guess his thoughts before he spoke; she showed great consideration for him; she tamed him with the disinterested gift of her heart."[3]

Obviously, to her, he was still a child. Yet she remained troubled by the fascination she could read in his look and by the naïve and pure expression of this first love. They were attached to one another, each in a different way. They enjoyed being together. While the haughty Inès was thinking lofty thoughts, Marie was penetrating the mystery of this young life ravaged by family tragedy. She alone understood his secret, passionate nature. They strolled in the extensive grounds. He listened rapturously as she sang and played the piano. She guided his first readings and taught him Italian. Tender toward him, she knew how to listen. Unlike Inès, she never lectured him. There grew up between them "an intimacy sealed with laughter, silence, and peace".[4]

Marie was quite devout; she could even be called mystical. With her, religion was more than a ritual. Fervent, every morning she would hear Mass in the country church in Louye, and Charles would tag along. Imperceptibly but firmly, she conveyed to him her devotion to the Sacred Heart, which would later have a decisive influence on his life. It was new to him, this Christ perpetually on the Cross to save sinful humanity.

Another boy in the same situation would probably have gone off hunting with his uncle instead of attending church with his cousin! And herein lies one of the keys to this complex, reticent individual. He would soon be intrigued by Marie as a woman. Through her he also discovered the mystery of the supernatural world. That came about because of the gnawing pain he kept inside, the wound inflicted when his mother and father had so suddenly departed. It is through this kind of pain that a person grows and changes. To the child wounded by his parents' inexplicable "betrayal", Marie showed the Cross of the One who also thought himself forsaken by his Father. The child's tortured heart welcomed this parental substitute. For Charles, love remained forever connected with pain. That realization came to him and buried itself deep inside, like a grain of wheat fallen to the ground. Would it sprout and grow ripe? For the moment, nothing was less certain.

[3] M. Castillon du Perron, *Charles de Foucauld* (Grasset, 1982), 40–41.
[4] Ibid.

After his two magical summer months, Charles went back to Strasbourg. And once again, eaten away inside, the boy—ordinarily quite placid—would abruptly express his mental state with sudden fits of uncontrollable anger. Thin-skinned, hypersensitive, he was growing more withdrawn. Exceedingly vulnerable and touchy, he would sometimes become impatient and aggressive.

The Morlets were not the Moitessiers. Certainly, the colonel and his wife were kind, generous, and affectionate. But how does one explain the fact that the grandfather's indulgence only fueled the boy's aggressiveness? Although an exaggeration, what Charles' Latouche cousin had to say later about the grandfather probably contains some truth: "His kindness was only equaled by his excessive weakness. Under less senile direction, this amazingly gifted boy, with his superior intelligence and heart of gold, could have become a remarkable man." [5]

In the Morlet household, Charles felt loved; he did not feel supported. He did not find there the strong guidance of the Moitessier household. The colonel had no power over the boy, not because the grandfather's character was weak—it was not—but because his moral code was conventional and not applicable to real life. He did what he could . . . at his age.

Charles did not have a chance to go to Louye a third time, in the summer of 1870. Napoleon had declared war on Prussia, a foolish act. He played into Bismarck's hands, giving the latter the opportunity to unite Germany and extend its borders. The French, unaware of what was happening, generally supported the war. And twelve-year-old Charles joined the crowd. In a letter to his cousin Adolphe Hallez, a naval officer, he writes: "At last Grandpapa will probably see his fortifications used for something. As for me, I too would like to kill Prussians." [6]

But "Grandpapa" harbored no illusions. Opposed to the Empire, he could foresee the tragic outcome. That is why he left Strasbourg and took his family to Rennes, in Brittany. Subsequent events justified his pessimism. The Germans had superior artillery and twice as many troops as the French. France's Alsatian divisions were defeated. Let down by Marshal Bazaine, Napoleon III was crushed at Sedan and surrendered. It was the end of the Empire.

But France refused to give up and was invaded and occupied. The Morlets did not wait for the pointed Prussian helmets to arrive. They took refuge in Berne, Switzerland. In a letter to Adolphe Hallez written October 11, 1870, little Charles fumes with indignation: "I would love to come

[5] G. de Latouche to MacCarthy, May 14, 1883.
[6] Quoted by Castillon, *Foucauld*, 44.

help you kill Prussians. Right now that task appeals to me more than doing my Latin and Greek." [7]

He did not get the opportunity. Paris fell January 28, 1871, and Bismarck imposed a harsh and humiliating peace. Alsace and part of Lorraine became German provinces; inhabitants who wished to remain French had to leave. The colonel and his wife chose to depart. Fortunate enough to have not lost their assets, they decided to go to Nancy (which would not be annexed but was still under temporary German occupation), where they moved into a single-family residence at 5, rue du Manège. An old quarter, an old building—a sad spot in spite of the cathedral nearby. The Rozières mansion had a marble floor and looked out on a courtyard planted with sycamores. Downstairs were three reception rooms; on the second floor, four bedrooms; on the third, servants' quarters.

With the school year nearly two-thirds over, Charles was not sent to the lycée. Father Delsor, a teacher from the Saint-Étienne middle school, acted as his tutor. The priest viewed his charge as "intelligent, taking an interest in his studies, very mild in temperament, more a girl than a boy". [8]

In another portrait, this one delineated by his cousin Pierre de Lagabbe, Foucauld's early maturity comes through: "He was old for his age. Instead of being interested in my games, he preferred to sit in the library and look through old volumes with my father. Although vigorous, he tended to be lazy when it came to physical exercise; he would rather do whatever could satisfy his intellectual curiosity." [9]

In October 1871 Charles entered the fourth-year class at the lycée in Nancy. There was a depressing atmosphere in this city where the defeat had been taken especially hard. The occupying German troops received looks of hatred as they paraded through the streets on horseback. Food supplies for the hardworking population were inadequate. The lycée teemed with students from Alsace and Lorraine. Like Charles, they had affirmed their French citizenship and dreamed only of revenge. The lycée mixed severity with nonchalance. In summer, students were obliged to take a 6 A.M. dip in the Meurthe. But back in the schoolyard they could revive by watching the scantily clad prostitutes of rue Saint-Joseph perform their morning toilette!

Charles proved to be a good student. He liked his teachers, who included Antoine Duvaux, an ardent anticlerical republican who would become a legislator and in 1882 Minister of Education, then under-secretary of state in the Jules Ferry government. And the boy, for once, had a friend. Gabriel Tourdes, like Charles, came from Strasbourg (born there in 1857).

[7] Quoted by *Bulletin des Amitiés Charles de Foucauld*, no. 66, 10.
[8] Quoted by G. Gorrée, *Sur les traces de Charles de Foucauld* (Éd. de la Plus Grande France, 1936), 19.
[9] Quoted by *Bulletin des Amitiés*, no. 119, 12.

His father, a doctor, served as dean of the Nancy medical school. Gabriel—obliging, friendly, honest, but not very exciting—was one of Charles' few childhood friends outside the family.[10]

Thanks to Gabriel, as enthusiastic a reader as Charles, the boy opened up a little, and most important, he felt less alone. At thirteen, he was still a chubby, round-cheeked child, introverted but curious about everything. On April 18, 1872, ardent in his faith, he made his First Communion and was confirmed by Bishop Foulon of Nancy, later a cardinal. Loyal to the magical memory of Marie Moitessier—and to the devotion of the time—he chose as a keepsake a picture of the Sacred Heart. Marie came from Paris for the ceremony, which made him happy. As a Communion gift she gave him Bossuet's *Élévations sur les mystères.*

But his interests lay elsewhere. He took part in the rejoicing of the French when the Germans left and French troops arrived in a Nancy bedecked with flags. There were the Tricolor, the people's jubilation, the sounding of the bugle, and one voice, that of a woman, Madame Émile Boutroux, who would express the emotion felt by all: "I burst into tears, and so as not to fall on my knees in prayer, I had to keep saying to myself: 'No, you're not in church; this is the flag of France!' "[11]

But his birthplace, Strasbourg, still belonged to Germany—a spear that remained imbedded in his flesh alongside the open wound left by the tragic death of his parents.

And time went by, with its ups and downs. Charles was entering that dangerous period, adolescence. At fifteen, quite mature for his age, he buried himself in books more and more. He got along well with his grandfather, who, according to pious observers, let him do "whatever he felt like", meaning simply—remember, we are talking about a nineteenth-century upper-class family—that he could read anything he wished. And he did not choose Bossuet! Instead, he preferred classical works, considered "licentious" by the right-thinking people of the time. Between Aristophanes and La Fontaine, he was delighted to discover an art of living diametrically opposed to the stark, dolorous Christianity that reigned in his milieu, except in the Morlet household. His teachers at the lycée did not counter his liberal, humanistic leanings. Although upright and competent, they were all atheists and displayed more interest in the form and beauty of classical works than in their content, unaware of its subtle, venomous decadence.

In October 1873, Charles began his last year of lycée studies. His rationalist thinking grew more marked. Little by little he was losing his faith.

---

[10] See their correspondence published in 1982 by Nouvelle Cité.

[11] Mme. Émile Boutroux, *Souvenirs,* 1912.

Why is faith lost? A weighty question that no one has ever fully answered. God creates man the way the sea creates the sandy shore, by drawing back. If the sea does not draw back, the shore cannot appear. Other biographers of Charles de Foucauld do not share this opinion. They lay the blame on his reading and on the "complete impartiality" of his secular teachers. It started with some doubts. Logical, since the profane authors contradict each other. And even the religious authors—what better proof than the diversity of religions and the heresies dividing believers. Nothing is certain. Nothing can be proved. Human reason is incapable of arriving at *the* Truth. The era was obsessed with positivism, and certain elites followed philosopher Auguste Comte's orders: "Replace the relative with the absolute everywhere." A Manichean split opened up: blind faith, for some people; for others, atheism based on rejecting tradition-bound dogma.

It was an age open to atheism. Renan had just published his *Life of Jesus*. Littré had completed his dictionary. Auguste Comte was indispensable to some of the elite in power. Scientism, anticlericalism, and secularism were in fashion. Catholics were losing ground, for preachers and catechists lacked the expertise to speak of the problems worrying educated young people and bothering consciences.

With Charles, it was not atheism yet; for him, the essence of God remained unknowable, and therein lay the problem. When tradition does not suffice, how can one cling to something unknown? Had he no spiritual guide? It may seem astonishing that Colonel Morlet and his wife, practicing Catholics, did not lend him support. He probably did not ask for it. He was undergoing no inner struggle, no questioning. None. God was drawing back gently, quietly, like the ebbing tide. The colonel was an esthete wrapped up in literature and archaeology; he was not capable of answering the boy's questions. But did Charles ask questions? Even gentle Marie, so mystical, and her impassioned mother, self-assured Inès, did not keep him from losing his faith. Except for summers, he lived far from them, and Marie was about to marry!

Charles did not find the lycée chaplain very interesting. Father J. B. Blanc had published a manual, *Complete Christianity, or Catholicism Elucidated for the Young*, for which little can be said: "labored and dry, tedious and unappealing" (Bishop Jacqueline). Between teachers he admired and this supremely self-assured canon, Charles chose the former. He preferred Voltaire, Rousseau, and Montesquieu to Bossuet, Pascal, and Lacordaire.

It must be emphasized that he did not become militantly, aggressively atheistic or anticlerical. That would go against the principles he derived from the masters of skepticism. To be an atheist, that too means certainty, dogmatism. Father Gorrée, one of Foucauld's spiritual biographers, writes: "The excessive freedom he enjoyed, the restless ardor of his passionate nature, the curiosity of a mind without guidance or supervision, all led him to books fatal to his religious faith, so that when barely fifteen he no longer could find in Christian convictions the necessary remedy for the agitation of his senses." [12]

Charles reached the same conclusion thirty years after the fact: "Reading widely gave me a liking for study but did me the great harm about which you know", he would write to Marie de Bondy. [13] "The philosophers are all at odds with each other. For twelve years I neither denied nor believed anything, despairing of the search for truth, not even believing in God. No proof seemed to me clear enough." [14]

His teachers? Could they have been bad teachers? "Just the opposite, they were all very respectful", he writes. Respectful of his freedom. But, "Even they do harm, in that they are impartial. Young people need to be taught, not by those who are impartial, but by believing, saintly souls", he would write to his brother-in-law much later. [15]

Still, is it fair for René Bazin to accuse the secular school of having made young Charles into "a student curious about everything, set on enjoyment, and sad, his mind filled to the brim with objections to a faith about which he knew little"? [16]

His loss of faith would be complete by the end of 1874, the year he studied philosophy; "And that was not the only calamity", he added. It can be assumed that, like others, he suffered the torments of the flesh. "I lived the way it is possible to live once the last spark of faith has been extinguished." [17] "At seventeen, I was all egotism, all impiety, all desire for evil; it was as if I had gone a little mad." [18]

Just like other young men, no better, no worse? Loss of faith and carnal impulses should not be lumped together.

Yet it is impossible not to make a connection between his state and Marie Moitessier's marriage on April 11, 1874. Michel Carrouges points out that "for him, this marriage resulted in a profound separation from the past." Marie was the only person who might have kept him from the tragic slide downward that followed his breaking with the family religious traditions.

In Paris' Saint-Augustin Church, twenty-four-year-old Marie Moitessier wed the dashing Viscount Olivier de Bondy, thirty. He was handsome, rich,

---

[12] Gorrée, *Sur les traces*, 20.

[13] Charles de Foucauld (hereafter CF) to Marie de Bondy, quoted by R. Bazin, *Charles de Foucauld* (Plon, 1921), 6.

[14] CF to Henri de Castries, August 14, 1901 (Grasset, 1938).

[15] Quoted by Bazin, *Foucauld*, 6.

[16] Ibid., 7–8.

[17] CF to Henri de Castries, August 14, 1901.

[18] CF to Marie de Bondy, April 17, 1892.

titled, cultivated, and charming. But in character, nothing like his father, a graduate of the École Polytechnique, a prefect, a peer of the realm, and a senator. The two families had encouraged this marriage. The two young people had been in no hurry. Why not? Something essential kept them apart. Marie was by nature religious, even mystical. Olivier, Catholic by tradition, remained a skeptic. Mass did not interest him. He did not accompany Marie to church, preferring society events, hunting, and horsemanship. In short, a marriage of convenience, arranged by the families.

Did Charles suspect that? What is certain is that he did not attend the wedding although invited, and, not to mince words, he was a bit jealous of the dashing Bondy. Committed to her marriage and set on having many children, Marie no longer took much notice of Charles. She distanced herself emotionally from her affectionate, rebellious little cousin. Charles was en route to losing his faith, or, to put it more precisely, to arriving at an adult consciousness minus metaphysical concerns. Marie was not the cause. But she alone could have caught up with him and accompanied him on this dangerous passage. Charles no longer felt held back by all that she had taught him to love, primarily the metaphysical world from which he was fleeing as fast as he could.

He completed the traditional secondary-school curriculum with good marks. What was he going to do with his life? From an early age, he had wanted to become an officer. Colonel de Morlet hoped he would go through the École Polytechnique first, as he himself had done. But Charles had no talent for math, and the military academy at Saint-Cyr seemed fine to him. In four years he would be coming into his inheritance. One day he would be the colonel's principal heir. That meant considerable wealth. He did not worry about the future, which he envisioned according to his tastes: not "becoming a general", but pursuing culture, traveling, seeing life, meeting women . . . He picked Saint-Cyr "because the entrance exams required less preparation". Why trouble himself with boring studies? His sole ambition was to "enjoy a decent life".

After being granted a dispensation for his age, Charles received his first baccalaureate degree on August 12, 1874, with an "above average". He then left Nancy for Paris, a change unwisely initiated by his grandfather. Suddenly, the sixteen-year-old boy was a boarder at a Jesuit institution on the rue des Postes (today, rue Lhomond), the famous Saint-Geneviève School.

Was it really too late for his faith? Surely not. Were the good fathers going to "rehabilitate" him, hold him back from the slippery slope?

Definitely not. Charles had too strong a personality not to take his experience to its conclusion. God had drawn back. Charles was not among those people who, through self-interest or desire to conform, adhere to their religion simply out of loyalty to family tradition.

At Saint-Geneviève's, no theologian could make him admit that "one equals three" (the dogma-mystery of the Trinity). Not only did he completely lose his faith, but, to the horror of the good fathers, he took no part in religious observances. Later, he would contradict himself (which explains the mistaken ideas of his biographers) in a 1901 letter to Henri de Castries: "All the objections that tormented me are resolved by a good Christian philosophy. But children are thrust into the world without being given the weapons essential to fight the enemies they find inside and outside themselves and which are awaiting them en masse as they enter adolescence." [19]

The Jesuits of Paris, for whom he would always have "the greatest esteem", did not keep him from loss of faith any more than had the chaplain of the lycée in Nancy.

What exactly did happen during his stay in Paris, those years of 1874 to 1876, which should have been so rewarding?

After his years as a day student in the Nancy lycée, the pampered child of the Morlet household found himself in a strict boarding school whose goal was to form an elite and, on occasion, to bring young rebels into line. Up at 4:40 A.M. Mandatory attendance at daily Mass. Harsh discipline, a heavy dose of mental work, little compensated for by infrequent recreational activities and almost no outings. A frugal diet. For Charles, it was hell.

The fathers remained insensible to his distress. They thought the overweight little aristocrat was on the road to ruin and that imposing an ascetic way of life would straighten him out. Not allowed to protest, he poured out his feelings in pathetic letters to his grandfather, begging to return to Nancy. In vain. Having lost his faith, naturally he rebelled against religious observance: Mass, Lauds, Vespers, confession, meditation, and so on. His masters tried to bring him back to more Catholic sentiments, but how could they reason with a rebellious adolescent who demanded "scientific proof of the Resurrection"?

The rift quickly deepened. Charles did not turn into a militant atheist; religion did not interest him. He declared himself a "freethinker", a label then in vogue. And since the colonel insisted he remain at the boarding school, Charles broke off all dialogue with the Jesuits. Theology no longer disgusted him even; he found it a dreadful bore, like Mass.

Nevertheless, in August 1875, he obtained his second baccalaureate degree, with an excellent grade in history. The questions dealt with the conquest of Algeria! He also excelled in geography.

[19] CF to Henri de Castries, August 14, 1901.

During summer vacation in Nancy, he begged Morlet to "release him from that hell". The colonel did not budge, shocked that the rebellious adolescent could be asking to leave such a fine boarding school.

And so Charles went back to school in October, to spend the year preparing for Saint-Cyr. The lava inside began bubbling up again. An eruption seemed inevitable. He started, so they said, to "go astray". Could he have been "depraved", as one of his biographers suggests? [20] It is easy to say that. Here again, biographers can do no more than refer to the confession coming much later, after 1900, and made out of humility: "Laziness was not the sole cause." [21]

Obviously! He had *never* been lazy. The laziness cited was an invention of the Jesuits to make the planned expulsion seem less shameful. "Depraved", then? What does that mean? Torments of the flesh that he did not know how to hide, unlike his classmates? Since Charles' own words have been used here so often, it would seem logical to quote him once more in this matter. For he expressed himself openly in an 1874 letter to his lycée friend Gabriel Tourdes: "You have to be very new at crime if you're terrified even though you *haven't done anything*, and you have to be unaccustomed to doing evil if you keep your remorse alive for such a long time." [22]

And as if to make more visible the fantasies overwhelming him, he wrote his signature thus: "Charles de F. nu, nue, nu, nue". [23] To repeat his 1892 confession: "At seventeen, I was all egotism, all vanity, all impiety, all desire for evil; it was as if I had gone a little mad." [24] A little mad from being cooped up. And, thus, rebellious. That is the key to his behavior. A spoiled child, in whom Colonel de Morlet had been unable to instill a gradual acceptance of discipline. And it was not just outward discipline. He found the Jesuits' mind control intolerable: obligatory confession, spiritual advisers, regulated piety, enough to turn anyone from true religion for life.

Michel de Suremain, head of the group Amitiés Charles de Foucauld, points out that the adolescent was bright, cultured, with an above average memory, and a strong liking for literature, history, and geography. He was not lazy. His academic preparation for Saint-Cyr was adequate. Then why? The tragedies of his childhood had left him vulnerable. His character had not yet been formed, or, rather, it had not yet been disciplined, for he did have character. He lost his faith, but after losing his family and his native

[20] J.-F. Six, *Itinéraire*, 25.
[21] CF to Marie de Bondy, April 17, 1892.
[22] CF to Tourdes, 1874, in *Lettres à un ami de lycée* (Nouvelle Cité, 1982), 54.
[23] A play on words with the Greek letter and the masculine and feminine forms of the French adjective meaning "naked".—TRANS.
[24] CF to Marie de Bondy, April, 17, 1892.

soil—his last points of reference. And he ended up in great danger.[25] Did
he really have a military calling? He did not show great enthusiasm for his
chosen vocation. He even declared it "boring". But there had occurred
the Prussian invasion, the humiliating defeat, and the annexation. Those
events affected him profoundly, along with the death of his parents. Like
other Frenchmen of the time, he had developed exaggerated patriotic
sentiments. His patriotic fervor took over the growing void left in his
heart by God's withdrawal. And, too, he so wanted to please his grandfather!

"You know what I think of boarding school", he would later write to
Marie de Bondy. "Fine for many; I found it detestable." [26] And in a letter to
Henri de Castries: "I lived the way it is possible to live once the last spark
of faith has been extinguished." [27] That tragic sentence sums it up well,
along with the ending of the letter: "I am bored to death." [28] What would
happen now? A scandal was avoided. In March 1876, with school in session,
the Jesuits sent their rebellious young man back to Nancy. Reason given:
"Laziness and disobedience."

It must be noted that he would not hold the dismissal against them. "I
took away from that boarding school a deep esteem for the Jesuits", he
would write to his cousin. What is certain: he did not find in their midst a
master who could understand him.

Relieved, he returned to Nancy, happy to be back with the Morlets. He
had never rebelled against his family. The colonel, deeply shocked but
resigned, provided a tutor so he could finish preparing for the Saint-Cyr
entrance exams. Charles did not care much for young Monsieur Dumont,
a mere twenty-one. "He's not very knowledgeable", he would confide to
his grandfather. "He is *ordinary*." Quite telling, this cruel remark from an
adolescent who was not ordinary.

How did the family react to the new Charles? Usually so open, he hid
from them his loss of faith. Not only from Colonel and Madame de
Morlet, but also from Marie de Bondy and from Mimi, the little sister he
loved so dearly. He did not want to cause them pain.

His cherished freedom regained, how would he use it? To wallow in the
pleasures of the flesh at last? "Tourdes, old boy, Friday I arrive in Nancy,
and I'm counting on you for every evening. I intend to enjoy to the full
what delights body and mind." [29]

[25] Michel de Suremain, *Bulletin des Amitiés*, no. 119, 12.
[26] Easter 1901, quoted by Bishop Jacqueline, *Lettres à un ami*, 55.
[27] CF to Henri de Castries, August 14, 1901.
[28] Quoted by Castillon, *Foucauld*, 55.
[29] *Lettres à un ami*, 49.

Horrors! Yet he was merely referring to books. But what reading! "Worldly" novelists: Bourget, Barrès, and Loti. *Poésies légères* and *Candide*, both by Voltaire, idol of the anticlerical bourgeoisie. *Lettres persanes*, by Montesquieu, also an anticlerical author, whom right-thinking people considered more dangerous than an atheist. The comic poet Scarron, scourge of chivalry and devotee of joie de vivre and elegance. Rabelais, droll critic of the decadent monastic life of his time and defender of a joyful skepticism and a materialism stripped of a moralizing and dolorous God, that colorful Rabelais whose works feature gross excess and coarse jokes of questionable taste. Erasmus, scourge of the depraved nobility and clergy. Mérimée, whom Charles considered the "number-one writer of the century", a conservative liberal who espoused tolerance and freethinking, a rationalist atheist although intrigued by the supernatural.

Who else? Charles felt very much at home with La Fontaine, no longer remembered as a notable freethinker attracted to sensual pleasure as well as to nature. "Sincerity and freedom", La Fontaine preached, to the delight of Charles after his struggle to escape from the good fathers. He recognized himself in La Fontaine's self-portrait: "I like gaming, love, books, music, the city and the country, indeed I like all that life has to offer." Like Charles, he hungered for all experience, but also for solitude and the inner life. "If you want to look deep into yourself, stay where you will be alone." "Rule over yourself. In solitude, you find the true pleasure of your own company." It cannot be pointed out too often that Charles loathed school dormitories and classrooms and, later, barracks and monasteries.

"I was so free, so young. There remained not a trace of faith in my soul." [30]

But he was not a true atheist, and deep in his heart he retained a longing for Christ and for the lost paradise of childhood, with its faith and certitude. And with its affection, for he remained tightly, viscerally attached to his family. He felt they loved him, he knew they loved him, even if they might not approve of him. For them, he was still "the boy with the unspoken prayer". [31] Would that love be enough to save an adolescent whom freedom and coming into wealth were going to expose to every possible danger?

In June 1876, he passed the entrance exams for the Saint-Cyr military school; he ranked eighty-second in the list of 412 successful candidates. And, at eighteen, one of the youngest. Not bad for a "lazy" student! He had worked very hard to please the colonel and to erase the memory of that embarrassing year with the Jesuits. And Morlet glowed with pride. What a fine officer he would make! And again, the colonel erred. With the

---

[30] Correspondence, April 17, 1892, February 24, 1893, in Bazin, *Foucauld*, 7–8.
[31] Ibid., 9.

approval of the family council, Morlet emancipated Charles, who, at eigh-teen, came of age legally. He would be taking possession of his fortune, which a Nancy businessman would manage while giving him an enormous monthly income, enough to satisfy his insatiable desires . . .

Brother Charles opened his eyes and recognized the familiar setting—his chapel in the uncomfortable Tamanrasset *bordj*.[32] His body wracked with pain, he could barely move from the spot where he had been crouched in prayer. The candle on the altar had gone out, completely consumed. Through the window slit came the light of a new day: December 1, 1916.

He rose and pulled aside the curtain separating his sleeping quarters from the chapel. He was surprised that no one had yet knocked at his door. He remembered that because of the drought the nomads had fled to the Adrar, more than three hundred miles to the south, and that the settled inhabit-ants, the Dag Rali, had fled the threat of the *rezzou* by taking refuge in the nearby mountains. At Tamanrasset, there remained only the former slaves, the Haratins too poor to venture far. They were probably outside under the wall, squatting in the sand as they waited for the marabout to finish his endless dialogue with the one God.

Brother Charles quickly perused an outdated newspaper, *l'Écho de Paris*, from November 2, 1916. "Day 822 of the war. Fighting around Bucharest. Shelling on the German and Belgian fronts. Continuing slaughter at Verdun. In Vienna, death of Emperor Franz Joseph imminent. In Paris, *L'Aiglon* performed at Gaumont-Palace. . . ."

Brother Charles decided to go somewhere other than the high-walled courtyard for a little fresh air. Since he had been advised not to leave the *bordj*, he climbed the seventeen steps leading to the parapet walk that topped the wall around his small, fortified castle.

Beyond the village, a desolate expanse, a vast horizon of dust and stones, the *reg*, always parched from the dry wind. Beyond, the desert. Charles watched as the sun rose in the east over the peaks of the Ahaggar. The long horizontal ridges of the Koudia took on gold and purple hues.

The fort, massive and forbidding, was built on a hillock overlooking the rocky plateau; the surrounding area had been cleared. An ancient ethel,[33] the color of a dirty lizard, grew near the dry wadi and provided the only trace of green in this mineral sea of sand and rock. In the distance, Charles could see the little village, scattered groups of pathetic cube-shaped clay

---

[32] *Bordj*: from *iborjet, iborjetin*, stonework tower. Not an indigenous word, but an arabized survival of the Latin *burgus*, from the Germanic *burg*, "castle". Foucauld himself did not use this term, taken up by the military after his death and, later, by visitors.

[33] Arab name for a variety of tamarisk found in the Sahara.

dwellings and a few abandoned *zeribas* (older-style huts of reed), housing non-nomadic Haratin families, determined cultivators of the tiny garden plots that afforded them a bare subsistence.

Farther on, a few hundred feet away, he saw the elongated shape of his dear hermitage, "the frigate", which he had resigned himself to abandoning upon orders from his military friends, taking along his treasures: the portable altar, the holy relics, the chalice and the ciborium, the monstrance, his vestments, books, manuscripts, medicines, and the supplies necessary for survival.

Then he looked down into the *bordj*. A squat building, made of *toub* (unfired clay bricks), without even a roughcast plastering, four angle towers joined by a thick crenelated wall over sixteen feet high, the door the only opening. This massive exterior, measuring around sixty-five feet on each side, sheltered the forty-five by forty-five inner courtyard, which had rooms arranged around its walls: the chapel adjoining the bedroom-office, two small bedrooms, a large food storage area, and a room containing weapons, ammunition, and a variety of equipment.

Brother Charles smiled. He was remembering the day he moved in, June 23, 1916, and the letter he had written on July 1 to his old friend General Laperrine, one-time commander of the Southern Territories:

> I give you the news of my move to another apartment and, indeed, to another quarter. After living on the Left Bank of Tamanrasset Oued,[34] and for eleven years in the hermitage you know well, I am settling on the Right Bank. A year and a half ago, with the Moroccan *rezzous* coming ever closer to the Ahaggar, operating regularly at Inzit and Timissao and threatening Abalessa, tempted by the large numbers of black and Haratin farmers in the area, I had the idea of building a little refuge, a tiny *kasbah*[35] where the population of Tamanrasset could take shelter should some of the Moroccan wanderers reach here.
>
> After thinking the matter over, questioning my neighbors, the Dag Rali, and ascertaining that they favored the plan, and talking with Saint-Léger and La Roche, a year ago I made up my mind to begin building, quite frugally, with just one workman, a Haratin from the village. My Tuareg neighbors urged me to live in the refuge, saying I would be closer to them, and that if the people did have to seek shelter there, it would be good to find the place inhabited and stocked with food and tools.
>
> Eventually I gave in and put up some structures that, without noticeably shrinking the courtyard—still quite adequate for receiving the entire village population, including neighboring nomads—made it possible for me to live here. I moved in a week ago, although the work is not finished, because to complete it I needed the beams, the doors, and the windows from the old hermitage.[36]

---

[34] Oued = wadi.—Trans.
[35] Here, a castle or palace.—Trans.
[36] CF to General Laperrine, July 1, 1916.

He had drawn up the plans himself, based on the medieval Berber fortifications he had observed on the slopes of the Atlas Mountains during his exploration of Southern Morocco in 1883: Saharan forts of the early Middle Ages, with thick rammed-earth walls, protecting villages and serving as grain warehouses and shelter for the villagers in the event of attack.

This fort did not come under the responsibility of the French military command, even though the army had furnished rifles to arm the population in case of attack.

The military nature of the project had not shocked Brother Charles, who recalled the fortified monasteries of medieval France and those of the Frankish Kingdom of Jerusalem. He knew that the small store of weapons and the three thousand cartridges would cause talk and an excuse for aggression by his enemies, the cruel Saharan rebels from Morocco and the Fezzan, longing for the good old days of the *rezzous* prior to the French conquest.

Was there real danger? Undoubtedly, and not just coming from Morocco. The general mobilization of 1914 had removed the majority of Africa's troops to supply the Franco-German front, which was devouring the elite of the French army. The Sahara was left with nothing but a few handfuls of Arab camel troopers and their French officers, threatened constantly from the northeast by the tribes of the Fezzan (South Tripoli) after the retreat of the Italians, who had annexed Turkish-held Cyrenaica and Tripoli in 1911. Confirmed troublemakers and professional pillagers, these tribes had been only too susceptible to the *jihad*, the holy war launched in 1914 by Resat Khan V, Sultan of Constantinople and ally of the Germans. An ideal pretext.

The plan of the Senoussi[37] was no secret: to invade the French Sahara, pushing toward Agadez and the Niger River. Once arrived, to replace France in black Africa, from time immemorial the private reserve of the Arabs—an inexhaustible source for slaves. The avowed purpose remained religious and was proclaimed in the mosques by the fundamentalist marabouts of Djarbout, Koufra, and Gouro: to drive out the Christians—French, Italian, and English—to spread Islam to all of Africa, to rebuild a great empire for the military-priestly caste.

With military assistance from the Germans and the Turks, the Senoussi had driven the Italians from Tripoli, appropriated some of their weapons, and pushed toward Algeria. On March 6, 1916, a thousand fanatic warriors, led by Sultan Ahmoud and armed with a cannon and machine guns, had attacked a fort on the northeastern border of Algeria, Djanet, manned by

[37] Founded in 1840 in Mecca, the Senoussi Brotherhood considered itself a fundamentalist political-religious organization created to oppose European penetration. Each branch of the brotherhood was headed by a religious leader (marabout) who proclaimed the *jihad*.

Sergeant Lapierre's fifty camel troopers. Alerted at Fort Polignac, Captain Duclos headed immediately to their rescue with 140 men. They arrived March 26, too late. The place had fallen two days earlier, and all of Lapierre's men were dead, wounded, or scattered in the desert. Threatened with destruction themselves, Duclos and his force withdrew to Polignac and barricaded themselves in the fort, harassed by Si Mohamed Labed, Senoussi leader in the area, who had roused the rebel Ajjer Tuareg and their neighbors, the Ait Lohen.

Once at Djanet the enemy was only 310 miles from Tamanrasset, whose sole protection lay thirty miles away at little Fort Motylinski with Second Lieutenant Constant and his thirty remaining camel troopers. Not much help could be expected from the loyal tribes of the Ahaggar, forced to flee to the Adrar Mountains because of the drought. (See map on page 233.)

Constant had alerted Foucauld on April 7. The hermit was aware that, henceforth, "Nothing but the good Lord could keep them from coming."

Nevertheless, he warned his loyal Tuareg nomads, scattered far and wide: Ouksem the Elder, leader of the Dag Rali Imrad; and Moussa ag Amastane, *amenokal* (head of the most noble family) of the Ahaggar, who was then 310 miles away, in the Adrar Oasis of southwestern Algeria. He advised Second Lieutenant Constant to retreat into the mountains, for how could he hold Fort Motylinski with so few men and weapons?

As for him, he would stay at Tamanrasset. To flee would be a mark of weakness, even of treason, vis-à-vis the still loyal Tuareg.

His action was well received. In May 1916, the tribes of the Ahaggar declared their loyalty. They had been spared. But for how long?

On June 16, Major Meynier's 650 men—the total strength of the Sahara—retook Djanet. Their position remained untenable, however, because of the distance from supply bases, and the French withdrew again. Like the Italian fort at Rhat, Djanet found itself once more in the hands of the rebels, who were harassing all of Algeria's eastern frontier. The Arabs of Tripoli had been joined by the Senoussi Kouans of the Tassili. Fort Polignac was threatened, and in September Fort Flatters, with its food convoys regularly plundered.

The rebellion of the Ajjer tribes of the Ahaggar threatened the whole Sahara and black Africa beyond. In vain Foucauld suggested a plan to Major Meynier, who was holding the last of the reserves at In Salah. The commander in Algiers, General Moinier, worried about the number of troops sent off to the French front, refused to go along with the plan.

On August 11, a caravan of nine camels had brought to Tamanrasset only rifles and cartridges, along with a stock of wheat and dates, which Charles stored in the *bordj*. In vain Constant had begged him to withdraw to Fort

Motylinski: "What will you do at Tam against a full-scale Senoussi attack? Ten cannon volleys, and your little fortress will collapse!"

"The fortress is only for protecting the population against an ordinary *rezzou*, a limited raid by enemy wanderers. In the event of an organized attack, we would seek refuge in the Ahaggar Massif, on Assekrem. I will let you know if that happens by sending Paul with a message in a hollow stick."

"If Fort Moty has not been captured like Djanet!"

"Come what may!"

Thus Brother Charles was quite aware of the danger. On September 1, he wrote to his friend General Mazel, commander of the Fifth Army in France: "We are on the alert here because of increasing activity by the Senoussi. Our local Tuareg are loyal, but we could be attacked by Tripoli Arabs. I have made my hermitage into a little fortress. Looking at my battlements, I think of the fortified monasteries of the tenth century. They have entrusted me with six boxes of cartridges and thirty Gras rifles, which take me back to our youth." [38] And to General Laperrine on September 30: "We have had a major alert. If the natives who surround me are loyal, I can defend myself." [39]

That is, if the assailants did not have a cannon as they had at Djanet. And if he kept up his guard, which would mean men armed with grenades taking turns night and day in the towers to prevent the enemy scaling the walls. For the moment, he had neither sentries nor grenades. Only God watched over him. Was that not what mattered most?

The *bordj* had been finished on November 15. Charles had worked side by side with the Haratins from Tamanrasset. Paul Embarek had begun digging the ditch, six and a half feet wide and more than three feet deep.

Brother Charles rested his glance on the wooden cross fastened to the top of the wall, over the entryway. Made with his own hands from two branches of the old ethel, no cross had ever been so humble, so rustic. He preferred crosses like that. While the red sun rose above the mountain, the hermit lost himself in the contemplation of the cross. Forsaken by the world, he rose far above the miserable place where he made his home. The Beloved was with him, merged with the blazing sun of the Ahaggar. "God alone is enough. Let nothing make you afraid."

---

[38] CF to General Mazel, *Bulletin des Amitiés*, no. 10.
[39] CF to Laperrine.

2

Scandalous Officer

The *rezzou* of Senoussi Beuh ag Rhabelli, on twenty fast camels from the Tassili, sped toward the peaks of the Ilamane, where it was to meet up with the Targui[1] rebel, Kerzou, who had instigated the failed September plot against Tamanrasset the year before. Objective: to kidnap the "white marabout" Charles de Foucauld, take him to Agadez alive, and hand him over to Kaoucen, the Senoussi leader who had been besieging the Nigerian oasis.

While the dromedaries advanced westward with a long stride, Beuh ag Rhabelli was recalling the events of recent days.

Everything had been decided in Rhat—the pearl of the Fezzan, just evacuated by the Italians, and the crossroads for caravans of salt, ivory, and arms. From Rhat, Si Mohamed Labed, Kaoucen's silent partner, relentlessly kept his allies and neighbors stirred up, those turbulent Ajjer tribes and the neighboring Ait Lohen. But he had failed with the tribes of the Ahaggar, in the center of the Sahara.

In Rhat, Si Mohamed Labed had received Beuh ag Rhabelli. They had discussed the uprisings in the Saharan oasis as a means of chasing out the Franks. At the moment, only the Ajjer tribes were in revolt. They hoped the Ait Lohen would follow. Perhaps the Dag Rali too, in spite of the close ties between Ouksem, the nephew of one of their leaders, and the marabout Charles, who had managed to take the young man to France with him. Perhaps Ouksem, and maybe after him the Ahaggar Tuareg's Moussa ag Amastane—the only leader to remain truly loyal to the marabout—would one day join the Prophet's holy *jihad*? Weren't they swayed by the Crescent's victories? Rhat, Djanet, Polignac! And imminent to the south, Agadez, Port of Green Pastures, now under siege by Kaoucen's *harka* (Moroccan irregulars)?

"Why does Moussa betray us?" Si Mohamed Labed had asked irritably. "What does he have to gain from the Franks, who are being crushed in France by our German allies, just as they were by our Turkish brothers in the Dardanelles?"

---

[1] "Targui" is the singular form of "Tuareg".—TRANS.

"One man on his own, the marabout Charles de Foucauld, keeps him ensnared in treason through magic spells", Beuh had replied.

"What? A man on his own, without arms, said to be poor or even destitute, isolated, thirty miles from a pathetic French garrison, is supposedly frustrating the holy Senoussi cause and holding our brothers, the Ahaggar Tuareg, in his power?"

"He is indeed, O servant of Allah! The marabout is not unarmed. He is not poor. He receives large sums from France and acts cleverly. He speaks the Tuareg language. Under the pretext of charity, he entertains many guests in his hermitage, which is at a crossroads for caravans. He gets people to talk."

"Do you think he is an army informer?"

"Probably. Fortunately, he does not yet have a telegraph, wireless or otherwise, that diabolical invention of the *roumis* [Europeans]. Also, he has an influence on the tribes' thinking."

"This cannot go on, and you have been chosen to bring it to a halt."

"Is he to be killed? That's simple. One merely has to buy a traitor from the Haratin village."

"We want him alive. Those are the orders. We need hostages to negotiate the withdrawal of the French garrisons. Charles the marabout rules over the Ahaggar, the very heart of the desert. Once he is fallen, discredited, chained, Ouksem will rally to the holy rebellion, then Moussa. Death would make him a martyr and anger Moussa. Alive, he will bring a large amount of gold. After we've humiliated him, we shall sell him back to the French, as we did with the Djanet prisoners. You will have your share, Beuh. Now, go! May the Most Holy guide your bullets and your spears!"

But Beuh ag Rhabelli himself was not that confident. Unfamiliar with Tamanrasset, he would be depending completely on the Targui Kerzou and his crew of pillagers. The white marabout seemed solidly entrenched in his little fort. And when Moussa departed, he must have left behind a few warriors who would be guarding the area around Tamanrasset. What could twenty or even forty men with only rifles and swords accomplish against the fort's thick walls? To demolish them would require a cannon. The Senoussi knew from experience that a few determined men posted in the towers could easily repel any attempt to scale the walls. Stocked with enough food and provided with a good well, the *bordj* could hold out for a month. As soon as the *rezzou* arrived, the marabout could dispatch a messenger to alert Moussa's warriors and the nearby garrison at Fort Motylinski. The *fellagha* (guerrilla fighters) raid might then end in a rout.

Unless Kerzou had a plan. That would be known in an hour, when the Targui rebel would be joining with the *rezzou*.

⚜

Tamanrasset, 6:15. The sun had risen and was climbing above the Koudia, the mountain ridge of the Ahaggar. The hermit heard the impatient bleating of a dromedary. The mail from In Salah! The important military post there, nearly four hundred miles from Tamanrasset, served as a station on the route to Algiers and France. Every two weeks communication between In Salah and Fort Motylinski took place, with a scheduled stop in Tamanrasset. The man, a camel trooper with the African army, had probably been riding for twelve days. He shouted: "Sidi Marabout! The mail has arrived!"

Brother Charles took him inside and fed him generously on flatbread and dates. But mostly the man was thirsty. While his guest ate, the hermit took the mail out of the postal bag. Recognizing Marie de Bondy's handwriting, his heart beat faster. Two letters from her! And two from Louis Massignon, his young friend who had been drafted. And the usual mail: the White Fathers of Maison-Carrée; the apostolic vicarate in Ghardaïa; Msgr. Bonnet, his faraway bishop. Newspapers from Paris and Algiers, a month old!

"Rest, Lazaoui. You can stay here. Tomorrow you'll be off to In Salah again, with the mail from Fort Moty."

The man shook his head. He seemed worried. Did he fear staying at the *bordj* because of a possible surprise attack? Obviously the hermit was alone and could not deal with an attack.

"When my camel has drunk, I'm going to the village to deliver the mailbag to a camel trooper from Fort Moty. He'll be back tomorrow with the bag for In Salah. I'll spend the night in Tam with my friend El Mehdi."

"I'll give you my letters before you leave tomorrow."

The man drew several buckets from the well and watered his camel. Then he mounted with a leap, waved good-bye to the hermit, and headed for the village, looking almost as if he were one with the hump of the animal, which lengthened its stride and melted into the gold of the sand.

Brother Charles returned to the bedroom, which also served as his office, and put down the mail. He seated himself at the desk cluttered with papers. He intended to write a letter to Captain de La Roche, the commander at Fort Motylinski. He would give it to the camel trooper who was coming that evening. As for the mail going to France, he had time. Lazaoui would not set out before the next morning.

He read his letters with delight and then once again became absorbed in his linguistic projects. After the enormous dictionary he had just completed—more than two thousand pages—after the grammar, he was going to elaborate on his work with a collection of poems, an unusual undertaking for a hermit! He bent over the text of a poem recited for him by Amenokal Moussa ag Amastane, who had composed the verses for a cousin with whom he was in love, the fair Dassine, the muse of the Ahaggar! Brother Charles had collected hundreds of other examples of Tuareg verse at the feet of Dassine, the living memory of the Sahara! Dassine, squatting on the sand with her *imzad* next to her on a string, transcended time and space. From a noble Tuareg family, wife of a retiring Targui named Aflan and older sister of Axamuk, who was Moussa's designated successor, Dassine (without making it obvious) actually ruled the Ahaggar tribe when Moussa was off in the Adrar hunting down moisture for the survival of the flocks, their only wealth.

Brother Charles put down his pen and smiled. Such was the paradox of Saharan civilization. Here in the desert, women, even married ones, had much greater freedom than in any Muslim country or even in France's aristocratic and bourgeois society, of which he considered himself a mediocre offspring. He went back to dreaming. What had he done with his life? In October 1876 he had entered famous Saint-Cyr, the special military school west of Paris.

If he had only known! How different reality from his dreams!

At first, everything had gone well. At the school there prevailed a spirit of revenge to which he had wholeheartedly subscribed. Proud of his class, which had selected the name "Plewna", he entered into the "spirit of Cyr". But it was not a school for young ladies. There also prevailed an ardent militarism, which Charles did not share. The school's discipline turned out to be harsher than that of the Jesuits! Dormitory. Up at 5 A.M. Exhausting exercise: riding, gymnastics, fencing, marches. Charles hated sports and anything violent. Intuitive, artistic, and literary, he did find at Saint-Cyr some "work for the mind": topography, military science, artillery, dimensioned drawing, ballistics, strategy for captains! A schedule so full he had to neglect his beloved Greek and Latin authors, whom he could get back to only on Sundays, and that without even having a room of his own.

He felt keenly the separation from his family, and camaraderie was not to make up for it. He did not fit in. He was different, physically and mentally. He had nothing of the soldier about him, this heavy eighteen-year-old with the puffy body and the fat face in which shone deep brown eyes occasionally animated by anger or passion.

Why did they scorn him, a young man of noble blood and great wealth? Because he was short? No. Flabby and potbellied, he was the antithesis of the brilliant officer. His arrival had very nearly turned into a disgrace. The military doctor had almost sent him packing, simply for "premature obesity"! Unfortunate consequence of the summer's family vacation, which a cousin would later recall: "Whenever the whole family gathered, we'd always dread seeing Charles head for the children's table, because he could gobble up all the cakes in no time."[2]

At Saint-Cyr, his uniform had to be custom-made since nothing in his size was to be found. For ten days he could be seen surrounded by his smart-looking comrades as he marched in civilian clothes, except for the Cyr garrison cap!

Awkward, he remained a "cossack". What was he doing at Cyr? The patriotism exacerbated by the occupation of his birthplace was no longer enough to give him the military spirit that the others were developing. He had hoped to fight and chase the Prussians from Alsace-Lorraine, and what did he see at Saint-Cyr, prestigious school for future officers destined to restore victory to France? An insipid concentrate of barracks and school-rooms, where cadets compiled useless treatises on fortifications! Soon the military spirit of revenge no longer motivated him. How could he over-look the fact that it also served as a useful cover for personal ambition? Here they loved glory just as the bourgeoisie loved wealth.

In the Second Company with Charles was one Philippe Pétain. "Nice fellow", Foucauld would say later. Charles' sergeant, Mazel, was to be the commander of the Fifth Army in 1915. And in charge of his dormitory, someone named Driant. Under the name Captain Danrit, he would pub-lish successful books exalting the glory of the army and the colonial em-pire. A heroic colonel, he was to fall at Verdun. One of the teachers, Lieutenant Dubail, would become Grand Chancellor of the Legion of Honor. And in the Third Company, a Sergeant Major Sarrail, unaware that he would become commander of the Third Army in 1914, save Verdun, and later head the Army of the East.

But in 1877 it was not yet the battlefield or heroic colonial adventures. Only the routine of a barracks-school. Boredom began gnawing at him. And yet, with the help of an exceptional memory and an unusually quick mind, he absorbed the curriculum without much effort. He needed do no more than glance at the lesson casually and in haste, and everything would be understood, assimilated, retained!

Thus, in his offhand way Charles passed the first-year courses at Saint-Cyr, placing 143rd out of 391. This ranking allowed him to choose the cavalry, the elite corps.

His concerns were not base. "I shall be spending my vacation in Nancy, because of my grandfather's health", he wrote his old lycée comrade, Gabriel Tourdes.[3] He hoped to be able to gorge himself on books. Oh! It would be good to read and translate Sallust, Horace, Erasmus!

---

[2] Quoted by René Pottier, *La Vocation saharienne du père de Foucauld* (Paris: Plon, 1939), 39.
[3] *Lettres à un ami de lycée* (G. Tourdes, 1874–1915) (Nouvelle Cité, 1982), 67.

In October 1877 he returned to Saint-Cyr for his second year. And boredom overcame him once more. "I am wholeheartedly bored here", he wrote to Gabriel Tourdes in January 1878. "So depressing to be able to read only 'theory' and revolting works on fortification, artillery, and so on. It all has a touch of the barbaric." [4]

Of what, of whom was he dreaming?

"Oh! If I could only be ten years older! I would probably not be in the service any more. I would be starting the life of an old bachelor, alone, in the country, in a nice little house. It is indeed good to be free and at peace, but it is hard to be alone. And yet, unavoidably, that is what I am condemned to." [5]

He had put into words his sense of foreboding. His guardian, his friend, the man who had replaced his father and whom he loved, Colonel de Morlet, died on February 3, 1878. Charles was deeply saddened.

"A whole period of my life is over now, peaceful family life, first readings, the happiness and calm that surrounded me with Grandfather close by. We were so happy, so unthinking, so confident of the future. In a single stroke my family has been taken from me, and my home, and my peace, and the carefree life that was so sweet. Never again shall I find all that." [6] "In a strange way, I have aged since a few months back. I had been asleep in my happiness and my carefree life. I awakened twenty years older." [7]

Twenty years? Yes, he would reach twenty on September 15, 1878. He was of age. And about to come into a double inheritance. The one from his parents and a portion of the one from Colonel de Morlet. Which proves that it never rains but it pours! An enormous fortune for this lost child: 353,500 francs (109,300 of it in real property) and 38,300 francs in property without usufruct, adding up to 391,800 francs. In today's currency, that would mean ten million francs [more than 1.5 million dollars], which could bring in an annual income of 500,000 francs [about 82,000 dollars]. This capital was managed by Charles' faithful business adviser in Nancy, Monsieur Laissy.

How was he going to use the veritable gold mine making him one of the richest officers in his Saint-Cyr class? After his beloved grandfather, there was no one to keep him from falling into a life of debauchery and gluttony. His second year was a disaster. Saved by his memory, however, he finished 333rd out of 386 in the Plewna class. In spite of this ranking, the loss of his first-class stripes, forty-five days of punishments and forty-seven days of confinement for carelessness, laziness, and unruliness, he was ad-

---

[4] Ibid., 69.
[5] Ibid., January 1878, 70.
[6] Ibid., February 5, 1878, 72–73.
[7] Ibid., April 13, 1878, 83–84.

mitted to the cavalry school at Saumur because of his good first-year
placement. He did get one benefit from his time at Saint-Cyr: he had lost
forty-five pounds!

A respite, the summer vacation spent with his Aunt Inès Moitessier, at
Louye, her château in the Eure. She was not good-natured, the lovely Inès,
and had little patience with this nephew who spent his days reading and
smoking, sprawled in an armchair or on his bed. She also felt sorry for him.
Did he not bear the burden of his paternal heredity? Wasn't he taking his
father's path? Working as little as possible. Loving pleasure, tobacco, alcohol, and fine dining. And the flesh . . .

"My dear Tourdes, I pass the time hunting and taking horseback and
carriage rides. I sleep late, I eat a lot and think little. Excellent conditions
for remaining healthy." [8]

And the place of God in all this? A blank. And Father Lanusse, the good
chaplain of Saint-Cyr, his cassock decorated with medals and face weathered
by the Mexican campaign, had not made Charles change his mind.

On October 31, 1878, Second Lieutenant Foucauld entered the École de
Cavalerie de Saumur. He had requested cavalry because of its panache, no
doubt, but also because he believed it to be not very tiring!

Saumur was an attractive, well-off little provincial city on the banks of
the wide and silvery Loire. The school had turned the town into the capital
of cavalry, complete with postcard photos: a horseman of the *Cadre Noir* in
his two-cornered hat and Imperial Guard boots; the riding ring; the
tackroom; everything having to do with horses!

Unfortunately, horses interested Second Lieutenant Foucauld very little.
He soon had a surfeit. To his friend Tourdes he wrote: "Some days there are
eleven hours of riding . . . and four hours of class. My days are spent on
horseback, my evenings are spent on horseback." [9] And it started at 5 A.M.!
Sometimes he managed to get a doctor's excuse from the chief medical
officer. But wasn't it Charles himself who had requested cavalry school?
And the others were very happy there! One only had to see them making
their way through narrow rue Alsace to the admiring looks of the populace,
magnificent steeds at a slow trot, brass gleaming, short coats immaculate, in
a nimbus of gold and dust as they headed toward the field of Verrie to
engage in acrobatic riding. Some were training for the Carrousel, the prestigious annual parade of the *Cadre Noir*.

But that sort of thing the young viscount no longer enjoyed, he who
had just come into his fabulous inheritance. There was Charles, enthroned

[8] Ibid., September 17, 1878, 95.
[9] Ibid., 104.

like a pasha in his room, number eighty-two, which he had furnished with light-colored cretonne curtains, mahogany bookshelves holding rare volumes, a soft bed, an upholstered easy chair, and a thick woolen rug.

Sundays he would shut himself up there with his favorite authors and feverishly make up for the school's Spartan diet. Spread out on his table, dishes prepared by the town's best caterers, along with fine wines. And since he found it a bore to eat and drink alone, he would invite one or another of his comrades, who were only too happy to take advantage of the little rich boy's gold mine.

"Come to my room Sunday. We'll imbibe!"

To help him "imbibe", Vallom was there, the evil spirit who would drag him into debauchery. For, unfortunately, it was two to a room, and Charles had the worst possible luck!

Antoine de Vallombrosa (soon to be Marquis de Morès), youngest son of the exceedingly rich Duke de Vallombrosa, was no stranger to Charles, who had encountered him at the Jesuit institution on the rue des Postes and at Saint-Cyr in 1877. Tall, slim, athletic, a good rider and sportsman, he had nothing in common with Charles except aristocratic arrogance and an unrestrained fondness for enjoying himself and squandering the family fortune.

Together they organized their free time, which would increase whenever bad conduct led to their being confined in their gilded room. Then they would use and abuse the town's best caterers. "It's Budan who's taking care of it": pâté de foie gras with truffles, petits fours, washed down with champagne. In the morning, Charles' barber would arrive to shave him. There is a story that he would ask to be awakened at 2 A.M. to finish his foie gras. When he was not on punishment, it was shopping in town, visits to the tailor, the bootmaker. In the evening, elegant suppers at Ragot's. For transportation, a brougham low to the ground. "After a good dinner, there's nothing like a good cigar, and to take you back home a nice little brougham, very low, so you don't have to go to the trouble of lifting your foot high to seat yourself in the carriage." [10]

Sprawled in his armchair, clad in white flannel pajamas sporting frog closures, he would smoke the world's most expensive Havana cigars, imported by a specialty broker. He would get "all stirred up" with trashy books. Since he could not receive young ladies in his room, he is said to have taken advantage of his outings to visit the "red-light district" on rue Courcouronne. But he soon tired of its demimondaines, the usual providers of entertainment for Saumur cadets. In the same way he imported the world's best cigars, he had the best-looking girls come from Paris, and he

---

[10] Quoted by Michel Carrouges, *Charles de Foucauld, explorateur mystique* (Cerf, 1954), 19.

set them up in a rented house near the school, generously sharing their charms with Vallombrosa. Sharing, orgies, fine dining. Did he take up the classic bet of the school's party animals? Thirty kilometers on horseback, three women, three bottles of champagne, all in three hours. Yes, there was nothing they did not say about Second Lieutenant Foucauld! "Engineer of debauchery, ascetic of sensuality",[11] convinced that sumptuous meals and a pretty woman's body would bring him happiness at last.

The story about devouring great mouthfuls of foie gras at night earned him the nickname *Le Porc* [pig]. His comrades took unfair advantage of his generosity, but out of jealousy they disparaged him. He was "fat Foucauld, greedy, revolting, and brutish."[12] Even Vallombrosa found him disgusting. "What do you expect?" was Charles' response. "Not every cavalryman can die at Reichshoffen!" Once, Charles would utter some terrible words: "I'm doing what my father did: I'm eating."[13]

His escapades extended beyond his room and the town. When not confined to quarters, he would take off. And even when confined to quarters, he would take off. One day he went to Tours for dinner disguised as a workman, complete with a false beard, only to be picked up when the police mistook him for an anarchist. No sooner had the lenient superintendent released him than it was his bad luck to run into General L'Hotte in person, the head of the school, an encounter that brought him two additional weeks of close arrest. He used the time to stuff himself.

There was also that incongruous, incomprehensible escapade: A runaway Foucauld—he had been refused leave—disguised as a beggar, seeking his bread in the countryside around Saumur, in the farms of the Maine-et-Loire. The gendarmes caught up with him just as he was about to leap from a bridge onto a moving train. Foucauld disguised as an indigent! Playing poor!

He was bored. He was tired of everything. He was running away like a child.

And now, an accounting: Charles had a total of twenty-one days of open arrest and forty-five days of close arrest, for a variety of offenses: poor work, incorrect dress, tardiness, failure to follow orders, unexcused absences. And the crowning touch: "Has 'forgotten' to collect his pay."

Barely passing his comprehensives (eighty-seventh out of eighty-seven), his final report was not an honorable one: "Conduct below average; scientific knowledge, none. Below average in his entire course of study. Social graces, none." And this harsh evaluation from the school's second in command: "Little military spirit. Insufficient sense of duty. A certain refine-

[11] Quoted by Charles Pichon, *Charles de Foucauld* (Éd. de la Nouvelle France, 1946), 38.
[12] Quoted by Marguerite Castillon du Perron, *Charles de Foucauld* (Grasset, 1982), 70.
[13] Quoted by Pichon, *Foucauld*, 34.

ment, well brought up, but frivolous, thinks only of enjoying himself. Very ordinary cavalryman."

And therein lay their mistake. Everything about that spoiled boy was out of the ordinary! And it was not all bad. The scenes of debauchery at Saumur and elsewhere have been exaggerated, blown up out of proportion to add some theater to Charles' tale.[14] But the harmful influence of the young Marquis de Morès-Vallombrosa has not been sufficiently emphasized. During vacations, he entertained Charles at his parents' sumptuous château, Abondant (six miles east of Louye, the Moitessier château), or at the family's equally sumptuous winter estate, a Gothic-Moorish château in Cannes.

Yet the two young men were not completely bad, for on January 3, 1879, Charles, with Morès as his sponsor, had been admitted to the Saint Vincent de Paul Society, which looked after the poor of Saumur.

Charles' tragedy consisted of having almost completely lost contact with the fine people who were his family. After Colonel de Morlet's death, he no longer saw his grandmother. In summer he would go to Abondant or Cannes rather than visit the Moitessiers. He still saw his gentle cousin Marie de Bondy at Louye, but she was so proper! Having gotten word of his escapades, Aunt Inès would reprimand him harshly and threaten to turn him out. He would take offense and go seek refuge at Abondant.

Morès was hopelessly lost. He was soon to resign from the army and marry a rich American. He indulged in a rabid anti-Semitism and set off on wild voyages of exploration all over the world, coming to a miserable end in the African desert, murdered by his guides.

And Charles?

With the sarcastic remark from Colonel Jacquemin ringing in his ears, "You leave in last place, I hope that ranking does not follow you, sir",[15] in October 1879 Second Lieutenant Foucauld was assigned to the Fourth Hussars in Pont-à-Mousson.

Since he was only an hour from Nancy, he planned to spend time in the apartment he still maintained there on the first floor of his grandparents' house, rue du Manège. He had little liking for the modest charms of the town of Pont-à-Mousson, where he had rented a studio apartment. The canal and the willow-lined Moselle delighted only fishermen, and he was not one. With a lack of artistic resources, the town's social life was limited and its ambiance austere in spite of the sometimes rowdy presence of the hussars and cuirassiers. So he also kept a place in Paris, a studio on rue de la Boétie.

[14] See General de Suremain's study in *Bulletin des Amitiés*, no. 99, 5.
[15] The colonel would have been quite surprised had he known that the class of 1978 at Saumur was to be named after Charles de Foucauld.

Once again Charles arranged for himself a life of luxury, which he strove to bring to a state of perfection. Smoking the best cigars and sampling the world's best foie gras were no longer enough. Thoroughbreds only in his prestigious stable! During leaves, he appeared before his family sporting the casual look that was to become his style: a dandy of the Belle Époque. He went to the theater. He smugly displayed his scholar's library, eighteen hundred rare bound volumes, acquired at great expense. A showoff, he liked to flaunt his wealth. He hated physical exercise but had an inquiring mind and a deep interest in geography, history, and travel. According to his ideas, to be socially acceptable one had to be quick, refined, and witty, never boring others nor speaking without having something to say.

Like so many of the other well-off young officers of his time, he sought a life in which pleasure greatly outweighed duty. Yet the confession uttered later, out of humility, need not be taken altogether seriously: "I was nearly dead, submerged in evil." [16] He arranged lavish late suppers at his apartment in Nancy. But when there was an alert, he would have to eat these meals in Pont-à-Mousson, doing so with his typical air of the gloomy, bored aristocrat. These nights were sometimes boisterous, and a few times he was evicted from his lodgings for disturbing the peace.

His relationship with the army remained ambiguous. His regiment, commanded by Colonel Beauvieux, included all kinds: aristocrats and lieutenants risen through the ranks. It was a harsh life; the forces remained at full strength because of the German threat, and the training proved intensive. Charles had no complaints about the Second Squadron, in which he served under the brilliant Captain Dalmas de La Pérouse. But the latter's adjunct, Captain Bressange, known as the Panther, would not put up with the young aristocrat's lack of discipline. Why the lack of discipline? It is easy to imagine that the more bored he grew, the more rebellious he felt. He loathed garrison life. But how can one remain an officer under all the constraints of military life and at the same time, thanks to money, yearn for freedom from all obligations?

Naturally, his reports were not very good. The review of August 1880 resulted in this qualified statement: "Being very young, this officer lacks firmness and enthusiasm. Of undeveloped character, he has much work ahead before he can perform at the level expected." Then, to soften the verdict: "He is upright, with sound judgment; he carries out his assigned duties well enough. But insufficient zeal and inclination. He might do better given proper guidance."

A perplexing account. His remarkable ability to synthesize continued to

---

[16] CF, "14° méditation", "Retraite à Nazareth", November 8, 1897.

astound. He was so gifted and his memory so remarkable that he could turn out reports almost effortlessly while others struggled over them for days on end.

At first Charles was happy with the good life; then, as at Saumur, once all the facile pleasures had been exhausted, he sank into ennui and dissatisfaction. It was an hour of extreme danger. He was almost killed while riding. He narrowly avoided fighting duels, the challenges occasioned by the lavish spending that offended many of the poorer officers. Because he was large and heavy for someone only five feet four inches tall, they called him "Father Foucauld".

Did he at least have some friends? He replaced the young Marquis de Morès-Vallombrosa with another aristocrat of the same vintage, a partying type. Jacques de Miramon, soon to be Duke de Fitz-James, was six years older than Charles and had but one goal in life: to have a good time. So history was to repeat itself! With the help of his new friend, Charles arranged lavish parties and huge feasts, thus winning high praise from Fitz-James: "How could one not love and esteem such a good comrade? With perfect tact and exquisite delicacy, he would let us benefit from his purse. I'd see him win heavily at cards, then lose deliberately without making it obvious. A real gourmet, he loved treating us!"

Then there was Mimi.

Her name was said to be Marie Cardinal. She was supposedly a dancer at the Paris Opera. Fiction.[17] The fact is that some of the well-off bachelor officers would make their weekends more pleasant by bringing down from Paris girls of easy virtue, demimondaines, and would speak of them as "dancers".

This daughter of a respectable Lorraine working man was twenty-four in 1880, well brought up, gentle, intelligent, charming. Being very independent, she had gone up to Paris, where she became an actress in a minor theater. The love affair was probably the first of any duration for Charles (then twenty-two). He moved her into his Pont-à-Mousson apartment, where they lived together as husband and wife. She dreamed of becoming part of the *beau monde*. Perhaps Charles really loved her. She proved a cheerful and patient companion. Unlike other demimondaines, she stayed in the background and did not make scenes. She loved him, and not just because of his money. Was she hoping for marriage? Probably. To him, the prospect was unthinkable. He even refused to receive her at the family home in Nancy and uttered the odious words, "No fox soils his own earth", the earth in question being the Foucauld mansion on rue du Manège.

---

[17] In *Bulletin des Amitiés*, no. 120, 11, General de Suremain looks at the question and separates fact from fiction.

Receiving word about what appeared to be a long-term relationship, Charles' family grew concerned; they feared marriage or ruin. But knowing how independent and touchy he was, they did not press the matter. True, the Moitessiers were ready to institute proceedings to impose legal restraints on Charles and assign him a conservator, but Mimi was not the sole reason: there were also his prodigious expenditures and his open-handed generosity to Morès-Vallombrosa.

The army, for its part, took this ordinary little matter seriously. Charles was flaunting Mimi. In July 1880 came the first punishment: "Consorting in public with a woman of loose morals."

The army could do no more. There were other more urgent concerns. The regiment was under pressure, almost on a war footing. Large-scale maneuvers were underway, and Charles' regiment was reassigned to Sétif, Algeria, as part of a routine rotation.

Earlier, on August 7, Colonel de Poul had replaced Colonel Beauvieux as leader of the Fourth Hussars. The new commander did not put up with the escapades of the young second lieutenant, and he wrote a scathing report to the general who headed the Sétif subdivision: "His marks at the cavalry school were poor. On July 12, 1880, he was punished with two weeks of open arrest for walking abroad, on a weekday, dressed in civilian clothes and accompanied by the woman of loose morals with whom he is living. The eve of our departure for Algeria, I forbade him to let the woman follow him there." [18]

The petty test of strength between the army and Foucauld had begun.

Disregarding the colonel's orders, Foucauld took his mistress to Algeria. The story goes that instead of acting with discretion, he bought a steamer ticket for "Madame the Viscountess de Foucauld"! He adored defiant acts that challenged the established order and the rules of his world.

Aboard ship, the farce continued. Since Mimi was sailing prior to his own departure, Charles commended her to the ship's purser, who fell for the hoax with no attempt to verify the status of his passenger. The sailor probably thought he was acting properly when he presented the lady to the sub-prefect of Bône. Marie played the game; she was a good actress. She was living her role and already saw herself as a viscountess. Besides, how could she turn back now?

When Charles disembarked a few days later, he was delighted by the success of the hoax. So he kept it up. And the truth did not come out until the arrival of the lawful spouses of the regiment's officers. The scandal was all the greater for having taken so long to surface. Colonel de Poul's report continues: "On November 24, Major Pelajont, commander of the regimen-

[18] Archives of the Ministry of War, in *Lettres à un ami*, 193.

tal detachment in Bône, in conformance with my orders, imposed on Monsieur de Foucauld two weeks of open arrest for having brought to Algeria the woman with whom he was living in France and for having refused to ensure the departure of said woman, in spite of my explicit orders. On December 22, the major imposed on Monsieur de Foucauld further discipline, two weeks of close arrest for 'his continued insistence on living, outside of wedlock, with the woman and his resistance to all counsel offered by the general in command of the subdivision'." [19]

The second lieutenant's "resistance" was indeed stubborn. But there was no army regulation that kept an off-duty officer from spending time with a lady, provided she behaved discreetly. Mimi lived at the hotel. He stayed in the barracks. Everything was according to the rules.

But the colonel persisted. His honor was at stake, and the army's, so he thought. He also felt like a fool, for all the young officers had taken Foucauld's side. To die for France, fine. But our private lives, no business of the army's!

After two weeks of close arrest, Charles still would not give in. The commander of the Constantine division sentenced him to thirty days behind bars. After which Charles joined his squadron in Sétif and appeared before his quick-tempered colonel: "What are your intentions regarding this woman?"

"They are unchanged, sir."

The colonel's report goes on: "In view of this officer's obstinacy, and with all possible means of chastisement having been employed, I see only one way of bringing to a close a situation that might otherwise lead to a serious breach of discipline: namely, a request that the officer be placed on non-active status, with no military duties." [20]

A major punishment, but not an unusual one. The Duke de Fitz-James had just been subjected to the same penalty. Charles had not been discharged from the army. He was temporarily on inactive status, without pay, for an undetermined length of time. They wanted to make him yield.

He retreated to Évian with his mistress. He ended up there, not out of devotion to her, but out of pride, as subsequent events would show. He had begun to love Algeria; the Kabyle people fascinated him. He had been devouring books and had carried out a few brief explorations. He was already dreaming of its mysterious southern regions, of the desert. The army, that was another matter. He loathed garrison life. He had not gone into the army to have an ordinary little career but to fight, to wrest his birthplace, Alsace, from the Prussians. And now? How was he to escape this impasse?

[19] Ibid.
[20] Ibid.

Évian, April 10, 1881. A lake, roses in bloom. The Hôtel de France, a splendid establishment, home to one hundred privileged guests taking the waters. Charles and Marie stayed in an annex, the luxurious villa Mon Désir. Évian's *Journal des baigneurs*, which listed the names of visitors of quality, was to mention "Madame and the Viscount de Foucauld".

The casino. Charles, black suit, black look, bristly mustache, watched wearily as Marie lost a few écus at baccarat. He was bored. He was tired of Marie, who dreamed of nothing but marriage, a substantial house, liveried servants, children.

Charles continued to fritter away his inheritance: staggering hotel bills, horse and carriage, gambling, fine dining, Mimi's outfits and jewelry. It did not help; nothing could fill the emptiness in his heart.

As for the family, the last meeting had provided no hope. He had flown into a rage over the case the Moitessiers were bringing before the court in Nancy; they sought a court-appointed counselor for Charles in view of his "squandering his fortune with wild bouts of spending". Aunt Inès characterized him as a "spineless weakling". He no longer wanted to see her—or her daughter Marie de Bondy. They still corresponded, out of habit, but he wished to forget her. Marie was expecting her third child. She led an increasingly austere existence, loathing the world and all those things that fascinated Charles. She loved only her children, her religion, and serious conversation. Moralistic, she was a perfectionist, an activist, and a worrier. She could not bear her cousin Charles' aristocratic casualness or his wild spending. And his women . . . horror, hell. Marie was in the hands of priests, "directors of conscience", and other pious types. One especially was guiding her with an iron hand: a curate at Saint-Augustin in Paris, Father Huvelin, who was also the mother's confessor—need more be said?

The weeks went by. The lovely month of May began, and the roses were in full bloom. On May 5, Charles, who had kept in touch with his comrades by mail, received a letter postmarked Sétif. The regiment was leaving for Tunisia to put down the rebellious Kroumirs. The officer began to wake as if from a dream. He rushed off to the hotel lobby and asked to see the newspapers, which he had ignored up to then. Algeria was on the front page, with bold headlines: "Revolt of Bou Amama"; "*Jihad* proclaimed in the South Oranais"; "Uprising of the Ouled Sidi Sheik"; "Fourth Chasseurs in Heavy Combat".

He read the article excitedly: "The War Ministry has decided to put the four squadrons of the African Fourth Chasseurs at the disposal of General Cerez, commander of the Oran Division. The troops, led by Colonel Innocenti, will be concentrated in Tafaraoua to help maintain order in the South Oranais."

Charles' regiment, the Fourth Hussars, stationed at Sétif to guard the Tunisian frontier, awaited its own call to action.

Charles avidly read the earlier communiqués. The origins of the crisis went back to 1879. Interested in extending their influence southward, the French had sent a mission to plan the layout for a railroad line to the South Oranais. In Tiout, the local people had shown hostility. The army then set up a military post in the area, angering the rebel elements led by the Oulad-Gharaba tribe's marabout, Bou Amama, who preached the holy war, or *jihad*. In 1880, a company of more than one hundred *goumiers* (tribal soldiers under French command) had received orders to stop him, but to no avail. The rebellion spread. The government equivocated. By February 18, 1881, the revolt had reached the southern region, where Bou Amama had also proclaimed the *jihad*. In the northeastern foothills of the Ahaggar, the members of Colonel Flatters' mission planning another railroad layout had been brutally massacred by Attici's rebels. In the South Oranais an officer on his way to arrest Bou Amama had had his throat cut. Thus, the sending in of massive reinforcements.

Charles de Foucauld rose from his chair, eyes shining with excitement. They were going to fight, and he was not there! He rushed to the villa.

"What is happening?" asked Mimi, alarmed.

"I am going to Lyon. An emergency. Don't worry."

Two hours later he was on the train. The next morning he appeared before the general of the Fourth Army Corps, Charles' commanding officer since the move to Évian.

"Monsieur de Foucauld! To what do we owe the pleasure?"

"Sir, I am respectfully requesting to be reinstated."

The officer, who knew Charles well, stared at him in amazement. "You do know the conditions?"

"Yes, sir. I am ready to break off immediately."

The general did not find this "conversion" credible. What was the rebellious young viscount up to this time? "Just what is going on, lieutenant?"

"Sir, I wish to fight! I am asking the minister to reinstate me. I accept all your conditions, and I offer to serve, if necessary, as a simple cavalry *spahi* [21] without a rank."

"Very good. Draw up your request for reinstatement. I shall send it on to the War Ministry, and the general who heads the cavalry office will decide what action to pursue."

"Will this be a long process, sir?"

The general smiled. He was pleased. The army was going to get back its enfant terrible. "Come now, Father Foucauld! I'm looking out for you!"

---

[21] A North African serving in the French army.—TRANS.

On May 14, the commander of the Fourth Army Corps sent the following dispatch to Paris:"The officer requests to be recalled to active duty and respectfully asks to be assigned to a regiment going to the field. He pledges on his honor that he will no longer see his former mistress, either in his own home or in his regimental garrison. I recommend that he be reinstated." [22]

On May 16, Second Lieutenant Charles de Foucauld was reinstated by presidential decree and given his old rank. His assignment was yet to be decided.

At El Mouellek in the South Oranais, May 19, a bloody battle pitted the rebels of Bou Amama against the French, who suffered a crushing defeat: sixty dead, twenty-two wounded, their convoy captured. Exhilarated by his success, Bou Amama headed north, pillaging and massacring as he went. The African Fourth Chasseurs received orders to move toward the South Oranais. The Fourth Hussars would probably be joining them. In Évian, Charles was stamping his feet.

On June 13 his assignment finally arrived: he was posted, not to the Fourth Hussars, his old regiment, but to the Fourth Chasseurs, then based in Mascara. After his last good-byes to Mimi, who received substantial financial compensation, on June 20 he sailed from Marseille for Oran. The campaign against Bou Amama had begun, and Charles found himself in the center of the action. A new man was soon to be born.

What had happened inside the head of this neurotic child, this profligate, party-loving young aristocrat, who, once he had landed in Africa, was to prove a remarkable officer? There are several conflicting explanations for this spectacular, unexpected turnabout. Some have seen it as a "generous impulse" and quote what Foucauld said to Louis Massignon in another context:"We must never hesitate to ask for those posts where the danger, sacrifice, and devotion are greatest. Honor, let us leave that to whoever wishes it, but danger, difficulty, let us always claim them." [23]

We are getting a bit ahead of ourselves! The Foucauld "finally transformed into his real self by eternity" had not yet been born. A letter from Saida dated October 8, 1881, is closer to reality. He writes his friend Gabriel Tourdes:"Naturally, I asked to go back to the army. An expedition like this is too great a *pleasure* to let go by and not enjoy. I am with a column that is maneuvering on the high plateaux. Very entertaining. I like camp life as much as I disliked garrison life."

"Pleasure, enjoy, entertaining." Perplexing words indeed.

Whatever the reason, definitely a turnabout. For he did undergo a

[22] *Bulletin des Amitiés*, no. 106.
[23] CF to L. Massignon, December 1, 1916, in G. Gorrée, *Sur les traces de Charles de Foucauld* (Éd. de la Plus Grande France, 1936), 311.

metamorphosis. "Father Foucauld!" In Africa the bookish party-lover with the flabby paunch, the habitué of gourmet restaurants, proved to be an excellent soldier and a leader. He endured the harsh constraints of African life, not only the dangers, but also the discomforts—and that is too weak a word. It is hard to picture "fat Foucauld", "Le Porc", on horseback under the sweltering sun of southern Algeria, he who only a few days before had been lolling on the leather upholstery of his coupé. His future friend, General Laperrine—who, along with Henri de Castries, Lyautey, and Motylinski, took part in the suppression—would later write: "Cheerfully putting up with the harshest trials, constantly risking his life, scrupulously looking after his men, he won the admiration of the regiment's experts, the old 'Mexicans'."[24]

What was left of the cynical playboy? "A charming little edition of Aristophanes, always with him, and a small remnant of snobbishness, which led him to stop smoking once he could no longer obtain his favorite brand of cigars", Laperrine concluded with a touch of humor.

So, why the change? A liking for action, a dislike for ennui? He had exhausted worldly pleasures, those of the table and the flesh. He knew they would never fill the emptiness born of his traumatic childhood and his loss of faith. But mainly it was his fascination with the Africa he had already glimpsed in Sétif. Thus, Charles de Foucauld's first "conversion": a deep love for the light and the vastness of the desert, its silences and starry nights. The call of Africa. The return to a primitive, wholesome life through the Berber peoples he was discovering. A feeling of power, too—for not all his motives were pure—as would be described by a fellow officer, the young camel trooper Psichari, recalling the exaltation of a youthful lieutenant at the head of twenty-five men, silently marching through the desert in search of the *rezzou*: "Africa! I can demand anything of her; for her, I can demand anything of myself. Because she is the earthly representation of eternity, she gives me the true, the good, and the beautiful."[25]

As J.-F. Six has stressed, God as yet played no part in the evolution of Charles' character and personality. There was even real danger in the "sudden surfacing of a wish for power, the frantic quest for knowledge, the mania to explore everything and fill in all the gaps",[26] which would take possession of the young officer. Who could predict to what heights or what depths those tendencies might lead him?

Until then, he had escaped from his neuroses, first, by dreaming, then,

[24] Laperrine, "Étapes de la conversion d'un houzard".
[25] Ernest Psichari, *Le Voyage du centurion* (Conard, 1922); English trans.: *A Soldier's Pilgrimage* (London: A. Melrose, 1917).
[26] J.-F. Six, *Itinéraire spirituel de Charles de Foucauld* (Seuil, 1958), 32.

by unbridled partying. Now he was escaping through action. The more violent the military action, the more it would serve his need.

Was there not also an unconscious desire to be rehabilitated in the eyes of his family, whom he had stopped seeing but had in no way rejected? His heart still bled from the lash of the whip inflicted by Aunt Inès' calling him "a spineless weakling". And Marie de Bondy, of course. And the other Marie, too, Marie de Blic, his delicate younger sister, so ill-prepared for her role as wife and mother, as traumatized as he was by the tragic death of their parents.

Africa! "A drunkenness that has naught to do with alcohol, an intoxication of sun, light, and bliss", said Lyautey, who served in the Second Hussars. Why was Charles drawn to these vast expanses, if not because there arose in him a desire for the absolute, "a thirst for freedom from all limitations"? [27]

He did not know it yet, but "the desert is an invitation and a purification for the soul." [28]

Six months in the field, on the high plateaux of Algeria and Morocco, hunting down Bou Amama's rebels. Soundly defeated at Kreider on July 9, 1881, the marabout retreated south, deep into the desert with his savage *fellagha*. The orders were not to pursue them. Let the vast desert do with them what it wished! Along with Attici and Ahmoud, Bou Amama found refuge in Tripoli, from where he pondered his revenge.

The Fourth Chasseurs' slow journey back to their base camp. Just as a cloud of sand raised by the wind must fall to earth, Charles was returned once more to daily life and to himself.

The balance sheet of the six months in action proved to be positive. He had made an excellent showing as a soldier. He was a true young leader, brave, concerned about his men, prepared to risk his own life. Accustomed to urban luxuries, he had withstood the harsh life of the desert surprisingly well. It was even a revelation for him: it seemed the expression of his inner self.

On December 4, 1881, Charles' special column was dissolved. On January 24, his squadron returned to its Mascara garrison, where Charles found once more the usual ambiance of army life. It made no difference that the officers he lived among were patriots; once the violence of war was finished, he had nothing in common with them. Nitpicking, meticulous, dedicated to the regiment and the military, their horizons were limited to weapons drills and horsemanship. With few exceptions, no intellectual

[27] Ibid., 34.
[28] Ibid.

curiosity, no real culture. An unimaginative sense of superiority vis-à-vis the native troops, with whom the French did not socialize in spite of living in their midst: all the lowly soldiers in the African army were Muslims. Indifferent to the peoples of the region also, whether they were Kabyles, Berbers, Arabs, or Jews. These ethnic groups who had somehow managed to coexist for a thousand years fascinated Charles, but how could he understand them without speaking their languages? And what French officer, except for bureaucrats devoted to administering Arab affairs, would dream of learning such tongues?

A profound malaise, an existential emptiness overcame Charles once again. Was he going to fall back into his dissolute existence? No, that did not appeal to him. An idea then much in vogue obsessed him: exploration. He did not yet have a specific destination. It could be Egypt or the East. Perhaps with the young Marquis de Morès-Vallombrosa, his evil influence from Saumur, who had just resigned from the army and was still shamelessly borrowing money from Charles.

A letter to his friend Gabriel Tourdes on October 2, 1881, showed his uncertainty: "When the column is done with, I'll try to go somewhere else, wherever there is some action." Where was there action? Tonkin? Charles was also thinking of the squadron of Algerian *spahis* serving in Senegal. A very popular assignment that he did not succeed in obtaining. Morès was planning to depart for the East. His father, the Duke de Vallombrosa, had cut off his credit; Charles loaned his friend one hundred thousand francs, a quarter of his fortune! And without the slightest guarantee. He decided to accompany the marquis and requested leave. The army said no.

A liberating refusal, the long-awaited excuse to break with the army. He turned in his resignation January 28, 1882, stating that he intended to make a "great journey to the East" with Morès. Exploration had become his obsession. He wrote to his friend Tourdes on February 18: "I have given my resignation. I detest garrison life. I find the profession overwhelmingly dull in peacetime. What is the point of plodding along aimlessly in a life that does not interest me? I would rather spend my youth traveling. That way, I shall learn about the world and will not be wasting my time." [29]

But life is never simple. He had forgotten about the family and the threat of conservatorship hanging over his head. The family had been dismayed to hear of his resignation and his loans to Morès. They summoned him to Paris. Rebellious already, he appeared before these relatives who claimed they were saving him from himself and from financial ruin.

The most vociferous was his legal guardian, his renowned uncle, Sigismond Moitessier . . . Aunt Inès Moitessier gazed down at him from the

[29] *Lettres à un ami*, February 18, 1882.

lofty heights of her righteousness. The Latouche branch was no less aggressive. Sigismond fired the first round: "When you went back into the army, we thought you were on the right path. And now you're resigning!"

"I want to explore the world! There are so many unknown lands! The East, Morocco, too . . ."

"That's insane", groaned Aunt Inès. "The country is closed off; they say a rebellion is raging. The Arabs from the north and the Berbers from the south are killing each other. The French are not about to intervene!"

"The rebellion doesn't bother me, quite the opposite. If there were no danger, there would be no pleasure in going."

"Fantasy of a spoiled child! Get married, Charles! Live according to your rank and make an honorable career in the army."

The voices rose. The threat was spelled out. They were going to cut off his allowance. The court at Nancy had already settled the matter: all that remained was the naming of a conservator. The litany of grievances was recited. Instead of living prudently on his income, in three years Charles had dissipated a quarter of his capital. They were shocked at his not having insisted on the repayment of the loans—totaling 104,000 francs—made to Morès-Vallombrosa who, after his February 15 marriage to an American heiress, had given up on the East and was planning to leave for the Dakota Territory.

"Money doesn't interest me."

"But how will you finance your journey to Morocco, when you won't even have your meager pay from the army?"

Stubborn Charles wanted to shout that this inherited money belonged to him and that he could do with it as he pleased. The court had decreed otherwise. Charles agreed that his cousin from Nancy, Georges de Latouche, would become his counselor; he did not want to hear any talk about a conservator!

Months went by. The army, hoping he would change his mind, delayed acting on his resignation. Charles was learning Arabic. By the end of May, he had come to a firm decision: he would explore Morocco. The country was still independent but lacked strong central authority; confusion and insecurity reigned there, created by petty tribal chiefs and *rezzou* leaders.

On June 12, the Nancy court, granting the family's request, declared Charles a "spendthrift", incapable of managing his financial affairs; they named as conservator Georges de Latouche,[30] forty years of age, formerly a

---

[30] Georges (1842–1895) was the son of Adolphe de Latouche, a member of the old Lorraine aristocracy. In 1842 Colonel de Morlet had taken as his second wife Georges' sister, Amélie de Latouche. In childhood, Charles was very close to this branch of the family, and he saw his cousin Georges during vacations at the romantic Latouche château, Birkenwald.

lawyer in Saverne, and a sub-prefect in Reims. Henceforth, Charles could not sign any bank document without first going through Latouche! In August the army, seeing that Charles was not going to give up, finally accepted his resignation. He had served the minimum period of enlistment agreed to upon his entering Saint-Cyr: five years. He remained an officer in the reserves.

Charles breathed a sigh of relief. For a few days, he felt unsure about the Moroccan exploration, so risky and still not funded. But he had abandoned the idea of following Morès-Vallombrosa and his nebulous projects to the United States.

⚜

Tamanrasset, December 1, 1916. Prostrate in the sand at the foot of the altar for some time, Charles rose slowly to his feet, whispering: "At the same time that you, through the invention of your love, kept my soul from being irretrievably submerged . . ."[31]

He smiled. Was it growing late? In the blue sky over Tamanrasset, the sun now stood high. Paul would soon be arriving to prepare his 11 A.M. meal.

On his way out into the courtyard, he thought nostalgically of the days when he was alone at the hermitage and had prepared his own bread. With a few scraps from packing cases, he would light a small fire under a large flat stone. While his cooking surface heated up, he would mix a cup of water with four cups of barley flour, adding a thimbleful of salt. Then he would knead this coarse, unleavened dough and use a stick to shape it into several thin, flat cakes. To transport a cake to the hot stone, he would first roll it around the stick. When the bread was golden, he would turn it over and cook the other side. It smelled good, and he would give thanks to God . . .

⚜

Some sixty miles to the northeast, the *rezzou* led by Senoussi Beuh ag Rhabelli had stopped. The heat was suffocating. Beuh uncovered the abandoned well that marked the spot where he was to meet the *fellagha*. A small patch of green indicated there would be water deep down. His men lowered the bucket fastened to the edge of the well. They brought up several quarts of water, muddy but cool. They gave thanks to Allah.

From behind a dune appeared the tall silhouette of a veiled man on a camel. There was an exchange of known signals. The Targui rebel Kerzou, deserter from the camel troopers' unit at Fort Motylinski, was the man

---

[31] Cf, "14° méditation", "Retraite à Nazareth", November 8, 1897.

chosen to carry out the raid on Tamanrasset; he approached the envoy of Si Mohamed Labed and greeted him. He did not like Beuh, who was younger and less experienced than he. But Beuh was the confidant of Si Mohamed Labed, who had put Kerzou in charge of the raid to capture the marabout Charles.

The *fellagha* sat astride a large white camel, a combat animal, fast and tough, the long-distance runner of the desert, capable of covering up to more than sixty miles without a stop. Kerzou missed the *rezzous* of the old days, before the arrival of the French. Back then the Targui warrior would carry in his right hand a long barbed spear, with a verse from the Koran engraved in the iron. In his left, there would be a light shield of antelope hide bearing mysterious signs in red ochre. At his side, the Targui saber, a strong straight blade with a hilt in the shape of a cross. All that was no more. Now, just a repeating rifle taken from the Italians in Rhat, a modern weapon that could kill a man at more than three hundred feet.

The two men greeted each other haughtily. Beuh seemed uneasy. He asked, "How do we proceed, Kerzou?"

"By nightfall we shall be in Tam."

"Do we have reason to fear Moussa's warriors?"

"His men are over three hundred miles to the south, grazing their flocks in the Adrar. If he has left some warriors in Tam, it cannot be many."

"And the soldiers of Fort Moty?"

"Two-thirds of them are gone. They are covering Moussa's tribe, which is being threatened by our brother, Kaoucen. The handful of camel troopers still at Motylinski has withdrawn inside the fort and will not venture out unless someone comes in search of them."

"The sedentary Dag Rali of Tam?"

"They have taken shelter in the mountains of the Koudia."

"The fort is ours then!"

"Attacking head-on is out of the question. There is no way of knowing whether the marabout has kept some men to defend the place. He is a former officer, experienced in desert warfare. We can only get in by surprising him."

"And how do you plan to do that, Kerzou?"

"Among my Amsel friends who took part in the failed plot of last September, I have a man I can count on, even though he is a black. El Madani ag Soba knows the marabout, who cured him of an eye infection."

"If he knows him, might he not betray us?"

"El Madani also knows where his interest lies. He cannot resist the lure of gold. He was involved in the September plot, when four of our Amsel friends were taken prisoner by the Fort Moty *roumis*. He knows he is a hunted man. He has nothing to lose."

"If the marabout cared for him and probably fed him too, how could he betray him? The Koran says: 'The one who loves you, even if he be a dog, you will love in equal measure.'"

"He is just a Haratin, a former slave. It is acceptable to make use of such a wretch. His soul belongs to sin." He hesitated, then went on: "The Haratin village is within spear range of the fort. They will not stir."

"You are certain?"

"They will not stir. They are too cowardly. We have only the Arab camel troopers to fear, our Muslim brothers who have betrayed the cause and serve under the colors of the *roumis*. But they are terrified, and as I have told you, they have withdrawn inside Fort Moty. The only risk lies in being seen by runners: messengers, mail carriers. That is why we shall operate at night, silently."

"If El Madani is sought by the Franks, he is hiding. How shall we find him?"

"I have friends in Amsel. They know where to find El Madani."

3

Exploring Morocco

From his room Brother Charles looked out at the deep blue sky over Tamanrasset, and he sighed. The clarity of space never ceased to amaze him; he responded to it with his entire being. The sky! The sky of "Tam", clear but for a few gold-edged, transparent clouds floating like spaceships, never dropping rain.

He wished he could leave the confines of the fort and see the thousands of colorful flowers blooming around the hermitage; they appeared with the morning dew but were dead by noon, withered under the pitiless sun. He wished he could cross the path of some poor Haratin, up early to work his little garden plot in the sandy, rocky ground: barley, a few vegetables from starts Charles had distributed, the seeds sent by Marie de Bondy. Must he always stay inside the *bordj*? Yes, that was better. Was he not a monk, once cloistered here in his hermitage behind a symbolic line of large stones and now enclosed behind the thick walls of this military structure? What did he need to look for on the outside? He had everything here, for he had God, the only necessity, and Jesus, a Real Presence in the consecrated Host.

This morning, December 1, 1916, he could not concentrate on his usual meditation: the Calvary of Jesus, who had given all so men might stop hating one another. And he, Brother Charles, had he too given all? Once again he became absorbed in his memories.

What an unbelievable adventure, his 1883 departure for the interior of a hostile, unknown Morocco! It had all begun in Algiers at the end of May 1882. He had moved into number 58 on the Valée Slope, in the working-class district of Bab-el-Oued, where he led the life of a poor student.

He, once the Viscount de Foucauld, poor! His last confrontation with the family had been a stormy one! He was in their power! A private talk with his cousin and conservator Georges de Latouche, since old Sigismond Moitessier had declared himself ready to forget his reckless nephew. Georges, forty, a most reasonable and respectable fellow. Bearded, conventional, moralistic, extremely serious, and determined to save poor Charles whether he liked it or not.

An emotional confrontation. Charles loved Georges as a brother, even though they had chosen opposite paths. His Uncle Moitessier and the fair Inès had advised the conservator to offer Charles a deal: if he stayed in the army, the income from his inheritance would be at his disposal. But Georges did not share their ideas. To refuse him the trip to Morocco might mean his returning to debauchery in response to the boredom of garrison life. Worse, he might fall into a depression (like his father!). To deny him any subsidy might lead to his involvement in a lethal spiral of indebtedness.

But if Charles undertook this crazy solo expedition to Morocco, he would be risking his life. Moulay Hassan, Sultan of Fez, had given a few Europeans permission to go into the northern part of the country. But the sultan controlled only a fifth of Morocco; the rest was ruled by *kaids* (local magistrates) and by independent tribal leaders, some of them troublemakers. Of course it was the "unsubdued territory" that interested Charles, including the southern edge bordering on the desert. The French Army could be of no help to him. It would not be going to Morocco. Not yet. Georges had asked, "Why Morocco?"

"The solo exploration of an unknown and supposedly dangerous country—that would be thrilling!"

Then the two who had been boys together seemed to communicate silently. It was as if Charles were saying, "Let me have this chance to come through at last, to prove myself, to become someone else, or rather to find my real self."

"Fine. In Algiers you should lay the groundwork for your trip to Morocco. But the life of luxury, that's over! You will have . . . 350 francs a month."

Charles was astonished. He would have 350 francs?[1] He had spent four thousand a month in his days of glory!

Then, suddenly feeling liberated, he burst out laughing. It was wonderful—money no longer meant anything to him! Had he ever had faith in it? Servants, carriages, fine dining, clothes, mistresses—an era gone forever. The essential lay hidden elsewhere, in the will to envision and realize some great enterprise. He fell into the arms of his astonished cousin. He was not through surprising them, Georges and the rest of the family! How he loved them, all told, those prudent, moralistic bourgeois, those aristocrats locked into their fine principles and their privileges.

Georges also laughed, relieved. He had been expecting tantrums. Or even worse: that Charles, bullied, would once again become a debtor, following that dishonorable path so dreaded by families. And yet here he

---

[1] Around ten thousand, in today's francs. In 1882 a worker earned about one hundred francs a month, or approximately three thousand in today's francs.

was, docile and pleasant, agreeing to lead the life of a poor, insignificant student in Bab-el-Oued. From whence had come this miracle? What had changed Charles? Africa.

Five months had gone by. The summer heat lay heavy over Algiers, the white city. On rue de l'État Major stood Mustafa Pasha's former palace, now devoted to silence and study, for it had become the city library. Charles had gazed upon the long shelves of books with love and respect. Books! He had rediscovered the grand passion of his youth. For months, he had been absorbed in books and manuscripts: exploration, linguistics, religion, wars, everything he could get his hands on. And the Koran also. In Algiers he had met historians, geographers, doctors, soldiers. He had thrown himself into the life of a penniless student and dedicated researcher. He was learning literary and conversational Arabic and Hebrew. And all this in anticipation of unknown Morocco, the Atlas, the desert.

An unusual personality ruled over the library and archives. Oscar MacCarthy, a sixty-seven-year-old Irishman, had been one of the first explorers of Algeria. Intrigued by the regions farther south, in 1849 he had almost reached Timbuktu. Bulging forehead, immense close-cropped head, full beard, weathered face dominated by gentle blue eyes. A small, spare man, his hands were never still, as if they were trying to grasp the elusive dream, the unfinished dream of his youth: to follow his exploration of Algeria with a journey to southern Morocco. The Atlas Mountains, the mystery of the Berber tribes . . . MacCarthy had not gone to Morocco, but he had read everything about that mysterious country. He was now too old to explore, worn out by his adventurous life. He could do no more than pass his enthusiasm on to someone younger. And now there was someone, a real godsend! Between MacCarthy and Foucauld, instant rapport.

"On the surface, Morocco appears to be a single political unit. But actually, there are one hundred troublesome tribes that Sultan Moulay Hassan is trying to bring together into a Sharifian kingdom."

"Is that possible?"

"Not without one of the great European powers. Germany? Spain? France? Our government's game is to persuade the sultan that he won't be able to gain true control without our protectorate, since only our army can end the looting, the corruption, the disturbances. Many of the *kaids* look at the example of Algeria, pacified and prosperous. They are hoping for a French peace to cement their shaky authority. The people, who live in dread of *rezzous*, know that their country's riches will not provide general prosperity without the help of our swords. There are a few young officers who understand this—Castries, Laperrine, Motylinski."

"Then why does our government hesitate?"

"It's a matter of the right time, internationally speaking. Also, they are lacking irrefutable documentation. They need an objective assessment of Moroccan disintegration and expectations." And the old explorer's blue eyes lit up: "Do it, Foucauld! I'm too old. Do it!"

"Without an escort?"

"No escort. It would only hinder you. You won't be pacifying or conquering, but gathering information. Since there are no roads, you will be exploring Morocco over its twenty-four hundred miles of trails. Choose the least known. European eyes have seen no more than a quarter of the country. Beyond Fez and Meknes, it is unknown territory once you go inland. The southern reaches are still a mystery, as are the mountains: the vast ranges of the Atlas hide in their fertile valleys an unknown civilization, the Berbers. Nothing is known about the Berbers, except that they fear the sultan. What do they expect from the French? Therein lies the problem."

"More than twenty-four hundred miles of trails! I have no money, sir. It would take at least twenty thousand francs."

"You'll only need a few thousand francs. Loading yourself down with baggage would only arouse the interest of pillagers. Disguise yourself as an Arab peddler or a pilgrim. Poverty is your means of survival. 'One thousand horsemen cannot strip a naked man', goes the Arab proverb. And no weapons, because you'll have to win over the population if you want them to talk to you. All you need is a mule."

Charles had listened to this speech in amazement. He had thought there was no way out of his financial predicament. And actually there was no predicament. This plain talk, which countered all the accepted standards, was just what he had been waiting for: to the nakedness of Africa he would bring his own nakedness. By stripping bare, he would conquer the immense distances. And by acting as a brother, he would conquer the hearts of men. For to know is to love.

"Disguise myself as an Arab peddler. But it would take me another year to speak the language perfectly. Why not as a Jew? Jews come from all countries. Everywhere in the Maghreb, Morocco included, people avoid them as if they were impure. They are all over: merchants, mule drivers, money changers. But people won't go near them, for they are also magicians . . . and moneylenders."

"The Viscount de Foucauld disguised as a poor wandering Jew?"

Charles smiled. He liked the challenge. To explore, on his own, the *bled es siba*, the unsubdued territory. That would be his response to the humiliation of the conservatorship: taking the humiliation as far as it could go.

MacCarthy nodded approval. "Your costume will make you a lowly creature and will allow you to go about unnoticed, with complete freedom. But you cannot travel alone. You must be accompanied by a real Jew, who will lend you authenticity. I know one. Part rabbi, part adventurer, part peddler. I shall introduce you. His name is Mardochée Abi Serour."

There was not much to like about Mardochée. Born in 1830 in a village in southern Morocco, he had grown up into a tall, strong, stooped man, prematurely aged. His long gray beard reeked of the snuff that he stuffed up his large, beaked nose. In his wrinkled face, below inflamed lids, the pale, tormented eyes showed a blend of wiliness and enthusiasm. He was a man of contradictions: belief in God and greed for money; fear of his own shadow and love for the adventure of travel; traditions and magic. Both lazy and energetic, he was motivated by curiosity and an overwhelming desire for gold—since his work earned him none, he tried to manufacture it by delving into alchemy. After his studies in Morocco, he had become a rabbi and had visited Palestine. Giving in to his commercial bent, he returned to Africa, where he embarked on wild speculative ventures, leading caravans to the Sudan. He was the first Jew to arrive in Timbuktu. He had barely escaped death a hundred times. He went on to work in Mogador, Oran, and finally Algiers, where he was eking out a living with small tasks for the Geographical Society. He lived in the ghetto, in a crowded, smelly room with his wife and four children.

Charles admired his old crimson caftan, well cut, but dirty and worn; his red skull cap with the black turban around it; the sandals that revealed clawlike, grimy toes: the true Syrian Jew so often seen in the Maghreb.

The project interested Mardochée. He would have done almost anything to escape the ghetto and his dull life in Algiers. He asked for 270 francs a month in salary, plus food, lodging, and incidentals, with an advance of six hundred francs. In return for which he would take Charles to the southern border of Morocco and bring him back to Algiers safe and sound.

Their departure was set for June. Before then, Charles would learn Hebrew, equip himself, and, most important, convince Georges de Latouche to release the five or six thousand francs needed for the enterprise. His conservator cousin proved reluctant, however, and Charles sailed for France to persuade him in person. He did not succeed. But he did not let that stand in his way. Once back in Algiers, he signed the contract, then presented the family with the fait accompli. Angry and worried, Georges wrote to MacCarthy and asked him to help break the agreement. Mardochée could not be trusted. He might lead his naïve client into an ambush or abandon him at the first moment of danger. As for Charles, he was inexperienced, an impractical dreamer, totally incapable of playing explorer.

But Georges finally relented and sent four thousand francs, with the possibility of two thousand more upon Charles' return. In Nancy, the family discussion had been emotional. Charles' sister, Mimi, was so worried that, secretly, she promised Mardochée a large bonus, eight hundred francs, if he brought her brother back alive!

On June 10, 1883, Charles met Mardochée at his hovel. The two of them prepared Charles' costume: long shirt with billowing sleeves, knee-length cotton trousers, Turkish vest in dark wool, hooded white robe with short sleeves, white stockings, sandals, and, to top it all off, a black silk turban over a red skullcap.

The same day they boarded the train for Oran. Thrilled, "Rabbi Joseph" was more than happy to put up with the scornful looks from the Arab workingmen crowded into the third-class carriage. Speaking in Hebrew, he went over his role with Mardochée. Henceforth he was to be Rabbi Joseph Aleman, a native of the Muscovy region. Driven from his homeland by the Russians, he had studied at a rabbinical school in Jerusalem. Now, "poor, but trusting in God", he was traveling through North Africa with his colleague to visit the pious Jews of the Maghreb. As for Mardochée, he was supposed to be looking for his wife's younger brother, who was somewhere in the Rif.

Out of necessity, the travelers were loaded down: a bag with a change of costume for the ex-viscount; a blanket, a few cooking utensils, basic food-stuffs, medical supplies; in two small cases, an explorer's tools, including sextant, compasses, barometers, thermometers, maps, paper. Charles also carried two thousand gold francs and some coralwork for trading—a way to get to know the local people. He had a letter of introduction from Monsieur Tirman, the Governor General of Algeria, addressed to Monsieur Ordéga, French ambassador in Tangier, who was to advise him and provide letters of introduction to various notable Moroccans.

In Oran, the pair left the train and went to a miserable inn. Charles was startled when the servant there addressed him familiarly as "*tu*". Now he knew firsthand the contempt of Arabs and many French for the Jews. Hatred of Jews was stronger here than elsewhere. Why? Age-old tradition. Refusing to blend in, guarding their religion like a treasure, Jews remained foreigners and thus made the ideal scapegoat on whom to blame the ills of society. Charles had come across anti-Semitism before, in Algeria. There the Arabs often instigated pogroms, with the French colonists looking on indifferently. Even in France, within rightist Catholic circles there was a persistent, deep-rooted anti-Semitism. One of the reasons for the estrange-ment between Charles and Morès-Vallombrosa had been the latter's active support of the sinister Drumont, author of a sickening, inflammatory work entitled *La France juive*.

With some delight, Charles had slipped easily into the role of rabbi, who was both a religious leader, therefore holy, and a Jew, therefore scorned. The paradox intrigued him, as well as the humiliation to which he found himself subjected, he who had been universally respected. He recalled the shock on the faces of haughty Inès Moitessier, the Latouches, the Bondys, and the Blics at his announcement that he would be venturing into the savage lands of the Barbary in the guise of a poor rabbi! That eccentric idea had scandalized them; for even in Charles' own milieu, behind the well-bred Catholicism, there prevailed a discreet, conventional anti-Semitism. Portents! On that June day in 1883, poor and scorned, making his way through the alleys of the Oran ghetto, he truly felt like a poor man, an outsider, and a Jew, and thus triply scorned. But who could have foreseen in that school of humiliation the commitment that was to be?

Charles recorded everything in his notebooks.

Oran, June 11. The Jewish Sabbath. A day of rest, travel forbidden. Mardochée went to synagogue and brought back two Jews: alchemists! By candlelight, Charles listened to the excited talk about their research: the philosopher's stone! And what was *his* philosopher's stone?

In the stagecoach, between Oran and Tlemcen, June 12. Contemptuous glances from the Arabs. One, pointing at Charles: "You know where that creature comes from? Straight out of Jerusalem!"

Tlemcen, June 13. Morocco was not more than forty miles away. Mardochée was seeking out Jews from the Rif, Spanish Morocco, to find out how to enter the country without being murdered or taken prisoner. Charles realized, worried, that his guide did not know Morocco at all, except for his birthplace, the distant village of Aqqa!

They bought bread and olives. Sitting cross-legged on the dusty ground in the square, they ate their meager supper. Suddenly, out of the Tlemcen Officers' Club came a group of young cavalrymen from the Chasseurs d'Afrique. As they approached, Charles recognized almost every one: Segonzac, Bessonneau, Jeanneret, Cavalcanti. What would happen if they recognized *him*? They walked right by, either paying no attention or casting contemptuous looks. One stared at Charles and made a face: "Look at the little Jew squatting there gobbling olives. He could be a monkey!" [2]

That evening, they finally found some Jews from the Rif. Mardochée supplied a bottle of anisette, everyone drinking from the same glass as it made the rounds. Tongues loosened. How do we get into the Rif? the rabbi wanted to know. Difficult and dangerous. It would be easiest to go to Nemours, the last Algerian port, and catch a ship for Tangier.

June 20. Tangier. At last they were in Morocco. They adopted the black skullcap, the blue handkerchief, and the black sideburns of Moroccan

---

[2] As told by Charles to his nephew, C. de Blic, in R. Bazin, *Charles de Foucauld* (Plon, 1921), 24.

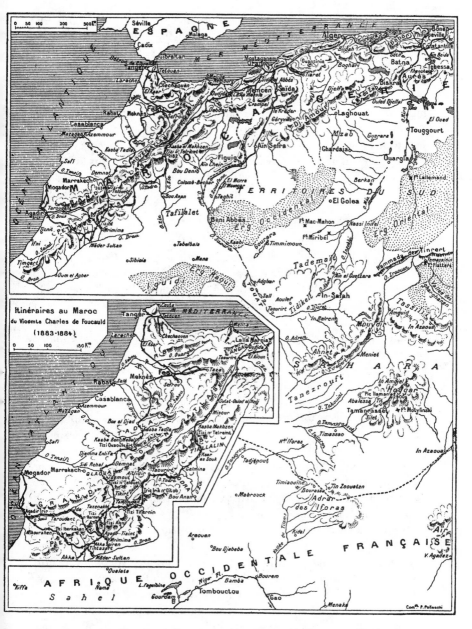

The author has not captioned this map, but the insert reads "Viscount Charles de Foucauld's route through Morocco (1883–1884)".

rabbis. Charles let the ritual locks grow down his temples; soon they would reach his shoulders. They disposed of their medical supplies and the small cases, which would only attract thieves. The scientific instruments were stuffed into a large goatskin bag, where they would not attract attention.

Charles did not find his visit with Ambassador Ordéga very encouraging. The country remained doubly closed. What was not under the sultan's authority was in a state of rebellion. The sultan saw in every visitor a spy sent to help prepare for a military invasion. In short, whether they were in the south or the north, Moroccans feared potential conquerors as much as they hated Christians, not to mention Jews! But the ambassador did give Charles letters of introduction to local chiefs possibly sympathetic with the French.

After buying two mules, they started out, heading for Chechaouen, arriving July 2. A lone Christian had preceded them, in 1863. Beyond, it was unknown territory. They were regarded with suspicion. Charles took his notes in pencil, secretly, using a tiny notebook only two inches square, kept hidden in his sleeve. When they stopped for the night, he would recopy his notes onto large sheets. After rising in the morning, he would unobtrusively climb to the roof of the home he was in, supposedly for the air, but in reality to take bearings. Besides his sextant, he would have the compass, the thermometer, and the chronometer. Meanwhile Mardochée would keep their curious hosts downstairs by fabricating some sort of explanation: those mysterious instruments were used for reading the future in the heavens, for communicating with souls, for revealing the sins of the Jews, for preventing cholera, for predicting the weather and the hazards of the road!

The barefoot travelers found it impossible to penetrate farther into the wilds of the Rif, where they had been greeted with insults and rocks. They went back toward Tétouan, then headed for Fez. They were to stay there more than a month, since the Muslim guide they had hired refused to travel during Ramadan.

Thanks to an introduction from a French friend, Charles was learning his role at the home of a Jewish family, the Ben Simons, who had received him graciously. Only the patriarch, Samuel, knew the viscount's identity. To the other members of the family, their friends in the Jewish quarter, and the marriageable young women who fluttered around him, the distinguished young rabbi had come there to round off his education.

MacCarthy's intuition proved good. In Fez, where the sultan ruled, people thought only of the French. Here, Charles wrote his cousin Georges de Latouche, "All the inhabitants dream of only one thing: the future arrival of the French. The sultan's authority is worthless, and the people are in constant danger from the violence and pillaging of the powerful Riata tribe. Thus they keep on praying to Allah to send them the French."[3]

The Moroccans were impressed by the prosperity of French Algeria, whose natural resources were ten times less than those of their own country. Charles heard Muslims at all levels of society asking: "When will the French come in? When shall we live in peace like the people of Tlemcen?" And Charles was appalled by the widespread social injustice: the agricultural people of rich Morocco saw the results of their hard work taken away by the sultan's tax collectors as often as by pillagers. If the north was under the sultan, what would he find in the south, where petty *kaids* and pillaging nomads fought over the farmers' harvests?

The hour had come for him to take the great leap, the discovery of the south. Thinking of it made him tremble. Not from fear, but from desire. A civilizing mission. The desire to serve France and to help the Moroccan people, so hardworking and so appealing. Pride, too: "Under no circumstances do I wish to come back without seeing what I have said I shall see, without having been where I have said I shall go", he wrote to Latouche.[4]

By plunging ahead, he would be justifying himself. If he succeeded— and wrote an original scientific, military, social, and political book that would pave the way for pioneers of civilization—he would be avenging himself on a grand scale for his wasted youth. As the geographer E. Gautier wrote later: "He was possessed by the secular rage to understand."[5] And not merely secular, as will be seen.

Before heading south, Charles decided to do some exploring to the east, going to Taza, a round trip of 180 miles.

A long march every day from dawn until nightfall. Mardochée dragged his feet. "He is the laziest creature you could hope to meet", Charles wrote Marie de Bondy on July 23. "And, besides that, a clumsy coward who does not know the first thing about traveling."

To reassure him, Charles hired some horsemen as bodyguards to get them to Taza safely. It was the only way to travel in the region without being killed. In every village, more was involved than just praying and chanting in the synagogue and blessing the babies held out to them: money had to be handed over to the local *kaid* in exchange for protection in his territory. "Without that protection, the people of the place you are just leaving will run after you with robbery in mind", Charles wrote his cousin Latouche. Even Taza lived in fear of pillaging. Thus Charles made sure he had some assistance, a young Sharif flanked by his two henchmen. And then he worried about being held up by this rather untrustworthy escort.

[3] CF to G. de Latouche, August 14, 1883, quoted by Bazin, ibid., 53.
[4] Ibid., 54.
[5] Quoted by L. Massignon, *Parole donnée* (Seuil, 1983).

The region seemed peaceful, but there were no roads at all, just paths of rammed earth. No more hotels or inns. They were welcomed at night in the villages by pious Jews; hospitality was the rule. They thanked their hosts with a gift: tea, sugar, a piece of coral jewelry.

As the trip progressed, the true character of each of the two explorers became more and more evident. Mardochée was lazy and cowardly, good mostly for cooking. Intelligent, sly, and a boaster, he thought he would be making an easy journey through Morocco. But nothing was easy in a land prey to a wealth of passions, political uncertainties, and troubles. As soon as he realized that, Mardochée had tried to restrict the trip to the northern area alone, the Rif, at the same time prolonging it so he could make more money. He had thought he could manipulate the young French tourist. He was wrong.

Charles, who was accumulating notes and topographic data, could not do without Mardochée, who gained him entrance to the Jewish communities. He proved intractable in his desire to reach the south, in spite of the increasing danger and practical difficulties: unhealthful food, highwaymen, extortion by the local *kaids*, the burning summer sun, parasites, more and more tortuous paths. He was happy in his role as explorer. He saw his true heroic nature coming to life. Beautiful, hostile Morocco, with the poverty of its living creatures and the sumptuousness of its natural setting, was turning him into a different man. A man.

From August 23 to 27 they stayed in Meknes, religious capital of the country. Then they headed straight south into the heart of Morocco, toward the mythical Atlas, whose immense ranges, rising to over thirteen thousand feet, bisect the country from the southwest to the northeast for nearly four hundred miles. The farther they journeyed from the large Sharifian towns, the less the sultan's authority was recognized. The uncertainty increased. For if the Jew was scorned, his presence was tolerated, out of habit. But the Christian was often threatened with death.

Charles was aware of the risks, writing, "Overwhelming greed is the rule everywhere. Lying and thievery in all forms. In general, banditry, armed attacks are considered honorable actions. . . . Even among the Jews, who fulfill scrupulously their duties toward God and make up for it by their treatment of men. . . . They talked to me frankly, as a brother, boasting of criminal activities, confiding to me their base sentiments." [6]

September found them in Bou el Djad, in the heart of unknown Morocco, about sixty miles from the ranges of the Middle Atlas; on the other side lay the great region of the south. A major incident came close to

[6] CF, *Reconnaissance au Maroc*, 1888.

ending the adventure. The Jewish community that received them was not deceived and denounced the false rabbi to the local grand marabout, an elderly Muslim leader held in great respect. He had the two travelers brought before him immediately. Fortunately, Charles was able to present a letter of introduction from a Fez *kaid*. Ben Daoud then gave Charles every consideration, even offering him young black women from his slave harem! He pretended to believe their story as translated by Mardochée.

Touched by the marabout's generosity, Charles ended up confessing the truth. Yes, he was a Christian, there to seek information, but not for the French government. He was no spy!

Odd behavior. But the Foucauld charm was at work. The marabout entrusted him to his son, Sidi Omar, and to Omar's son, Edris, who was a *hadj* (one who has made the pilgrimage to Mecca). Edris, the same age as Charles, got along with him very well and served as his guide. He had returned from Mecca by way of the French cities of Algeria and thought of nothing but French civilization and ways. Edris even compromised himself to the point of entrusting to Charles a letter for the French ambassador in Tangier, requesting that official observers be sent to Morocco! And he admitted, "If the sultan knew about this, he would cut off my tongue and my hand!"

Thus Charles found himself in the middle of some minor political intrigue. Apparently, the local elite thought only of the arrival of the French and were getting ready for it. Edris had become his inseparable friend. He took the Frenchman to visit Tadia. They said good-bye to each other on September 23 with embraces and promises to meet again.

"How rich this country would be if the French ruled it!" exclaimed Edris.[7]

Three months had already gone by since their departure, and they still had half of Morocco to discover, the most inaccessible regions, completely unknown, the area beyond the Atlas Mountains. They finally reached the foot of the Middle Atlas at Kasba Tadla; they proceeded alongside the range, went around it, then crossed the Grand Atlas through the Tizi n'Telouet Pass (altitude, more than 8,600 feet), with snowy peaks towering over them. Charles was the first European to discover this fabulous land, ruled by the lords of the Atlas from their crenellated *ksour*.[8]

There was an incident on October 26. Charles relates: "I saw only three small caravans that day. The leader of one entered into lengthy discussions with my escort. He wanted to rob me, and he suggested that my men work

---

[7] Ibid., 259–67.
[8] The plural of *ksar*, fortress.—TRANS.

with him, offering them half the loot. Wouldn't they gain more that way than by continuing? Ridiculous work, following a Jew around! My men, who had their prejudices, rejected his offer. He could find no words strong enough to express how idiotic he thought they were!" [9]

After they had crossed the third range, the Anti-Atlas, the landscape changed; the desert appeared, dotted with wondrous oases that would be irrigated by melting snow from the nearby mountains.

What they saw on November 12: "The Sahara and the palms are bordered on the north by the crest of the ridge of the Anti-Atlas. At the foot of the mountains, an immense, nearly infinite plain begins. Gray, undulating, it stretches south to the horizon. The dry bed of the Drâa, nearly two miles across, runs through it, and beyond there is the great desert stretching to the Sudan. Everywhere, the plain, undulating or level, sandy or rocky, always barren and solitary. The only traces of life are to be found in a few oases, where black specks stand out here and there in the distance." [10]

He marveled at the evergreen forest of palms and the hardworking, dark-skinned Berbers dressed in indigo cotton from the Sudan. The plain of the river Drâa unfolded before the travelers; here lived tribes not under the sultan's authority. Charles' notes piled up.

"Claiming a need for silent, solitary prayer, I would go off a ways, covered from head to foot by a long *sisit*. The folds of the garment concealed my instruments. A bush, a rock, a hillock would keep me out of sight." [11]

For while what he wrote might not give him away, sketches were a different matter, evidence of the kind of activity indulged in by spies.

They stayed in Tisint from November 14 to 16. People there were friendly. They suspected he was French, but no one said anything for fear of jeopardizing his safety. He made friends with Hadj Bou Rhim, who twice risked his own life to protect Charles. Touched by this trust, Charles admitted he was a Christian.

That this journey was affecting him deeply comes out in letters to his family: "Harsh beauty of the landscape, seen under indescribable light." [12] And in his travel notes: "A night of destiny, following the twenty-seventh day of Ramadan. Then the demons too come out of the earth, which explains the night of prayer to avoid their temptations. The contemplation during such nights leads one to understand the Arab belief in a mysterious night, *leïla el Kedr*, when the sky opens, angels descend to earth, the water

[9] CF, "Itinéraire au Maroc", article for the Société de Géographie, later included at the beginning of *Reconnaissance au Maroc*.

[10] Ibid.

[11] CF, "Retraite à Nazareth", 1897.

[12] *Bulletin des Amitiés*, no. 77, 14.

in the sea turns fresh, and all that is inanimate in nature bows down to adore its Creator." [13]

Not conscious of the dangers lying in wait for him, even pretending to be unaware that his pockets were nearly empty, he went on alone across the Anti-Atlas toward the Drâa, toward the desert to which he seemed irresistibly drawn. He was stopped at Mrimima on January 3, 1884, and threatened with death. He could not even head back toward Tisint, where he knew he would be protected by Bou Rhim. Through a beggar, Charles sent him a distress call. The *hadj* came with a force of twenty-five men and set him free.

So he was safe in Tisint. It was time to think about the journey back. Naturally, he planned to return through the eastern region with which he was not yet familiar but which was so dangerous that he had been forbidden to enter the country from that direction. The rumor spread that he was a Christian with plenty of gold, and the pillaging bands in the area were salivating. More than ever, it would be impossible to travel through Morocco without protection from the local *kaids*, which meant having an abundant supply of gold. He no longer had any. He dispatched a message to Latouche asking him to send the promised two thousand francs. The only means: a bank transfer. The nearest bank was nearly two hundred miles to the west, in Mogador, which was on the Atlantic coast.

On January 9, Charles left Mardochée to wait for him in Tisint and took the Agadir road, with the *hadj* as his escort. A number of incidents marked this trek to the coast. Besides the usual pillagers, he had to deal with warring rival tribes, who were killing each other in the name of the Prophet.

On January 28, an unrecognizable Charles—thin, bearded, filthy, clad in dirty rags, a peddler's sack over his shoulder—knocked on the door of the French consulate of Mogador. The secretary, a Monsieur Zerbib, was disgusted by the sight of this Jewish beggar who wanted to speak with Monsieur le Consul. Charles smiled wearily, astonished at reassuming his old personality: "I am the Viscount de Foucauld, cavalry officer. I have come to cash a check on the Bank of England. The consulate has probably been apprised."

Thinking it was a joke or a scam, the secretary showed him the door. Charles, whom the Maghreb had taught patience, went out, sat on the step, then entered once more. The secretary rushed toward him with a threatening gesture. Charles gave him a withering look: "Let me have some water and show me where I can wash and shave."

Such authority emanated from this odd beggar that the secretary complied and directed Charles to the washroom. Suspicious, he watched though

---

[13] CF, *Reconnaissance au Maroc*, 164.

the keyhole. He saw the wandering Jew remove all kinds of unlikely objects from his pockets and his sack: barometers, sextant, thermometers, and a whole array of writing and drawing supplies.

A few minutes later, Charles, presentable, made his entrance into the office of the chancellor, for the consul was away. Monsieur Montel received him pleasantly, but he had no news. The Bank of Mogador had not received any funds for him. The chancellor smiled: "Do not be alarmed. We are going to send you home. A ship is leaving Mogador for Marseille in a week's time, via Casablanca and Tangier."

"Thank you, but that is out of the question. I shall be returning on foot, through the Sous, the Atlas, and the Rif."

"Some four hundred miles in unsubdued territory? Two to three months of travel?" The chancellor's astounded looks expressed the one question: "Why?"

"If you leave saying that you are going to do a thing, you do not come back without having done it. I shall write my family and ask for money. In anticipation of the transfer order, could you tell me where to find Mogador's most modest Jewish inn, where I'd be able to get credit?"

The dumbfounded bureaucrat acquiesced. An hour later, Charles, settled in a small hotel run by a Spanish Jew, was writing his sister to ask her for money. He knew that dear old Mimi, only too happy to learn that he was alive, would not refuse him. Then, no longer concerned about the future, he began writing up his travel notes. He would be spending forty-five days in Mogador, working twelve hours a day, before finally receiving on March 14, 1884, the two thousand francs transferred from the Bank of England, the funds that were to allow him to finish his travels as he had planned.

Escorted by his friend Hadj Bou Rhim, he went by way of Agadir again and through the fertile valley of the Sous. Once again, the pencil races across the pages of the notebook: "The Sous, surrounded by cultivated fields, winds through the tamarisks; giant olive trees shade the stream, and perched above its shores are two tiers of villages. The Sous' plain is a vast surface of red earth, without a stone. It is nearly twenty-five miles wide! For three days I shall be traversing this marvelously fertile plain." [14]

An El Dorado, virtually untapped. Sixty miles of a fertile valley, irrigated in summer by the melted snow streaming down from the Atlas.

After crossing the Anti-Atlas again, on March 31 Charles rejoined Mardochée in Tisint.

The return journey was to be harsh. On April 13, 1884, he bade farewell to that miracle of the desert, the now-flooded Drâa Oued, which spread green over the sands, dotting them with amazing oases.

[14] Ibid.

He went through the Anti-Atlas once more, then the Grand Atlas, and began the slow trek north. He had been forced to hire three armed Arabs to protect him from pillagers. The protectors proved more dangerous than the bandits! In the middle of the desert, on May 12, two of the three guards attacked him, planning to take all. Mardochée tried to defend him but was driven back. Their only weapon, a revolver, was in their baggage and out of reach. Were the two travelers going to be executed? No trail, no witnesses. But the third guard, Bel Kacem, did not go along with the idea. They argued for hours, while Charles sat on the ground and waited philosophically, deaf to Mardochée's wails.

The three guards rose at last. A verdict had been reached. Life or death? It was life. Bel Kacem had prevailed. A hard-won compromise: the two travelers were cleaned out. The two bandits stole nearly everything: baggage, supplies, money. Yet Charles was left with what, to his thinking, was the essential: his notes, his sketches, his scientific instruments. And the two mules.

After a two-day walk along the Moulouya Oued, they arrived in the little village of Debdou, exhausted. They asked some hospitable Jews to take them in. Their hosts brought them water and washed their feet. Then Charles stood up, took the pan of water and washed his face and beard. The others looked at him, scandalized! A pious Jew never washes his beard! Exposed, he confessed his identity and begged not to be betrayed, for the country was not safe. They sold their mules, and, after renting two fresh ones, they set out again, with a caravan of Jews.

The travelers arrived in Oujda on May 22. The next day they crossed the Algerian border, entering the country at Lalla Marnia. The journey was over. It had lasted eleven months, instead of the planned five. Charles had lost forty-five pounds. He was exhausted but happy. He was alive, a miracle that did not cease to astonish him. He had changed completely. One word could describe it: "expanded". He had left the army embittered, withdrawn, rebellious; now he was liberated, opened up, victorious.

After dismissing Mardochée,[15] Charles slowly headed toward the only inn in Lalla Marnia. And strangely enough, as if he wished to prolong the mystification, he refused to reveal his identity right away. Need to upset? Instinctive solidarity with the scorned Jews? But he could not get out of it this time: the innkeeper, Papa Lapique, unceremoniously turned away this grubby beggar in tattered garments. Charles had a hard time persuading him to go on his behalf to the commander of Mogador's rather sizable

---

[15] Having collected the promised bonuses, on his return to Algiers, Mardochée bought mercury and became engrossed in his alchemy experiments involving the transmutation of metals; he died of mercury poisoning.

military garrison. Lavergne, the head of the battalion, was dining with his officers.

"Commander Lavergne, there is a beggar who wishes to break down my door. Since I refused him entry to the inn, he has become haughty and threatens to complain to the Oran Division! He refuses to give his name and expects to be able to speak with you."

"Tell him that the commander does not receive people without knowing who they are."

Returning to the inn, Lapique obtained a scrap of paper from Charles on which the mysterious traveler had scribbled: "Viscount Charles de Foucauld, lieutenant in the African Fourth Chasseurs."

Astonishment. Charles was brought into the officers' mess. But no one recognized him. Then, spotting an old comrade from Saint-Cyr, Charles looked deep into his eyes: "Greetings, Maumené. What are you up to here?"

"Foucauld! *Père Foucauld!*"

Finally recognized, he was fêted by one and all. Henceforth, he would be a hero, the hero of the day, the first Frenchman to risk his life in the successful conquest of the three Atlas ranges.

Undeniably, from the scientific point of view, his achievements were remarkable. Before him, fewer than four hundred fifty miles of trails had been mapped; he recorded more than seventeen hundred additional miles and three thousand elevations. He corrected the old survey of the course of the Drâa and brought back thousands of observations, one hundred thirty-five drawings, and twenty maps. Now it was a matter of finishing his book, *Reconnaissance au Maroc.* So he set himself up in Algiers and devoted himself wholeheartedly to this major project. Was that all he did?

Murky, unclear, this period in his life, evoked by two lines in a letter to Marie de Bondy: "Coming back from Morocco, I wasn't much better than I had been a few years earlier, and my first stay in Algiers had consisted of nothing but evil."[16] Which has led Abbé Six to write: "The voyage of exploration barely over, he threw himself into evil once more. Why the same mistakes all over again?"[17]

But what mistakes? Should this confession of Charles' be taken literally? It was made after his conversion, when he had a tendency to exaggerate such things out of humility. There is nothing to demonstrate that he resumed in Algiers the life of debauchery he had led in Saumur and Pont-à-Mousson. In the first place, his travels had worn him out. And his time was taken up by his book, on which he said he worked day and night. And lastly, he had no money. Latouche was keeping him on a short rein.

---

[16] CF to Marie de Bondy, September 20, 1889, *Bulletin des Amitiés*, no. 49, 106.
[17] J.-F. Six, *Itinéraire spirituel de Charles de Foucauld* (Seuil, 1958), 37.

Everything shows that, far from falling into debauchery, Charles was instead thinking about an honorable conclusion to the woman question. But first he spent the summer in France: he was in Paris, then at Tuquet, the Moitessiers' summer residence near Bordeaux; he went briefly to Nancy to dispose of his apartment and then on to Les Landes for a short session of military training. Finally, October 1884 found him back in Algiers, where he was about to live through an episode quite natural and ordinary for a young man of twenty-six.

Her name was Marie-Marguerite Titre, and she was twenty-three. Her father, Commander Titre, was a widower, semi-retired but very active. Head of the topographic section of the Algerian Nineteenth Army Corps, he had spent twenty years in the army's geographic service. He served as vice-president of the Geographical Society (Algiers branch), whose president was Oscar MacCarthy, the keeper of the library; it was of course in that center of North African culture that the commander had run into Charles. He had invited the explorer to his home in Britraria, had introduced him to his daughter, Marie-Marguerite, and the inevitable happened: the two young people fell in love.

Beautiful, loving, spontaneous, bright, and artistic, Marie-Marguerite was a very moral young woman with a strong character. A fervent believer, she had converted to Catholicism after the death of her mother, a Protestant. In short, a totally attractive person. The only point on which the young couple differed concerned faith: Charles was an agnostic. He had been honest in warning her about this when he proposed marriage: "When we are married, I shall leave you completely free to do as you wish in matters of religion. But as for me, I shall not practice, because I am not a believer."[18]

To which she replied with gentle obstinacy: "I feel that through me you will be converted."

And there the matter rested. Delighted, Commander Titre gave his consent to the match.

Shortly afterward, Charles left for France, where he was to spend the summer. In August, he was with the Moitessiers at Tuquet, a small eighteenth-century château Sigismond had bought in 1884, after selling Louye, which was too large for them. At the beginning of September, Charles was to travel to Nice for a visit with his sister, Mimi, who had married a banker, Raymond de Blic, on December 30, 1884.

Charles of course told his relatives of his engagement. Total opposition. He fell apart, even becoming ill. The three women in the family who mattered most to him presented a united front: his aunt, Inès Moitessier; his

[18] Account of Marie-Marguerite Titre, *Cahiers CF*, no. 25, 38.

cousin, Marie de Bondy; and his sister, Marie de Blic. And of course, the uncles, the brothers-in-law, the male cousins. The reasons put forth seemed unarguable. She was not of his world. Commander Titre was a Protestant, something of an agnostic, in fact. A remarried widower, he had wed his mistress. He did not have money; Marie-Marguerite would have no dowry. Under these circumstances, Charles, whose fortune had been eaten into rather extensively, could not raise his children properly and would be forced—horrors!—to send them to the state-run secular schools. And his daughters would have no dowries. In short, this marriage would be the archetype of the *mésalliance*. These people enmeshed in their prejudices had never laid eyes on the young woman.

Charles, after a brief struggle, surrendered. He broke his engagement.

Of course, "God moves in mysterious ways", and, four years later, the young viscount would write to Marie de Bondy: "I needed to be saved from this marriage, and you saved me." [19] That is rather brusque for an epitaph, however. Apparently he suffered a long time because of this broken romance, but he would recover.

For the moment, he was looking for an escape from his pain. He did not find one. Yet, even before the publication of his book, he was fêted everywhere, and it was up to him whether he wanted to reap the rewards of his work in Paris or in Algiers. On June 20, 1884, he had been admitted to the Geographical Society of Paris, his name proposed by Oscar MacCarthy, who had written to Maunoir, the secretary general: "Rarely has anyone worked so long and accomplished so much." On January 9, 1885, this prestigious society, presided over by Ferdinand de Lesseps, had granted its highest award, the gold medal, to "this voyager with a great future". He was also given academic honors at the Sorbonne. At the gold medal ceremony on April 24, 1885, Henri Duveyrier[20] had stated:

> Sacrificing far more than his comforts, having made and kept to the very end far more than a simple *vow of poverty and misery*, having renounced for nearly a year the considerations due one of his military rank, Monsieur the Viscount de Foucauld has conquered us, through the extensive and detailed information that brings new perspectives to almost everything hitherto known about the geography and the political conditions of Morocco. Thanks to him, it is truly the opening of a new era. One is hard put to know which to admire more: his findings, so beautiful and so useful; or the

---

[19] CF to Marie de Bondy, September 20, 1889, in G. Gorrée, *Sur les traces de Charles de Foucauld* (Éd de la Plus Grande France, 1936), 69.

[20] Duveyrier, 1840–1892, famous explorer and geographer of North Africa and the Sahara, one of the first to describe the Ahaggar. A wholehearted supporter of Foucauld.

devotion, courage, and material self-sacrifice that made it possible for him to obtain such findings. [21]

All this newly won glory now weighed on him, and although his book was only half finished, he thought only of departing again. Beset by his demons once more, his ambition was to cross the Sahara and reach black Africa.

Having wrested a thousand francs from his conservator, on September 14, 1885, he sailed for Algiers from Port-Vendres.

So there he was, in the South Oranais. In spite of the region's chronic state of insecurity, Charles traveled with an unarmed escort and only a horse and two pack mules. His diet was exceedingly frugal. Crossing the Amour *djebel* (mountainous region), he plunged into the desert, visiting the Laghouat and Ghardaïa Oases, then El Golea, where he made friends with an officer-interpreter, Motylinski. He headed northwest and ended up in Touggourt. He let the dazzling beauty of the desert sweep him away, with its dunes like the waves of some petrified sea and the dry beds of its wadis submerged by the sands. But who could quench his thirst for the absolute, which felt to him like a deepening void, a chasm, a summons? Fascinated by the solitude of the desert, he left his escort and struck out alone. Night was falling. Stretched out on the sand, he gazed at the billions of stars, relentlessly questioning them, watching in vain for a reply or at least a sign.

After crossing the Sahara from west to east, he reached Gabès in Tunisia, from where he sailed for France. He was at his sister's in Nice by January 23, 1886, as restless and unsatisfied as ever. It seemed as if nothing could fill the void in his heart.

Tamanrasset, December 1, 1916. 10:30 A.M.

Three knocks on the door of the fort. Brother Charles snatched himself away from his meditation. It was probably Paul. The former Haratin slave was coming to prepare food, as he did every morning.

Brother Charles headed toward the fort's only door: a low opening protected from the outside world by a wall thirteen feet long and a ditch seven feet wide, three feet deep, spanned by a narrow footbridge.

To reach this door, Charles had to step over a brick barrier, bending to avoid a low beam. The barrier kept the door from being opened wide. In case of attack, an airtight chamber could be created by filling the corridor with sand; then it would require a cannon to enter the fort.

Brother Charles smiled when he thought of these protective measures,

---

[21] *Bulletin des Amitiés*, no. 72, 12.

which he would have judged unworthy of him had he not built the fort with the sole aim of sheltering food supplies from the Moroccan *rezzous*; he had also foreseen that he might have to take in that little group of sedentary Haratins forced to remain at Tamanrasset, should there be an attack by the Senoussi rebels from Tripoli, who were now at Djanet, the Algerian frontier post fallen to them March 24.

Such defense measures would have made no sense if the *bordj* had not sheltered large stocks of food meant for holding out in case of siege as well as for alleviating the endemic famine in this drought-stricken region. The Tuareg nomads had gone three hundred miles south, looking for pastures to sustain their flocks. But the former slaves, the Haratins, remained chained to the soil by their poverty.

This stock of food meant putting up with something dreadful: weapons! Thirty military rifles and six crates of cartridges, entrusted to Brother Charles by the army. Just reviewing those numbers in his mind irritated the hermit, so imbued was he with the spirit of pacifism ever since he had left the army thirty-four years earlier. But what could be done? It was a war situation. There would be no survival rations without the fort, to which the Haratins might flock in the event of an attack, especially if the nearest little French garrison, thirty miles away at Fort Motylinski, should have to retreat to In Salah, leaving the Ahaggar completely defenseless.

Providing, of course, there was not a surprise attack and these poor black people, men, women, children, and the elderly, had time to run to the *bordj*, more than sixteen hundred feet from their miserable shacks built of dried bricks and reeds.

Brother Charles opened the first door and, standing in the chamber, asked, "Who is it?"

"It is I, Paul."

Brother Charles continued down the corridor and opened the second door. An imposing black man slipped inside quickly, shutting the door behind him, then headed for the courtyard, where he would light the fire.

Paul Embarek was in the prime of life. In Beni Abbès, in 1902, Charles had bought him his freedom for four hundred francs, three times the price of a camel; Paul was then fifteen, very strong and not very bright, a black slave captured in the Sudan. Subtle, contradictory ties bound together master and servant. To escape from poverty, the freed slave had attached himself to the Christian marabout; he had even accepted learning his catechism, without going as far as being baptized. But that was enough to allow him to serve Mass, until Charles the priest had been authorized by the pope to say Mass without a server.

Paul was a liar, a thief, and a lecher and would probably never change; daily contact with a holy man seemed to have no effect on him. Unfathomable mystery! Several times, Charles had turned him out for bad behavior. He always came back, not at all contrite, like a big thief of a cat, seeking from the priest only food and protection. For years, Brother Charles had not been able to do without him. There was no one else at Tamanrasset to serve Mass. Moreover, despite his laziness, he was a good gardener and a passable mason. "I shall keep him unless his faults become close to crimes, reminding myself that Jesus kept Judas. I am somewhat attached to him." [22]

A less than satisfactory servant for the hermit, turned out, taken back, in 1915 Paul Embarek found a wife in Tamanrasset and after that no longer lived with the hermit but in the village. He then came to the hermitage and later to the *bordj* only to prepare meals and do building work.

"Two camel troopers from Fort Moty, Bou Aïcha and Bou Djema, arrived in the village this morning on business", Paul announced. "They will stop by to visit you tonight before heading back to Fort Moty."

Brother Charles, followed by Paul, went to the food storage room, picked up a wooden bowl, measured out wheat from a cloth sack, filled the bowl, and handed it to Paul Embarek.

The black man went back into the courtyard and lit a fire of old boards beneath a flat rock. While the rock was growing hot, he put the grain in a small mill of the kind used by the Berbers of the Moroccan Atlas, and he began grinding by hand. The mill cracked the grain but did not make flour. Paul took the cracked wheat, and with no leavening added, mixed it up and shaped a flat round bread that would be baked on the heated rock. Altogether, three loaves of flatbread were to be prepared: one for the priest, one for Paul, and a third for the poor.

While Paul was grinding his wheat, Brother Charles returned to the food stores, opened another sack, and filled an old pot with hard, dry dates, to which goat hairs had stuck. He placed the pot next to Paul. Once the loaves had been shaped and were cooking, Paul took the pot of dates and prepared the dish known as *khefis*. He added a little water to soften the fruit and keep it from burning and placed the pot on the fire. He stirred the mixture, turning it into the indigestible paste that would make up the rest of the hermit's dinner, along with a pitcher of water from the well. He, Paul, preferred to crunch on the dry dates. Brother Charles was unable to do that: he had no teeth!

Fifteen miles to the northeast, near the region's farming center, Amsel, Senoussi Beuh ag Rhabelli and his *rezzou* had stopped.

[22] CF to Father Huvelin, March 3, 1898.

Suddenly, from behind the dunes a husky young black man loomed up, clad in a piece of unbleached cotton tied at the waist. He came forward, and Kerzou introduced him: "El Madani ag Soba. He is on our side and will be our guide to the marabout's *bordj.*" Then, turning toward El Madani, he went on: "I see that you did indeed receive my message. I also see that the cursed *roumis* of Fort Motylinski have not caught you."

The black man began shaking, rolling his bloodshot faience eyes. "Do not be afraid, El Madani. We shall protect you. Look, our men are not only armed with the blue men's traditional sword but also with fine Italian rifles seized at Ghāt: there is a jinni hidden in each one."

The black man was still rolling his anxious eyes. He muttered, "And afterward? What good will that do me when I'm hiding in the mountains living on roots and a few dates? Even in Amsel, my brothers, the Haratin rebels, are terrified of being shot by the *roumis.* Holy war has been declared, but the French have not left, unlike the Italians."

"Not yet. Have patience. The justice of Allah cannot be long in coming. You will guide us to Tamanrasset, El Madani. And once we have made off with the marabout, you will receive the reward for your services, which will enable you to withdraw to Djanet or Rhāt, where you will be safe among us."

El Madani's eyes continued to roll, but now it was from greed. He had never owned anything—not land to work, not even a couple of goats. He had never seen money, that marvelous thing which allowed the race of Tuareg lords and the French masters to do anything: to eat their fill, to own wives and a real house, to travel. Shaking, he asked, "How much?"

"Twenty pieces of silver."

The thought of such a large amount left him breathless. Then he became bold. Now anything seemed possible. Even hating these Berbers who had enslaved his ancestors and who today were asking him to betray the marabout. Pretending to be shocked, he shouted, "Only twenty pieces of silver in return for a burial! Let's say one hundred pieces! That's not expensive for a life!"

"The marabout's life is to be spared. Mohamed Labed wants him living, for a trade with the *roumis.*"

"Aha, then he will bring a thousand pieces! The marabout is sacred to his people. Without counting the treasures you will take away from the fort. I have seen them: the supplies of excellent grain, of couscous, of dates; and there's all the wine, the cloth, the weapons! The weapons!"

The bargaining proceeded, their voices low. Beuh was growing impatient. Finally they settled on thirty pieces, payable when the marabout had been seized and properly tied up and placed atop a camel, ready to be transported to Agadez.

"How do you plan to go about this, El Madani? Is the marabout alone?"

"He lives alone, but he is often visited by armed men from In Salah and Motylinski. There is also Paul Embarek, that vile black who takes part in his sorcery."

"How can we get inside the fort?"

"There is but one door, and it is heavy. The marabout keeps it shut day and night, with a lock and a bolt. No one could break it open."

"What about scaling the walls?"

"Out of the question. From the bottom of the ditch around them to the crest, the distance is four times the height of a spear. Only trickery will work."

"Is there a password?"

"I don't think so. The marabout opens when he recognizes the visitor."

"He knows you, El Madani."

With this word that could be taken two ways, the traitor bowed his head. But why this? After all, they were not going to be harming the marabout, were they?

Some shadows loomed up in the dark. The Tuareg reached for their weapons.

"Do not be afraid", said Kerzou. "They are our men. Tuareg rebels, supporters of Sultan Ahmoud. Ait Lohen nomads staying near the Ajjer."

"Can you trust them?"

"Yes. They are all relatives of mine, won over to the Senoussi cause, haters of the Franks. They are on horseback and armed."

"What kind of weapons?"

"Old rifles from the 1870 war, stolen from the French. But they also have the swords and spears of desert warriors and know how to use them."

"How many are there?"

"A good fifteen. Ready for anything if a share of the booty is theirs. They will not be unwelcome if there is resistance and we have to besiege the fort."

4

Conversion

One is always only at the beginning of love.
—Father Huvelin

Brother Charles' salt-and-pepper beard shook slightly as he recalled that decisive year in his life, 1886.

Back from Algiers, on February 19 he made his home in Paris. Paris! Preparations for the World's Fair were underway. Monsieur Eiffel was building his tower, which some Catholics called "the new Babel". Between the fiacres, a Daimler sped along the streets at twelve miles an hour. General Boulanger was minister of war, and there was talk of war against Germany.

Charles rented a bachelor apartment at 50 rue de Miromesnil, in the Saint-Augustin district, not far from 42 rue d'Anjou, where the Moitessiers and Bondys lived together. A few nice pieces of furniture. On the floor, thick Moroccan wool rugs, on which he slept. Shelves holding rare books, and on the walls some watercolors, along with a few drawings he had brought back from Morocco. A valet was his only servant. The days went by, solitary and studious. Dressed in a jellaba and Turkish slippers, his thoughts were all of Morocco, Algeria, the Sahara, deepest Africa. Voyages, exploration, and heroic deeds. His friend Fitz-James, who ran into Charles during that period, did not recognize him: "He was quite changed, my fat Foucauld! He had become thin. And no more parties, no more ladies, no more fine dinners! Devoted to his work!"

Charles got along well with Olivier de Bondy, and most evenings he visited Inès Moitessier's drawing room, where the family would gather. But his days were entirely devoted to finishing his book, *Reconnaissance au Maroc*. Now he had to go to the heart of the matter and make a collection of dry notes into a living work imbued with the spirit of the adventure and all that had fascinated him: the journey, the unknown, the wide expanses of those virgin lands, the deserts, the fantastic peaks of the Atlas; and in the midst of the chaos of the sands, that improbable life found flourishing in an oasis or in a finger of good earth deep in the valleys where the wadis flowed.

Charles signed a contract with the publisher Challamel, 27 rue Jacob, which would later adopt the name "Société d'éditions géographiques, maritimes et coloniales" and would be famous in the world of sailors, explorers, and travelers.[1]

He often saw Henri Duveyrier, the famous explorer who had given him a helping hand and had encouraged him to write his book. Duveyrier himself had gotten his start in 1860 through a voyage of exploration followed by a book. Like him, Charles was to exploit without delay his newfound fame, which would not last. Paris was quite fickle! For Charles did not have many cards to play. After setting up his little apartment, he had barely enough income (for he was still under conservatorship) to live there with his valet. Struggle along like that in Paris? Or, once he had convinced his cousin conservator, use his capital for a great exploration that would bring him lasting fame? That was the only alternative, and of course he did not hesitate. He was changed, certainly, but he had never been able to strike a balance between mediocrity and madness. The whole problem was to avoid choosing the wrong form of madness.

While he waited for Georges de Latouche to be convinced, Charles would don his black suit and dine on Sunday evenings with his neighbors, the Moitessiers. There he rubbed elbows with men of politics, Orléanists, who left him indifferent and sometimes, as he put it, "wordless and overwhelmed".

It is surprising that he kept his distance from the concerns of the day. Aristocratic society found itself shaken by two rising, antagonistic forces: the liberal, money-making bourgeoisie and the workers, both influenced to some extent by atheistic and anticlerical ideologies. Himself a freethinker, Charles remained unmoved as the guests unanimously waxed indignant over the legalization of divorce, the expulsion of religious orders, the secularization of government, the egalitarian positivism of those in power, and the first stirrings of the labor union movement. He did appreciate, however, the way Inès Moitessier led her guests to express themselves, never taking sides herself. Certainly, it was a royalist ambiance, loyal to the traditional Church and the pope, but with a certain liberalism, and no hypocrisy. And most important, it was never boring at the house on rue d'Anjou, although there was neither frivolity nor license.

Besides these gatherings, Charles sought out the family atmosphere of more private evenings at rue d'Anjou, with the Flavignys, the Countess

---

[1] Today, "Éditions maritimes et d'outre-mer", affiliated with the publishing group Ouest-France.

Armand de Foucauld and her son, and other relatives who might be passing through: the Foucaulds from the Périgord, the Lagabbes, the Latouches, the Morlaincourts. And above all, his cousin, Marie de Bondy.

Twelve years had gone by since her marriage to Viscount Olivier de Bondy, a reasonably successful union. Marie had given birth to five children (one had not survived). Charles adored these little cousins; upon his return from Morocco he seemed to them a legendary hero as he emerged from the dark shadows where the family had hidden him because of his youthful escapades.

Marie was now thirty-six. Despite the unfortunate Algiers romance, which had left a taste of ashes, Charles still felt drawn toward his cousin, not a carnal attraction, for she was as much the mother he had lost as she was the ideal wife he would never have. For him, she represented the archetype of the *anima*, "the feminine mirror of his spiritual yearnings" (H. Didier).

An odd couple, the Bondys! Wealthy, cultured, courtly, entertaining at times, an ardent royalist, Olivier de Bondy was as shallow as Marie was deep. He thought only of enjoying himself: hunting, riding, clubs. She, serious and sometimes distraught, created a gulf between them that he could not cross. A Voltairian, he would go to his club when she went to Mass. Not interested in society, she reigned over her little family. Although living the life of the privileged, she made great demands on herself. Of a mystical nature, religion was her real passion.

Yes, an odd couple. She put up with Olivier's aristocratic nonchalance and his frivolous occupations. Although he did not find her very entertaining, he had come to terms with her absorption in serious books and parish meetings. In short, they got along well. Yet, in spite of her heavy family and social responsibilities, a feeling of loneliness hung over Marie, and she went more and more often to the confessional of her spiritual adviser, Father Huvelin, at the nearby church, Saint-Augustin.

Imperceptibly, Charles and Marie drew closer. Charles was still feeling isolated emotionally. Whether it was from fatigue or from disgust over his past and his inglorious breakup with Marie-Marguerite Titre, he remained celibate, something that surprised him. "Celibacy became sweet to me, a heartfelt necessity",[2] he would later write, as if he felt a need for this form of asceticism to understand what was happening to him. An astonishing transformation, which preceded and heralded what was to be a radical

[2] "Retraite à Nazareth", one of the primary sources where C. de Foucauld recounts his conversion ("14ᵉ méditation" extract from Foucauld's account of his retreat at Nazareth from November 5 to 15, 1897, published in *Écrits spirituels* [Gigord, 1923]. The two other primary sources are his 1901 letters to Henri de Castries [Grasset, 1938] and his letter of February 21, 1892, to Henri Duveyrier, *Bulletin des Amitiés*, no. 83, 3–8).

upheaval for him. He was becoming detached from the flesh. A certain Sigmund Freud, who had just opened his office in Vienna, would have observed that "this sweetness, this heartfelt necessity" was a prelude to a sublimation of the libido into the higher (let us say, spiritual) activities that were occupying him increasingly and were not intellectual activities. Later, Charles would attribute this unexpected change to God, who had his conversion in mind: "You forced me to be chaste, deflecting me from evil by the gentlest and the strongest means; it was not through my goodwill, but in spite of me. . . . Little by little the terrain was being cleared." For, "You cannot enter a soul where the demon of vile passions reigns." [3] God demands all. He takes the place of ordinary passions. That is the price which must be paid.

God? But who is God?

He would often read the Koran, remembering the peoples of the Maghreb and their fervor, which had awakened in him these religious concerns. And indeed, Islam had left its mark. "Islam has produced in me a profound upheaval", he would later write to Henri de Castries. "Observing this faith and these souls living with God as a continual presence has allowed me to glimpse something greater and more true than worldly occupations." [4]

Did Islam tempt him, as Laperrine suggested in a letter to Nieger? [5] Charles himself said, "Islam appealed to me too strongly. I was very attracted to its simplicity of dogma, hierarchy, and morality." And above all he liked its unity—as Louis Massignon was to write in recalling Charles' "contact with this dominant faith, which burns the believer to ashes beneath the unreachable sun of divine unity." [6] But Charles had more to say, writing to Henri de Castries: "But I could see clearly that Islam was without a divine basis and that the truth was not there." A radical judgment on his part, rather surprising. But much he had read in the Koran about the life of Mohammed shocked him; the Prophet had become rich; he had undertaken wars of conquest and had encouraged his followers to pursue the *jihad*, without necessity. He had also indulged in all the pleasures of the senses, and his rule relegated woman to the role of mother and instrument of pleasure.

Father Six has the right idea about the temptation of Islam for Charles: it was "in essence, a religious seduction".[7] And therein lay the problem. Like human love, conversion is a matter of the emotions, not of the

[3] Ibid.
[4] CF to Henri de Castries, July 8, 1901 [Gasset, 1938].
[5] General Nieger, "Laperrine et le P. de Foucauld", *Construire*, no. 13, 182.
[6] L. Massignon, article, *France-Maroc*, March 15, 1917.
[7] J.-F. Six, *Itinéraire spirituel de Charles de Foucauld* (Seuil, 1958), 45.

intellect. Certainly it was the desert and the contact with Muslim (and Jewish) religiousness that had shaken Charles so deeply. But "suffering alone does not bring about conversion. There must be the working of grace. Something divine that is impossible to explain."[8]

Thus he turned away from Islam to bury himself in the little book Marie de Bondy had given him for his First Communion, Bossuet's *Élévations sur les mystères*. Earlier this dry work had put him off, but now he appreciated its subtle depths and especially, he said, its "warmth and beauty". He found in it shock phrases disturbing to his old skepticism: "My soul, reasonable soul whose reason is so weak, why do you claim that you exist and yet claim that God does not?"

One passage in particular vibrated in the deepest fibers of his being: "Let us form in ourselves the Holy Trinity, unity with God, knowledge of God, love for God. And since our knowledge, which for now is imperfect and obscure, will depart, and since the love in us is the sole thing that will never depart, let us love, let us love, let us love. Let us do without end what we shall do without end. Let us do without end in the temporal world what we shall do without end in eternity."

What a change of focus for someone who had once enjoyed only pagan literature, Greek and Roman, and erotic writings. "I find those works [now] empty and distasteful."[9] He was no longer seeking absolute truth—it seemed unattainable—but virtue, which he found in these moral teachings and above all in the example of Inès and her daughter Marie.

That year, 1886, Charles spent a calm and happy summer at La Barre, a splendid country estate of 4,500 acres in Berry. Here Olivier de Bondy's father—once a prefect and peer of France, later a senator—offered his guests a life of luxury. The gigantic château with pink towers and a keep was almost uninhabitable, but it boasted a romantic terrace overlooking the Creuse and wonderful grounds with flower beds, a tropical greenhouse, and an orchard of five thousand trees, presided over by Marie de Bondy.

At La Barre, Charles took boundless pleasure in his cousin's strong and quiet presence. With Marie, he had everything. The atmosphere of family tenderness so long denied him, shaded with a discreet sensuality. A solid Christian faith, well established and applied to life, for these privileged aristocrats saw no contradiction between their ways and the poverty of Jesus. These were good people, who walked the straight and narrow; they were devoted to their children and their spouses; they practiced charity and treated their servants with respect: What more could one ask?

[8] Ibid.
[9] CF, *Écrits spirituels*, 79.

Marie's influence became decisive. And Charles began to question: "Since she possesses such an intelligent soul, the religion in which she so firmly believes cannot be the madness I think it." [10]

Much more than intelligent. "Such a beautiful soul aided You, but through its silence, gentleness, kindness, and perfection." [11]

But there were new developments. In September 1886, Charles took military training in Tunisia, which complicated an incident sparked by an act of impetuosity on his part back on July 14. Moved by the news of the banishment of the Duke d'Aumale, and probably encouraged by Olivier de Bondy, a militant Orléanist, Charles, who had never been mixed up in politics, felt obliged to send a telegram to the colonel in charge of his old regiment, the Fourth Chasseurs of Africa, then stationed in Tunis: "As sole officer of the corps presently in Paris, may I extend him greetings on behalf of the officers of the Fourth Chasseurs and tell him that our regiment, which distinguished itself under his leadership, will honor the glorious general who led it to victory?" [12]

Instead of dismissing the matter as the inconsequential action of a "vain and excitable" (as he characterized Charles) young reservist, the colonel reacted strongly. He sent a fiery report to General Boulanger, the war minister, who, initially a supporter of the Duke d'Aumale, had recently dismissed him. The affair turned ugly. The military bureaucracy, now on the side of the Republic, suspected a conspiracy. It felt that Foucauld had "incited the head of his corps to carry out an act of disobedience and had disregarded his duty to the military". And they suggested that the minister "determine to have this officer's case brought before the president of the Republic in order that he be suspended from his duties for a year and not be called up during that time". [13]

Of which Charles was given notice on September 18. Distressed, for he still valued his title as a reserve officer, Charles then went to Tunis, where he may well have been under arrest, for he declared later that he had to spend three weeks there.

This minor affair is not lacking in interest. It intensified his break with the army, where he no longer had a future. In short, it isolated him even more, forcing him to turn elsewhere, to a place he did not yet imagine.

[10] "Retraite à Nazareth", in ibid.

[11] Ibid.

[12] Fourth son of Louis Philippe, the Duke d'Aumale had distinguished himself in 1843, fighting against Emir Abd el-Kader on the high plateaux of Algeria. In 1886 the Third Republic, to forestall the return of the pretender, had dismissed the duke from the army and exiled him, along with the other members of the royal family.

[13] *Bulletin des Amitiés*, no. 84, 18.

He planned to return to Paris October 15. But an event hastened his return: "a surprising event", he said, without further elucidation. Was Marie de Bondy on the verge of death? Marguerite Castillon du Perron, in her biography, speaks of "madness suddenly overcoming him: his soul was abruptly opened, revealed, scarified." [14] Father Six is inclined to think it was a mystical state, "a touch of the Being". But that would not have caused the sudden return to Paris.

Few specifics are to be found. Eleven years later, in his "Fourteenth Meditation", Charles would limit himself to saying: "By what devices, God of goodness, have you made yourself known to me? . . . Astonishing circumstances, unexpected solitude, emotion, illnesses of dear ones, deep and intense feelings, return to Paris in the wake of a surprising event." [15]

Which could mean any number of things. Marguerite Castillon thinks that his agitated state was the result of Marie de Bondy's serious illness (paratyphoid), which may have made Charles realize just what he felt for her. Did his feelings go beyond the permissible? It is difficult to get a clear answer from Charles; whenever he has given Marie's important influence its due, he has made of it a spiritual influence: "Beauty of a soul whose virtue had appeared to me so beautiful that my heart was irrevocably ravished." [16]

Was it, as described by Marguerite Castillon, a question of "a raging flame that sharpens and deepens every pain suffered", of "an emotion of terrifying force", and of "unconscious ambiguity". Or did he simply love her "with an unobtrusive tenderness", "with a supremely sweet and gentle intoxication"? [17]

In his "Fourteenth Meditation of Nazareth", written in 1897, Charles would, of course, be much more discreet. According to his account, everything happened on the spiritual plane: "At the same time, you were strengthening my ties with beautiful souls. You had brought me back to that family, object of passionate attachment in my youth. I was living in their midst in such an atmosphere of virtue that my life was rapidly restored: it was spring returning life to the earth after winter. You had driven the evil from my heart; my good angel had found its place there again, joined by an earthly angel."

Step by step, Charles was heading toward the major crisis, the upheaval, the metanoia. In the fall of 1886, he was shaken but in no way converted: "My heart and my spirit remained far from you [my God], yet I was living in an

[14] M. Castillon du Perron, *Charles de Foucauld* (Grasset, 1982), 151.
[15] "Retraite à Nazareth".
[16] Ibid.
[17] Castillon, *Foucauld*, 152.

atmosphere much less corrupt. Little by little the terrain was being cleared. You had broken down the barriers, made the soul malleable, prepared the ground by burning the thorns and the bushes." [18]

Shaken on the level of faith, it was not yet a question of Christ. Charles expressed himself clearly on this, addressing him in the "Meditation": "After receiving so many acts of grace, it [my soul] was still not acquainted with you. You were acting continually in it, and it did not know you. . . . At the beginning of October 1886, after six months of family life, I admired and wanted virtue, but I did not know you." [19]

Everything about this conversion is surprising. God had been given back to him in Africa, thanks to the stark beauty of the landscape joined to the religiousness of the Muslim and Jewish peoples. But it was still an undifferentiated God, the God of Voltaire, not a person, not the God incarnate, whom he did not realize he sought. There then arose in him a sort of tender call, seemingly to a God unknown to him, a God closer to him than he was to himself. "To be aware that you are accompanied but not to know the One who accompanies you is a dreadful mystery", points out Marguerite Castillon. One evening he entered a church. There, bathed in the gentle candlelight, he sat down before the altar and whispered, "My God, if you exist, let me know you!" [20]

He no longer pushed away this "temptation", for it was filling the emptiness in his heart at last: happiness, deep and lasting joy. Or at least the promise, for nothing was yet accomplished. He was waiting then—passionately, as with everything he undertook. For in this situation, waiting and surrender were the perfect form of action. A stripping bare, as in his vision of the African desert.

Once again, he plunged eagerly into the little book by Bossuet that Marie had given him. Now each sentence set him aflame: "Oh, God, how poor is my soul! It is only chaos before you have begun to untangle all its thoughts!"

Chaos, that is obvious. There was nothing but agitation in his head. But faith? The light of faith? Bossuet's response: "When you begin, through faith, to make the light of faith break through, it is still imperfect until you have given it substance through charity and until you, who are the true sun of justice, burning and radiant, have set me aglow with your love!"

He understood. Faith was the key to everything. It was given. But there was also love. Step by step, he walked in the darkness toward the little flame he could still see shining at the end of the tunnel of his ignorance. Once

---

[18] "Retraite à Nazareth".
[19] Ibid.
[20] CF to Henri de Castries, August 14, 1901.

again rose the cry from his tortured heart: "My God, if you exist, let me know you!"

A pathetic plea. "You would not be seeking me if you had not already found me", an inner voice kept saying. Yet, a remarkable feature of this conversion that was taking place: Charles' praying to a God he had not yet met. How can this contradiction be resolved? Ah! "You would not be seeking me if I had not already found you!" In the desert of Africa, as in the desert of the city and that of his heart, Charles had suspected God's existence, detected his perfume, perceived the discreet shadow from his light. He had received that "touch of the Being", that all-embracing, sweet sense of a Transcendence that surrounds and guides us. He had not yet seen its face or received its light.

In October 1886, in Paris, Charles had long discussions with Marie de Bondy. Gradually, silently, that mystical and ardent soul was pushing him in the direction he wished to go. How happy she was when he finally exclaimed: "How fortunate you are to believe!" But he then added: "I seek the light and I do not find it!"[21]

His feelings were complicated and unsettling. In his contacts with Marie and to a lesser degree with Inès, his rational side was also called upon: "In Paris, I found myself with people who were extremely intelligent, virtuous, and Christian. I told myself that maybe this religion was not absurd", he wrote to Henri de Castries.

And, already the summer before, in the country, at La Barre, "I found the example of all the virtues, and along with that good minds and deep religious convictions", he wrote to Henri Duveyrier.

Charles was no less specific in his "Meditation of Nazareth", already quoted: "You drew me to virtue through the beauty of a soul whose virtue had appeared to me so beautiful that my heart was irrevocably ravished."

And his conclusion, logical: "Since this religion is not madness, perhaps it is where the truth lies. Let us study this religion. Let us find a teacher of Catholic religion, an educated priest, and let us see what there is in it."[22]

And that announces the appearance of the second key character in the conversion and also in the life of Charles de Foucauld: Father Henri Huvelin, the curate at Saint-Augustin's, and Marie and Inès' regular confessor.

In 1886, he was forty-eight years old. A graduate of Paris' École Normale, his teaching degree was in philosophy; his other major fields of study were Greek and history. He had completed his education at the French seminary in Rome, where he received a degree in theology. A teacher at the little

---

[21] Quoted by R. Bazin, *Charles de Foucauld* (Plon, 1921), 93.
[22] Ibid.

seminary of Saint-Nicolas-du-Chardonnet in 1864, he could look ahead to a high place in the Church. But that was not his chosen path, and he also abandoned the idea of becoming a monk. Mystical and ascetic, he happily turned to the life of a simple parish curate, at Saint-Eugène's initially, then from 1875 at Saint-Augustin's, where he soon became a force in the confessional and in the pulpit.

His success there (most notably, he converted Littré)[23] stemmed from his verbal enthusiasm, his impassioned faith, and his learning. In 1880 his health began to deteriorate. The penitent ascetic life he had imposed on himself from an early age was not unconnected with his poor physical condition, which lasted until his death. In those days, medicine had no way to relieve the painful rheumatism afflicting him.

Thus, in 1886, this man who had been an athlete in his youth could be seen dragging himself to the church, head bent, face puffy beneath the tufts of curly gray hair. But in the prematurely aged face glowed the light of his clear blue eyes, a reflection of his loving, passionate soul. As soon as he climbed into the pulpit, there would emanate from him the presence of him to whom he had given all.

Sundays, he preached as many as five times at Saint-Augustin's, where his listeners felt small and humble under the enormous nave. For several years, he had even delivered lectures to young people in the great crypt. Adults flocked there also. Paying no heed to the pompous, erudite style of preachers of his time, he spoke to the heart, simply, shaking up his rich parishioners, recalling that Christ had come first to save the little folk, the suffering and the poor. To love them. "When we wish to convert a soul, we must not preach: we must show our love."

People also came to his confessional, for he had the gift of discernment. They also came to his home at 6 rue de Laborde, a little apartment cluttered with books and papers. Sitting there, pain and intelligence on his face, "resigned to the crowd as well as to illness", with a cat on his lap, he would receive visitors of every sort, young and old, aristocrats and servants. They would first be surprised by his severity, then astonished upon seeing him weep, as he shared their misfortunes or deplored their shameful acts. He would respond to praise by saying modestly that he had never converted anyone: "Only God converts." Was his physical suffering the price he paid for his charisma? Like the Christ with whom he identified, he bore the evil of others and assumed it in his flesh. "Suffering purifies us, ennobles us, gives us charm", he would say on Sundays before his splendid, dumbfounded listeners.

Did Charles hear him at Saint-Augustin's? It is likely, for even if he did

[23] The liberal politician and scholar Maximilien Littré.—TRANS.

not practice, he liked going into churches to sense the undefinable perfume of transcendence raising mediocre man above his petty destiny. Evening was his usual time for such contemplation, when the silence of the church was like a bit of desert within the bustle of Paris. It is also possible to imagine Charles at morning Mass, surrounded mostly by servants and working people.

On October 30, 1886, Charles de Foucauld rose early.[24] He ate no breakfast. His mind aflame, he left his apartment and headed for Saint-Augustin's. A decision had been made. He would meet Father Huvelin. Marie had advised him to do so, but she mentioned it to no one, since no actual appointment had been made. Charles hoped to see him after one of his lectures. But the priest had recently stopped delivering them, worn out by a nearly fatal attack of bronchitis. Charles then decided to see him anonymously in his confessional, where he could be found before the first Mass.

Since it was very early and the church had just opened, there was as yet no one in the confessional, in the nave's third chapel, on the right. Father Huvelin was there. Charles leaned toward him and, without kneeling, murmured in a voice overcome by emotion: "Father, do not be surprised. I do not come for confession. I do not have the faith. I only wish to learn some things about the Catholic religion."

Father Huvelin fixed his eyes on him: "You do not have the faith. Have you never believed, then?"

"Yes, thirteen years ago. But right now, I am unable to believe. There are all the obstacles of the mysteries, the dogma, the miracles."

"You are mistaken, my son. What is missing now, in order for you to believe, is a pure heart. Go down on your knees, make your confession to God, and you will believe."

"But I have not come for that!"

"That does not matter. Go down on your knees and say the *Confiteor*."

Without really understanding what was happening to him, Charles knelt and confessed at length, covering his entire life. When he would pause, a gentle silence extended over all things, barely disturbed by the soft rustlings of the pious folk gathering in the adjacent chapel to hear early Mass. Finally, the priest granted him absolution: "*Deinde te absolvo . . .*"

Charles was filled with joy and a peace he had never thought possible.

"Have you eaten anything?" the priest asked.

"No."

"Receive Communion."[25]

---

[24] It is not known for certain whether it was October 29 or 30.
[25] "Retraite à Nazareth" and letter to Henri de Castries.

Charles rose to his feet. He felt astonishingly light and at the same time possessed by that incomprehensible joy. In one moment, all his doubts had been swept away. He did not believe, he knew! He headed toward the altar of the Virgin. "*Introibo ad altare Dei.*" I shall approach the altar of God. It was as if he had become a child again, the child he had been before the death of his parents. He had found his father again. Then he received the Body of Christ; he would never again be hungry or thirsty.

Strange, that order from Father Huvelin: "Receive Communion." And it was definitely an order, issued by a priest ordinarily retiring, patient, a listener. At that time the rules about receiving Communion were rather strict. Certainly, Charles was not a stranger; Father Huvelin had run into him at the Moitessiers', and Marie and Inès had mentioned him. The priest had seen him in Saint-Augustin's, at night, a furtive shadow submerged in the darkness of the church. Perhaps he had been waiting for Charles. He let himself be guided by one of those lightning flashes of intuition not unusual in true spiritual advisers.

Charles had chosen well. He, so temperamental, immediately asked Henri Huvelin to instruct and guide him on this new journey, this perilous exploration inside himself, which was going to lead him to Christ, the thousand obstacles along the way being the arguments set up by the rational human brain. This time, Charles was no longer stuck at the 1 = 3. For the explanation of the existence he would lead against his very nature lies in what was central to this conversion: a total adherence to this mad premise of a Christ-God, a man-God, a God incarnate, always present, loving and living in the Eucharist. Why? Charles saw, he received the light, he felt the love, and he was fulfilled.

Yes, astonishing, this conversion. Nothing human involved; it proceeded from the supernatural. Thus Huvelin the theologian stayed in the background. He did not try to convince this very special penitent through arguments addressed to his intelligence. Only God can convert, and he does so by going for the heart. Father Huvelin would give the key to this conversion later in introducing Charles to the abbot of Solesmes: "He makes of religion his love." Father Huvelin saw what others had not seen, even Inès, even Marie, more persuasive in her silences than in the words she must not have failed to address to him in her efforts to convert. He had no need for reasoning, because he had already applied reason to the whole matter. "He needed only one word to catalyze an experience that had reached its culmination." [26]

"Make your confession", that is, relinquish yourself, your ego, your

---

[26] Cardinal C. Martini, "Charles de Foucauld, une religion d'amour", homily, Milan Cathedral.

pride. "Receive Communion", agree to receive the One who is Love, by giving yourself to him in return. And it was the effusion of the Spirit that brought about and carried through the conversion, the metanoia: "As soon as I came to believe there was a God, I understood that I could not do otherwise than live only for him." [27]

A lightning-swift, irreversible conversion. For Charles was not a half-hearted creature. As has already been seen, in his life it was all or nothing, whether for good or evil. God invited him to love him. He said yes without reservation. It was not only God in whom he believed, but in a person, a face, that of Christ, who suddenly enveloped him in his love. And he responded to that love at once, without reservation. Jesus became for him "the only model". Having found Christ, he wished to imitate him. What does this poor and persecuted Christ say? "If you wish to be perfect, sell your possessions, give your money to the poor, and follow me." Thus, Charles' dedication to poverty, which sprang up at the same time, that desire to humble himself, "the most powerful means we have of joining with Jesus and doing good for souls".[28]

On leaving Saint-Augustin's, Charles was overcome by "that infinite peace, that dazzling light, that unfailing happiness".[29] And nothing would ever be as before. He was so thoroughly "converted" that he wanted to go at breakneck speed, frightening even Father Huvelin himself! Right away he was leading the life of a monk: prayer, *lectio*, strict asceticism, and, most notably, complete obedience to Father Huvelin.

But here the priest stepped in to moderate his enthusiasm. Why? "He wanted to see him set out slowly and secretly on the road of sacrifice, a path where it would no longer be pride that set each step in motion", wrote J.-F. Six.[30] Religious vocation? That was to be seen. No hurry. For the impetuous convert, an intolerable situation. "Why wait? I want to be a monk, live only for God, and do that which is the most perfect, whatever it might be." [31]

In light of the good priest's sermons, it is possible to imagine his response: "God has visited you, and you believe you are giving. It is very easy to think that, as long as he sustains you. But let the hour come when you no longer feel anything. Then you will be allowed your turn to give."

"I do not understand!"

"You are not the owner of what you feel. No! You own nothing. You only receive. The grace of God . . ."

[27] CF to Henri de Castries, August 14, 1901.
[28] CF to Marie de Bondy, December 1, 1916.
[29] CF to Henri de Castries, December 1, 1916.
[30] Six, *Itinéraire*, 74.
[31] CF to Henri de Castries, December 1, 1916.

"What? Some day I will stop receiving?"

"Indeed. That is what John of the Cross means by the dark night of the spirit. The hour when we no longer receive is a merciful delicacy of God to allow us our turn to give to him at last."

"Waiting is hard."

"If there is no limit to what God asks of us, it is because there is no limit to what he wishes to give us." [32]

And Charles put questions to him. The dark night of the spirit? Let him first go through the tests of time and insensibility, which would come as surely as night follows day. Father Huvelin advised him to learn about the "mysteries" and, most important, to pray and to strip away his old self. Mass, confession, Communion, as often as possible. But such devotion was not fashionable, and Charles had good reason for thinking that he was still too much a sinner to be worthy of approaching the Communion table. Father Huvelin, very much ahead of his time, brushed these scruples aside impatiently: the Eucharist was not a reward reserved for the just but a force to take one to Christ, who gives himself to sinners first. That attitude meant Charles could relive daily the miracle of his conversion: the Real Presence of Christ in the Eucharist was not a symbol but a living reality, and the wonder of that never left him.

In the family, they knew nothing as yet. Except for Marie, who kept the secret. Inès returned home one day very excited: "I saw Charles at Mass, and he received Communion!"

The family was shocked. How could this former profligate dare approach the Communion table?

Why did he not talk to his loved ones, since he was so sure of his future course? Of course, his milieu did not like outpourings of emotion, which were almost a taboo. One did not talk one's love affairs over with the family, and, for Charles, it was indeed a matter of the heart. A thunderbolt.

This odd lack of communication was compounded, early in 1888, by his behavior—strange to say the least—apropos of what had until then been the major event of his life: the exploration of Morocco. If he did want to be an explorer, he would need contacts; yet he abandoned the scientific world and the geographers who, a short time before, had fascinated him. He divided among his nephews the precious souvenirs from Morocco: weapons, burnous, jellaba, as well as his military hats, the shako from Saint-Cyr and the kepi from Saumur. He was no longer interested in the management of the fortune he had jeopardized, and he still refused to get after his debtor, Morès-Vallombrosa. The predictions of Laissy, his financial

[32] A. Gilbert-Lafon, *Échos des entretiens de l'abbé Huvelin* (Roblot, 1917).

manager, were gloomy; Charles went so far as to give his sister, Marie, his silverware to thank her for money she had given him. The family, upset, saw no salvation for him but a marriage with a good dowry. Strangely enough, Father Huvelin went along with that idea. Not yet trusting in Charles' religious vocation, he was on the family's side: one of Monsieur de Richemont's daughters, a pious young woman with a substantial dowry, was thought to be a good match. But Charles spurned all advances, saying to himself over and over: "As soon as I came to believe there was a God, I understood that I could not do otherwise than live only for him. My religious vocation dates from the same hour as my faith. God is so great! There is such a difference between God and everything that is not God." [33]

A year went by. In February 1888 Charles came up against that wall, the dark night of the spirit about which Father Huvelin had warned him. An echo of the crisis can be found in a letter Henri Duveyrier wrote that same month to Maunoir, secretary of the Geographical Society, both men dismayed at seeing the young viscount abandon his exploration projects: "I feel a sincere affection for Monsieur de Foucauld. He is a rare person and, I fear, a man either stricken with an irreversible illness or else suffering a profound emotional disturbance. He deserves to be treated with consideration." [34]

What was going on in Charles' mind? Once again, he was hanging back before the mysteries of dogma. As soon as illumination no longer supported him, he sank. And yet he clung to obedience without a murmur. A difficult confrontation. Father Huvelin was shocked by the syncretism of his thought: "A religion consists of an organic whole. It must not be denatured by mixing in foreign elements such as the Koran!"

Charles would later admit to Henri de Castries: "At the beginning, faith had a number of obstacles to overcome. I who had doubted so strongly, I did not come to believe everything in a single day. The miracles of the Gospel seemed to me hard to believe." [35]

And so Father Huvelin quickly changed his approach. Enough theology. Since Charles had been illuminated, faith was going to suffice for everything. Let him devote himself to imitating Christ and reading and meditating on the Gospels. Let him forget what he had been and become a child again.

Charles understood that the only path for him lay in renunciation and submission to an experienced guide. What followed was astounding: the blind obedience shown by this man who had been so long a rebel, know-

---

[33] CF to Henri de Castries, December 1, 1916.

[34] In G. Gorrée, *Charles de Foucauld intime* (La Colombe, 1952), 50; and M. Carrouges, *Charles de Foucauld, explorateur mystique* (Cerf, 1954), 120.

[35] CF to Henri de Castries, December 1, 1916.

ing neither God nor master, defying his family and the army. Charles Pichon writes, "Now he is living his religion from within; his sensibility and his intelligence are transformed; they are on a higher level, they are expanding, they are soon ordering themselves according to the absolute. He allows the inexplicable as a fact acceptable to his reason instead of reacting as if it were a distressing scandal or physical torture." [36]

Father Huvelin patiently set out to crush his ego. The priest still saw the influence of Islam in the overweening desire for perfection that excited Charles. Jesus, in his humanity, was not glorious; he remained "poor and meek at heart". Like him, let Charles strive to take *the last place*.

That phrase moved him deeply. "Jesus has so taken the last place that no one has ever been able to wrest it from him", Father Huvelin said repeatedly. [37] This pithy quote from the priest led Charles to his personal vocation, which resembled no other: not missionary, not ecclesiastic. It was much more than the return of the biblical prodigal son, whose behavior was logical and in his own interest. Charles was not "returning to the path of righteousness", as his family put it. Possessed by a passionate love, he threw himself unrestrainedly into the way of total asceticism.

What was going to happen now? Charles had once and for all given up further journeys of exploration. For eighteen months he obeyed Father Huvelin, who advised him not to hurry into the religious life. His desire to be a monk only grew stronger. He read eagerly the lives of the Desert Fathers; but there were none today. "While desiring to exhale all that is in me before God and lose myself totally in him, I do not know which order to choose. The Gospels showed me that the first commandment is to love God with all one's heart and to enclose everything in that love. The first effect of love is imitation." [38]

What order would best imitate Jesus? He did not want to preach—he felt unworthy—or do mission work, which involved preaching. He did not feel called to that and did not wish to become a priest. "Thus, I should imitate the hidden life of the poor and humble workman of Nazareth." [39] He wanted to be lowly, reduced to nothing, to "exhale all and be totally lost".

Summer 1888, once again at La Barre, indescribable happiness at being with Marie de Bondy. From there, on August 19, she took him to visit the Trappist monastery at Fontgombault, eighteen miles away. [40] In ruins. A

---

[36] C. Pichon, *Charles de Foucauld* (Éd. de la Nouvelle France, 1946), 168.

[37] Father Huvelin, sermons, March 1887, quoted by Gorrée, *Foucauld intime*, 64.

[38] CF to Henri de Castries, December 1, 1916.

[39] Ibid.

[40] The restored Abbey of Fontgombault is very active today. It houses more than one hundred Benedictine monks, who live, pray, and celebrate the liturgy strictly according to the traditions of the order of Saint Benedict.

miserable place. A handful of poor monks eked out a living working the land with their hands. Charles waxed enthusiastic over the poverty, the detachment, the silence, the peace, the adoration, the fraternity. The powerful words of Bossuet came back to him once more: "O eternal God, draw me out of time, fix me in your eternity! As I wait, grant I may pray unceasingly and spend my days and nights in contemplation of your law."

Contemplation! In the old Romanesque church, he contemplated the miraculous statue of Notre-Dame-du-Bien-Mourir[41] and realized that first of all it was a question of dying to oneself. Would he be a Cistercian? On his way out of the church, he received another shock. Marie describes it: "He had seen a brother in a habit so dirty, so patched, that this poverty had seduced him."

For Charles, this humble lay monk was Christ. The last place was there! The most obscure task in the poorest of monasteries! Obviously, Marie, like the rest of the family, would have liked a more "intellectual" order, the Benedictines.

Charles, moved, said good-bye to Marie. They exchanged a secret pact: never to hide anything from each other. To share their joys and sorrows.

After that blissfully happy stay at La Barre, Charles said a final farewell to the army, following his final session of training as a reserve officer, when he conducted himself so well that the Duke d'Aumale incident was forgotten. On taking off his uniform for the last time, on September 19, he received his final report, a glowing one: "Devoted officer, conscientious and hardworking, equal to his duties. Fine platoon leader."[42] But for him that era was gone forever.

On returning to Paris, he learned of the success of his book, illustrated with his own drawings. Unanimously praised in scientific circles, the work went beyond detailed geographical descriptions. There was in it inspiration that rang true, an expansion of the spirit, the lyricism of a poet whose soul rejoiced over the starry nights of the desert, the harsh solitude, the gigantic rocky masses of the Atlas, the cool oases amid the burning sands, the poor men with pious souls. A writer had been born.[43]

He was encouraged to depart again and achieve new exploits. Departing was indeed at the center of his thoughts. But for another kind of journey, an inner one; for another kind of adventure, a spiritual one.

[41] *Bien mourir* = to die a Christian death.—TRANS.
[42] Gorrée, *Foucauld intime*, 65.
[43] A costly volume to produce, *Reconnaissance au Maroc,* 495 pages, was not to be reissued until 1934, then again in 1939. In 1985, Éditions Aujourd'hui published the facsimile of the 1888 edition, minus the appendices and the atlas.

Following Father Huvelin's advice, he decided to go on a pilgrimage to the Holy Land.

Tamanrasset, December 1, 1916. 11 A.M.

Brother Charles was roused from his memories by a gentle knock on the door; Paul Embarek came in, preceded by the delicious odor of the well-browned bread he had just removed from the hot stone in the courtyard of the *bordj*. He also brought in the pan with the cooked dates. He put a loaf of the flatbread on the table, laid another aside in the cupboard for the poor, kept the third and crouched on the sand to wolf it down. Brother Charles reprimanded him. The tall black man leaped up, rattled. Brother Charles said the *benedicite* and sat down at the table, now cleared of its pile of papers.

The bread, dusty with ashes and still smoking, was as hard as wood. Charles broke up the loaf and put the pieces in his wrought-iron bowl. Then he picked up the pan of dates, dipped his fingers into the thick mixture, removed the pits from the fruit, and poured the hot paste over the morsels in the bowl. He stirred everything together with his wooden spoon, adding a little—very little—soft, rancid butter. The stewed fruit had turned into a sort of dough, the traditional *khefis*. Brother Charles took hold of it with both hands, kneaded it, crushed it to release the remaining liquid. Then, his thoughts elsewhere, he took little mouthfuls of this bland, sweet putty, all the while under the mocking gaze of Paul, who was spitting date pits onto the sand floor and chewing up his flatbread.

When there were European guests, Charles did not dare offer them *khefis*, which usually did not do their stomachs any good. The hermit would serve the date mixture only to the Tuareg notables, who knew how to appreciate it. For French guests he would open a can of corned beef, that everyday army ration the soldiers referred to as "monkey". As for Brother Charles, he never ate meat. His vegetarian diet forbade it, along with eggs.

He washed down his indigestible repast with large swigs of pure water. That was his sin of gluttony. But no, he had no regrets about not drinking that muddy, mucky water from the dryish wells of the desert as a form of penance!

At the end of the meal, another sin of gluttony: Brother Charles poured himself a cup of coffee, an old mixture from the day before, with no aroma, reheated in the coffeepot over the ashes of the courtyard fire. He never used sugar, considered a delicacy. Paul, of course, had a right to a lump.

Paul told him, "The two camel troopers from Motylinski are still in the village. They will stop by this evening to pay their respects and to get your messages before heading back to Fort Moty. They would rather ride at night."

Twelve miles to the northeast, the *rezzou* of the *fellagha* had been obliged to slow down its camels while passing through the rugged desert of the Koudia. High atop his dromedary, the Senoussi Beuh ag Rhabelli was talking with the Targui, Kerzou. The Targui was a simple man, a nomad, but not a shepherd, for he had never worked with his hands, God forbid! A pillager and a Targui noble, his tent was not large, but he was well born, with no black Haratin slave blood in his veins. He regretted the days of the *rezzous* that his elders would recall in the tent, between songs accompanied on the *imzad*.

As for Beuh, in spite of his cruelty and lack of scruples, he was a sophisticated young man. He claimed to have studied the Koran with the marabouts of Alexandria, but more likely it was Tripoli. Very politicized, he secretly looked down on the Tuareg, and, along with his master Mohamed Labed, he dreamed of the restoration of the Ottoman Empire, with its emirs. These all-powerful officials of the sultan would once again serve in colonized territories, exploiting the working population, robbing them without violence through the imposition of taxes, to be supplemented by *bakshish* (bribes).

Beuh explained his "revolution" to the Targui: "The great sultan reigning in Constantinople, leader of the believers, has declared a holy war against all the territories of the French and the English, who are enemies of the German kaiser, the sultan of the *roumis*. The agent of the *jihad* is the Senoussi sect, and to it belong most of the marabouts of the Tripoli region, but also those of North Africa and the Sahara, soon to be joined by the Islamic lands of black Africa. I am responsible for contacts with the tribes of the eastern Sahara, the Ait Lohen, traditionally hostile toward the French. The Tassili is my favorite territory. A mythical region rich in history."

"And Kaoucen?"

"He is the spearhead of the Senoussi Order. He has five hundred battle-hardened warriors and is going to take Agadez, the pearl of the South. It is he to whom we shall hand over the marabout Charles, who opposes the will of Allah and is trying to convert the Tuareg to Jesus the prophet, whom they call the Christ."

Kerzou nodded his head while pulling up his *litham*,[44] which had slipped

---

[44] A *litham* is a veil covering the lower part of the face.—TRANS.

down over his chin. All this high-level political talk was beyond him! One thing seemed understandable to him: pillaging! And the marabout Charles' *bordj*, that was the cave of Ali Baba!

5

Toward Giving All

When Brother Charles recalled his first pilgrimage to the Holy Land, he was filled with reverence. Jerusalem, Bethlehem, Nazareth! According to biblical tradition, Palestine, the land of pilgrimage, offered a new start after a metamorphosis, a setting off in the steps of Jesus.

Arriving in Jerusalem December 15, 1888, he found a snow-covered city. Was that a sign? And of what? From the slopes of Mount Scopus, Charles, standing in the stirrups, contemplated three thousand years of history. How many massacres in God's name? Here three religions fought for space. Who would win the Mosque of Omar, the Basilica of the Holy Sepulcher, or the Wailing Wall? What dialogue would there be among the divided sons of Abraham?

At the Basilica of the Holy Sepulcher, amid the odor of incense and the soft litanies of heavily bearded Greek monks, he searched in vain for the Tomb. In the eleventh century, Hakim, the sultan of Cairo, had destroyed it. He looked for Calvary. In its place, he found only mosaics, gold, silver, grilles, and ostensoria, all the miscellaneous clutter of human piety. How to picture Jesus there, nailed to a cross, Mary prostrate at his feet? On the polished stone there was only a silver plaque marking where the cross had been.

"The dome of the Holy Sepulcher, Calvary, the Mount of Olives rose before me. I had to think differently and place myself at the foot of the cross." [1] Do those words mark the moment of the revelation that if he wished to follow his crucified God in every way, his life would not be made up of gentle contemplation but of suffering and rejection?

Charles left Jerusalem and on Christmas arrived in Bethlehem, an Arab town bustling with life. He searched for the manger and the grotto of the Nativity. At the presumed site loomed an enormous basilica with a Turkish soldier standing guard. Here too men had replaced the simplicity of the divine with pretentiousness. Shocking uproar on Christmas night when the faithful battled to get into a church that was too small. Pilgrims or tourists? He then closed his eyes and humbled himself before God: "Jesus, Mary,

[1] CF to Father Jérôme, December 21, 1896.

Joseph! Indescribable sweetness of praying so near them in the grotto."[2]
And they lived again in his heart.

In Nazareth, January 10, 1889. A peaceful site: in an amphitheater of hills planted with olive trees stood little white houses; the narrow streets were lively with merchants and humble craftsmen. He was again following the path of Jesus, not the Crucified of the Resurrection, but "the humble craftsman lost in abjection and obscurity".[3]

And it was here that he heard at last the answer to his appeal. Something very strong and very gentle: to humble himself in the midst of the Holy Family, become its domestic servant, silent, in the last place, to conform to the unique model of a Christ poor and as yet unknown, a Christ obedient and obscure. "Jesus *descended* to them and came to Nazareth. Throughout his life he descended: by becoming flesh, by becoming an obedient little child, by becoming poor, abandoned, exiled, persecuted, tortured, by always putting himself in *the last place.*"[4]

Once again, Charles was deeply affected by what Father Huvelin had said: Our Lord "has so taken the last place that no one has ever been able to wrest it from him." But Charles would later write to Marie de Bondy: "I thirst to lead at last the life I seek, which I have glimpsed, guessed at, while walking through the streets of Nazareth where once trod the feet of our Lord, humble craftsman."[5] A life also glimpsed in the Jewish ghettos of Morocco, where he had been schooled in abjection and humility through that virulent anti-Semitism he knew as a Jew among Jews: the very route chosen by Christ, who had wished to become incarnate in the most humiliated people on earth.

Back in Paris on February 14, 1889, Charles announced to Father Huvelin and Marie de Bondy that he might become a Trappist, in some poor and secluded monastery. Marie did not approve of this choice. She was unduly alarmed about the rigors of the practice of mortification—the Trappists of the time had a reputation for severe asceticism. Father Huvelin, although he liked the Cistercians and had once considered entering the order, agreed with Marie. Knowing Charles was not fit to work with his hands, he would rather have seen him in the Benedictines. Accordingly, he advised a retreat at Solesmes.

Obedient, on April 25, Charles presented himself to the prior, Dom Delatte, with the following letter of recommendation from Father Huvelin:

[2] Ibid.

[3] CF to Marie de Bondy, June 24, 1896, in G. Gorrée, *Sur les traces de Charles de Foucauld* (Éd. de la Plus Grande France, 1936), 88.

[4] CF, "Méditation sur saint Luc".

[5] CF to Marie de Bondy, June 24, 1896.

"Dear Reverend Father, the Viscount Charles de Foucauld who delivers this to you is a former officer, an intrepid voyager in Morocco, a devout pilgrim in the Holy Land, a thorough gentleman, a very good Christian, who makes of religion his love."[6]

But Dom Delatte was not fooled, and it was he who, in May, sent Charles to make a retreat at Soligny, the Trappist monastery in Normandy founded by the abbot de Rancé, who had reformed the Cistercians. To Charles, however, this famous abbey seemed too organized, not sufficiently "poor", in the literal sense of the word.

Throughout 1889, he could not decide: "The Gospel and reason do not teach us which of the three lives of our Lord—the hidden life of the worker, the solitary life in the desert, the life of the missionary—we should lead, since they are all equally perfect. We must silence our own arguments, lend our ears to the voice of the Spirit, and observe where God is pushing us, obeying his impetus. As for how to recognize where God is pushing us, the only infallible means is to heed the words of a wise and holy spiritual adviser: 'He who listens to you listens to me.' "[7]

Father Huvelin, unfortunately, made no pronouncement, merely emphasizing that it would have to be a strong community, given Charles' unstable personality.

At the La Barre château once again, on August 14, with Marie de Bondy, a month-long stay, a time of sweetness and heartbreaking sorrow that would leave a permanent mark on him. He wanted to get used to thinking of himself as merely the "oldest son" of that incomparable woman. First gesture of giving all to God.

Once back in Paris, on September 20, 1889, he told her again what he had never stopped telling her: "You did me good at an age when I was hard to reach. What good have I received that I have not received from you? Who led me back to the good Lord? Who gave me Father Huvelin? The first religious book I received, you had given to me. It is you who took me to the Trappist monastery. Through the picture on your table, you introduced me to the Heart of our Lord."[8]

But he had to tear himself away from the sweetness of the family atmosphere in order to choose the religious community where he would be forever cloistered. As always, he leaned toward the most radical. Would he be a hermit? He could not make up his mind.

On September 20, Charles bought Saint Teresa of Avila's famous work, *The Book of Foundations.* "How beautiful it is!" he wrote Marie de Bondy. From that time the works of the great Teresa were to make up his basic

[6] *Bulletin des Amitiés,* no. 93, 9.

[7] "Commentaire de saint Matthieu", *Écrits spirituels* (Gigord, 1923), 194.

[8] CF to Marie de Bondy, September 20, 1889, in Gorrée, *Sur les traces,* 69.

religious reading, after the Gospels. On October 15, 1889, he even made a retreat at a Carmelite monastery, Saint-Denis, but stayed only a few days.

Where would he go? Although tempted by the Franciscans, he did not really want an active order. He always found the Benedictines too intellectual, "not abject enough". The Carthusians were too cut off from the world, from the poor especially. He like the Cistercians best, and Father Huvelin finally accepted his choice.

But which monastery? Fontgombault, the poorest, was too close to La Barre. Finally, Father Huvelin uttered the name "Notre-Dame-des-Neiges". He knew its founder well, a certain Dom Polycarpe Marthoud, whose brother had been a fellow student at the seminary in Rome. Located in a forbidding, lonely part of the Ardèche, this abbey was the highest in France (altitude, 3,300 feet) and therefore the coldest. The community was poor by choice. At that time, all the Cistercians lived by working the land; the arid climate here was a guarantee of poverty. And if that monastery was not harsh enough for Charles, there was the Trappist house in Akbès, Syria, a remote priory founded by Dom Polycarpe in response to the expulsion decree of March 29, 1879. He had withdrawn there to live out his last years.

On October 20, Charles received a warm welcome at Notre-Dame-des-Neiges from Father Eugène, prior and novice master. But he stayed only ten days. He was still making up his mind. On the advice of Marie de Bondy, he made a retreat on November 22 at the Jesuits' Villa Manrèse, in Clamart. Father Soyer, a friend of Marie, welcomed him paternally: "What are you seeking?"

"A life in accord with Christ's, one in which I can share his poverty, his humble work, his hiding away in obscurity in Nazareth. His *abjection*." [9]

That word comes up often in the spirituality of Charles de Foucauld. It has to be understood within the context of the spirituality of Father Olier, founder of the Saint-Sulpice Seminary, and that of Cardinal de Bérulle, both of whom Father Huvelin would cite when instructing Charles. Jesus is "abject" because it is through him that God *descends* to his creature of dust and mud. He is abject, too, in his Eucharist, "where he lies wrapped in what is most common in nature". This makes understandable Charles' fascination with the Eucharist, which consists of the Divinity's *descending* into the bread to be offered man. But above all, *abjection*, as understood by Charles (from *abjicere* = to reject), is this God incarnate through love and rejected by his own.

Back in Paris, he finally made up his mind. "God is calling me, and he is calling me to the Trappists", he wrote his sister. He would serve his novitiate

[9] *Écrits spirituels*, 83.

at Notre-Dame-des-Neiges, then he would go hide away at the Akbès Monastery. He wrote Father Eugène, "At this hour God in his mercy has deigned to make known to me his will in all its clarity. Thus I now respectfully ask the Reverend Father Abbot to accept me." [10]

On December 11, he said his final farewell to his sister (then living in Dijon): "Growing closer to God does not mean that people forget each other. After this, you know my silence will always mean there is nothing new concerning me. I shall interpret your silence to mean the same. For those who are close to God and have their hearts filled with him, it is hard to find those little things to say that make up the content of letters. It is better to pray for those one loves and offer jointly with them the sacrifice of separation." [11]

Mimi choked back her tears as she said good-bye. There is no doubt that for him, too, the reality of separation from the family was terrible, causing pain that he would have to assume daily.

After having disposed of his Nancy apartment (for the last year he had not been under court-imposed restrictions), he returned to Paris on December 18. The most difficult thing was still to be done.

On January 15, 1890, Charles heard Mass at Saint-Augustin's, in the chapel of the Virgin, where he had been converted. Beside him was Marie de Bondy, her heart broken as they received Communion together for the last time. They had decided never to see each other again.

Then, in silence, the two of them went to Marie's home on Avenue Percier. He dined there and would stay until 3 P.M. Then he went to rue de Laborde to say good-bye to Father Huvelin, who was confined to bed. Afterward he went to see Marie one last time, "for the last time in this world".

"I was seated next to you, in your drawing room, looking first at you, then at your clock." [12]

Why abandon everything? Could he not stay in Paris near his loved ones, near her especially, and be a parish priest, like Huvelin? Did God require complete sacrifice?

"To make to God the greatest sacrifice in my power by leaving forever those I love. In a Trappist house, far from all those I love. . . . O Lord, with all my soul I renew this offering of my entire self, given so that I shall never take a breath that is not for you." [13]

Every January 15 he was to write to Marie. He would never forget: "I see you still. It seems to me as if it were yesterday."

[10] *Lettres à mes frères de la Trappe* (Cerf, 1969), 19.
[11] CF to Marie de Blic, December 11, 1888, *Bulletin des Amitiés*, no. 97, 4.
[12] CF to Marie de Bondy, January 15, 1900.
[13] CF, note of January 15, 1895, *Bulletin des Amitiés*, no. 97, 5.

7:10 P.M. He rose. She blessed him. She could not hold back her tears. He wept also. It was a "sacrifice which cost me all my tears, for since that time I no longer weep; I feel as if I have no more tears. The wound of January 15 is always the same. The sacrifice of then remains the sacrifice of every hour." [14]

Stopping at his apartment before he headed for the railroad station, he wrote in his notebook, addressing God: "I thirst to make for you what is for me the greatest possible sacrifice, that of leaving forever my family, who were my happiness, and of going far from them to live and die." [15]

The night train carried him south. The morning of December 16, he got off at a deserted little station: La Bastide-Saint-Laurent. He set out on foot through country overrun with briar. A wood of young pines, hills. On the high plateaux of the mountainous Vivarais, a modest monastery: Notre-Dame-des-Neiges, nestled in a wild site, a valley surrounded by windswept peaks. In the distant horizon, Mount Lozère and the Cévennes.

The monastery was surrounded by little snow-covered peaks. In the rocky valley, thin patches of green. Monks could be seen here and there; dressed in gray work habits, cowls lowered, they were planting young pines and beeches to be used as firewood for cooking and heating—but only in the scriptorium and the infirmary. A lonely spot except for a few isolated sheepfolds. There were six months of snow and wind to be endured here. A few plantings of oats and wheat, which the monks, by the sweat of their brow, managed to wrest from the marginal soil. Between these little fields, fallow ground where they grazed their flocks. A feeling of great peace emanated from this harsh site, where the essential remained hidden, invisible. The monastery, a large white granite structure with a slate roof, had been founded in 1849 by Dom Polycarpe at the request of Dom Chautard, the abbot of Aiguebelle. The farm buildings surrounded the main structure. [16]

The brother porter greeted Charles with a warm smile and led him to the small guest room, then left him alone. Although well pleased by the silence, the solitude, and the religious peace to which his whole being aspired, he was still heartbroken by the separation. He could not keep from writing to Marie de Bondy immediately: "Yesterday was harsh, but still sweet, because I could see you. I am not accustomed to the idea that our good-byes were for always. So little past has separated us, how can we be so completely separated in the future? I know it, I wish it, and I cannot believe it. Now, still, I feel I am very near you, yet my eyes will never again

[14] Ibid., 7.
[15] CF, *Écrits spirituels*, 83.
[16] The monastery we know today, a most unusual structure, is not that of 1890, which was destroyed by fire in 1912 and rebuilt higher up.

see yours. How could I not be wholly filled with grief? But I must draw strength from my weakness and make the weakness itself serve God; I must thank him for this grief and make of it a gift to him. Losing you, I have lost as much as it is possible to lose." [17]

He offered to God this huge sacrifice, consoling himself with "the order he has given me to place you first in my prayers and everywhere throughout my life".

Then his suffering overwhelmed him again: "It is true that without you I do not live. How sweet you made those last days, those last hours. Thank you for yesterday, thank you for everything, thank you for its beginning and its end. May we one day find ourselves together at the feet of the Lord, possessing him as we possessed him yesterday morning; may he bless us as you blessed me last evening, a sweet blessing, thank you, a good and salutary blessing. So lovely for me to leave like that. For every sweet moment you have given me, all the good you have done me, thank you." [18]

Although he is putting everything on a spiritual plane and offering his despair to God, it would be hard to imagine a more intense love letter. As Father Six points out, "A heartrending letter, in which his strongly emotional nature is seen in its pure state." [19]

The next morning, Charles presented himself to the abbot of Neiges, Dom Martin, a young monk with a kindly, intelligent expression. The son of a peasant, he was only thirty-four, two years older than Charles. When he saw the viscount, he smiled: so this is the terrible Charles de Foucauld, the rebellious Saumur cadet, the intrepid explorer of Morocco! Beneath the face that was trying to look humble, the monk saw the dark, passionate, indomitable look!

"What do you know how to do?"

"Not much, Most Reverend Father."

"Call me Father. Do you read?"

"A bit . . ."

"Here, other than prayer, what we do is mostly manual. You will be helping in the kitchen. You will be sweeping. You will go into the woods to cut the shrubs for making brooms. Father Eugène, our prior and novice master, will instruct you."

That very day, Charles entered the community as a postulant. After an unusually brief probationary period (nine days), on January 26 he donned the white habit of the novice and took the name Brother Marie-Albéric. Henceforth, wholly a monk, he felt fulfilled. The only thing that upset him was not having a little cell for himself, as did the Benedictines, the

[17] CF to Marie de Bondy, January 16, 1889.
[18] Ibid.
[19] J.-F. Six, *Itinéraire spirituel de Charles de Foucauld* (Seuil, 1958), 99.

Carthusians, and the Carmelites. Here, life was entirely communal: refectory, work, sleeping quarters. It also bothered him to have to obey and be accountable, even in very small matters.

But he threw himself totally into the fraternal monastic life. He took on—clumsily—the most humble tasks, finding happiness in humility. He did not suffer from the cold or from the strict, meatless diet. Up at 2 A.M., to bed at 7 P.M. Only one full meal, at 2:30 P.M., and three light snacks. During Lent, there would be only one small meal, at 4:30 P.M. In the Trappist monastery everything was done with a calculated slowness, so the spirit could be left free to enter into prayer. For prayer was everything there. This slowness surprised Charles, that tense and active person. To his sister, he wrote: "No sound from outside reaches us. It is solitude and silence with the good Lord. They treat me very well here, with a charity full of tenderness." [20]

He needed kind treatment. He was so clumsy with his hands that the monks kept him away from farm work. He chopped kindling, made garlands for the church, swept the floors, polished the chandeliers, served in the refectory, weeded the cemetery, repainted the crosses. This aristocrat who had spent his life being waited on had no problem fitting into this community of poor monks, most of them from the country. The abbot was amazed. Already more than austere in his habits, Charles set an example through his daily eight hours of religious practices and through his humility, as he strove assiduously to be the last in everything. In 1920 René Bazin questioned an old monk, a wheat harvester and cattle drover, who had known Brother Albéric well: "I talked to him just like to a peasant. I saw him every day. He never refused to help anyone. He was as handsome as a second Francis of Assisi." [21] Remembering his strange novice later, Dom Martin would say, "I had never encountered anyone with such qualities except in books." [22]

Offices, adoration, *lectio*: the Scriptures, the breviary, the *Imitation*, the works of Saint Bernard and Bossuet. He also sought sustenance from the Psalms, which he soon knew by heart. He felt in tune with the great mystic Teresa of Avila and followed her teachings to the letter. Through *The Interior Castle* he learned that holiness is possible here below since everything is possible with God if one effaces oneself to become one with him. That is why everything begins with self-effacement.

That, he understood from being at Neiges. He wrote to his sister: "Their agricultural work is salutary for the soul. While occupying the body, it accords the soul the power to pray and meditate. And it creates such

[20] CF to Marie de Blic, February 18, 1890, in Gorrée, *Sur les traces*, 74.
[21] R. Bazin, *Charles de Foucauld* (Plon, 1921), 104; also in Gorrée, *Sur les traces*, 76.
[22] C. Pichon, *Charles de Foucauld* (Éd. de la Nouvelle France, 1946), 181.

compassion for the poor, such charity for the worker! We become very conscious of the price of a crust of bread once we see for ourselves how hard it is to produce!"

At last his fascinated mind, dazzled by the Absolute, consented to come back down to faith stripped bare, to the humility of God's creature, the trust of the child. Louis Massignon, the famous Islamicist who later became Charles' friend, understands his passage from Islamic mysticism to Cistercian mysticism: "It was in Morocco, in the Arab desert, that he found himself in the presence of Islam, and the contact with this dominant faith, which burns the believer to ashes beneath the unreachable sun of divine unity, acted as a catalyst to bring his unbelief back to Christian doctrine, which proclaims the pre-excellence of charity over faith. And his gaze, going beyond the empty *mihrâb*[23] in the bare mosque, rested on the sacrifice offered in the white, image-free nave of the Cistercians."[24]

As for self-effacement, he obtained it through grace and love. Father Eugène, his novice master, was not much older than Charles and not always easygoing. Of modest rural background, he was sometimes incredibly touchy, and Charles demonstrated his saintliness by obeying him to the letter, while missing the subtle, thorough guidance of Father Huvelin.

Father Eugène quickly recognized Charles' merits: "This fine young man has cast off everything. I have never seen such detachment and, along with that, overwhelming modesty. He can boast of having made me weep and feel my lowliness."[25]

So Brother Albéric had no problems? Far from it. He still found the separation from his family terribly painful. And his lively spirit soon felt frustrated by the strictness of the rule. That was his weak point. He had tasted too much freedom to be able to give it up within a few months. Through the Cistercian rule, he made great efforts to follow to the letter "the beloved Jesus", but he was still conditioned by the impulses of his heart. He was more hermit than monk, but he did not know that yet. Insensibility and restlessness were no more spared him than any other novice. He attributed them to what he called temptations to obedience of mind: "I do not receive joyfully enough the manual tasks they assign me", he confessed. The whole business is subtle. He obeyed. He wanted only the will of God. But what unexpected resistance he put up, which he could not control! He could not manage to detach himself fully from the world he had left behind. He wrote to Henri Duveyrier: "I entered the Trappist order through pure love. I love Christ, and I could not bear living a

---

[23] A *mihrâb* is a niche in the wall indicating the direction of Mecca.—TRANS.
[24] L. Massignon, in *France-Maroc*, March 15, 1917.
[25] M. Castillon du Perron, *Charles de Foucauld* (Grasset, 1982), 204.

life other than his. The greatest sacrifice for me, so great that all the others do not exist, is the permanent separation from a beloved family and a few friends—among whom you are one of the first—to whom my heart is attached with all its strength. Love of God, love of men, that is my whole life, that will be my whole life, I do hope." [26]

But Charles was already looking beyond the Trappist house. In accordance with the rule of Saint Benedict, he venerated Dom Martin: "In all things, look upon your superiors as upon our Lord himself." With his critical spirit, the novice could not help but find the abbot timid and overscrupulous, ruling the community too "softly". He dreamed of a radical asceticism.

He began to think about Notre-Dame-du-Sacré-Coeur in Akbès, Syria, the poor, isolated priory under the authority of Notre-Dame-des-Neiges. It would provide an even more radical break with his past.

After making his worldly goods over to his sister,[27] Charles de Foucauld took leave of the monks, all of them sorry to see him depart. Accompanied by Dom Martin, on June 26, 1890, he arrived in Marseille, where the abbot said Mass at Notre-Dame-de-la-Garde. The next morning Charles sailed for Alexandretta, Syria. He wrote to Marie de Bondy: "I think I feel all the waves, which, one after another, are taking me far away." [28] Waves [*lames*], tears [*larmes*] . . .

Tamanrasset, December 1, 1916, 11:30 A.M.

It was growing hot behind the thick walls of the fortress. Brother Charles knew the poor would not be making their visit until nightfall, many hours away. It was quiet; he could work.

He carefully reread the pages of his Tuareg dictionary. Then he recopied the latest poems gathered here and there, to be used to illustrate the dictionary entries. The poetry dealt only with love and war. Odd to see this old hermit, who had renounced all forms of violence and the joys of human love, bent over his copies of these fiery verses:

> My parents had kept me from leaving for the *ahal*;
> And yet I had already taken part in other fêtes,
> Those celebrated with bullets and gunpowder!

---

[26] CF to Duveyrier, April 24, 1890, in *Bulletin des Amitiés*, no. 97, 10.

[27] Which made possible her 1893 purchase of a château, Barbirey, near Gissey-sur-Ouche, Côte d'Or.

[28] CF to Marie de Bondy, June 27, 1890.

The *ahal*! That *fête galante* under the communal tent, at night, the place where unmarried girls, ardent young widows, and even the spurned, would flock to meet young bachelor warriors! The most beautiful woman presided, her braids dressed with butter, the skin between her nose and lips painted blue, her body draped in a flowing multicolored gown. She would play the *imzad*, a hollowed-out gourd with one string, from which she drew harsh sounds that grated on the nerves and mingled with hoarse songs meant to bewitch the heart.

The men had glossy braids, held close to the head by the *litham*, the blue veil of the Tuareg. Their bodies were wrapped in the long, bright indigo *tekamest*, the fabric newly dyed and rich with embroidery.

> This year my eyes have seen
> Dates such as the hand gives not to the mouth.
> But this year, my eyes have also seen
> A filly whose love has wounded me.
> But, oh, Géggé, how harsh for the heart is your love!

The pages of Tuareg poetry piled up on Brother Charles' table and fell onto the sand floor. And the hermit kept writing, writing. And when he ran out of paper, he turned over envelopes from old letters. His inkwell was soon dry. Then he went to his reserve supply, an ink he had made himself, a combination of camel urine and charcoal, which left on the paper the strange odor of caravans.

At the same hour, around twelve miles to the northeast, the *rezzou* led by the Senoussi Beuh ag Rhabelli and the Targui *fellagha* Kerzou had stopped at the Kébir well to let their dromedaries rest. The men got their mounts to kneel; then they threw themselves awkwardly on the ground. With their hands they scratched at the sand, which became damp, then muddy. A silty mixture appeared, but that was all. So they would have to do without water until Tamanrasset. And there they would drink the fortress' fresh, cool water . . . diluted with that famous Communion wine the great marabout was said to bring from France by the barrel! The marabout out of commission, they could get as drunk as they wished. May the Prophet forgive them! This would certainly not be the first such instance under the Crescent! Reward for the kidnapping: the pillaging of the fortress. Weapons, ammunition, foodstuff, liquid silver. Kerzou was talking. He knew. When he was a corporal in the camel troopers, serving under the French at Fort Motylinski, he had been to Tamanrasset and had gone inside the fortress. He was telling his story, exaggerating . . . And the others crowded around, eyes shining with greed, mouths open, tongues hanging out like dogs trained for the hunt.

"All around the central courtyard, there is a line of rectangular sheds, so many little warehouses stuffed with food and equipment."

"Why so much food? It is said the marabout doesn't eat."

"He's happy with a little gruel since he doesn't have any teeth. The food is for fattening the lazy Haratins from the village. That's how he hopes to convert them!"

"What kind of food is there at the fortress?"

"Grain, wheat especially. Dried dates. Millet and couscous. And lots of canned goods brought from Algiers and France!"

"And in the cans?"

"Beef, which they call monkey! And milk."

"Oh! Milk cannot be canned. Are you talking about cheese?"

"No, it's definitely milk. Milk in the form of powder!"

The men looked at each other in amazement. They knew the marabout was skilled in magic and necromancy, but turning milk into powder! Dried milk!

"And . . . the treasure? Silver? Gold, maybe?"

"There's that too. Do not be impatient, brother. The *roumis'* fortress has walls nearly seven feet thick and more than twenty-six feet high. To get in, you'll have to fight. The marabout is powerfully armed. He is a former cavalry officer. He will not let his throat be cut as if he were a Haratin slave!"

El Madani, the Haratin traitor, heard that remark. His dark face became grayish, his look unfathomable. He hated those Berbers!

6

Cistercian Monk

Charles de Foucauld tore himself away from compiling poetry and once more became absorbed in his memories.

On June 27, 1890, the steamer from Marseille brought him to Alexandretta, Syria, from where he would set out for Akbès and nearby Cheiklé, the world's poorest and most isolated Trappist house, where he hoped to hide away in obscurity the rest of his life. He was possessed by the spirit of sacrifice. "Painful to see the shore slip away", he wrote his sister. A physical separation from his last tie to the world.

Piraeus, Thessaloníki, Smyrna, Mersin. After twelve days at sea: "To-morrow I shall be in Alexandretta, and I shall bid farewell to the sea, last tie with the country where all of you breathe." [1]

Finally the port of Alexandretta appeared on the horizon. They were in Syria, a province of the Ottoman Empire. On the jetty, a Cistercian monk awaited the arrival of Brother Albéric. Brother Étienne was flanked by three rather sinister-looking armed horsemen, which made Charles smile. The monk explained; "The back country is infested with bandits. So, in exchange for cash, the Turkish authorities supply us with these three *souwari* (police officers)."

Riding mules, they headed across the mountains. A two-day trek on steep paths carved out of the rock, overlooking wild ravines. Once they had crossed the Nur Mountains, they went through forests and moors until they reached the town of Akbès. Four more miles and then, looking out into a valley—elevation two thousand feet—Charles finally saw Notre-Dame-du-Sacré-Coeur, a priory under Notre-Dame-des-Neiges. [2]

The monastery, an ambitious project for such a desolate region, was being built amid a stark landscape of green oaks and briar. Here Kurdish shepherds grazed their meager flocks of sheep. The monastery under construction was going up at the entrance to a wild valley, through which ran a stream. From the heights above the valley, the Marach Plain could be seen, 250 miles of brush and desert stretching from Antioch Lake, a silvery glim-

---

[1] R. Bazin, *Charles de Foucauld* (Plon, 1921), 110.

[2] An abbey is autonomous, and its community elects an abbot. It may found priories, to be headed by superiors (priors) named by the abbot of the mother abbey.

mer to the south. To the north rose the snowy summits of the Taurus Mountains.

The place was called Cheiklé,[3] a miserable hamlet, a few huts of dried mud, abandoned in 1860 during the massacre of Armenians by the Turks. The village was under the Adana *vilayet* (administrative division); administratively, it was in Turkey (eastern Anatolia), just over the border from the Aleppo *vilayet* (Syria).

A rudimentary gate opened into the farmyard. On the right, temporary buildings, of wood and adobe: the stable and the barn. On the left, the bakery, the kitchen, the forge, a shed. Farther back, the monastic buildings, also temporary: refectory and scriptorium, of clay and wattles, the roof boards covered by thatch or sheet metal, like the other farm buildings. Only the church—without a belfry—and the chapter house, both of dressed stone, offered a contrast to the settlement's extreme poverty. There was no real dormitory yet; in winter the monks slept in the hayloft above the stable, in summer over the refectory under a low sheet-metal roof. Charles recounted, "An establishment à la Jules Verne: a jumble of barns, livestock, cottages, all crowded together from fear of incursions and thieves."[4]

The monastic property, nearly three hundred acres, was surrounded by a cirque of mountains covered with oaks and umbrella pines. Here and there, big gray rock formations with caves. In winter wild animals from the mountains would venture near the monastery grounds: wolves, panthers, bears, and wild boars. For eight years, about twenty work-hardened, weary monks had been tilling the reasonably fertile soil, growing wheat, barley, and cotton and maintaining a vegetable garden and a vineyard. Enough to feed the little community, a dozen Kurdish workers, and the fifteen or so Christian orphans who ranged in age from five to fifteen and had been sent there by the three Lazarist missionaries in Akbès. Obviously, the founder, Dom Polycarpe, faced with the possibility of the community's having to retreat from Notre-Dame-des-Neiges, had set his sights too high. Thus the buildings of dressed stone had not been completed. There was not enough income to finish erecting a large traditional abbey. The markets were too far away to sell what the monks produced. So any money would have to come from France, but Notre-Dame-des-Neiges, the motherhouse, was very poor, also.

Charles was delighted with this forbidding site. He could not have imagined any place more suitable for burying himself. And yet the monastery was so isolated that he wondered what purpose it served. Sensing that

[3] Pronounced Cheurlé.
[4] *Bulletin des Amitiés*, no. 86, 6.

the newcomer had some unanswered questions, Father Étienne explained: "This country is a mixture of ethnic groups: Arabs, Kurds, Armenians, Syrians, Arameans, Greeks, Levantines, Europeans. And of religions: Shiite and Sunni Muslims, Orthodox Christians and Roman Catholics, Maronites, and Uniates. Our monastery was created amid this mixture of infidels and somewhat lax schismatic Christians. The Trappist house has caused a sensation here."

Silence. The monk continued: "In the first century of the Church, Christian hermits lived in the mountain caves nearby. The valley was uninhabited. This harsh solitude attracted the Trappists. At first we lived in tents. It was hard. The population was hostile. Without financial resources, worn out by fevers, shivering in winter, suffocating in summer, the handful of monks around Dom Polycarpe has held on. A great monastery, three-stories high, will be built . . . if the money comes."

Shocked, Charles looked at him. He had seen the grim poverty in the surrounding villages. Why not conform to that life? He had also noticed that the monastery employed lay workers. But he said nothing.

The monk understood his unspoken questions. He smiled: "If you have come to suffer, you will not be disappointed. Each day the Lord brings us, we expect pillaging and massacre, for this country is infested with hungry bandits and Muslim fanatics."

"Is it possible to convert them?"

A fatalistic shrug from Father Étienne. Only God converts. That was certainly what Charles thought, already firm in his conviction not to preach, but to pray, love, welcome. And to share a life of great poverty.

The prior, Louis de Gonzague, was actually the brother of Dom Martin, the abbot of Neiges. He received the newcomer paternally and put him in the hands of Dom Polycarpe. The asceticism and holiness of the former abbot of Neiges affected Charles deeply. The old monk lived in a hut with a thatched roof. Charles recounted, "He, so well educated, he who so loved study, with what joy he plunged into humble manual tasks! When he no longer had the strength to spade the ground, he washed clothes. Finally, he had to be content with mending them." [5]

For Charles, up at 2 A.M., exhausting work began, eight hours a day, added to his eight hours of spiritual activity. Depending on the season, he cleared the ground, gathered hay, harvested crops, or picked grapes. He carried heavy rocks for finishing the wall around the property, washed the orphans' clothes, sawed wood for cooking. The usual tasks. But he was not finding that enough. He wrote Father Huvelin: "You hope that I have sufficient poverty. No. For rich people we are poor, but not as poor as I was

[5] J.-F. Six, *Itinéraire spirituel de Charles de Foucauld* (Seuil, 1958), 31.

in Morocco, not poor like Saint Francis. I deplore it but do not make a fuss over it. Another matter about which I keep silent and obey. Gradually, without calling attention to myself, I shall be able to obtain some privileges allowing me to practice poverty better." [6]

He did know peace, however, as he wrote his sister on January 3, 1891: "My soul is experiencing a profound peace, which grows daily. It increases faith, which calls for gratitude. I am where the good Lord wants me to be. In a year, I shall make my profession. In my heart, I long to be bound through those vows, but I am already bound through my every wish." [7]

In spite of the threat of cholera, which had already struck the monastery annex—the victim, a Turk working at the orphanage—he was happy, as he wrote on May 11, 1891, to his old school friend from Nancy, Gabriel Tourdes, now a judge in Saint-Dié: "It is impossible to describe the peace and calm in which I have lived since coming to the monastery. There is nothing comparable to this peace. 'I leave to you my peace.' I feel it here, a peace unknown to the world, which I had not come here seeking and of which I had no inkling, but which God confers on me in his infinite goodness." [8]

Now sure about his vocation, in July 1891 he resigned as a reserve officer and asked to be listed as an ordinary soldier. He wrote Marie de Bondy: "I am pleased by this step. I left behind everything that was material, but there still remained a wretched complication, my rank, and it pleases me to have thrown it out the window." [9] Such a step also meant he no longer had to attend the required reserve training sessions. Now he could be called up only in time of war.

His mind and heart full of joy, perhaps, but his body did not keep pace. Too much physical labor and, more serious, too ascetic a life. In August 1891, he fell ill. His feet were in bad shape. They put him to work in the library, which should have thrilled him. But he did not find the setting suitably poor. Dom Polycarpe had to reprimand him to make him eat and sleep and to curb what the monk called "his somewhat excessive love for bodily mortification". How far was Charles going, when he managed to shock even this saintly monk devoted to absolute poverty? Dom Polycarpe wrote to the Abbot of Neiges, Dom Martin: "Brother Albéric is still the little saint you know and behaves as he did when you had him at Notre-Dame-des-Neiges. He always sets an example, often makes us joyful, and sometimes frightens us. Keep praying hard for him. His perfection is too great to be lasting."

---

[6] CF to Father Huvelin, November 5, 1890, in l'Abbé Huvelin (DDB, 1957).

[7] CF to Marie de Blic, January 3, 1891, in Bazin, *Foucauld*, 117.

[8] *Lettres à un ami de lycée* (G. Tourdes, 1874–1915) (Nouvelle Cité, 1982), 147.

[9] CF to Marie de Bondy, July 16, 1891, in G. Gorrée, *Sur les traces de Charles de Foucauld* (Éd. de la Plus Grande France, 1936), 81.

But Charles, unperturbed, pursued the course he had set for himself. Would he, as he hoped, be a humble lay monk devoted to manual labor until the day he died, or would he become a choir monk and a priest, which involved a long period of study? Nothing had been said to him, and he had not asked any questions. He tried to leave his future to the will of the Lord, as expressed by his superiors. In spite of everything, he could not help thinking about the matter, as he recalled Father Huvelin's radical remark: "In all things, one must state one's preferences, one's strong dislikes, and then do what one is ordered to." Thus Charles wrote to Marie de Bondy: "If they talk to me of studies, I shall state that I have a very strong preference for staying up to my neck in the wheat fields and the woods, and an extremely strong dislike for whatever might tend to draw me away from that last place which I have come here seeking, away from that abjection into which I wish to sink ever deeper, and then, when all is said and done, I shall obey." [10]

He banished even those thoughts, which he called his forbidden garden. God was with him, that was enough.

The father prior, Louis de Gonzague, did not share Dom Polycarpe's misgivings. He wrote to Dom Martin, Abbot of Neiges, on February 4, 1892: "When I am suffering greatly, I have only to glance at Brother Albéric in the church to feel comforted." And, on February 23: "If we are not too unworthy, God will make of him a true saint!" [11]

The vocation of a saint involves obeying and not asking oneself questions about one's future. Charles did not yet know it, but his superiors had made up their minds quickly about Brother Albéric's future. They had taken note of his good education, his moral and intellectual qualities, the ease with which he read Latin and Greek, his ability to give orders . . . and his inability to do farm work: he would become a priest, and they already saw him as novice master, successor to Dom Polycarpe.

Brother Marie-Albéric pronounced his provisional vows on February 2. They shaved his head, leaving only a crown recalling that of Christ insulted. To his great consternation, he was called to the choir in the church, a sign that showed the intentions of his superiors, which did not fail to upset him. Fortunately, he knew nothing of the letter written by Dom Martin to the general chapter of the Cistercians: "I dream of one day seeing Brother Albéric succeed Father Louis de Gonzague."

And the latter felt much the same, writing to Marie de Blic, February 4, 1892. "Our brother Albéric seems an angel in our midst. He only lacks

[10] Ibid., November 4, 1891, 81.
[11] Quoted by M. Castillon du Perron, *Charles de Foucauld* (Grasset, 1982), 211.

wings. What a saintly companion! Dom Polycarpe tells me that never in his long life has he met a being so entirely devoted to God. In spite of his amazingly austere life, he enjoys excellent health."[12]

Sole problem, the priesthood: "I foresee that I shall have to wage a serious struggle against his humility, and in the end, in keeping with our order's rules on obedience, this is not something we can order him to do."[13]

Well, maybe not . . . Two months after he had taken his vows, they asked him to begin his theological studies. In that wasteland? At the little community of Lazarist missionaries in Akbès, a saintly priest, Father Destino, very learned, was competent to teach him.

Once again Charles obeyed, with regret, after raising a few timid objections: "I did not hide that this new vocation has no attraction for me", he wrote Marie de Bondy. "They replied that it had been decided: I stopped insisting." Then he added, "I may need your support. It is a very grave moment, for I am entering that critical period when many vocations are shipwrecked."[14]

He was more than content with adoration and contemplation in "abjection". Why complicate that with dogma, the whole intricate scaffolding raised by theologians to support faith?

But he obeyed. Twice a week, he went off to Akbès accompanied by a novice. They would leave Cheiklé at 4:30 A.M., after Matins. Taking steep shortcuts, they had an hour's walk through the mountains. They were back by 9 A.M. And Charles would be relieved to return to his humble work: sawing wood and mending the little orphans' clothes. "And to think there are people who claim that becoming a monk is a way to avoid the problems of everyday life!" Charles wrote Marie de Bondy with a touch of humor.

Actually, it only looked as if he had given in on the principle of "staying in last place". Studies, the priesthood? "That is what God wants of me *at the present time*", he wrote Marie de Bondy on May 10, 1892. Alarmed by his austere life, his beloved cousin suggested that there would be greater mortification in agreeing to what they asked of him than in his being allowed to pursue his own desire for a life so austere that it disregarded the respect one owes one's body.

In August 1892, he fell ill. Under the sheet-metal roof of the dormitory, the heat was infernal. No rest. The doctor detected a pulmonary lesion, consumption, tuberculosis—in those days, usually incurable. Charles was overjoyed. He would at last find God and escape from this base world! But

[12] Quoted by Bazin, *Foucauld*, 120.
[13] Ibid.
[14] CF to Marie de Bondy, April 26, 1892.

mysteriously, his health returned. Writing to Marie de Blic, Dom Polycarpe hinted at a miracle: "This came about quite suddenly, and surely we cannot attribute it to the medicines given him." [15]

Charles was genuinely distressed, but, once again, he obeyed.

During this period, he suffered even more cruelly over what he considered to be a lack of charity within the very heart of the community. He burned, but others did not: in spite of himself, he deplored it. And yet, the rule was respected: offices through the night, silence, solitude, work, worship, asceticism, fasting; no trips, no visitors. The community seemed content with being in a kind of rut, but Charles could not bear it. He deplored a "spirit of worldliness" he thought had taken root in the cloister, not to mention "inappropriate behavior". He dreamed of a life of the "strictly necessary", not imagining that this would vary from one individual to another, as Saint Benedict wisely pointed out in his rule.

After that came more solid criticism. There was not enough love; treating each other well seemed an effort. They took for granted the separation between choir monks and the brown-clad lay brothers, who performed most of the manual labor and were exempt from some of the religious activities. [16] Toward each other, the monks did not practice true charity. But where was true charity, true poverty? Charles found them by going into miserable huts to watch over the dead. He found monastic life, even lived in poverty, too safe and secure.

Already, his thinking went against the tendencies of the period! At the request of Leo XIII, in September 1892, the general chapter of the Cistercians met in Rome to make plans for bringing together the two existing congregations, the common observance and the strict observance founded at Soligny by Abbot de Rancé. Charles saw this as a threat to monastic austerity as he would have liked it to be: radical. Inevitably, the Cistercians would conform to the less strict rule.

On October 20, 1892, the general chapter voted for unification. Dom Sébastien Wyart was elected abbot general, and Charles waited anxiously for the practical details of the change. The gap separating him from the community continued to grow. He did not understand the Trappist way of life, which consisted of moderation and balance, as called for by Saint Benedict in the early rule that was later taken up by Saint Bernard. Added to his lack of comprehension was the malaise arising from his superiors' understandable desire to see him choose the priesthood: he could then become a superior too, a role suited to his talents, since he had neither the skill nor the strength to be a manual laborer. Well, he still aspired to "the last place". He

---

[15] Quoted by Castillon, *Foucauld*, 215.
[16] This distinction began to disappear after Vatican II.

felt caught in the trap of the obedience to which he had committed himself when taking his vows. Even his last recourse, Father Huvelin, agreed with the Cistercian superiors: the priesthood and less austerity.

And now along came a papal brief allowing the Trappists to season their greens with butter and oil! To Marie de Bondy, he wrote: "We no longer have our beloved salt and water cuisine. You will understand that I miss it. A little less mortification, that means a little less given to the good Lord. A little more spent, that means a little less given to the poor. Where will this stop; are we on a slippery slope?"[17]

One meal a day during Lent was now a thing of the past. The pope forbade fasting after noon.

In June, the new constitution arrived at last. To Marie he wrote: "Very austere, fine in every way, and yet it is not as much poverty as I would like, it's not abjection as I might have pictured it. My desires along these lines have not been satisfied."[18]

And so he became increasingly tormented, although he was experiencing moments of great peace at the foot of the altar. As much as Marie, Father Huvelin remained the chosen confidant of his torments. Charles was entering the dark night of the spirit. First of all, he judged himself harshly: "My soul always full of misery, pride, vanity, confidence in my judgment, harshness toward others and indulgence toward myself, cowardice, timidity. Still, alas, lacking charity, I am lukewarm, restless, without gratitude or repentance."[19]

How, in the name of charity, to keep from judging others harshly? "Is it essential to accept novices who have genuine virtues and who seem not to be causing the community any difficulty, but who seem to be seeking some ideal of monastic life unknown to me, a sweet, calm, pious life of ease with all the necessities and not a few luxuries, and who follow the rule only moderately? Or is it essential to receive only those who have decided to seek our Lord at whatever cost, to follow the rule and to walk with our early fathers in the footsteps of our Lord?"[20]

In another letter to Father Huvelin, he was more specific: "I am troubled at times. Around me I do not see the necessary virtues practiced or even valued. I see that the spirit of worldliness has taken root here among us all, when it should be far, far away. Poverty is a beautiful thing, blessed and divine, and men find it repugnant."[21]

The crisis erupted on August 26, 1893. He began to have doubts about

---

[17] CF to Marie de Bondy, May 21, 1893.
[18] Ibid., June 27, 1893.
[19] CF to Father Huvelin, June 14, 1893.
[20] Ibid.
[21] Ibid., July 8, 1893.

the final vows coming up in eighteen months. He was still asking for "the last place, poverty, abjection, manual labor, austerity in everything". He was seeking perfection by the imitation of Christ, thus the desire for the cross and the final martyrdom, which he saw as the culmination of the mystical wedding. He did not wish to become a priest.

For the first time he thought about starting a new order, a community in line with his ideal of the "radically humble". He spoke of it to Dom Polycarpe, his confessor, who responded with silence and disapproval.

Charles, suddenly doubtful, asked accordingly: "Does this idea come from God, the devil, or my imagination?"

"Stop thinking about it for the time being. Wait for an opportunity that God will create, if indeed this idea comes from him."

But Charles thought about it constantly and on September 23, 1893, opened his heart to Father Huvelin: "Might there not be a way to establish a little congregation to lead this kind of life, to make a living solely from the work of our own hands, as did our Lord, who did not live off collections or offerings or the labor of workers from the outside?"

His plan: "Renounce completely the holding of property, whether collective or individual." There he touched on the historic evil of religious orders, often rich in a world of poverty. "Make the giving of alms an uncompromising duty. If a monk has two habits, he gives away one. If he has food to eat, he gives to those with none, saving nothing for the following day. An obscure life, a life of work and prayer, and not two kinds of monks as they have at Cîteaux, but one kind, as Saint Benedict wanted." [22]

But he did not spare Saint Benedict either: "None of the complicated liturgy of Saint Benedict. It closes the door of our monasteries to Arabs, Turks, Armenians, who are good Catholics but do not know a word of our languages." [23]

So he was seventy years ahead of Vatican II! His dream: spiritual life would be built around the Mass, an event involving the entire community, with long silent and solitary prayers. "Little nests offering a life of devotion and hard work, a refuge for the souls in these countries whom God calls to serve him and to love him, nothing more!" [24]

But was it not his pride that drove his desire to be a founder? He knew himself to be a weak and miserable sinner. But he reassured himself: "If the idea comes from God, it is he who will make it grow, soon gathering the souls equal to being the foundation stones for his house." Charles would at once fade away, "into the nothing that is my place".

[22] Ibid., September 23, 1893.
[23] Ibid.
[24] Ibid.

And the final argument to convince himself and Father Huvelin: "Our Lord has said that when we have sinned greatly, we must love greatly." [25]

Having put forth the idea that had been obsessing him for two months, he waited for Huvelin's opinion. But to his great disappointment, the priest, perplexed, did not reply.

What then was this order he dreamed of founding, in which "absolute poverty"—which he confused with "imitating Jesus in all things"—would be the rule? He began by asking himself an appropriate question: "Does God give me such wishes so that I may sacrifice them to him or so that I may carry them out? " [26] The crux of the matter is that he refused to "side so readily with not practicing the virtue that our Lord so diligently practiced and that one would expect to see in the cloister". [27] But was he not making the assumption that his desires reflected reality? Christ has never asked mankind to lead an overly austere life, but only to love God and one's neighbors as oneself, an agenda difficult enough!

At times Charles transposed his cultural model onto Christ's, which was quite different. For the ex-viscount, from a cultural point of view, working with his hands made him "abject"; he was doing the job of an inferior. That is why, once having decided to "be the last", he saw himself as a manual laborer, forgetting that, in Jesus' Jewish society, manual labor was not looked down upon. But Charles was conforming to the rule of Saint Benedict. "They shall truly be monks in living from the work of their hands, as did our fathers and the apostles." In seeing himself as the last, it was logical to reject the priesthood. Jesus did not belong to the priestly class, a privileged group in his day, as in many ways it still was at the end of the nineteenth century, in spite of the strictures of anticlerical governments and the persecution of missionaries.

His criticism of his order was harsh; yet it was not an era of monastic decadence. He remained hostile to the division between lay monks and choir monks, which perpetuated the divisions in society. He opposed the hiring of lay workers from the outside to perform the backbreaking tasks. He was hostile to the collective holding of property, which was the rule in all monasteries. He called for radical poverty, observing, "As for poverty, they want none of it." He also found the monastic liturgy too complicated, inaccessible to the poor, and for use in church he would have liked the "everyday language" of the country instead of Latin. Finally, he was inspired by the reforms of Teresa of Avila ("create little groups, little dovecotes, like the Carmelites", he said) and went even farther. Although Teresa

[25] Ibid.
[26] Ibid., September 22, 1893.
[27] CF to Marie de Bondy, August 26, 1893, in Gorrée, *Sur les traces*, 82.

rejected property, she accepted alms, and Charles could not go along with that.

Having no call to be a hermit, and unable to fulfill his calling as a monk with the Trappists, he wanted to create an order to fit his own exaggerated vision. Was this pride? No, because he planned to remain the last in all things. He wanted only to do Christ's will. But how to distinguish what came from Christ and what came from him? His faith so complete, his feeling of fusion with Jesus so strong, he was blinded and incapable of heeding any advice from his superiors. After all, Saint Bernard and Saint Teresa of Avila had left their monasteries to reform them. It is the tragedy of reformers to have to choose between the voice of God whispering in them and the voice of their superiors, who are the guarantors of tradition but also of a certain spiritual comfort and material security, without which a community could not survive and recruit.

Charles ended up concurring with his voices, which could not deceive. Thus, his desire to break away: "Since there does not exist here the meeting of souls I have always sought, or anything that resembles it, or anything that replaces it, must I not try to create it?" he wrote to Father Huvelin on September 22, 1893. While assuring the priest that he would follow his orders, Charles' determination to go his own way came out clearly in the letter, although he was doing everything according to the rules, for he went on to say: "Is this a dream, an illusion from the devil, or a thought or invitation coming from the Lord?" He was experiencing a painful conflict between submission and stubborn loyalty to the inner call he could not betray. Under the circumstances, it is understandable that Father Huvelin hesitated for a year before replying!

So the trial of strength continued. His superiors tested his obedience. And in everything—or almost everything—he was perfect. "A true saint", they said. Not only in accomplishing his humble tasks, but even more so in studying theology and becoming what he did not want to be! He managed to do what he did not like and even ended up finding his studies not unpleasant, for they expressed the will of God through the will of his superiors: "Theology is interesting; it does not equal experiencing the poverty, abnegation, and mortification that come from doing manual labor. I study through obedience, having resisted as much as I saw fit." [28]

He knew his purgatory would come to an end. He admired Dom Polycarpe and did well under his guidance. He remained convinced that God would make them all change their minds. The most important thing was not to rush them. Obedience was sacred. Any rebellion could only be a trick of the devil. And it was also important to listen to them devoutly as

---

[28] Letter of May 23, 1893, quoted by Bazin, *Foucauld*, 123.

they warned him against stubbornness and "a mind of his own". Was his desire to be a founder truly of supernatural origin? Was it not proper to wait for a sign from God? So he was waiting. He had all the time in the world. On this point, patience, he had truly changed.

All the same, it was hard. He looked ahead to a sad Christmas in 1893. Still no reply from Father Huvelin. Either the priest was making up his mind, or he did not want to interfere with the Cistercians' spiritual guidance. What was Charles to do?

On the advice of Dom Polycarpe, he put himself in the hands of the Virgin. "In a time of great suffering, around Christmas 1893, not knowing where to seek refuge, fearing deceit by the devil, I put myself completely in her hands. I remembered the mother's heart of Our Lady of Perpetual Help, and I put myself in her hands like a child, asking her to hold me up and to make of me, not what I would like, but what she herself would like, for the greater glory of her Son, according to his will." [29]

But deep down he was unyielding: "It is up to this good Mother to inspire the abbot and Dom Polycarpe when the time comes—if it does come as I so desire— for our Lord to let me follow him more closely." [30]

He finally received a letter from Father Huvelin, on January 29, 1894: "Continue your theological studies. Concentrate on inner virtues, and especially on annihilation of the self. As for exterior virtues, perfect your obedience to the rule and to your superiors. As for the rest, *we shall see later.* You are most definitely not made to lead others. Can you not find here what God is asking of you, in the life you are in now? " [31]

Charles was deeply distressed. But he obeyed, hanging onto the words: "As for the rest, we shall see later." The "rest", his desire to be a founder!

Father Huvelin could not hide his opposition from Marie de Bondy: "I am alarmed by this life he wishes to enter into, by this Nazareth where he wants to go live, by this group he wishes to create around him! More and more, he will be taking his own ideas to be the voice of God speaking to him. The beauty of the purpose to which he believes himself called will conceal from him everything else, especially the unworkable. He wants too much; there is a constant search for better things that throws his spirit into a state of agitation. But I do not expect that we can keep him with the Trappists. It is obvious he will not stay." [32]

On the surface, Charles obeyed. But deep down, he was unyielding. He wrote Marie de Bondy: "Father Huvelin tells me to keep on with theology. He would like to see me a deacon. He tells me to try to find right here

---

[29] CF, *Considérations sur les fêtes de l'année,* November 14, 1897.

[30] CF to Marie de Bondy, January 14, 1894.

[31] Quoted by Gorrée, *Sur les traces,* 85.

[32] H. Huvelin to Marie de Bondy, August 9, 1894, in Bazin, *Foucauld,* 127.

what God is asking of me, in the life I am in now. Everything calls me in the opposite direction, but I remain in Huvelin's hands. I am doing and shall do what he has told me to do. I will ask only not to take my solemn vows. Time, or death, or God, at any rate, will take care of the rest. But I still hope the Lord will allow me to follow him in the path he shows me." [33]

But what path? Mortification is not an end in itself. "A part of me is in heaven. With the other part, I love, I must love, it is my sweet and urgent duty to love passionately my fellowman. To understand man's purpose. To seek truth." [34]

And everyone stuck to his position.

On October 15, 1894, the abbot of Staoueli Monastery in Algeria died. Father Louis de Gonzague, the prior at Cheiklé, was elected his successor. But he was reluctant to leave Cheiklé, where there was no monk qualified to replace him. To allow him to keep Cheiklé under his authority, the mother abbey of Notre-Dame-des-Neiges turned the priory (which was not autonomous) over to Staoueli. Thus Dom Louis de Gonzague remained the superior at Cheiklé, and he named Father Étienne acting prior. The latter wrote to Father Huvelin on November 20, 1894: "I am counting on your influence to lead Brother Albéric to make his solemn profession. As for the priesthood, we are in no hurry, and if he is opposed to it, I shall not pressure him." [35]

The following year, 1895, was a time of waiting and uncertainty. Brother Albéric finished drawing up his rule, outlined in 1893. Nowhere did he make any concessions: total gift of self, generosity in the extreme, but a disregard for the limited human stamina of the ordinary monk.

At the end of July 1895, faced with the obligation of renewing his temporary vows, Charles refused. He even thought of leaving, since everyone was against him.

Writing to his sister, Mère Clémence, Dom Polycarpe proved quite harsh: "He dreams of founding a new order ten times more austere than ours, and with that as an excuse he is refusing to make his solemn profession. On our behalf, may Saint Francis Xavier cure him of this mental illness!" [36]

Now everything depended on Father Huvelin, whom Charles had sworn to obey completely. Finally, after ten months of embarrassed silence, on September 13, 1895, the priest gave in. With regret, he grudgingly approved Charles' decision to leave the Trappists for a religious life more in keeping with his vocation.

[33] CF to Marie de Bondy, August 9, 1894.
[34] CF to Louis de Foucauld, November 28, 1894, in Gorrée, *Sur les traces*, 86.
[35] Quoted by Six, *Itinéraire*, 157.
[36] Dom Polycarpe to Mère Clémence, February 15, 1895, in Castillon, *Foucauld*, 223.

On October 25, 1895, Dom Polycarpe died without having changed his opinion. Father Huvelin, once he recommended to Charles "annihilation of the self and perfection of obedience to the rule", stopped answering letters; but on December 25, he did an about-face. Charles weathered the blow and submitted. He took up his theological studies again, "faithfully, diligently, but with little success, for I am old and have no memory".[37]

Had he given in? It would be hard to say. "My soul is still exactly the same. Nothing has changed since autumn. With time, my fixity increases."[38]

In vain he sought a compromise solution: while remaining connected to the monastery, he could live outside it, as a hermit, in the caves above Akbès, establishing some "little dovecotes" with a few very poor monks. Or instead he could just be a lay "friend of the monastery", living at its gates. His requests were turned down. Monk he was, and monk he would remain, and he would be called to high posts, in line with his abilities. Everything conspired to make him into an important person. Not only would there be the priesthood separating him in church from the lay brothers, but he had already been slated to become novice master! "How happy I would be to obey him!" exclaimed the current holder of that position, Father Philomène.

And that was the danger seen by Charles, who wished more than ever to remain in last place: "A prideful thought torments me: I might have even been a superior in the next two years!" he cried out to Father Huvelin.[39]

Once again, he hoped for death. He had escaped it twice: cholera, then tuberculosis. A third opportunity presented itself. Would this be the one?

In November 1895, the Christians of Armenia, who were subjects of the Turkish sultan, Abdul Hamid II, rebelled and demanded independence. The sultan used the situation as an excuse for genocide. He sent their traditional rivals, the Muslim Kurds, to fight against them and also offered massive support from the Ottoman army. The conflict affected the Akbès region. Adding to scenes of "unspeakable horror" were the winter weather and widespread disease: cholera, tuberculosis, and the influenza that had already carried off Dom Polycarpe. Fleeing the massacres, Armenian communities in distress took refuge in the mountains, where they were decimated by famine and the bitter cold. Although the Turkish military authorities had been ordered to look out for them, the two Catholic establishments of Akbès and Cheiklé faced danger from bands of pillagers and Muslim fanatics. The French consul in Alexandretta invited the Trappists to take shelter there, but to no avail. They did not want to

---

[37] CF to Father Huvelin, December 1895.
[38] Ibid.
[39] Ibid., January 16, 1898.

abandon their orphans and the local Christians who worked at the monastery. A screaming crowd laid siege to the Cistercian house, in spite of the presence of eight Turkish soldiers. Charles the officer came back to life. He organized the defense, and when they were about to be overrun, he thought up a way to trick the enemy. Trappist Bonaventure Rabbath tells the story: "Inside our walls, large chimney pipes were hoisted up, and men armed with hunting rifles shot into the pipes to make it seem as if the monks had some powerful artillery."

Although the Christians in the surrounding villages were massacred, the monastery was spared.

But in March the situation took a turn for the worse. The Turkish unit in Cheiklé and the one protecting the Lazarists in Akbès were both withdrawn. Charles was pleased, however: "It is better to suffer with our brothers than to be protected by the persecutors." Perfect imitation, he thought, also included martyrdom!

His wish came very close to being granted! The president of the Society for the Propagation of the Faith received the following telegram on March 28: "Trappists and Lazarists in Akbès are under siege by the Kurds. Without immediate help they will be massacred." The monks themselves sent an appeal for help to the French consuls in Aleppo and Alexandretta, who contacted Constantinople on their behalf. But it was not until the end of April 1896 that the sultan's forces cleared out the valleys. Father Bernardin, the subprior of Cheiklé, tells the story: "Countless atrocities during those terrifying days. For three solid days the monastery was under siege from thousands of Kurds eager for murder and pillage. Through unexpected luck, the *moutessarif* [head administrator of a region] Khayri-Bey had been making his rounds in the region and hurried here on a forced march with his two hundred Turkish regulars, who forced the fanatical hordes back into their mountain territory." [40]

Charles would write to Marie de Bondy: "At the end of March, Akbès and all the Christians within a two days' radius should have perished. I was not worthy. Pray that I might be converted and that, in spite of my being a miserable creature, I might not be turned away again from the heavenly gate once held half-open for me." [41] "In Marache, the closest city, only ten leagues away, the Turkish garrison killed forty-five hundred Christians within two days." [42] Everywhere, frightful massacres: 110,000 Armenians murdered and four thousand dead from cold and hunger. Villages burned, leveled, the survivors finished off or stripped of everything. Writing to France to ask for "alms for these poor folk dying of cold and hunger in

[40] *Bulletin des Amitiés*, no. 87, 14.
[41] CF to Marie de Bondy, in Gorrée, *Sur les traces*, 88.
[42] Ibid., May 3, 1896.

their ravaged land",[43] for the first time Charles regretted not being a priest so he could have gone from village to village at the height of the persecution to encourage those unfortunate persecuted Christians to die for their God. He remarked in a letter to Notre-Dame-des-Neiges, "If ever you are called to those countries where the people sit in the shadow of death, bless without restraint and give of yourself body and soul." [44]

It should be noted that the attack against the Trappist monastery at Cheiklé was launched the night of March 26–27. Exactly one hundred years later to the day, on the night of March 26–27, 1996, there occurred the attack and kidnapping of the monks at the Cistercian house in Tibhirine, Algeria.

It was a deeply distressed Charles who, on February 2, 1896, agreed to renew his provisional vows for a year. His superiors had laid down their conditions: within the year he would have to choose; no further postponement would be granted him—such was the rule of the order. Solemn vows to the Trappists, combined with the priesthood, a permanent commitment to Cheiklé, where they would be grooming him to become prior. Otherwise, he would be sent back to secular life. Charles hoped secretly that they would keep him on at Cheiklé simply as a servant, but nothing was definite.

He had accepted Father Huvelin's decision, but all the same he begged him for permission to contact the order's highest authority in Rome, which meant Dom Wyart, abbot general of the Cistercians. On June 15, 1896, Father Huvelin finally gave in: "I had hoped that you would find with the Cistercians what you are looking for, sufficient poverty, humility, obedience. I am sorry that cannot be. There is too deep an impetus toward another ideal. I do not see that you will be able to halt such movement. Speak plainly to your superiors of the invincible impetus that, no matter what you do, has long been moving you toward another ideal. No, I do not think that you are called to higher duties; I see that you feel lifted up in another direction." [45]

Charles immediately wrote to Dom Wyart, asking for a "dispensation from his simple vows", that is, permission to live outside the community, as a hermit; otherwise, release from his vows, which would mean a break with the Order.

And he began to fine-tune the rule of the "Little Brothers of Jesus", the new order he was planning to found. He kept the classic regulations from the rule of Saint Benedict: eight hours of work and eight hours of prayer, lifelong commitment to one house, strict seclusion, perpetual silence. But

---

[43] CF to Father Huvelin, January 16, 1896.

[44] *Lettres à mes frères de la Trappe* (Cerf, 1969), 117.

[45] Father Huvelin to CF, June 15, 1896, quoted by Bazin, *Foucauld*, 131.

he eliminated the monastic offices because they were in Latin; he wanted his little community to be suitable for illiterate brothers. The offices were replaced by prayer, the rosary, and five hours of adoration of the Blessed Sacrament.

When it came to asceticism, Charles' rule was extremely strict, not to say inhumane. An inadequate, unbalanced diet. Seven hours of sleep, completely dressed, on the dirt floor, with neither mattress nor pallet. No underwear, no change of clothes, bare feet (sandals for outdoors). No property, even collectively owned, thus no material security. No stocking of food or supplies. The monk would assume responsibility for his existence by his manual labor alone, refusing offerings, even if his work did not provide enough to live on. No borrowing, no debts. Besides there being no storage of provisions, "it is forbidden to turn away anyone asking for food." Which, in a poor country, comes down to dooming oneself to starvation. Thus the expression "to die for Jesus", included in the rule, meant what it said.

"It shall never be permitted to refuse anyone who asks, should we have to give the last sou, the last crust of bread in the house. And if we have nothing, we shall invite the guest or the pauper to come in, and we shall go begging for him."

Poverty and the "last place" still obsessed him:

> To live solely from our manual labor. No gifts, no honoraria for saying Mass, no collections for the poor. Nothing, absolutely nothing, not in cash, not in kind. Only two exceptions: if there is no bread, we shall go out and collect the necessary dry bread but not money to buy it. And the same with medicine and food for a seriously ill brother or guest. The work shall be of the lowliest sort, that performed by the country's poorest class. Tasks simple enough so that all, the educated and the ignorant, the strong and the weak, can carry them out within the walls of the brotherhood. This labor shall provide occupation for the body alone, leaving the mind free to meditate and pray while the fingers work.

The number in the brotherhood would not exceed eighteen, young and old, literate and illiterate, all equal. "There shall be no distinction between fathers and brothers, lay or otherwise. All shall be equal, and all shall be called brothers." No laic could become a priest, but the order would accept priests who wished to become brothers. No perpetual solemn vows. Simple vows for a year, renewable. The brothers would establish themselves in cities or neighborhoods where the poor lived, building houses like theirs. The "monastery" would have only three rooms: one for the brothers, one for guests, and a chapel. They would not buy land; it would be leased.

"We shall not reclaim what we have loaned. Lawsuits shall be forever forbidden. We shall let ourselves be shorn like lambs, and not only shorn, but slaughtered. It shall be forever forbidden to carry or possess arms, or to strike anyone, even for reasons of self-defense." [46]

Upon reading this revolutionary rule, which Charles dispatched to him July 12, 1896, Father Huvelin was dismayed. He replied on August 2: "Ah! My son, your letter has caused me pain!"

He enjoined Charles to stop judging the other monks.

> Make yourself very small, go huddle in some hidden corner of this monastery you are in. We follow our Lord and are with him wherever we obey him, wherever we humble ourselves, there where we work, there where we have surrendered ourselves. A house is built for us in our hearts, or, rather, we let a house be built in us by the hands of Jesus, he of the humble, gentle heart!
>
> You wish to be a founder? A director of souls? My child, I cannot see you in that role! Your regulations are unworkable and have frightened me. . . . The life you had embraced [with the Cistercians], you were judging, you were no longer a participant. It was no longer the spirit of the religious life, but a spirit apart. How worried I am! I am suffering unbelievably. Take simple obedience as your light. Above all, do not found anything. If you are resistant to the spirit of the Cistercians, lead a different life, but do not draw any companions into it, I beg of you.

Since he was aware that his entreaties would do no good, he added:

> What pain I feel! If they refuse to grant what you ask, consider the matter closed, stay where you are, see in their decision the will of God. And, in obscurity, wait! Concentrate on your studies. Develop your mind and widen your horizons. There in the East, you could render service to your order by showing its beauty, its strength, and its grandeur; immerse yourself in mortification and, above all, in humility.

Humility, the absence of pride, and no extremes. For that, he needed a wise rule backed up by centuries of use.

> As for mortification, you will never find it to be enough. You need to be defended against this thrust toward the infinite, which leads to anxiety and keeps you from settling on something specific. Such a thrust is possible only for hearts that never tend toward the extreme.
>
> [He ended:] Put yourself at the disposal of your superiors. Accept their decisions with simplicity. Study theology. Above all, do not found anything! If you continue to feel this way, you will not be able to remain with the Trappists. In that case, lead a different life, at the gates of a community, in the abjection you desire. [47]

The permission he had sought! Brother Charles was overjoyed. He felt himself transported by an irresistible longing.

But Father Huvelin had also written: "Obey your superiors", so Charles was waiting for an answer from Dom Wyart, the abbot general of the

---

[46] "Règle de 1896", in Gorrée, *Sur les traces*, 120–30.
[47] Father Huvelin to CF, August 2, 1896, in ibid., 89.

Cistercians. And once again it was as though time had stopped. The superiors remained torn. What to do with this person who was so troublesome, yet from whom they expected wonderful things? If they let him live on the outskirts as a hermit, there would be shame and possible divisiveness in the community, which was certainly not going to react with enthusiasm. If they kept him in the monastery as a servant or a lay monk, the situation would be worse; from the heights of his virtuous "abjection" he would continue to cause difficulty for the community.

The affair would be played out between Dom Louis de Gonzague, who, knowing Charles well, did not want to lose him, and Dom Wyart, the abbot general in Rome, who did not know him at all. But the latter had been conditioned by Dom Louis at the last general chapter of the order: "He is an exceptional individual. He is as stubborn as a mule, but he is humble of heart. Holy obedience will make him come round. Have him here with you in Rome, have him study theology at the source, two years at the Gregorian University, the supreme reward for a *normal* monk. Then he will agree docilely to the priesthood and be qualified for the highest responsibilities in the order."

But was Charles a *normal* monk?

He finally received Dom Wyart's answer, September 10, 1896: "Go to our monastery in Staoueli, where instructions will be given you by Dom Louis de Gonzague."

Fearing the worst, Charles set out at once. An hour after his September 23 arrival in Marseille, he boarded the Algiers steamer.

He was greeted by a triumphant Dom Louis de Gonzague: "Here is the decision of your superiors. Before making up your mind about the future, take some time for reflection. You will study theology at the Gregorian University in Rome for two years."

Charles was filled with dismay. Rome, university! He could imagine nothing worse. He pulled himself together immediately. Father Huvelin had written: "Take simple obedience as your light." Love alone would guide him. "Why did I go into the monastery? Because of love, pure love. Sacrifice is nothing more than the supreme test of love." [48]

Tamanrasset, December 1, 1916, noon.

The Ahaggar sun beamed down on a deserted landscape. It was siesta hour in the Sahara, in the hamlet of the Haratins and in all the nomad camps around. Even pillagers still out wandering stopped in the shade of a tamarisk.

[48] Quoted by Six, *Itinéraire*, 104.

But Charles de Foucauld went on working. Refreshing naps were not for him.

Breaking away from his memories, he returned to his anthology of Tuareg poetry. In order to ask forgiveness for the somewhat frivolous nature of this project, he pushed back his chair and knelt on the ground, his arms on the table. He prayed at length, looking straight at the altar's tabernacle. Then he roused himself from this joyful contemplation. He had to get his mail ready for the camel trooper postman from Motylinski who would be stopping by soon.

First there was a letter written three days earlier, to the mother abbess of the Poor Clares of Nazareth. He read it over before sealing it: "I am still alone. On Christmas night, your old and faithful servant will be with you at the feet of Jesus. I shall pray for France."

Brother Charles knelt on the ground again, his head on the table, resting in his arms. He prayed at length, like a thirsty traveler drinking clear water. Then he sat up and slowly read the letter from Marie de Bondy. Although she never complained, something of her despair came through in the letter. After losing her husband, she had raised four children alone. Now, the oldest was making her suffer and no longer came to see her. Charles picked up his pen.

> Thank you for the letters that arrived this morning, along with the can of cocoa. You keep on spoiling your old son!
>
> How could you not feel weighed down after the anguish of these years of war? Here below Jesus has shared his chalice with you too often and you have drunk from it too faithfully for him not to share generously with you his heavenly glory also.
>
> Abasing ourselves is the most powerful means we have of joining Jesus and doing good for souls. When we are able to suffer and to love, we can do much, all that is in our power to do in this world. We feel that we are suffering; we do not always feel that we love, and that is one more source of great suffering. But we do know that we want to love, and to want to love is to love. We find that we do not love enough. We shall never love enough, but God, who loves us more than a mother, has told us he will not reject the one who comes to him.
>
> You can tell how often I think of you.[49]

At that very moment, ten miles to the north, the *rezzou* had set out again through the mountainous region of the Koudia. In the lead, perched on his camel, Kerzou, the rebel Targui, once a corporal at Fort Motylinski, rode along beside the Senoussi Beuh ag Rhabelli. Behind them, in a long line, the thirty-eight *fellagha* camel troopers.

---

[49] CF to Marie de Bondy, December 1, 1916, in Gorrée, *Sur les traces*, 312.

Abruptly, the Senoussi spoke: "I don't understood the double game of Moussa and Ouksem. How can they be for Allah and against him at the same time?"

Kerzou smiled knowingly. Evenings, at the French camp, the subject had often come up. He had heard the post commander, Captain de La Roche, discussing it with his lieutenant, Constant. Kerzou answered Beuh: "Moussa ag Amastane was named by the French to be *amenokal* of the Ahaggar Tuareg, replacing Attici, who had taken up our holy cause but was defeated at Tit. He sought refuge in Tripolitania and died there three years ago, before he could seek revenge. The French gave Moussa the scarlet jellaba and a medal they call the Legion of Honor, which all the French officers would willingly die for. Moussa used to be only a petty noble chieftain like so many others, so it is in his interest to play the game of the French. And it is the same for Ouksem, the chief of the Dag Rali. But the other Tuareg want something besides a medal and honors. They regret the days of the *razzias* [raids by *rezzous*]. They do not stop badgering their *amenokal*: 'What do the French contribute to us, except for their roads and their future railroad, all of which will one day render useless our traditional caravans of weapons, grain, and salt?' "

Kerzou exploded: "Moussa did what his father never would have! He gave up the tent of the proud desert nomads and had a brick house built. And he stays there, in one place, at least for part of the year. He is no longer a true Targui, even if he does keep—with the blessing of the Franks—six slaves and four black women!"

"If the French lose their war against the Germans, the Turks will drive them out of Africa. Then the good old days will return. That is why Moussa and Ouksem play a double game. But we shall certainly be able to make them choose their camp. Besides, young Ouksem, heir of his adoptive father, has already chosen. He is virtually ours!"

And so the *fellagha* chatted to relieve the tension as they approached Tamanrasset for the attack.

7

Rome

Take simple obedience as your light.

Still kneeling on the sand in his bedroom-chapel, Brother Charles continued recalling the events of his life.

He had sailed from Algiers on October 27, 1896, arriving in Rome several days later. His first act had been to enter a church; prostrate before the Blessed Sacrament, he pledged to live according to God's will. Everlasting discussion! Where was God? How did he express his will? In the heart of a poor wandering monk? Or in the heads of the monk's superiors, always full of plans?

Then he went to ring at the monumental door of the Cistercian headquarters, 95 Via San Giovanni. They were expecting him. His reputation for holiness had preceded him. Dom Louis de Gonzague, the new prior of the Staoueli Monastery, had not failed to keep the abbot general informed.

A letter from a novice, Brother Yves, gives an account of Charles' behavior: "At Staoueli, he lived on nothing. He was content with eating the vegetables in his soup, without tasting the soup or anything else, and that was his one meal for the day, at noon. He slept only two hours. He would stay up until midnight in the little chapel of the infirmary, where he could see the Blessed Sacrament. At midnight he took a short rest, and at 2 A.M. he would be in the choir with the community. How edifying for the other monks! In church his eyes never left the Blessed Sacrament! *He did not believe, he saw!*" [1]

Charles had resigned himself to being tested in Rome. He wrote to Marie de Bondy: "My desires have in no way changed, but I am obeying with simplicity and with the confidence that, following this lengthy test, the will of God is going to manifest itself clearly, whatever that will may be." [2]

---

[1] Letter from Father Yves, quoted by R. Bazin, *Charles de Foucauld* (Plon, 1921), 135.
[2] CF to Marie de Bondy, October 2, 1896.

And to Father Jérôme at Notre-Dame-des-Neiges, he wrote: "I shall most likely spend three years here. A test to which I am trying to submit in the best manner possible, with obedience and gratitude." [3] "Old, ignorant, unused to Latin, I am having great difficulty with my classes. I shall be a dunce in theology just as in everything else." [4] "The habit of asking what one should do, even regarding little things, has a thousand good results: it gives peace; it teaches us to conquer ourselves; it makes us look upon earthly things as nothing; it leads us to perform a host of acts of love. To obey a confessor is to obey God; and to obey is to love; of all acts of love, obedience is the most pure, the most perfect, the most elevated, the most disinterested, the most reverential." [5]

Even if his superiors were wrong? Especially if they were wrong! For "even if our confessors did not make us do the thing most perfect in itself, the love, the humility, and the good will that form the essence of our obedience would make our act that much more pleasing to God because of those virtues accompanying it." [6] "When we love, what is sweeter than giving to the one we love? Especially if we give something with which we do not want to part, then what is sweeter than suffering for love, than giving all the blood in our heart to the one we love?" [7]

But in private, his heart bled. He wanted to imitate the poverty of the Christ of Nazareth. But, "now they are telling me that I may be mistaken, that you, Lord, are not allowing me to follow you so closely." [8]

Two months went by. Charles concentrated on his theology, but he still had not seen the person who had called him to Rome. Dom Sébastien Wyart was on the road, making his regular visits to the monasteries. Secretly, Charles was pinning all his hopes on him. He wrote to Marie de Bondy: "It will seem obvious to him that God does not wish me to be in a Trappist house, at least not as a priest." [9] But he was not altogether sure of that, as he confided to Father Jérôme: "If they say to me: you are going to take your solemn vows in ten days, and then you will be ordained, I shall obey . . . with joy, certain that I am doing God's will." [10]

On January 16, 1897, Dom Wyart finally returned to Rome. The following morning, Charles was summoned to his office. According to custom, he

---

[3] CF to Father Jérôme, December 7, 1896, *Lettres à mes frères de la Trappe* (Cerf, 1969).

[4] Ibid., November 19, 1896.

[5] Ibid., November 29, 1896.

[6] Ibid.

[7] Ibid., November 8, 1896, in G. Gorrée, *Sur les traces de Charles de Foucauld* (Éd. de la Plus Grande France, 1936), 91.

[8] CF, *Méditations sur l'Ancien Testament*, Genesis 30:1–21.

[9] CF to Marie de Bondy, January 15, 1897.

[10] CF to Father Jérôme, January 24, 1897, in Gorrée, *Sur les traces*, 311.

knelt at his feet, closed his eyes, and submitted. Suddenly a flash of inspiration came and certainty as to how to act. He had rehearsed his plea, his speech; and now there was nothing, no speech, no will of his own. Contrary to all human logic, he decided he would not speak. In advance, he was giving in to the decision of his superiors, whatever it might be. Well, it could only be negative. They would make him "toe the line". And in advance he accepted it, because obedience is the very stuff of love.

He opened his eyes, kissed the ring on Dom Wyart's extended hand. The abbot motioned him to his feet. For a few seconds there was a touching exchange of looks between the venerable abbot general and the spirited little monk with the ardent expression. The abbot smiled paternally. Behind the ardor, he saw only humble submission.

"You are taking theology courses at the Gregorian University. For a monk, it is of great benefit to drink at the purest source of religious instruction."

Charles humbly bowed his head in agreement. As he remained silent, the abbot continued, his voice conveying a touch of anxiety: "Brother Albéric, the moment has come to examine God's plans for you."

But Charles kept silent. Total surrender of his will. Let God act alone. A silence that cried out: "Decide, I shall obey."

Dom Wyart understood, and he was deeply distressed. "Withdraw, Brother Albéric, and tell me in writing the state of your soul. Then I shall call a meeting of my council, and we shall deliberate."

The abbot dismissed him. They had remained together only a few minutes, but the essential had taken place, the inspiration of the Holy Spirit. Dom Wyart did not need a long speech. Nor even the written report he had requested. He knew already that Brother Albéric's immediate superiors—Dom Louis de Gonzague and Father Étienne—had been mistaken. Theology would not bring fulfillment to this ardent child. He could not be satisfied with courses, be they Roman or Gregorian! Schooling would not quench the fire burning in him and make him a good monk, inconspicuous among the others. But what, then, since he did not want to move up through the hierarchy?

Charles felt a mixture of satisfaction and despair. He had given all. Now he only had to accept the irreparable. As for the written plea, he would not produce it, any more than he had the spoken one. He wrote to Father Jérôme: "Obedience is the most perfect of the levels of love, that on which we cease to exist as ourselves, on which we die as Jesus died on the Cross, the highest level of love, incorporating all the others and surpassing them. Let us always obey with our entire soul, and we shall always love with our entire soul. Let us give this highest level of love." [11]

[11] Ibid., January 24, 1897.

146 CHARLES DE FOUCAULD

But so far nothing had been halted.

"When God sees this perfect obedience in his children, he always gives special wisdom to their confessors", Charles had also written to Father Jérôme.[12]

The superiors remained torn. How could they deprive the order of such a man, and maybe even of such a saint? But how could they go against the will of God, which seemed to be expressing itself by his very silences? Dom Wyart and Father Robert Lescand, Charles' inspired confessor in Rome, finally became convinced that the order had to open its gates wide for this flaming bird whom it could not long keep caged. And the council, meeting January 23, 1897, unanimously agreed.

That very day, Dom Wyart summoned Charles, who had been expecting the worst: the priesthood, followed by ascent to various offices in the order, he who dreamed only of ascending to Calvary.

"You are free, my son. You can follow the particular vocation that seems good to you. After prayer, study, and reflection, the fathers recognize in you a special vocation outside the rule. That is what the council has decided, unanimously. May God guide your footsteps."

Charles was overwhelmed. He had a hard time containing his joy. Dom Wyart's look grew more serious, as if he were pondering all that awaited this child just rendered almost unbearably free.

"You will have to follow your vocation without further delay, with all your heart, and in keeping with God's will. As far as the matter of vocation is concerned, you shall remain in obedience."

"To you, Father?"

"No. It would be best to speak with Father Huvelin, as you did in the past."

"Yes, Father. Along with my obedience to you, I have never abandoned my obedience to Father Huvelin."

"Where do you plan to go?"

"I would like to be a 'familiar' in a humble monastery in the Holy Land. Father Huvelin will choose the place."[13]

Charles was exultant. He had succeeded in obeying his inner voices while at the same time respecting monastic discipline.

"Dom Wyart has provided me with the strongest moral certainty that can exist on earth that this is God's will", he wrote to Raymond de Blic on February 11, 1897. And in his *Écrits spirituels*, the following: "The will of God is that I follow this attraction, which draws me out of the monastery toward the life of renunciation, humble work, and deep obscurity I have so long envisioned."[14]

[12] Ibid., November 29, 1896.
[13] Cf. letter to Marie de Bondy, late January 1897, quoted by Bazin, *Foucauld*, 141–42.
[14] Cf. "Retraite à Nazareth", in *Écrits spirituels* (Gigord, 1923), 84.

But most surprised of all was Dom Louis de Gonzague, who had thought sending Charles to Rome would tame him. He was shocked by the decision. He wrote his brother, Dom Martin, on February 11, 1897:

> He is leaving the order to go to Palestine and live the life of a hermit. It is a misfortune and very painful for me. I would have thought that in Rome they would not rush through the matter so cavalierly, but admittedly, the fellow is amazingly tenacious in his desires and his will. And, actually, in our order, he had sincere affection for several persons but very little for the order itself. He is the perfect example of our nineteenth-century nobility: courageous, generous with his blood and his money, saintly sometimes, as is the case, but incapable of lasting obedience or submission to the discipline of a leader. He may become a saint. I hope so, but it would be by following his own lead, not by obeying. He has, I think, made too many great and beautiful sacrifices for God to allow him to stray, and that, in my opinion, is his only real safeguard as he sets out on this extraordinary path he has chosen.

Learning of the annoyance of Louis de Gonzague, Dom Wyart wrote him: "Let me tell you that, taken as I was with this incomparable soul, I used every means to try to keep him for you. I shall tell you in detail the battles engaged in to win the desired victory for your paternity. God, in very clear fashion, inflicted failure on me. Who can resist God?"

And Dom Louis, writing to Marie de Blic, ended up acknowledging: "By leaving us, Brother Albéric has caused me the greatest sorrow I have felt in my entire life. In the seven years I have seen him a Trappist and faithful to all his religious duties, I have grown to regard him as a true saint. Moreover, that is the impression he has left here." [15]

Father Huvelin's agreement still had to be obtained. Faced with Charles' joy, he melted: "I am touched, moved by your letter. I have nothing to say." [16]

No, nothing. He approved, what happiness! "Your ideas differed too much from what you could accomplish at the monastery for you to stay there." Just the same, he was sorry: "Wherever we are, we can practice the life of Nazareth, be forgotten, live obedience, live the cross."

Wherever, and even—and especially—in a Cistercian monastery!

"You will be leaving! I foresaw that long ago!"

Ah, the dear, good priest! But the rebellious child had only himself to blame for what was to happen: "God arranged the Cistercian life for you as the only solution, as the only voice that could guide you in total security."

"Security", that was the least of Charles' concerns! Acrobat of God, he chose to work without a net.

And now, where to go? "Like you, I picture the East. Akbès, Staoueli? Impossible. The same thoughts would come visit you there, the same

---

[15] Dom Louis de Gonzague to Marie de Blic, in Bazin, *Foucauld*, 143.
[16] Father Huvelin to CF, January 27, 1897.

comparison between the life you were living and that which you are now pursuing." Father Huvelin seemed to be suggesting a Franciscan monastery, but "not *in* the community, but in its shadow, asking only for its spiritual resources while living in poverty at the gatehouse."

As for founding an order, patience! "Live your life. Then, if souls come, live the same life together, without regulations, without anything. Do not provide a rule."

And now, go ahead! Here Father Huvelin's words are those of the mother worried at the thought of seeing her favorite son set out on the harsh roads of the world. Charles at first refused the steamer ticket generously offered by the Cistercians; he wanted to go to the East *on foot*, like the poor pilgrims of yore. But Huvelin said no: "Accept the passage without further ado. Spare yourself these initial complications, at a time when you will need all your strength and composure."

And to his inhuman offer to write the family less often or perhaps not at all, Father Huvelin replied, thinking of Marie de Bondy and Marie de Blic: "Here there are some loving souls who would suffer greatly. Write a little more often at first, a little less later."

And now, he had to follow through. *Descend*, that is. He had to forge ahead on the inner road leading to perfection and to love-imitation. "Descend . . . All doors are open to allow me to cease being a choir monk and descend to the rank of familiar and valet. Once again, I am in the hands of God and obedience." [17]

So he would not be a priest. That was a choice, which he no doubt regretted. Referring to Father Jérôme, then soon to be ordained, he wrote: "There is no vocation in the world as great as that of the priest. He is no longer of this world, but already of heaven. The priest is something transcendent, surpassing all. What a vocation! I would like to have been a priest. But I was unworthy." [18]

He would be departing. He was in a hurry to leave behind opulent Rome and the pomp and splendor of the Vatican, to lose himself in the footsteps of the poor and persecuted Christ: "To be a servant, a valet, a familiar, to head for those distant shores where so many souls are lost, where an abundant harvest perishes for lack of workers. There where we can do more good for others, that is where we are at our best. Selflessness, devotion." [19]

On February 14, 1897, before Dom Wyart, Charles de Foucauld renewed his vows of poverty and perpetual chastity, adding the vow "to possess no more than a poor workingman can have". As for the vow of obedience,

---

[17] CF to Father Jérôme, January 21, 1897, in *Lettres à mes frères de la Trappe*.
[18] Ibid.
[19] Ibid., January 24, 1897, in Gorrée, *Sur les traces*, 93.

Charles may no longer have had to follow the Cistercians, but he was tied to Father Huvelin more than ever.

On February 17, he sailed from Brindisi aboard the Jaffa steamer. Looking ahead to the inspiration of the Holy Land, his heart overflowed with joy.

⚜

Tamanrasset, December 1, 1916, 1 P.M. Still at his table, kneeling on the sand, Brother Charles was writing:

> To Second Lieutenant L. Massignon. Military Postal Service.
>
> Very dear brother in Jesus, this morning I received your letters of October 3 and 9, moved at the thought of the very great dangers you are perhaps going to encounter, that you are probably already encountering. You have done a fine thing by asking to join the troops.[20] We must never hesitate to ask for those posts where the danger, sacrifice, and devotion are greatest. Honor, let us leave that to whoever wishes it, but danger, difficulty, let us always claim them. Christians, we should provide an example of sacrifice and devotion. That is a principle to which we must be faithful our whole lives, in simplicity, without asking ourselves whether any pride enters into this conduct. It is a duty, let us do it, and let us ask the beloved Bridegroom of our soul that we may do it in all humility, in complete love for God and our fellows. Walk this road in simplicity and in peace, certain that it is Jesus who has inspired you to follow it.
>
> If God spares your life, your household will be that much more blessed, because by devoting yourself more fully, you will be more united with Jesus, and you will have a more supernatural life. If you die, God will keep Madame Massignon and your son without you, just as he would have kept them for you. Trust that God will give what is best for his glory, what is best for your soul, and best for the souls of others, since you ask of him only that, since everything that he wants you want also, wholeheartedly and without reservation.
>
> Our corner of the Sahara is at peace. I pray for you with all my heart and at the same time for your household. This will reach you around Christmas and January 1. Look for me to be very near you on those two days. A happy and holy year! May God keep you and protect France! May Jesus, Mary, and Joseph keep you with them your whole earthly life, at the hour of your death, and through eternity. I embrace you with all my heart as I love you in the heart of Jesus.[21]

Brother Charles closed his eyes. When he opened them, his gaze rested on the tabernacle on the altar. Then he picked up his pen and dipped it in the inkwell:

---

[20] Louis Massignon first fought in the Dardanelles, in 1914, then he requested to be sent into combat on the German front. His family and Paul Claudel tried to have him appointed to the Foreign Ministry! He was finally assigned to the front at Thessaloníki. See chapter 15.

[21] CF to Louis Massignon, December 1, 1916, in ibid., 311.

To Madame Raymond de Blic.
  My dear little Mimi . . .

He could see the tormented face of his beloved sister. Tears welled up in
his eyes. Would he ever see her again?

Ten miles to the northeast, the *rezzou* of Beuh ag Rhabelli, guided by
Kerzou, had stopped. They were early. The *fellagha* were taking a rest near
an abandoned well. A little patch of green grew there, showing there
would be water under the surface. A man lowered the bucket fastened to
the rim. He brought up several quarts of water, muddy but cool. They
gave thanks to Allah. Then they crouched on the sand in the shade of a
tamarisk.

"Tell me about Ba Hammou's double game", Beuh asked Kerzou.

The Targui waited a long while before he replied, enjoying the soft, hot
sand after being uncomfortably perched on his swaying camel. At last he
said: "Ba Hammou is the *khodja*, the confidant, of Moussa, who is *amenokal*
of the Ahaggar because the French approved him and some of the tribes
elected him. When Ba Hammou is not at Tam, he frequents the pasture
lands to the southeast with the tribe of Moussa. He is there now. That
means he is near our brother Kaoucen, who is laying siege to Agadez. Ba
Hammou probably keeps him informed as to the movements of Moussa,
the only person who might interfere with our operation against the fort of
the marabout. That is why we have received the order to act quickly."

"But is Ba Hammou working for the marabout too? I have even heard
that he is teaching the satanic sorcerer your language, Tamasheq, knowledge
he plans to use in turning the people of the Ahaggar away from the true
religion."

"Yes, the marabout is also making what he calls a 'dictionary'. And a
'grammar', too, I believe. All this is dangerous for Islam. But Ba Hammou
knows what he is doing. A member of the sect of the Kadria, he is thereby
under orders from the Senoussi. Moussa, as I have said, also plays a double
game. He is involved with the Islamic revolt and the French at one and the
same time. He and Kaoucen probably exchange information, through Ba
Hammou. Allah will be the judge!"

8

Gardener for the Poor Clares

After seven days in steerage with the immigrants, Charles de Foucauld stepped off the ship at Jaffa February 24, 1897, then made the long pilgrimage to Jerusalem on foot. Still dressed "like the poorest of the peasants of Palestine", he went on to Nazareth, arriving March 5, jubilant. Night had fallen; it was cold. So as not to disturb anyone, he slept at the gate of the Franciscan monastery where he expected to be hired as a servant, a house suggested by Father Huvelin.

The next morning he presented his letter of recommendation to the brother porter, who recognized Charles from his previous trip. But they did not need a servant here, not even an unpaid one. "Go see our sisters, the Poor Clares, or the Franciscans on Mount Tabor."

Still smiling, Charles presented himself at the convent of the Poor Clares. Or rather, first he presented himself to God. Without asking anyone for anything, he entered the chapel and prostrated himself before the altar. So oddly dressed, he could not escape notice, with his striped tunic and hood, a huge chaplet hanging from his belt. The solemn eyes glowed with passion in the unshaven face. His feet, bare but for the sandals, were bruised and dusty from the long journey. He looked more like a run-of-the-mill beggar than a genuine pilgrim. Uneasy, the sister gatekeeper, who had seen him enter, remarked to the nun with her, "I'd better keep an eye on that man. I'm afraid he might be a thief."

Then, without asking for anything, Charles headed toward the Franciscan house at Mount Tabor, six miles away. There, he confessed to a priest, and, not concealing his identity, he asked for work. The Franciscan to whom he spoke, Father Voisin, happened to be chaplain to the Poor Clares of Nazareth. He advised Charles to return to the nuns, and he discreetly informed the abbess of the true status of this peculiar indigent.

On March 9 Charles appeared at the convent of the Poor Clares once again, but this time he asked to speak to the abbess.

Mother Marie-Ange de Saint-Michel had been waiting for him with curiosity. In spite of the parlor's thick grille that stood between them, their eyes met, and the abbess was not fooled. The beard may have been heavy, but the features were refined, the eyes sparkled with intelligence, and the language was elegant. The miserable getup did not make any difference; this was definitely Viscount Charles de Foucauld, the ex-Cistercian, whom they had announced. What tragedy had brought him so low? She describes the meeting: "All he had was a small handwritten copy of the Gospel and his indescribable outfit, calculated to make him an object of total contempt. Yet, under the shabby, unkempt exterior, one could see the man of the world. His speech gave him away." [1]

"What can I do for you?"

"I would like to do manual labor here, Reverend Mother. Any gardening chores that you would be so kind as to give me."

The abbess was startled by his request. Then she smiled: "There is no lack of work here, but you could not come inside our outer wall."

"I want no more than to live outside the convent, provided that I am given permission to come and pray in the chapel."

"We need a sacristan and a man who can do our errands in town and some work around here. What salary would you like?"

"No salary, Mother. Just a little bread."

More and more surprised, she agreed. "You may stay in the gardener's house." Through the window, she pointed out a rustic cottage.

Charles shook his head. "Couldn't I have an ordinary hut in the shadow of your walls?" He had noticed beyond the courtyard, some three hundred feet away, a wooden hut leaning against the convent's outer wall, a kind of storage shed. "That would do very well for me", he said.

Again, she agreed. He had won. The last place with the poorest of nuns, the daughters of Saint Francis and Saint Clare.

"To embrace humility, poverty, renunciation, abjection, solitude, suffering, as did Jesus in the manger. To care not for human grandeur, or rising in the world, or the esteem of men, but to esteem the very poor as much as the very rich. For me, to seek always the last of the last places, to order my life so as to be the last, the most despised of men." [2]

For Charles, the life of his dreams had begun. He swept, he ran errands for the Poor Clares, he served Mass. He stayed in the cramped tool shed, barely seven feet square, and lit only by an unshuttered window. The sisters had given him two trestles, on which he placed two boards to make a writing table. A stool. For sleeping, a straw pallet and a blanket. He was more than satisfied.

His attempts to garden were pathetic. "He was incapable of planting a head of lettuce", one of the sisters would say later. He did not even know how to use a spade. He was not good with his hands, and willingness made

[1] S. Chauleur, *Charles de Foucauld et mère Marie-Ange* (Éd. Saint-Paul, 1946), "lettres au chanoine Caron".

[2] CF, "Retraite à Nazareth", 1897, in *Écrits spirituels* (Gigord, 1923).

no difference. The sisters laughed without malice at his awkwardness. He repaired the convent wall. They had him sort lentils and peel vegetables. Unobtrusively, the mother abbess kept an eye on him, astonished by his desire to do what was right, by his thirst for poverty, and by his shining faith. She left him all possible freedom, which he used and abused by adoring and contemplating in the chapel or meditating in his shack and by writing about the Gospels, in which he was constantly discovering new depths of meaning.

Everyone in the monastery now knew who he was and from whence he had come. To please him, the sisters pretended they thought he really was a poor wanderer the mother abbess had taken in out of charity. "He leads a life more angelic than human, a very contemplative life", the abbess said.[3]

Charles was jubilant. To his cousin Louis de Foucauld, he wrote: "God let me find here what I was seeking: poverty, solitude, abjection, very humble work, total obscurity, imitation of Jesus. Love imitates, love wants similarity to the one loved. Keep my secrets, Louis. These are secrets of love that I am confiding to you. I am very happy. The heart has what it has been seeking for many years. Now all that remains is to go to heaven."[4]

He was in heaven. His shack stood by itself in an establishment for nuns, on the outskirts of the little city. He would rise at dawn and go to the Franciscan friary to serve early Mass in the crypt, then he would go back to the Poor Clares.

The sisters were concerned when they saw him living on nothing but bread and water. He finally accepted a few figs and almonds. The mother abbess wrote, "We are delighted, hoping that some fruit will temper a bit the harshness of his perpetual fast."[5] But, hiding these treats in his large pockets, he would distribute them to the poor children who came knocking at the door of his hut. He even gave them his bread and his miserable garments!

He gave up his mattress and slept on the bare ground, a stone for a pillow. But he slept so little! Always silent, he spoke only if asked a question. Yet he remained cheerful and affable, his heart and mind overflowing with the divine joy that filled him.

That joy started to trouble him. It gave him a guilty conscience, which he tried to relieve by greater austerity. The mother abbess said; "I have never met anyone who carried a disdain for riches and man-made objects so far, or anyone so self-sacrificing and self-demeaning. His clothes were falling apart."[6]

[3] Chauleur, *Foucauld*.
[4] CF to Louis de Foucauld, April 12, 1897, in R. Bazin, *Charles de Foucauld* (Plon, 1921), 147.
[5] Chauleur, *Foucauld*.
[6] Ibid.

Once, a priest who had come to preach a retreat was offended by the sight of a servant spending so much time in the chapel. He advised the sister gatekeeper: "Tell that unfortunate man to go work. He mustn't waste away his whole workday."

"He is a nice young fellow, but not too bright", the Poor Clares' chaplain had said of him when he first arrived. Charles thoroughly enjoyed that kind of humiliation. Once, another priest, noting how thin he was, invited Charles to finish the leftovers from the meal Charles had just served him.

The Passion of Christ humiliated remained his obsession. As a human being, he felt responsible for that deicide, and from that sprang his desire for mortification as redress. In his "Resolutions at the End of a Retreat", we read: "Penance consisting of fasts and vigils. No special instruments of penance, except the scourge. One meal a day, no set time, taken while at work, without stopping the work to eat it. Bread and water." [7]

Just as he ate very little, he slept very little, only enough to get by: between three and six hours, sometimes two. He would get up when he awakened, even if it was the middle of the night.

Fortunately, he stayed in touch with Father Huvelin, who, delighted at first to see him "finding a burrow in the shadow of the chapel of these poor holy daughters", soon tried to moderate his austere habits: "Remain what you are. Just add a little sleep. Let the sisters add to your diet the little things they will judge appropriate." [8] For the essential lay elsewhere: "Remain humble, poor, obscure, and unknown. Nourish yourself on the Psalms, which give such vivid expression to the feelings that feed the soul united to God or in search of him." [9] "Keep your soul open to receive his gifts." [10]

Charles knew that from experience: the center of his life was not penance but love, which he found in contemplation, in adoration of the Blessed Sacrament, and in the Eucharist. His faith in the Real Presence was total: "You are there, my Lord Jesus, in the Holy Eucharist. You are there but a few feet from me, in the tabernacle. Your body, your soul, your humanity, your divinity, your entire being is there in its double nature! How close you are, God!" [11]

He loved. "To pray is to think of God with thoughts of love." "The best prayer is the one in which there is the most love. It is so much better because it is loving", he wrote to Marie de Bondy. [12]

[7] "Retraite à Nazareth".
[8] Father Huvelin to CF, May 1, 1897.
[9] Ibid., May 13, 1897.
[10] Ibid., June 22, 1897.
[11] "Retraite à Nazareth".
[12] CF to Marie de Bondy, February 3, 1897.

"I thought I had given up all when I left the Trappists", he wrote his sister. "I have now been given more than enough. I am enjoying to the full being poor, dressed as a servant and a worker, in this low state which was that of Jesus." [13]

Father Huvelin shared his enthusiasm. "How I bless Nazareth! Yes, that was the place! "[14]

But he was still trying to moderate him: "Do not ask for anything out of the ordinary. Be satisfied with what is possible and do not seek anything unusual." [15] "Do nothing but stay in the hands of God, ready for everything that he will ask of you." [16] But unwisely, he also said: "Do what is most perfect, or what seems to you the most perfect." [17]

Charles did not allow himself to be swallowed up by the joy of the mystical life. His concern for the poor never faltered. When he went into town, the children would follow him about. Even those who had thrown stones at him when he first came, ridiculing the foreign wanderer, now ran after him with shouts of joy, and "their uplifted bare arms and their dancing and their eyes surrounded him with light".[18] His hut was soon overrun by children and the poor of all ages.

His reputation for holiness was spreading, but some superficial minds considered him a gentle dreamer. He seemed outside the world, living only in adoration. The sisters had asked him to rid the area of a jackal making night raids on the henhouse. They entrusted Charles with an old hunting rifle borrowed from a neighbor, whose son showed him how it worked. The former cavalry officer lay in wait, then tightened his fingers around . . . his rosary beads; he sank into, not sleep, but the deepest contemplative prayer. Carried away in God, he let the sisters' enemy escape with the spoils from the henhouse.

For the first time, he went by the name "Brother Charles of Jesus"; that, along with nothing more than "Nazareth, Holy Land" was how he asked friends and relatives to address their letters. Clad not in a monk's habit but in a workman's blue tunic, he tried to go about unnoticed; but he soon became a personality in the town, and his true identity came out. Few could understand how he had managed to end up a servant in the poorest of monasteries in a forgotten country, a neglected colony of the Ottoman Empire.

One day, no longer able to contain himself, a Salesian lay brother from

[13] CF to Marie de Blic, November 25, 1897.
[14] Father Huvelin to CF, August 26, 1897.
[15] Ibid., July 13, 1897.
[16] Ibid., July 29, 1897.
[17] Ibid., August 26, 1897.
[18] Bazin, *Foucauld*, 153.

Nazareth questioned Charles when he ran into him on the street:
"They are saying many things about you. I would like to know if they are
true."

"And why, exactly?"

"They say that you were of high position in France."

"And what position would that be?"

"You were a count!"

"I was just an ordinary soldier."

"What is your secret, Brother Charles?"

"The more I gave up, the more happiness I found!" [19]

The key to this happiness was his living faith, his contact with God,
made possible by forsaking the ego. This letter-confession to Father Huvelin, dated January 16, 1898, goes to the very heart of his life:

> My life proceeds in great peace. During the day, I work while it is light. In
> the morning and evening and part of the night, I read and I pray. Rosary,
> stations of the cross, and silent prayer. Having no clock, I do not know how
> long I sleep. I sleep well, and at night I ask my good angel to awaken me
> when God wishes. I think I sleep about five-and-a-half hours. Once I am up,
> I say Matins, then I meditate by writing about the Gospels and the Psalms,
> until the angelus. Then I go to church. I receive Communion every day, and
> I confess once a week, to a Franciscan.
>
> Sundays and days off it is infinitely sweet to spend all my time in church,
> reading and meditating at the foot of the tabernacle, there in the lonely little
> chapel of the Poor Clares. I look at the tabernacle, and these are days of
> delight.
>
> Holidays and Sundays, I eat the same meals as the Clares, coffee in the
> morning, dinner at noon, a light supper at night. The other days I live on
> bread. Up to now I have been taking two meals. But there is so little
> mortification in my life, I suffer so little, that since yesterday I have begun to
> take only one meal, as I did for so long in the Trappist house, but that will
> just be for the winter. From Easter to September 14, I shall take two. If I eat
> nothing but bread, it makes no difference whether I eat it at one hour or at
> another. I thought it right to do this little trifle for God. I do not wear the
> hair shirt. My only form of mortification is the scourge.[20]

It may appear to have been an uncomplicated life, but it was not, because of his "perfectionism". He was a worrier. His confession included a
list of self-accusations, in order of importance. *Half-heartedness:* "Prayers
said hastily, Mass heard most inattentively, presence of God maintained
poorly." *Cowardice:* "Lazy about getting up. Sometimes I go back to bed
instead of rising the first time I awake." *Gluttony:* "Voracious appetite,
eating too much." *Lack of charity:* "Not praying enough for others and

[19] Quoted by Bazin, ibid., 156.
[20] CF to Father Huvelin, January 16, 1898, from volume of correspondence, 59–60.

judging some too harshly." *Pride:* "I think about rising in the world, becoming a superior with the Cistercians."

Actually, his principal temptation was to visualize *somewhere else*, to go beyond. He was unable to live at peace in the here and now. From whence came that temptation? Did he not have everything he wanted there in Nazareth?

"This temptation exists. I see it only as a trick of the devil to torture me. Or at least to distract me for several days at a time. I have wondered if my readings in theology might not be tempting me toward grandeur. But my studies are good for me; they make me love the Church and my neighbor; they straighten out my thinking; they transform my inner life. Sometimes I have said to myself that it might be better to put aside my books and ink and paper and be content with my chaplet. In all things, I shall do as you say. Bless your little child who lies at your feet with respect and such tender gratitude." [21]

To become that little child once again would have made him completely happy, but that was an impossible dream. He was what he was and would have to accept it.

He who so badly needed support now had to lend support to his loved ones. Not just his delicate sister, Mimi, but also Marie de Bondy, who was going through bad times. She had recently lost her husband, then her mother. Her sons were turning out badly, especially the eldest. She had financial difficulties. She no longer expected anything from life and sought refuge in duty and a tragic mysticism fed by suffering. In a spirit of sacrifice, Charles had suggested to Father Huvelin that he might stop writing her. The priest talked him out of it. "She needs you!" He took responsibility for her spiritually. But he was so far away!

No, he was not as well balanced and serene as he appeared to be or as he claimed in his letters. His nature remained full of contradictions, of highs and lows. Certainly, he knew moments of boundless joy. But anguish was a fundamental component of his psyche. Moreover, it was one of the forces motivating him. Like all mystics, his periods of exaltation were sometimes followed by black periods, which he tried to overcome by increasing his mortifications. "Aridity and darkness, everything is painful for me, even telling Jesus that I love him. I must cling fast to the life of faith. If at least I could feel that Jesus loved me! But he never tells me that he does." [22]

During this time his desire for martyrdom grew. In his spiritual notes, in which he has Jesus speak, on June 6, 1897, he had written: "Think that you are to die a martyr, stripped of everything, stretched out on the ground,

---

[21] Ibid., 60–63.
[22] CF to Louis Massignon, June 6, 1897.

naked, unrecognizable, covered with wounds and blood, violently and pain-fully killed, and do you wish that it were to happen today? Consider that your whole life is to lead you toward this death. And see thus the insignificance of so many things. Think often of this death, both to pre-pare yourself for it and to judge things at their true value." [23]

Like Pascal, he despised the body, the flesh, because he measured the distance between the God who filled him with joy and human nature, so weak. Night brought him no rest. He stayed awake, his soul consumed. As soon as morning came, he would whip his poor, rebellious body to tame it. He feared neither suffering nor death but hoped and prayed for them. He feared only "displeasing the divine Master" and straying from him, falling back into the dark night of the spirit. He feared sin, the devil. And so he was excessively scrupulous; that went along with his anguished nature. According to him, his sins were his lack of attentiveness and his lack of feeling, especially during adoration; his inability to imitate the divine model, his inability to love boundlessly, for he was held back by "all that remained in him of the human and the unconsumed, the carnal and the untrans-formed", writes Marguerite Castillon.

Finally, the "evil" that made him suffer was that he could never succeed in "being nothing", that is, he could never kill his ego, with which he had grappled the day of his conversion.

But how could he "be nothing"? Even dressed in rags, fasting and mortifying himself, he would never be *poor* in the ordinary sense of the word. He would never be able to hide his aristocratic birth, his education, his culture, and his intelligence, all of which gave others that much more reason to consider his present life "saintly", a word already uttered by every one of his former superiors. And he felt that in this reputation lay the real danger: an insidious pride. Which explains why he intensified his mortifi-cations. Wherever he went, people were astonished, not to say shocked. He traveled on foot. If he had to be burdened with a mule, he would walk beside it. He refused money from any source and begged for bread on the road. He would sleep under the stars, like a real beggar. But he was not a real beggar, nor would he ever be. He was richer than the sultan of Constantinople, and he knew it.

Father Huvelin himself could not resolve the paradox: "Not to seek the exceptional, at the same time striving for the utmost perfection." It is obvious that Charles thought only of the exceptional, even in abjection and obscurity. And most significant, in *imitation*: "Like Christ, we shall always have the cross. Like him, we shall always be persecuted. Like him, we shall always appear to be defeated. Like him, we shall always in reality

---

[23] "Retraite à Nazareth," June 6, 1897, in *Oeuvres spirituelles* (Nouvelle Cité, 1974–97).

be triumphant. And that insofar as we are faithful to grace, insofar as we let Christ live in us and act in us and through us." [24]

To satisfy his thirst for activity, at the request of Father Huvelin he wrote his *Méditations*. Here again he fell into excess: three thousand pages in three years! They make up almost the entirety of his *Écrits spirituels*, which from a literary point of view do not reach the quality of works by John of the Cross and Teresa of Avila, his models. But he did not write with a literary purpose. He was pouring out his heart.

In early 1898, on a pilgrimage to Galilee, Charles finally reached the greatest of spiritual heights, mystical illumination. He merged with Christ, his model. He saw him on the roads of Palestine, where he had written the story of salvation: "Gift of an exceptional intimacy, which seemed to have been accorded him as a never-to-be-exhausted treasure" (Castillon), and which explains the rest of his heroic adventure. He felt "the kiss of Jesus' lips on his face, Jesus' hand, which he was allowed to hold for a long while".[25] He saw Jesus: "Some days, toward night, your hand is raised to bless your child." [26] Pressed against his chest on April 7, 1898, day of the Passion, "the nuptial day", Charles actually felt Christ's heart beating against his own. And he asked himself: "Who entered me? Who united with me in a union that has no earthly name, that the mind does not comprehend? In a divine union. You united with me, Lord, by means of a divine miracle and in a supernatural way."

And the unutterable dialogue begins: " 'Ask. Ask with faith, my child.' 'May your heart be consoled to the fullest by all men. I find nothing I desire more fervently than that.' " [27]

And so Charles reached the heights of mystical union. He would know other such moments, but never of the same intensity. With the naïveté of a child, he gave an account of his experiences in the *Écrits spirituels*, never imagining that someday people could read it.

Back in Nazareth, the light of the living God was still so apparent in his face that the Clares no longer had any doubt: this beggar who had landed at their door and had become their obedient servant was indeed a saint!

Yet he could not be satisfied with this happiness in God, the egotism of which he soon began to dread. Doubt gripped him once more: "The soul sees itself rejoicing, gloating, receiving much", he wrote to Father Huvelin.

---

[24] CF to Father Caron, June 30, 1897.
[25] CF, "Méditations", in *Écrits spirituels*, February 28, 1898.
[26] Ibid.
[27] Ibid., April 7, 1898.

"But it does not give back, it remains useless. And the more I rejoiced, the more I wanted to work."[28]

He even came to miss the Trappists! "A wish to return to the obedience that embraces every moment, the obedience through which every act becomes an act of pure love."[29]

After coming to Nazareth in search of abjection and obscurity, he found happiness there! A situation he thought intolerable in a world where "so many souls are lost or in pain."[30]

He mortified himself and judged himself a "miserable being, so worthless, so helpless, so inept". But it was all in vain, for he became the cherished child of these good nuns, and he did not know what awaited him!

Mother Marie-Ange de Saint-Michel, abbess of the Nazareth Poor Clares, had of course kept her superior informed about Charles. Mother Élisabeth du Calvaire, fifty-seven, abbess of the Poor Clares of Jerusalem, was, despite her frail look, a strong woman of the Teresa of Avila type. Born in Sarlat in 1841, she had pursued her vocation against family opposition. Abbess of the Clares in Périgueux, in 1876 she had founded a monastery in Paray-le-Monial according to the strict primitive observance; then she had left her country with fourteen nuns to found in 1884 Sainte-Claire de Nazareth, the first Poor Clare house in Palestine. In 1889 she left Mother Marie-Ange in charge and went to Jerusalem, founding the house there, which she now headed. Her task was not easy. The two convents, being poor, survived only because of gifts from France.

At first Mother Élisabeth had been amused by Mother Marie-Ange's enthusiastic descriptions of her strange "domestic", "that unpaid servant who dresses like a pauper, talks and writes like a scholar, and prays like a saint".[31] Then she began to worry: "Aren't these daughters dupes of one of those eccentric characters not unheard of in the Holy Land?" Finally, intrigued, curious—a feminine sin!—she asked to see this phenomenon.

To keep from distressing Brother Charles, Mother Marie-Ange merely asked him if he would go to Jerusalem to deliver a personal letter to her superior. Delighted by the idea of a second trip to the Holy City, Charles set out on July 7, 1898, refusing to travel in the ordinary manner. No mount, no baggage, no food, no money. He would go on foot to Jerusalem (seventy-five miles), begging for his bread along the way. Sleeping briefly here and there under porches, he made the usual five-day journey in three

---

[28] CF to Father Huvelin, March 3, 1898.
[29] Ibid.
[30] Ibid., March 8, 1898.
[31] Quoted by Bazin, *Foucauld*, 167.

days, edifying the occasional traveling companion: "During the entire journey, his lips never ceased moving in prayer." [32]

Twice he walked for twelve hours straight, in sandals, fasting on the second day so he could receive Communion at Nābulus, where he arrived exhausted, his feet bloody.

Finally, on the third day he sighted the walls of Jerusalem, joy in his heart. The convent of the Poor Clares had been built outside the city, on the road to Bethany, opposite the Mount of Olives; there was a magnificent view of the Holy City. Since it was late, Charles did not dare disturb the sisters, and he slept on a rock near the convent gate.

The next morning, he was taken into the parlor, where, according to the strict rule, the mother abbess, concealed by a dark green serge curtain, spoke to him from behind the grille. They could not see each other, and that was a shame. For he would not see her round cheeks, her sparkling eyes, her resolute expression. And she would not see the flame burning in his eyes, the feet battered by the journey. But she heard him, and from his first words, forgetting about the letter he had brought her, she was conquered. Through Mother Marie-Ange, she already knew who he was, but she did not grow bored hearing him. She questioned him. He told her of his childhood, his conversion. She asked, "What has been your greatest sacrifice?"

"Separation from my family. Once I was with the Trappists, I suffered greatly. Not because of the community, since everyone there was very kind to me. But the thought of my family constantly tormented me. I said to myself at times: always, always, always; never, never, never. To live here always, never to see them again." [33]

Silence. She too knew the burden of separation. But silence could not separate these two beings with a great love of the Absolute. She exclaimed: "There is no question of your starting out again. They have told me that you arrived exhausted, with bloody feet. You shall stay with us a few days. We shall put you up in the chaplain's apartments."

"Outside your enclosure, leaning up against the thick wall, there is an empty hut not far from another hut occupied by a black couple."

"Our caretaker and his wife. You could use the other hut."

After he left, the mother abbess said to one of her nuns: "Mother Marie-Ange is not mistaken. He is truly a man of God. We have a saint in the house." [34]

Charles spent four days in Jerusalem, "happy to be retracing Jesus' footsteps once more". He returned there in September 1898, again on foot,

[32] Quoted by D. and R. Barrat, *Charles de Foucauld et la fraternité* (Seuil, 1958), 42.

[33] CF, *Le Voyageur dans la nuit* (Nouvelle Cité, 1979), 59.

[34] Quoted by Bazin, *Foucauld*, 168.

although Mother Marie-Ange had ordered him to leave with a mule! This time he stayed until February 18, 1899.

Mother Élisabeth was hoping to keep him there. Clearly they were enthralled with one another. Charles reported their conversations to Father Huvelin.[35]

Because she already had great plans for him, she asked in surprise: "Why aren't you a priest?"

"I wanted to leave my order. To remain in the last place. Francis of Assisi never served as a priest."

"The last place can also be attained by evangelizing with all the accompanying contradictions, difficulties, failures, slanders, persecution."

"I wish to imitate Christ."

"You could imitate him in his public life, instead of imitating him in his hidden life."

"I have nothing to live on."

"Once you are a priest, you would be our chaplain, here in the shadow of our enclosure. Here or in Nazareth."

"Such a prospect is not in accord with my vocation."

Silence. Then she struck home: "Take holy orders to become our chaplain, Brother Charles. Be our priest as long as you wish. While serving here, prepare some disciples in the shadow of our cloister. When you have a sufficient number, and the moment has come, you shall go with them where the Holy Spirit leads you."

He trembled. It was too good to be true! She pushed her advantage: "If you are to have disciples, in order to prepare them you really should be a priest."

He fought back, weakly. How could he not see the hand of Providence in this unexpected offer? After arriving as a beggar and turning into a servant, now he was being offered the opportunity to found, something for which he had long hoped and prayed. Then he felt pride gently nudging him. He immediately stepped back. "To found, there has to be a call from God. There has to be a mission. I cannot give one to myself."

"But one has to do something for one's fellow man. Your time seems to have arrived. You are forty years old."

"I think guiding souls is what I am least fit for in this world."

"If we waited to act until we were fit to do something, we would never act. What does your spiritual adviser think?"

"In his last letter, Father Huvelin said: 'Open your heart wide to receive what God gives.'[36] But he has also told me: 'Do not found.'"

---

[35] CF to Father Huvelin, 91–97, and Bazin, *Foucauld*, 173.
[36] Father Huvelin to CF, March 16, 1898.

"Speak to him again. The context has changed."

When asked, Father Huvelin remained perplexed. Naturally, it delighted him that Charles was finally considering the priesthood. He had to admit that what he had not been able to obtain in twelve years of guidance, a weak woman had obtained after a few conversations from behind a curtain! Charles confessed to him ingenuously, "The abbess is a spiritual mother to me: head of ice and heart of fire; indomitable strength of character." [37]

Mother Élisabeth had awakened in him his most secret desire: to found. It became an obsession. But first, he had to convince Father Huvelin, whom he had promised to obey. "There is in me a secret desire to found a community. I envision the rule of Saint Benedict, but simpler, freed of the multitude of vocal prayers that burden it. And more poverty, more work; less ceremony, so that much time can be given to silent prayer and the inner life and to practicing charity at every opportunity." [38]

In a letter written October 22, 1898, he elaborated: "I dream of something very simple, resembling the communities of the early days of the Church; a few souls gathered together to lead the life of Nazareth, to live from their work, like the Holy Family; a small family, a small monastic household, very small, very simple, contemplating Jesus, in one of those solitary places in the Holy Land, in the simplicity of early times." [39]

As to the possession of goods in common, on that point he remained inflexible; everything was to be set up with adoration in mind.

But Father Huvelin refused to give his consent. "Stay in deep obscurity. Leave things as they are. Wait for an unmistakable sign." [40]

And so Charles continued to be torn. He wrote to Father Huvelin: "When I consult my head, it replies: for now, meditation. Later, priesthood and spiritual guidance of the Poor Clares. And if God wills it, the formation of a little nest of adoration. When I consult my heart, my inclinations: close all your books, never pick up a pen, remain a servant. And if the day comes when the nuns weary of you, go into the wilderness, and every day or two ask to be given for the sake of charity a crust of bread and a little water. Father Huvelin, you alone can reconcile my heart and my head."

He felt he was unfit to be a founder, judging himself "helpless, incapable". Just "a small child, definitely not through innocence and humility, but small through docility and a soul that is not yet fully formed, that has not grown, that has remained infantile, creeping along." [41]

---

[37] CF to Father Huvelin, October 15, 1898.
[38] Ibid.
[39] Ibid., October 22, 1898.
[40] Father Huvelin to CF, December 30, 1898.
[41] CF to Father Huvelin, February 8, 1899.

Father Huvelin continued to refuse his request. No foundation. Charles acquiesced. He had also been disappointed in his attempt to find at least one companion. In September 1898 he had gone to Akbès in hopes of recruiting Brother Pierre, a former novice, whom he had known at the Trappist house and whose late father was an Armenian Orthodox Christian. But Pierre declined the invitation to follow him. He had gone back to live with his mother. His mother! How well Charles understood that! So Charles was still "the little workman hidden in the shadow of Saint Clare". He would remain the only hermit at Sacré-Coeur.

But the repressed desire to be a founder was taking its emotional toll. Once again, he was tormented by his peaceful happiness, which, to his mind, seemed egotistical. He confessed to Father Huvelin, "My usual state is pleasure in the presence of Jesus. I think it would be better to work at bringing others that pleasure rather than enjoy it all alone." [42]

Thus his desire for activism always found justification in the legitimate obsession of the Christian: he could not be the only one saved. If the Christian's first duty is to love God, the second—indistinguishable from the first—is to love one's neighbor as oneself.

In waiting for the sign, he succumbed to the sweetness of living in the shadow of Jerusalem. He wrote his sister, "I live like a hermit, receiving everything I ask for and working as I wish, when I wish, at light tasks they ever so tactfully provide me so that I can say I am earning my keep. I don't know why the mother abbess had me come here, for I am not much use. Her aim is to be able to practice charity and to overwhelm me with acts of generosity. She is a saint." [43]

He enjoyed a solitude he found satisfying. He saw few people and came to the monastery gate like a pauper to receive his food. At noon, a milk soup, four figs, a spoonful of honey. Evenings, a piece of bread. He did not go into the city but gazed upon Jerusalem from the heights of his retreat. He could see the gilded cupolas of the sanctuaries, the palaces, then, in the distance, Bethany and the mountains of Moab and Edom rising like a somber wall on the other side of the River Jordan. And he would marvel that "God spared his puny, shorn lamb the slightest breeze." [44]

He observed the offices, and he slept two hours a night on two boards covered with a mat, a rock for a pillow. His few visitors marveled at his kindness and at the joy emanating from "this man without a house, without a family, without wealth, and without position". He was dubbed "the holy hermit of the Poor Clares". He called his neighbors (the black couple) "my brother" and "my sister", which overwhelmed the poor

[42] Ibid., March 8, 1898.
[43] CF to Marie de Blic, October 15, 1898, quoted by Bazin, *Foucauld*, 169.
[44] Ibid., 170.

scorned folk. But this gentle, humble man knew how to act forcefully when the need arose: one day he amazed the sisters by turning out, *manu militari*, a group of Italian beggars noisily occupying the monastery court-yard.

Patiently Mother Élisabeth continued to talk to him of the priesthood, but he would counter her with his usual argument: the last place. For to his eyes, nothing was more grand than a priest. Her answer to that: "If you have received gifts, increased by study and long years of spiritual activity, was it only so you yourself could make use of them?"

"Being a priest means a public role. I am made for the hidden life."

She began to dream: "Ah, if I were a man, I would not hesitate. To spread a new blessing on earth or to keep it in the heavens . . . One more Mass, that is an act of grace for mankind!"

But he shook his head stubbornly. Then, she played her last card: she enjoined the community of Poor Clares to pray. Moved, Charles finally said: "Speak to Father Huvelin."

Which she did. Obviously, the vicar of Saint-Augustin's also hoped that Charles would become a priest. Charles knew that, so he was expecting a positive response. After all, to be a priest was to imitate Christ fully, for he was the supreme priest, offering himself at the altar daily. But Charles wanted to hold on to the unique aspects of his semi-eremitical vocation. Thus no parish, no monastery, no mission. Since what he was seeking did not exist, he would have to found an order so he could become his ideal: a silent, contemplative priest with an austere life and a fixed abode. But Father Huvelin did not agree.

On February 18, 1899, Charles was back in his shed in Nazareth, in the shadow of the Poor Clares' house. "Intense need for solitude", he wrote. Once again, with all his being, he sought to bury himself, to "contemplate the Beloved". On March 10, he received from Father Voisin the cord of Saint Francis of Assisi; he tied the Franciscan rope around his waist.

Patiently Father Huvelin had renewed his spiritual guidance. His letters flowed like honey: "Stay in the peace of this blessed retreat. Take what God gives, without searching in agitation. Make use of things as if you were not using them, employing them only in the service of God, and with detachment from yourself." [45]

"We obey in silence. We do good by what we are more than by what we say. We do good by being of God, by belonging to God. Yes, stability. Gather moss. Let the grace of God penetrate, grow, and solidify in the soul. Avoid agitation and endless new beginnings. It is true that we are

---

[45] Father Huvelin to CF, April 18, 1899.

always beginners, but at least it is always in the same way and the same direction." [46]

And in answer to a question from Charles, who, sleeping only a few hours nightly, would doze during offices. "Do not fret over depriving yourself of sleep, and do not set a minimum for which to strive. Such a minimum does not exist, because you will always think you ought make it even lower. Get as much rest as you need in order to be able to think clearly. Do not take a humiliation as a fault but as an opportunity for gentle, agreeable humility. That is what you are doing with the unfortunate slumber to which you sometimes succumb. It is not an act of infidelity." [47]

This wise advice apparently went unheeded. Charles was letting agitation regain its hold on him. He was too happy in Nazareth; it could not last! He was enjoying a "life of delights, living in clover".[48] He decided he would leave the Clares, for the same reasons he had left the Trappists. Ah! That vow of stability imposed by Saint Benedict.

In April 1900, not long after he had taken as his device *Jesus caritas*, with a heart and a cross, he was offered an opportunity that would allow him to combine the priesthood with the founding of a new order. The "Mount of Beatitudes" was up for sale, and Charles glowed with enthusiasm. Here, on this little grassy hill overlooking Lake Tiberias, Jesus supposedly delivered the Sermon on the Mount, the Beatitudes. The place was wild and somewhat hostile. Charles could already picture himself there, solitary and inspired, offering the Holy Sacrifice amidst Muslim shepherds. Under these conditions he would accept the priesthood. But not to become the most reverend father abbot of a traditional monastery or the chaplain-idol of the holy daughters of Nazareth!

He immediately sought permission from Father Huvelin. But the vicar proved completely opposed to a purchase that would require a large sum— thirteen thousand francs—which Charles obviously did not have. He doubted the place's authenticity and did not want to see Charles mixed up in what seemed to him a dubious transaction: the sales agent, Lendli by name, was handling the matter on behalf of the Franciscans and also claimed to represent the Turkish government. Huvelin could not see Charles isolated on the "mount", without financial support. And why did the Franciscans not want the land? "I see nothing but objections, and your willfulness frightens me", he concluded.

Charles was upset by this response, but for the first time he ignored his mentor; he went back to Jerusalem. On June 17, 1900, he turned the

[46] Ibid., July 18, 1899.
[47] Ibid., October 26, 1899.
[48] CF to Father Huvelin, April 26, 1900.

payment over to Lendli, the thirteen thousand francs having been generously provided by Marie de Blic.[49] Then, plunging ahead at breakneck
speed, June 22 he met with the Latin patriarch of Jerusalem. He needed
Bishop Piavi's consent to establish a new order. While he was at it, he
would ask him for the priesthood . . .

Dressed like a beggar, he appeared before the patriarch without any
letters of introduction. Bishop Piavi barely listened and then dismissed
him. "He sent me away rather briskly", Charles would write to a friend.[50]

On his return to Nazareth on July 4, Charles learned that the so-called
salesman of the Beatitudes was a crook. He had taken off with the thirteen
thousand francs! Philosophical, Charles accepted this new setback with
detachment. "Let us not attach too much importance to the events of our
lives or to material things. They are simply passing dreams",[51] he wrote his
sister as a kind of funeral oration for the stolen money, which Marie would
never see again.

But something remained following this incident. Charles was still determined to become a priest. But he would have to leave. In Nazareth he had
given himself over to mystical union with Christ and had forgotten about
union with mankind. What good was it to have given up his life as a reveler
to become a "mystical reveler", another form of egotistical pleasure? He
wanted to imitate Jesus. Mother Élisabeth was right. Jesus had left his
hidden life of contemplation in Nazareth to throw himself into the world
and serve there. Clearly, Christ wanted him elsewhere: "As soon as his will
summons one here or there, one must run, fly, give up solitude, throw
oneself among men." [52]

Leave, for where? "The wilderness." Not to bury himself as he had done
three times—at Neiges, Cheiklé, and Nazareth. But to dwell among the
most disinherited of the earth and bring them the good news of Christ.
For him, wilderness meant the deserts of Africa. Suddenly he recalled his
travels in Morocco.

And also, there was the temptation of martyrdom. In June 1896, learning
of the death of the Marquis de Morès-Vallombrosa, murdered by his own
guides while exploring the Libyan desert, Charles had said: "Within the
great charity that abounds in heaven, there is nothing but prayer and love
for those Muslims who have spilled his blood and who will perhaps spill
mine."

The wilderness. Jesus too went into the wilderness. "We must go into
the wilderness and abide there to receive the grace of God. It is there we

---

[49] Around four hundred thousand in today's French francs.
[50] CF, June 26, 1900, quoted by Bazin, *Foucauld*, 178.
[51] CF to Marie de Blic, July 21, 1900, quoted by Bazin, *Foucauld*, 178.
[52] CF, *Écrits spirituels*, 114.

cleanse ourselves, rid ourselves of all that is not God", he wrote Father Jérôme.[53]

The wilderness. But not to preach there as did those fine missionaries, the White Fathers with the long patriarchal beards. His inner vision illuminated, Charles could see Mary sanctifying Saint John through the Visitation, the pregnant Mary silently carrying Jesus. "Just as do those monks and priests dedicated to contemplation in all the mission lands. They come there to evangelize and sanctify wordlessly, while carrying in silence Jesus, the living image of the evangelical life. O beloved Mother, it is your very own mission, the first with which Jesus entrusted you, that you have deigned to share with us by calling us to this life." [54]

He heard the voice crying out in the wilderness: "In all the pages of his books, God commends to us his poor children, his disinherited children. Let us heed his voice, let us be the fathers, the brothers, the children of these unfortunates. Let us be their consolation, their refuge, their shelter, their hearth, their paternal home. . . . Let us concern ourselves with those who lack everything, those of whom no one thinks. Let us be the friends of those who have no friends." [55]

All Tamanrasset is contained in those generous words.

But first, to be a priest. Since Bishop Piavi wanted nothing to do with him, he would return to France and ask the archbishop of Paris to make of him a kind of independent missionary priest: no parish, no monastery. As a formality, he asked for Father Huvelin's approval, but, receiving no answer, he sailed from Jaffa for Marseille on August 8, 1900, traveling fourth class, with no luggage other than his breviary. Meanwhile Father Huvelin had replied July 25: "Stay in Nazareth." But the letter arrived after Charles' departure. An irresistible force was now propelling him toward what he had always rejected: the priesthood.

Tamanrasset, December 1, 1916, 2 P.M.

Brother Charles, kneeling on the sand in his chapel, was reciting with fervor the office of None:

> Lord,
> Spread this evening the true light,
> Light of life, day without end.
> And when death strikes,
> Gather us unto your light.

[53] CF to Father Jérôme, May 31, 1898.
[54] CF, *Considération sur les fêtes de l'année*, July 2, 1898 (Nouvelle Cité, 1987).
[55] CF, "Retraite à Nazareth", in *Oeuvres spirituelles*, 1898.

Then he rose and went to the gate of the fort.

The procession of poor had begun. But the word "poor" did not mean much here. All the Haratins were poor. But some of them, like Paul Embarek, worked. Paul was poor, since he had nothing except the clay hut he had built for carrying on his romance with Tablalt and the tiny garden he maintained at the foot of the high arid plateau, a fragile pocket of soil constantly threatened by drought and by the sand that had to be painstakingly removed. The little chores he did for the priest were paid in grain, three pounds a day. Paul was pleased, for the priest had increased his salary. When he had first arrived, he would receive only two pounds (worth around twelve cents), which he would take home every evening after his work was done.

Worst off were former slaves with no work, the infirm elderly, repudiated wives, and orphans. Paradoxically, the abolition of slavery had increased their misery. Nowadays, a man or woman who could no longer do the work would be cast aside by the master without a second thought. Why should he be burdened with such people?

Charles knew them well. In Helouat and his wife, Shaket, and their three sons, Fadimata, Lilli, Azoum; their two daughters, Fota and Tekadeit. They had also taken in a niece, for no one is more generous than a pauper. Similarly, Tiloul, a woman who owned nothing but her reed hut, supported several elderly, infirm aunts. To all these folk, Charles would give a handful of wheat or a few dates, something to keep them from starvation for another day.

Despite their poverty, the nomads and the sedentary Tuareg had a few animals. This one might rent out his camel; that one might keep goats, source of a little milk. Sheep provided meat, milk, and wool, which the women used for knitting, a skill taught them by young Ouksem after his trip to France. And actually, the men had taken up knitting too. It was better than simply talking all day long with nothing to do. A real revolution, of which Brother Charles was proud!

The *rezzou* of Beuh ag Rhabelli had reached the Drîn well. A small caravan carrying rock salt between Tassili and Bilma was unlucky enough to pass by. It had no escort. The merchants expected to get away with merely paying the usual tribute but were disappointed. Armed only with blades, they could not defend themselves against the *rezzou* and were only too happy to have their lives spared. Kerzou had been unable to resist the bait and diverted two of his men to escort the stolen caravan to a hideout in the Ajjer. Enormous blocks of salt weighing more than forty pounds each and a dozen pack camels, what a fortune! In vain Beuh tried to dissuade him. Were they not going to need their full strength to capture the fort?

"There you won't be finding any twenty cakes of salt, but grain, canned goods, weapons and ammunition, maybe even gold."

The merchants, cleaned out, walked toward Hirafok, the road to Taman-rasset forbidden them so they would not sound the alarm.

The *rezzou* set out again. The Tuareg were pleased. This profitable bit of plunder heralded better times ahead for the *rezzous* once the Franks had been driven from the Sahara.

9

Priest of Jesus Christ

Charles de Foucauld arrived in Paris on August 8, 1900, and, rather embarrassed, appeared before a stunned Father Huvelin. His face was gaunt with fatigue, but his flashing eyes showed unwavering determination. At the sight of this prodigal son, the vicar immediately melted with tenderness. He said later, "The cannonball was fired, and who could stop it? He was well aware of my opinion, but something stronger impelled him, and all I could do was admire and love him. A very holy soul."[1]

After this emotional moment they talked.

"And what do you wish to do now?"

"What would God like me to do? That which consists of the greatest love. The greatest love is in the closest imitation. Where shall I find the closest imitation of the life of Nazareth? In the order of the Little Brothers of the Sacred Heart of Jesus that I wish to found with other souls. Therein lies what God would like me to do."[2]

"But how can you discriminate between what is the divine will and what is your own?"

"By the object's appeal to my secret desires; by an inner impulse that I feel has to be followed. While I am experiencing these attractions and impulses, I gauge their durability and their nature. Time and grace allow me to discern. If the action considered stems from God's will, eventually it becomes imperative." Charles bowed his head and added in a humble tone: "And an inner impulse can be authenticated by humbly submitting it to the scrutiny of one's spiritual adviser . . ."[3]

Father Huvelin was baffled. Why did he, a miserable priest burdened with poor health, have to be the one to settle this emotional debate between God and the passionate creature who had one day stepped into his confessional? Spiritual adviser! Then he faced up to it. Summoning the little strength he had left, he tried to understand, to *discern*.

Charles' life was indeed centered on the imitation of the living God. But how could he carry that out in practical terms? He could not stand

---

[1] Quoted by Bazin, *Charles de Foucauld* (Plon, 1921), 182.
[2] CF, "Retraite de diaconat", in *Oeuvres spirituelles* (Nouvelle Cité, 1974–1997), 531.
[3] Quoted by R. Quesnel, *Charles de Foucauld, les étapes d'une recherche* (Mame, 1966), 116.

living in an ordinary monastery or even nearby, outside the gates. He could not help comparing the life led by monks with the exigencies of the evangelical life, summed up in the radical "forsake everything and follow me". Under these conditions, he could do nothing but live like a hermit. Yet he needed others: therein lay his weakness, his only weakness, heritage of his childhood desertion. He also wanted to give of himself to others, directly, physically. Accordingly, he hoped to live his own rule with a few select companions. He wanted a community designed to suit him. In that case, was he still being faithful to his vocation, or was he confusing his own will with that of God? For he was setting up, without compromise, a rule of his own that had not even received the approval of the Magisterium.

Father Huvelin saw in this chosen being a disturbing alternation between euphoria and anguish, between doubt and determination. The most painstakingly devised plans were abandoned in favor of uncertain enterprises, such as the Mount of Beatitudes monastery. Incapable of settling down in one place, was he really amenable to the working of grace? Was he really seeking the last place? Was he still faithful to the original call? He seemed so fickle, so unstable, at times the slave of the intense forces of a volcanic temperament.

Certainly, he was noble. He sought perfection. But that made him lapse into excess. His rule seemed utopian. And how could he reconcile the exigencies of a solitary life devoted to adoration with the need to be accessible to humanity? He had such a personalized concept of the hidden life, so much fierceness and exaggeration in his desires, and a tendency toward willfulness that he had not yet overcome. And yet he remained obedient and was still faithful to the base on which his vocation stood: the imitation of Christ, with whom he felt merged, in a genuine mystical communion. [4]

Father Huvelin opened his eyes. Charles was waiting, humble and submissive. The priest smiled. "You must be defended against this movement toward the infinite, which results in restlessness and your never settling in one place. Such movement is possible only in hearts where there is never excess." [5]

Never excess! When the heart is overflowing, let it burst with love and the presence of God!

"Dear Father Huvelin, this is not one of those undertakings that attains success through human means; it is the breath of the Holy Spirit, to be pursued in simplicity of heart and with the zeal and faithfulness of love." [6]

[4] Ibid., 100–112.

[5] Father Huvelin to CF, August 2, 1896, in G. Gorrée, *Sur les traces de Charles de Foucauld* (Éd. de la Plus Grande France, 1936), 89.

[6] "Retraite d'ordination", in *Oeuvres spirituelles*, 534.

Father Huvelin surrendered: "I have no more advice I can give you. Keep your heart ready, and let it be filled with what Christ wishes to place there."[7]

Charles hoped to receive the priesthood quickly and called upon the good relationship between the vicar of Saint-Augustin's and the "ordinary of Paris", Cardinal Richard. And in addition the archbishop could be asked to back up his request to Rome for approval of the order of the Hermits of the Sacred Heart or Little Brothers of Jesus. But the archbishop took no interest in him. Neither in his priesthood nor in his monastic plans. His Eminence had no use for a little gyrovague who had spent the last ten years wandering between the Cistercians and the Franciscans.

Never mind! Charles would go to Rome and see the pope. And he had another reason for going to Rome: Mother Élisabeth had entrusted him with taking the first steps toward the creation of a convent there to support her two communities in Palestine.

Endowed with Father Huvelin's blessing and some financial help, he left Paris. He had not been to the World's Fair, nor had he seen Marie de Bondy. It was extremely painful for him to know that she was so near. But they had vowed never to see each other again in this world. Marie did not even know he was in Paris. Nor did she know that he was going to Rome, where she herself was heading for Jubilee Year events. They may have even traveled on the same train, she in first class, he in third . . .

Charles did not go directly to Rome. He planned to stop at Notre-Dame-des-Neiges to ask his former abbot for the priesthood, which they had denied him in Jerusalem and Paris. Leaving the express train at Valence, he boarded the local, which huffed and puffed its way up the slopes of the Vivarais. He finished his journey on foot, praying constantly, his heart joyful at the thought of seeing again the beloved monastery that stood alone on the high plateau. Arriving incognito at the gates of the abbey at nightfall, he mingled with the half dozen beggars waiting there. At the appointed hour, the brother porter came out to greet them: "Enter, my friends! Good soup and a place to sleep await you!"

He had not recognized Brother Albéric in the dusty garments of Brother Charles. Thoroughly delighted by his anonymity, Charles ate thick soup and black bread with the paupers, then he slept beside them on the straw of the barn. It was only the next morning that he revealed his identity before going to early Mass. After the office, he knelt before Dom Martin, the abbot, and kissed his ring. Then he explained.

Dom Martin was happy to see his novice. Notre-Dame-des-Neiges was open to him if he wished to prepare for the priesthood. Since he was no

---

[7] Father Huvelin to CF, May 7, 1901.

longer a Cistercian, they would ask the bishop of the diocese (Viviers) to ordain him. It was as simple as that.

But already, Charles wanted to leave. For where? Rome, to obtain approval for his fraternities. Dom Martin succeeded only in getting him to give up his Middle Eastern costume, giving him the sober black frock of a Trappist oblate.

After arriving in Rome the night of August 29, Charles looked for a place to stay. Having refused the aid offered by the abbot of Neiges, he did not have a sou. First he knocked on the Cistercians' door; but Dom Wyart was away, and Charles was not so bold as to ask for lodging. Then he went on to the headquarters of the Capuchins with Mother Élisabeth's letter for the father general. He was not at home either. They agreed to put him up, but for only four days. Would that be long enough to gain an audience with the pope? Obviously not. Would the pope see him at all?

On September 3, he sought lodging from the Fathers of the Blessed Sacrament, who turned him over to the Bassettis, a devout family on Via Pozzetto. While waiting for his papal audience, Charles visited the tombs of the apostles and the Roman basilicas "to earn the indulgence of the Jubilee". On one such visit, he ran into a Capuchin missionary just back from Ethiopia. This priest, apostolic vicar of the Galla people, admitted he had come to Rome to be made a bishop.

Africa! Charles was startled. Bishop André Jarosseau describes their meeting:

> When I mentioned to him our Abyssinia, his whole being trembled, and he soon asked me to take him with me to work for the conversion of the Ethiopians. His look—pathetic, mortified, sorrowful, but at moments illuminated—reminded me of my seraphic father Saint Francis. This touching similarity led me to accept his offer, and upon that, we set out together on a walking tour of the holy basilicas so as to earn the indulgences of the Grand Jubilee.
>
> During our walk, we happened to go by the door of the community of the Fathers of the Blessed Sacrament. He asked me if he could go into the house to greet someone he knew and to obtain a letter of recommendation I had asked him to provide me. What happened in this house, which must have been inhabited by the angel of the Bedouins of Tamanrasset? He never came out. And that is how it was that the mission to the Galla tribes never had the glory of numbering Charles de Foucauld among its missionaries.[8]

The anecdote demonstrates Charles' uncertainty regarding his future. But he remained openly fascinated by Africa.

---

[8] *Bulletin des missions catholiques*, December 12, 1924.

He finally saw the pope September 6. But to see is not to have dealings with. It was merely a general audience, not the private one he had been unable to obtain. The radiant gaze of Leo XIII—age ninety—met the burning gaze of Charles de Foucauld, which then disappeared amid the sea of faces. As for the order he wished to start, Charles found himself referred to Vatican bureaucrats, who told him to go through hierarchical channels, that is, consult his bishop.

Just as Charles had not seen Marie in Paris, he did not see her in Rome. "I was deeply moved at finding myself once again near you, here in this Rome where you were just a short time ago", he wrote her on September 3.[9]

After his return to Notre-Dame-des-Neiges on September 29, Charles buried himself in a blessed spiritual retreat interrupted by intensive theological studies. Dom Martin had given in to his wish not to live among the community and had set him up in a little cell in the attic of the church. He reached it through the sacristy staircase, outside the enclosure. From his cell, he could reach a little gallery from which he could witness the offices without being seen. He spent his nights up there in contemplation. The brother sacristan would bring him one light meal a day. The father subprior gave him instruction in theology.

On October 7, 1900, a joyful Dom Martin conferred upon him the minor orders. The abbot wrote Marie de Bondy, "I have had this pleasure. It is the greatest of my life." Then Charles went into retreat for the subdeaconate. Again, he wondered about his future. Father Huvelin was urging him to return to the Holy Land and become the chaplain of the Poor Clares. Material security with the sisters, stability, the sweetness of the contemplative life. But Charles increasingly envisioned a small community, the Hermits of the Sacred Heart, in "that African Sahara where so many souls are without evangelizers", he said.

On December 22, 1900, Bishop Bonnet of Viviers ordained him a subdeacon. "Bonds especially sweet and strong", Charles wrote Marie de Bondy, unaware that he was torturing her. "They contain the solemn vow of chastity; it is most definitely a marriage."[10]

Then Father Léon Laurens, a young priest from the diocese of Mende, began to teach him to say Mass. "His spirit was taken over by prayer. The *Introibo ad altare Dei* was enough to plunge him into 'distractions' in the manner of Saint Ignatius. So accustomed was he to the exercise of being in the presence of God, where he was totally submerged in mystical union, that he would enter into that presence at the slightest opportunity,

---

[9] CF to Marie de Bondy, in *Bulletin des Amitiés*, no. 75. In the same issue, see Father Sourisseau's detailed study on C. de Foucauld's 1900 stay in Rome.

[10] CF to Marie de Bondy, December 24, 1900, in Gorrée, *Sur les traces*, 111.

sometimes in spite of himself. Recovering, he would throw himself at my feet and ask for forgiveness. I was deeply affected. One only had to see Brother Albéric for a few minutes to receive the distinct impression that one was in the presence of a saint." [11]

He was ordained a deacon March 23, 1901, in Nîmes, by Bishop Béguinot, Bishop Bonnet being ill.

It was during the retreat for the deaconate that Charles changed the expression "Hermit of the Sacred Heart" to "Little Brother of the Heart of Jesus", which would henceforth be his own. He no longer saw any contradiction between the priestly function and the essential poverty. Together, they were the offering of himself in full to God's will, the giving of himself to the very poor, even to the point of martyrdom, if need be.

On June 8, Dom Martin and Brother Charles climbed into the light cart that was to take them to Viviers for the new priest's ordination. "Bring enough food for both of us", the father abbot said. Around noon, feeling hungry, he suggested to Charles, "Let us stop a while to lunch in the shade of these trees." Charles stopped the horse and took a small package from his pocket. In it were six dried figs and four nuts. He shared them with the dumbfounded abbot, then he offered him the water bottle.

On June 9, 1901, in the cathedral in Viviers, a deeply fervent Charles de Foucauld was ordained by Archbishop de Montéty, a Lazarist, archbishop of Beirut and onetime apostolic delegate in Persia. Bishop Bonnet, present at the impressive ceremony, was so overcome that he had been unable to officiate himself. He was already genuinely attached to this strange man of God. Charles, henceforth priest of the Viviers diocese, was never to carry out his functions there, but he had a place always in the bishop's heart. Charles would write to Marie de Bondy, "For me, he is still the best, the most tender and loving father. What wisdom and what strength of character." [12]

While Charles was encountering almost everywhere obstacles to the foundation of his order, Bishop Bonnet was the first in the hierarchy to welcome it, encourage it, and approve of it: "Yes, I approve of your planned Union of Brothers and Sisters of the Sacred Heart of Jesus. But if God wants it to become a reality, how many obstacles it is going to encounter and how much suffering will be required before it wins its place in the sun of the Holy Church!" [13]

Dom Martin and Father Charles de Foucauld headed back to Notre-Dame-des-Neiges the same day, arriving at 1 A.M. Charles spent the rest of the night in adoration in the church, remaining until the morning of June 10, when he would celebrate his first Mass there.

[11] *Bulletin des Amitiés*, nos. 4–5, 60.
[12] CF to Marie de Bondy, April 11, 1902, in Gorrée, *Sur les traces*, 146.
[13] Quoted by J.-F. Six, *L'Aventure de l'amour de Dieu* (Seuil, 1993), 55.

Marie de Blic, his sister, was nearby! Intense emotion. With Marie de Bondy out of his life,[14] little Mimi was his only connection with his tragic childhood, with his vanished parents. Aged forty in 1901, married for sixteen years to banker Raymond de Blic—an upright, exacting man, a perfectionist—who had given her six children, she was worn out from her heavy household responsibilities at the Château de Barbirey. Scrupulous, delicate, she was still the anxious little girl who feared sin and denied herself pleasure. Detesting social activities, she liked only reading and study, blossoming only in the education of her children, who wore her out. Practicing an unconscious Jansenism, like her brother, she imposed mortifications on herself, but, unlike Charles, without ever having the fulfillment of mystical union.

Mimi had arrived at Notre-Dame-des-Neiges the night before. Charles, gone to Viviers, had left a note for her: "I am going to sit and have a long chat with you. Wait for me in your room. Make sure that you have a good meal after receiving Communion. Rest assured that your coming here is truly a joyous occasion for the community, which, full of illusions about me, loves me a thousand times more than I deserve." [15]

At 6:30 A.M. Charles, who had not slept all night, was present at the community's early Mass. Then at 7:30 A.M. he celebrated his first Mass. Mimi was there, hidden in a little lateral chapel outside the cloister, reserved for visitors. Through a grille, Charles gave her Communion. She wept. She knew that, after the long face-to-face chat in the parlor, she would probably never see her adored brother again.

And now? Father Huvelin, who did not think him mature enough to embark on a spiritual adventure alone, advised him to remain at Neiges another year to gain a more profound sense of his vocation. "Keep your heart ready." [16] "Wait until you are given a nearly irresistible push toward the mission you seem to have received." [17]

But Charles thought only of leaving, of making a deep commitment without delay. To go where? "I must go not where the land is the most holy but where souls are in the greatest need. In the Holy Land, priests and monks are present in great numbers, and there are few souls to win", he had already noted in his "Retraite de diaconat".[18]

[14] But he wrote to her on April 23, 1901: "Since God made you the first instrument of his mercies toward me, it is from you that they all flow. If you had not converted me, brought me to Jesus, and taught me little by little, word by word, what is pious and good, would I be at the point where I am today?" (CF to Marie de Bondy, April 23, 1901).

[15] Quoted by Bazin, *Foucauld*, 189.

[16] Father Huvelin to CF, May 7, 1901.

[17] Ibid., May 29, 1901.

[18] CF, "Retraite de diaconat", in *Oeuvres spirituelles*, March 1901.

The African Sahara still fascinated him. "My place is in the desert. To establish myself *over there*, to be a priest and a hermit, for I believe that would be to the great glory of God, even if I remained alone, and even more so if he were to send me companions", he noted in his *Écrits spirituels*. Naturally, he was thinking of Morocco. But Morocco was still impenetrable.

In a letter to his friend Henri de Castries,[19] dated June 23, 1901, he spelled out his intentions: "We would like to found on the Moroccan frontier, not a Trappist house, or a great rich monastery, or a large farm, but a small and humble sort of hermitage where a few poor monks could live off some produce and a little barley harvested with their own hands, in a small cloister, in penance and adoration, not preaching but giving shelter to all comers, good or bad, friend or foe, Muslim or Christian. This is evangelization, not through words, but through the presence of the Most Blessed Sacrament, the offering of the divine sacrifice, prayer, penance, the practice of evangelic virtues, universal and brotherly charity, sharing down to our last mouthful of bread with every pauper, every guest, every stranger who arrives, and receiving every human being as if he were a beloved brother." [20]

He wanted to go where the most deprived dwelled. In Africa, "among the most abandoned flocks, the lame, the blind, and the poor. I think there are no people more neglected."[21]

Father Huvelin finally gave in: "Go where the Master calls you", he told him on July 15, 1901.

The southern reaches of Morocco and Algeria are vast. Where would he go? Aïn Sefra, Taghit, Igli, Beni Abbès? Those regions were not yet pacified and, in addition, were forbidden territory even for the African missionary order, the White Fathers. For Charles, just one more reason to go there. On August 22, 1901, he wrote to Bishop Bazin, apostolic vicar of the French Sudan and Sahara, who resided in Bamako: "The memory of my companions who died without the sacraments in the expeditions against Bou Amama twenty years ago, in which I took part, impels me to leave for the Sahara. I humbly ask Your Excellency for the privilege to set up,

[19] Count Henri de Castries, ahead of Foucauld at Saint-Cyr, was a legendary figure of the North African conquest. Officer and geographer, in 1876 he had carried out a study in Morocco that influenced Foucauld. In 1881, Lieutenant de Castries, whom the indigenous people called Bou Serr, "man of the secret", had taken part in the campaign against Bou Amama, but he had refused to see Foucauld because of his bad reputation. After Foucauld's exploration of Morocco, the two became friends. Foucauld would later refer to him as "my best friend, my brother, my very soul". Their correspondence began in 1901 with this first letter.

[20] Quoted by Gorrée, *Sur les traces*, June 23, 1901, 113.

[21] CF to Father Caron, April 8, 1905, quoted by Bazin, *Foucauld*, 187.

between Aïn Sefra and the Touat, in one of the French garrisons without a priest, a small public oratory and also permission to be joined there by companions, if Jesus sends me them, priests or laymen, and to practice there with them adoration, my being the chaplain of this humble oratory, without title of curate or vicar or chaplain, and with no subsidy, our living as monks in prayer, poverty, work, charity, without preaching, without traveling, silent and cloistered. Charles de Foucauld, unworthy priest." [22]

On August 25, Father Huvelin sent the prelate the following letter of recommendation: "You will see in him heroic devotion, unlimited endurance, a calling to influence the Muslim world, humble and patient zeal, obedience within his zeal and enthusiasm, a spirit of penance with no thought of censure or harshness." [23]

And Dom Martin had already written his letter on July 15: "Never in my life have I seen a man who comes so close to the ideal of holiness. Never had I seen outside of books such marvels of penance, humility, poverty, and love of God." [24]

But the northern Sahara territories were no longer the responsibility of Bishop Bazin. Bishop Guérin had just been named apostolic prefect for the Sahara, his seat Ghardaïa. Dom Henri, prior of Notre-Dame at Staoueli, wrote him on September 5: "This is the most beautiful soul I know. Of unbelievable generosity of spirit, he walks with giant steps along the road of sacrifice, and he has an insatiable desire to devote himself to the redemption of the infidel. He is capable of everything, except perhaps of accepting too strict a guidance. I have been edified by his heroic virtue. There is in him the stuff of several saints. His mere presence is an eloquent sermon, and, despite the apparent oddness of the mission to which he believes himself called, you may receive him with total confidence." [25]

For good measure, on September 1 Father Huvelin also wrote on his friend's behalf to Bishop Livinhac, superior general of the White Fathers of Maison-Carrée near Algiers:

Much enthusiasm, but much good sense. Much zeal, but much obedience. His love of mortification is a need that comes from his love of God. I have seen his vocation grow. I have seen him become more sensible because of it; it has made him more humble, more simple, more obedient. His problems at the Cistercian house came from his reluctance to receive holy orders. He did not dare!

Nothing bizarre or extraordinary, but an irresistible force that impels, a strong implement for rough tasks. Firmness, a desire to go the limit in love

---

[22] Quoted by Bazin, ibid., 192–93.

[23] Ibid., 191.

[24] Ibid., 192.

[25] Ibid., 196.

and giving; never discouragement, a little harshness formerly, but that has been tempered! Let him come at his own risk, see him in action, and judge.[26]

And Bishop Bonnet of Viviers, on September 5, 1901, wrote his own letter to Bishop Livinhac: "He broke off his career to give himself completely to God. He has acquired a reputation as a saint here, and our priests seek as if it were a great act of grace the pleasure of a few minutes in his presence." [27]

If he knew about them, these letters must have been most disturbing for the modest, "unworthy priest". But he might have recognized they were necessary after the series of bitter rejections he had endured in his somewhat too independent efforts to approach the patriarch of Jerusalem, the archbishop of Paris, and, finally, the Vatican.

And now, it was time to go! Following the advice of Major Cauchemez, Charles chose Beni Abbès, a large and prosperous oasis in southern Algeria, near the Moroccan border. Morocco, where he had hoped to go, was still inaccessible. France would not occupy it until 1906 (Treaty of Algeciras), with the protectorate agreement signed later, at Fez in 1912. Not a single Catholic priest resided in Morocco. The White Fathers were established in northern Algeria, but none of them crossed the parallel of Ghardaïa, on the threshold of the Sahara, the great unknown.

One last problem remained to be solved: the French administration, under the influence of the anticlerical government of Waldeck-Rousseau, was not fond of priests. Charles received a recommendation from his old classmate Major Lacroix, who headed the Department of Indigenous Affairs in Algiers. At the military outposts, they awaited with curiosity the arrival of Saint-Cyr and Saumur's onetime renegade, the ex-viscount and partygoer, Charles de Foucauld, *Père Foucauld*!

Early in September, Charles left with sincere regret that "little nest", Notre-Dame-des-Neiges, and from Marseille sailed for Algiers. He was heading toward his destiny, this man who would henceforth be known as Father de Foucauld, Foucauld the African!

Tamanrasset, December 1, 1916, 3 P.M.

Loud knocking at the door roused Brother Charles from his memories. He slipped through the narrow passageway and, without asking who was there, opened the massive door. A large fellow, a black Haratin, stood before him. The hermit offered him a friendly greeting.

[26] Ibid., 194.
[27] Ibid., 196.

"I am hungry", said the man. "I have eaten nothing all day. I would like alms."

The priest looked him over uncompromisingly. The black man was about twenty-five. Certainly, he was quite thin, but he appeared in good health. He was big and strong without being muscular. "Why aren't you working at the farming center?"

"It is closed. There's no water."

"But there are other ones, at Tit and at Abalessa . . ."

"I've been there. They don't need me."

Brother Charles had his doubts. They all lied. The Haratins were natu-rally lazy. Because manual labor was looked down upon by the ruling class, the Tuareg. So he did not allow himself to feel sorry for the man. In the courtyard, he showed him a little wooden box that served as a form for bricks. "Make me twenty bricks, and I'll give you a measure of wheat." An easy hour of work. He had only to retrieve clay from the bottom of the dry bed of the wadi, wet it, knead it, and pack it in the mold, then let the brick dry in the sun, since firing was not used here.

"No", said the black man, looking stubborn. "I'm tired."

"Fine, then go on your way."

"You aren't going to give me anything, Sidi Marabout?"

"Yes. Some good advice. You have to work to live."

And he showed him out.

Since the sun did not set until around 5 P.M., the Senoussi *rezzou* kept the dromedaries from moving along too speedily. They would have to arrive at Tamanrasset under total darkness. Yet it was too much to hope that so many camels could pass by the Haratin village without being noticed. Beuh ag Rhabelli pointed this out to Kerzou, who knew the region: "Will we have to neutralize them? There's a danger they might alert Fort Motylinski."

"No. They will stay out of our business. The Haratins are the children of slaves or of freed Sudanese and Nigerian slaves. They are not very energetic. Over the centuries their people were enslaved by our *rezzous*. Some are of mixed race. They live in extreme poverty because of the stupid French laws freeing them."

"What do you mean?"

"Fifty years ago, in the Ahaggar we had three thousand slaves serving six thousand freemen. Our people, the Tuareg nobles, treated them well. Never beaten, as well fed as horses, they did light work in the gardens or tending animals. By freeing them, the French turned them into paupers. The rich nomads and the sedentary farmers who used to own them, often for prestige, no longer wish to employ them, for they are lazy. As a result, they wander and steal to survive. To help them feed themselves, the French provide work by building useless roads and all those brick houses, which do not equal the traditional tent or the *zeriba* made of rushes. This work out in the hot sun tires them, and they miss the good old days of slavery!"

They laughed an ominous laugh. But the black man, El Madani, did not laugh with them.

"So, you don't think that one of them would go to alert Fort Moty?" Beuh asked again.

"Even if they wanted to, they have no mounts. It would take them a whole day and part of a night to reach the fort, more than thirty miles away. By that time, we will be far away to the southwest!"

Drawing by Foucauld. In April 1900, in Nazareth, Foucauld adopted as his device *Jesus Caritas*, with a heart and a cross.

10

Hermit Priest at Beni Abbès

Love is at work. It is indefatigable.
—Milan Kundera

Charles de Foucauld disembarked in Algiers on September 10, 1901, and went to stay with the White Fathers in their motherhouse, Maison-Carrée. This order of African missionaries had been founded by Cardinal Lavigerie in 1868 to evangelize the continent. In 1901, it was headed by a holy priest from the Aveyron, fifty-five-year-old Bishop Livinhac, who greeted the new arrival warmly, surprised, at the same time, by his unusual vocation. If he did not want to be a parish priest or a monk, why did he not become a missionary, like the White Fathers? And why did he wish to settle in the southern desert region, where even members of the African order had not yet been permitted to do their work?

"Pacification in the south is far from complete. Beni Abbès, where you are planning to go, is the farthest point of French penetration. The army is the only presence; it not only provides security but also acts as the governmental authority and takes care of mail and transportation. I doubt they will be willing to have you there."

"I have an appointment in Algiers with Major Lacroix."

"Ah? You know the head of Indigenous Affairs?"

"He is an old classmate."

A few days later, the two men embraced. Major Lacroix was a fine example of that noble and disinterested, patriotic and enthusiastic officer trained by the French Army to colonize Africa. Today "colonization" is a pejorative term, but it had no such connotation at the beginning of the century, when it meant establishing a little order in countries where famine and endemic disease reigned and the only law was force. The settled population lived under constant threat from *rezzous*, bands of pillagers. The people of the north, Arab and Tuareg, considered the south with its blacks their traditional preserve of slaves.

"You will have all the necessary permits. And everywhere you go in Africa, you will be welcomed by the army as a brother."

"By the army, maybe. But the government authorities? They are not fond of 'clerics'."

"You are not a cleric like others, *Père Foucauld*! And it is very much in the interest of France to let you work in Africa. You wish to convert the natives? What better way to make them good Frenchmen? "

Charles nodded his approval. His ardent soul also burned with the purest patriotism, which had its roots in the army. If he had been pulled away from a dissolute and self-centered existence, he owed that initially to the army. But deep in his heart, he had but one country, that of Christ, who had said, "My kingdom is not of this world", and the priest wanted to make that country known within these still neglected lands.

Then Charles met Bishop Charles Guérin of Ghardaïa, apostolic vicar of the Sahara and his direct superior in the hierarchy. Immediately they formed bonds of true friendship. They had in common that they loved God above all else. In 1901, the young missionary, son of an orientalist archaeologist, was a mere twenty-nine. A teacher of Arabic and novitiate director for the White Fathers of Maison-Carrée, he had just been named to his post by the archbishop of Algiers and now had full authority over the massive Sahara region. His was a bright presence. In Africa, he was realizing the promise of a scholarly, pure, and noble youth, in self-effacement and in the desire to sacrifice himself for the Christ who had filled his life. He and Charles shared the same fascination with Islam, based essentially on its mysticism.

Writing to Marie de Bondy, Charles did not spare praise for his new friend: "He is a holy, charming soul. Loving, gentle, humble, intelligent, prudent, very fine, angelic, he has the kindness and perfection of an angel." [1]

On his side, Guérin was no less enthusiastic: "For your family it is a great blessing to have such a relative, just as it is for my mission to have such an apostle", he would later write to Marie de Bondy. He saw in him "admirable virtue" and added: "A true saint such as he is inevitably does good. He cannot help but make radiate around him something of the gentleness and kindness of the Jesus who is henceforth his whole life." [2]

He supported Charles' projects from the beginning and gave him all the authorizations he needed to become established at Beni Abbès as chaplain of the military garrison and as witness of Christ among the local tribes, the only priest for two hundred fifty miles around. Accustomed to the rather solemn paternalism of the White Fathers, with their long patriarchal beards, Guérin was utterly charmed by this poorly dressed, small, dark-haired man

---

[1] CF to Marie de Bondy, June 28, 1902, in G. Gorrée, *Sur les traces de Charles de Foucauld* (Éd. de la Plus Grande France, 1936), 150.

[2] Quoted by R. Bazin, *Charles de Foucauld* (Plon, 1921), 197.

with his exemplary humility, who would have seemed quite ordinary had it not been for the deep-set brown eyes sparkling with intelligence, kindness, and passion, which glowed in the thin face of an Eastern ascetic.

Bishop Guérin knew what he was doing. French black Africa was on the way to being converted to Christianity by his order of missionaries, whose principal tool was the sermon. The White Fathers were fathers in every sense of the word: they had paternal authoritarianism and nobility. But what was accepted by pagan black animists was forcefully rejected by the proud Arabs, the ardent Berbers, and the Tuareg, all steeped in their own religion. To convert them, other weapons would be needed. They would have to be charmed. A saint would be needed. Might this "little brother of Jesus" be the one? Charles wrote to his cousin Marie, "The work being entrusted to your child is admirably beautiful. To sanctify the infidels in a place where even Saint Augustine has not gone. Pray that I may be faithful."[3]

After spending a month in the Cistercian abbey of Notre-Dame-de-Staoueli, near Algiers, where Father Prior Henri had received him "as a dear brother and friend", on October 15, 1901, Charles, his many permits in his pocket, took the train to Aïn Sefra, via Oran.

Father Henri tells the story to Dom Martin, the abbot of Neiges: "All the difficulties have been ironed out, one after the other. Protectors and friends appeared as if by magic. I looked over the few things he had packed, and we arranged for his receiving food supplies regularly. All that remained was to find a banker, and Mme. de Bondy agreed to accept that responsibility."[4]

The Arab telephone or, rather, Major Lacroix's telegraph worked well. Charles was greeted warmly at every stop. At the end of the line, Aïn Sefra, General Cauchemez welcomed him in person and put him up in a beautiful room, whose soft bed the apostle would scorn, sleeping on the floor as he usually did. The next morning, Lieutenant Huot, who was on his way back to Beni Abbès, approached him, offering a horse and an escort. Thus Charles could cover the twenty-five hundred miles of paths in complete safety, a trek he had planned to make across the desert alone and on foot!

At the military posts, the old comrade received a warm welcome. Arriving at Taghit, he was moved to tears. There, the head of the garrison, Captain Susbielle (who would become a friend), wearing a sky-blue kepi and a light-colored dolman, had led out fifteen *mokhazni* (Arab soldiers) draped in their robes. They galloped toward Charles in a cloud of sand. The

[3] CF to Marie de Bondy, September 26, 1901, in Gorrée, *Sur les traces*, 136.
[4] Dom Henri to Dom Martin, in *Bulletin des Amitiés*, no. 104, 3.

captain had told them in advance: "The man you are going to see is a French marabout. He is coming to live among you and the poor people of the desert, to stay here always. Receive him with honor!"

The horsemen came to a halt, dismounted, and approached to press their lips to the hem of Charles' robe, the first homage paid by the men of the desert to the apostle of the Sahara. That day, very moved, Charles celebrated his first Saharan Mass, probably the first Mass ever said in that spot.

A large oasis, almost two miles wide in some places, Beni Abbès spread out on the left bank of the Saoura Oued, in the middle of a vast palm grove. Tumbling down from the Atlas Mountains of Morocco in spring, streams of melted snow would swell the Saoura, irrigating some seven thousand date palms before disappearing in the desert. Dunes and two cliffs surrounded the oasis. From their heights, the thirsty traveler could see a miracle of life: green fields, springs, fountains, around which crowded the many caravans arriving from Algeria and Morocco. Under the benevolent shade of the palms there thrived apricot, peach, and fig trees, grape vines, and plantings of barley.

In the middle of the palm grove rose the fortified village of the Berbers of the Abbabsa tribe, settled farmers, some one hundred and fifty households. Covered streets, stone and earth ramparts, interrupted only by one massive gate. A place where it seemed as if men stood eternally on the defensive. At any time bands of Moroccan pillagers could swoop down on them from the desert.

On the edge of the palm grove a second village, also surrounded by high walls, sheltered Arab nomads, shepherds of the tribe of the Rehamna, or Imrad. They lived in tents. Camels, donkeys, and a few goats grazed nearby. The third *ksar*, on the outskirts of the palm grove, was the home of the Haratins. These former slaves, black or of mixed race, worked at planting and harvesting for the non-nomadic Imrad Berbers, who owned land. The Haratins' *zeribas*, miserable huts of reeds or branches, could be seen up and down the ravine that rose toward the plateau. All told, fifteen hundred indigenous Muslims who did not mingle with each other.

On the plateau stood the structures of the fourth group. The French had built a large fort, a *bordj*, "the redoubt", housing three companies of sharp-shooters and one of light infantry, about eight hundred soldiers, two hundred of them from Metropolitan France. They were led by Captain Regnault and a handful of commissioned and noncommissioned officers in love with Africa, obsessed by the desert.

From the plateau, a spectacular view. To the north and east stretched the pink sands of the Great Western Erg, some of its dunes more than six hundred feet high. To the west, another plateau, rocky and barren, the

Tafilalt. Beni Abbès was situated at the confluence of two deserts: the sandy South Oranais and the rocky Hamada, which stretched all the way to Morocco.

Charles' heart beat faster at first sight of such beauty, silence, and solitude—a summons to prayer. The desert for adoration; the oasis for charity.

He settled in at the *bordj*, warmly welcomed by the young officers. Father Huvelin had advised him to introduce himself as "Father Charles de Foucauld, former officer", but he would have none of that, for he thought of himself as the servant of all, Brother Charles of Jesus. But, in spite of him, it became the practice to call him "Father de Foucauld", and the name of father was also dear to his heart.[5]

Charles remained at the *bordj* only a few weeks, the time it took to build the hermitage, which stood sixteen hundred feet from the oasis, in the middle of a piece of land he had purchased. These twenty-two acres, formerly owned by a local *kaid*, were on the plateau, between the redoubt and the oasis, and belonged to Charles thanks to the generosity of Marie de Bondy. She had paid a premium for them: 1,070 gold francs, or around 35,000 French francs (about 5,700 dollars) in today's currency. For the moment, the site was nothing more than a *reg*, uncultivated desert strewn with pebbles, except for two depressions whose arable soil nourished a few wild palms. Water could be found only by digging deeply.

Captain Regnault assigned a few of his Algerian sharpshooters to clean out the old wells and the two springs. Following Charles' specifications, they erected a rustic hermitage, his *khaoua* (brotherhood), using clay bricks and stones, with earth for mortar. The roofing of reeds over the posts and beams of ethel and palm would not withstand a storm, but it rained here once a year at best, alas!

On December 1, 1901, the chapel of Notre-Dame-des-Neiges was finished, and Charles' heart beat with joy. All it lacked was the bell (which had been commissioned at Staoueli), for if the soldiers did not know the hour, they would be unable to attend Mass. But would they attend? For the chapel walls, an officer had drawn four figures of saints, and Charles had drawn a large Christ with open arms and the Stations of the Cross. This was

---

[5] In the first rule drawn up for the Little Brothers of Jesus (1896), the founder expressly states: "All shall be equal and all shall be called brothers. The superior is called 'brother servant'." The second rule (1897) specifies "brother prior", stating, "All bear the name 'little brother' since they should be made very small through humility. No little brother shall bear the name 'father', not even priests or the prior. The prior is called 'brother prior'." In his *Retraite à Beni-Abbès* (1902), chapter 37, Foucauld specifies: "To have myself called brother and not father."

the only room that would have the luxury of a rug—camel hair—and mats to cover the sand floor.

He slept in this very meager chapel, fully clothed, on the step of the altar, near the tabernacle, "like a dog at the feet of his master",[6] he said. But he found himself so comfortable there—too comfortable!—that he ended up moving into the adjoining sacristy, barely five feet long. When a soldier expressed his astonishment, Charles declared: "On the cross, Jesus was not lying down."[7]

Later the brotherhood would have two cells adjoining the chapel, one for him, the other for guests, then a room for receiving the local people, a rustic infirmary, and a few army tents for supplies. In each room, there were sayings on the walls to encourage meditation. In one corner of the garden he dug his grave, an old Trappist custom. Around his little structures, he raised a low wall; beyond, he outlined the limits of the cloister in pebbles. Pitiful enclosure! When Brother Charles was seeing visitors out after dark, he would stop suddenly, bend down, and feel around for his pebbles. "I can go no farther, here is my cloister wall. Good night!"

As he told his lycée friend Gabriel Tourdes, in a letter written near the end of 1901, he was happy, "living from the work of my hands, unknown by all and poor and enjoying to the full the obscurity, the silence, the poverty, and the imitation of Jesus. Imitation cannot be separated from love. Whoever loves wishes to imitate, and that is the secret of my life. A priest since last June, I immediately felt called to go to the lost flocks, the most neglected souls, so I could carry out my duty of love among them. I am happy, very happy, although I am in no way seeking happiness."[8]

He led a life as regular as a Trappist monk's but harder. Up at 3 A.M., he divided his time between work (seven hours) and the spiritual duties of prayer, *lectio divina*, and offices (twelve hours). He slept only five hours (his rule called for seven hours).

His relations with the inhabitants of the oasis, settled and nomadic, were excellent. "The people are very pleasant. After dreading the arrival of the French, they seem pleased by it and recognize that for the first time in generations they can gather in their crops, which the pillagers used to appropriate."[9]

The non-nomadic Berbers, wary at first, came to see him. Very soon, they were venerating "Marabout Khaouia Carlo", Brother Charles, the man of God to whom they could speak freely because he knew their language. His territory, his symbolic cloister wall, became sacred. "A *zaouïa*

[6] Bazin, *Foucauld*, 198.

[7] Ibid., 205.

[8] CF to Gabriel Tourdes, 159.

[9] CF to Henri de Castries, October 28, 1901, in Gorrée, *Sur les traces*, 137.

[refuge] of prayer and hospitality", he said, modeled after those Muslim brotherhoods which, when he was in Morocco, had provided him shelter and without preaching had shown him the image of God. Petty theft, so common elsewhere, was unheard of in these places. It was possible to leave any object unguarded even at night; meanwhile, the slaves would be wandering elsewhere to steal a little food.

Brother Charles ought not to have been too hopeful, however. The non-nomadic Berbers maintained their fidelity to Islam. All they expected from the French was "trade to make them rich". But they were not fanatics, and, in spite of the weight of tradition, Charles hoped to convert them.

As for the nomadic Arabs, he held out very little hope. "By nature harsh and cruel, obstinately Muslim but not really practicing their religion, they are quite ill-disposed toward the French", he wrote to Bishop Guérin.[10] And the slaves, with no religion, vegetated in hate, despair, and apathy.

Fortunately, there was the garrison. All the commissioned officers and most of the noncommissioned ones were Christians, more or less practicing. But among the European sharpshooters, quite a few wild fellows! Good or bad, Brother Charles would invite them all to come and share a brotherly evening. They were not to find any alcohol there! "This poor man offers you what he has", he would say, proffering his pitcher of cool water or a bowl of "desert tea"—an infusion of plants—along with some dates and a little barley bread he had kneaded himself. Just a few things, he thought, but more important was the burning saintly heart he offered without reservation. In his company, the rough soldiers were so overwhelmed that some of them dared not return. But any visitor who came with an open heart filled him with delight. "I cannot get over their being willing to come and hear me", he wrote Marie de Bondy. Boundless joy!

He felt quite close to some of the officers, such as Regnault and Susbielle. The latter recalled, "We would sit down on the ground in front of the brotherhood, contemplating the great sand dune and the great silence of the Sahara. And there we would pass hours I found too brief."

With his springs now flowing, Brother Charles sowed barley, planted two hundred fifty palms, some fig and olive trees, and put in the orchard the seeds Marie de Bondy had sent. While waiting for the trees to bear fruit, he regenerated the wild palms by creating *seghias* (irrigation ditches) to carry water directly to their feet. Exhausting work that he could not carry out alone, especially since the hermitage had to be built at the same time. Water was a major problem. For nine months, from October to June, the daytime temperature never went below eighty-five degrees. In the

[10] CF to Bishop Guérin, February 4, 1902.

three months of the summer it would rise to 105 degrees and sometimes as high as 120. The ground would dry out. Fortunately, manpower was not lacking, and Charles hired two Haratins, of mixed Arab and black blood. But they refused to live at the hermitage, for sharing the hermit's meals— a little barley gruel, a bit of bread, a few dates—amounted to starvation. The army supplied Charles with grain, vegetables, and canned milk; but he gave it all to the poor.

Thus Charles wrote to Dom Martin, begging him to find among his novices, "a soul willing to follow me and ready for martyrdom, starvation, and faithful obedience." [11]

For the time being, to solve the problem of manpower and also that of his apostolate (since the Arabs and Berbers remained hostile to Christianity), he had to recruit by resorting to slaves, still numerous at Beni Abbès.

On January 9, 1902, he redeemed his first slave, what an event! "The greatest joy of my life", he said, as he placed an *ex-voto* on the altar of Saint Joseph. The slave was a twenty-year-old black man, whom the Arabs had carried off four years before during a *razzia* in the Sudan (Mali). Charles gave him the name Joseph du Sacré-Coeur. He redeemed him thanks to a gift from Marie de Bondy, but at a premium. What a sight it must have been, the young fellow repeating after Charles that "henceforth, he would have no master other than God." But he was a Muslim. Charles hoped that he would be converted, "and of his own accord: I shall apply no pressure of any kind—complete freedom!" [12] He ended up sending Joseph to the White Fathers in Algiers. He did not say why, but the reasons can be guessed: faint interest in religion, poor work habits, the complaining of a man poorly fed.

A second slave, redeemed July 4, 1902, a twenty-five-year-old man, worked for a while in the vegetable garden, then took off. On July 12 Charles bought still another, this time a four-year-old child whom he christened Abd Jésus (servant of Jesus); he ended up turning him over to Bishop Guérin. In September he bought a young father from Tafilalt, but he let himself feel sorry for the man and sent him home to his wife and children. His last purchase was Paul Embarek, fifteen, who would become Charles' longtime servant. [13] Paul was willing to entertain the possibility of baptism . . . at some later time. Even counting his one willing convert, Mama Hakem, an elderly blind mulatto whom Charles supported, the results here were negligible. Thus Charles found himself facing the

[11] CF to Dom Martin, September 16, 1901.

[12] Quoted by Bazin, *Foucauld*, 216.

[13] Redeemed September 14, 1902. Not to be confused with Paul Bonita, redeemed February 27, 1903. The latter was the son of Mohamed ben Ombarek, which caused the confusion about the names in some biographies.

CHILDHOOD

Portrait of Charles as a child. Good student, conscientious, hardworking, he sometimes exploded in violent tantrums. He loved solitude and nature. (*Blic family photograph.*)

Élisabeth de Foucauld, née Morlet: a pale face, gentle and sad, framed with sensibly coifed black hair. Her melancholy appealed to the children. Something mysterious clouded her life. Here, with Marie and Charles. (*Blic family photograph.*)

School picture, Saint-Cyr preparatory class. (*National Archives.*)

Charles de Foucauld starting Saint-Cyr, 1876. He was eighteen, a hypersensitive, withdrawn adolescent beginning to open up. And yet, "I was all egotism, all vanity, all impiety, all desire for evil; it was as if I had gone a little mad. I was so free, so young. There remained not a trace of faith in my soul."

Second lieutenant in the Fourth Hussars at Pont-à-Mousson. Did well at Saint-Cyr, but last in his class at Saumur; he had wearied of everything. "I hope this ranking does not follow you, sir!" quipped his colonel. This dandy of the Belle Époque loved to strut, but he could be noble and was fascinated by travel. (*Blic family photograph.*)

CONVERSION

Charles in 1886. He had just explored Morocco. He was famous. Then came the meeting at Saint-Augustin's, the lightning-swift conversion. A man, Father Huvelin, a woman, Marie de Bondy, were the instruments of Providence. (*Blic family photograph.*)

Father Huvelin, vicar of Saint-Augustin's in Paris. A loving, patient priest who listened and who hungered for God. (*Photograph from Mme. Louis Lefébure.*)

Marie Moitessier, future Viscountess de Bondy, a bright figure who lit up young Charles' surroundings and led him to God. (*Forbin family photograph.*)

WITH THE TRAPPISTS

The Cistercian abbey of Notre-Dame-des-Neiges (Ardèche) made Foucauld into a monk and, later, a priest. An isolated, forbidding place. This poor, needy agricultural community admitted him as a novice in 1890. "I entered there through pure love."

ABOVE The abbey in 1890. (*Collection of the Abbaye d' Aiguebelle.*)

RIGHT A scale model, made by the abbey of Notre-Dame-des-Neiges.

ABOVE The Trappist house of Notre-Dame-d'Akbès in Cheiklé, Syria. Twenty monks built a monastery in this wild setting, where the howling of wolves could be heard. Foucauld pronounced his temporary vows here in 1892. But "Brother Albéric" did not find the house poor enough. (*Collection of the Abbaye d'Aiguebelle.*)

LEFT The only photograph of Foucauld in the black cassock of the secular priest. Picture taken in 1900 at his sister Marie's home in Barbirey with his nephew and godson Charles, whom he hoped to see become a priest. The boy would go into the navy and become an admiral! (*Blic family photograph.*)

IN BENI ABBÈS

In 1901, Foucauld settled in Beni Abbès, a major Saharan oasis, crossroads for caravans from Algeria and Morocco. Despite the French fort here, there was a constant threat from *rezzous*. (*Ofalag photograph.*)

Foucauld in front of his hermitage, surrounded by poor blacks, slaves, and freemen. "I live from the work of my hands, unknown by all and poor and enjoying obscurity, silence, the imitation of Jesus, inseparable from love." His vocation flourished here. The desert for adoration, the oasis for charity. (*G. Gorrée collection.*)

ABOVE In 1905, General Lyautey, commander of the Oases, paid the hermit a visit. Deeply moved, the future marshal later wrote: "He is the most lofty spiritual figure I have ever encountered. No doubt that he has an essential place in the order of the world." Here, they are in front of the hermitage. (*Petites Soeurs de Jésus, Rome.*)

LEFT Brother Charles became the friend of the proud Tuareg and of the poor black slaves he strove to redeem. "The man you are going to see is a French marabout. He comes to live among you and the poor people of the desert", Captain de Susbielle stated. He is shown with Brother Charles and the young slave Abd Jésus, whom Charles redeemed. (*Regnault family collection.*)

In 1901, Bishop Guérin, apostolic vicar of the Sahara, warmly welcomed Charles to Beni Abbès. He afterward said of the hermit: "A veritable saint such as he inevitably does good." Above, in front of the hermitage with little ex-slave Abd Jésus. (*Collection of the White Fathers, Algeria.*)

Foucauld in Beni Abbès: "To share my bread down to the last bite with any pauper, any stranger who appears, receiving every human being like a beloved brother. My ordinary inclination is for solitude, stability, silence. But if I believe I am called to something other, I obey. Love always obeys when it has God for its object." (*Photograph from the Petites Soeurs de Jésus, Rome.*)

PACIFICATION TOUR

ABOVE Foucauld in a Tuareg camp. Saroual fastened with a leather belt, long indigo gandoura; a blue veil, the *litham*, masks the white faces of these men whose origin is unknown. (*Cahiers C. de F.*)

LEFT The tent in which Brother Charles celebrated Mass when he was traveling in the desert. Day is just breaking over the white sands of the Tidikelt; it is the holy hour of the Eucharist. (*Cahiers C. de F.*)

BELOW A stop at the oasis of Silet, on the edge of the Tanezrouft. A Targui has come. "One must love them in order to be loved in return", Brother Charles always said. (*Ofalag photograph.*)

THE HERMITAGE OF
TAMANRASSET

ABOVE The first hermitage (1905). A hut of stones grouted with clay, covered with reeds. In front of the tent, the hermit rejoices: Tam is the poorest village in Africa.

BELOW The 1910 hermitage, "the Frigate". Father Charles would say to visitors, "As you can see, it's very comfortable. You may sleep in the chapel. The altar step will be your pillow. I say Mass at five A.M." (*Photographs from the Forbin family and the Petites Soeurs de Jésus, Rome.*)

FRIENDS

ABOVE The beautiful poet Dassine, the muse of the Ahaggar, playing the *imzad*, next to her husband, Aflan, dressed for war. In the Ahaggar, women safeguard the traditions. (*Cahiers C. de F.*)

LEFT Brother Charles in Tamanrasset, 1909, with his adopted "son" Ouksem, a young Targui of good family. (*Photograph by Félix Dubois, Blic collection.*)

Colonel Laperrine, pacifier of the Sahara. He opened to Foucauld the forbidden routes of the Ahaggar. A legendary figure of the African army, he was the consummate cavalry officer. His rank showed in his expression, his bearing, and his soul. The desert was his kingdom, his passion. His men called him "the Saharissime". (*Cahiers C. de F.*)

VISIT TO FRANCE

ABOVE In 1913, Foucauld took his young friend Ouksem to France: a veritable round of châteaux! Here, with Marie de Bondy, who is gazing tenderly at "her old son", worn out by his ascetic life. Afterward he wrote her: "Now that I have seen you, it is as if this long separation never existed." The man on the left is Marie's son-in-law, the Marquis de Forbin. (*Forbin family photograph.*)

LEFT Charles de Foucauld in France, 1913. (*G. Gorrée collection.*)

In the heart of the Ahaggar, Charles built a modest hermitage on Assekrem, which overlooks a rugged massif, a natural fortress for the Tuareg. The chapel here, of stone grouted with clay, stands at 9,200 feet on a narrow plateau battered by the winds. No water, no vegetation, but a splendid place, barren and wild, which invites prayer and contemplation, "the most beautiful solitude in the world", he was to call it. (*Photograph from the Petites Soeurs de Jésus, Rome.*)

Charles de Foucauld with Abd Jésus, the little slave he redeemed in Beni Abbès. (*Forbin family photograph.*)

Paul Embarek at the end
of his life. In Beni Abbès,
Foucauld had redeemed
and freed this black slave
captured in the Sudan.
Catechumen, he served
Mass. "I am somehow tied
to him", the hermit said.
He was never baptized.
(*G. Gorrée collection.*)

Above, Brother Charles photographed
at In Salah by Doctor Béraud, who said,
"This serious man was all smiles, which
seemed somehow poignant in that
emaciated face marked by asceticism."

Charles remained very close to the
army. He used to invite officers and
soldiers to share a brotherly evening;
"The poor man offers you what he
has", he would say with a smile.
(*G. Gorrée collection.*)

THE FORT

The hermitage/fort was built in 1915 according to Foucauld's specifications and was modeled on the old Moroccans *bordjs*. It was supposed to shelter the population of Tamanrasset, under threat from the *rezzous*. "On seeing my battlements, I think of the fortified convents of the tenth century", he said. He was struck down in front of the entry (below) after a year of famine in which he had given away all his reserves. (*Photographs from G. Tairraz.*)

"Let us concern ourselves with those who lack everything, those to whom no one gives a thought. Let us be the friends of those who have no friends, their brother. The love of God, the love of men, that is my whole life, that will be my whole life, I hope. When we can suffer and love, we can do much, the most that one can do in this world." (C. de F.)

"To be consumed in adoration, to immolate oneself with Christ for the salvation of men. To live in Tamanrasset without power, without possessions. To efface oneself and finally abolish the self, until the buried seed sprouts." (C. de F.)

(Photographs from the Petites Soeurs de Jésus, Rome.)

problem of slavery, which dragged him into a political spiral he had not anticipated.

Upon its occupation of Algeria in 1830, France had decreed the abolition of slavery, which was widespread among the Muslim peoples. But there was an enormous gap between theory and practice. The sensibilities and interests of the tribal chiefs and marabouts, the major slaveowners, had to be catered to in exchange for their loyalty.

Ever since his arrival in Beni Abbès, Charles had rebelled against this state of affairs: "Please be so good as to tell me the policy on slavery", he wrote to Bishop Guérin on January 15, 1902. The reply: "It is through an *order* of General Risbourg, confirmed by Colonel Billet, that slavery is allowed to continue."

Charles' retort, February 7, 1902, in a letter to Dom Martin:

> It must be made known to whom it may concern: "this is not legal." It is hypocrisy to put on stamps and everything else, "liberty, equality, fraternity, human rights", you who fetter slaves and condemn to the galleys those making a lie of what you print on your banknotes; you who steal children from their parents and sell them publicly; you who punish the theft of a chicken and allow that of a human being. We should not interfere in temporal affairs? But when the government commits a grave injustice against those entrusted to us, it is necessary to tell it so, for we represent on earth justice and truth, and we do not have the right to be sleeping sentinels, mute dogs, indifferent pastors. Voices must be raised so that France will know of this injustice and thievery. I have informed the apostolic prefect. I do not wish to betray my children, to be a bad shepherd. It frightens me to sacrifice Jesus to my calm, my cowardice, and my natural timidity. [14]

And since the good abbot of Neiges was advising moderation, Charles retorted: "You defend too readily a state of affairs that destroys souls." [15]

His letters to his superiors not receiving any satisfactory responses, Charles wrote on April 1 to his friend Henri de Castries, the conscience of Algeria, the upright peacemaker: "The great scourge of this country is slavery. There is no solution for our shame and our injustice except emancipation." He noted the inhuman working conditions: irrigating the palm trees with goatskins filled from wells was an exhausting chore. If they stopped, they were beaten. If they escaped, they were pursued with gunshots. "They are bludgeoned daily", stated an indignant Charles. They are lazy? But did they choose to work without pay? And could it be surprising that, poorly fed, they stole to survive? "No human power has the right to fetter these unfortunate creatures, whom God has created as free as you and me." He was furious when some runaway slaves seeking refuge with the

[14] CF to Dom Martin, February 2, 1902.
[15] Ibid., March 17, 1902.

French authorities were returned to their master, who then killed their travel urge by cutting the tendons in their feet.[16]

In reply, de Castries offered to bring up the question with Denys Cochin, a deputy whose special interest was the abolition of slavery. The matter was in danger of being made public. On June 28, Charles wrote to Bishop Guérin again:

> Nothing has changed. Not only do those enslaved remain so, but slaves are being bought and sold every day with the full knowledge of the Arab bureaus, which consider themselves obliged to accept such an attitude because of discipline and orders received, despite the personal feelings of the fine officers there. Enormous, monstrous injustice. Here slavery is pushed to the outer limits of barbarism. The harshness of it makes family life impossible. If a slave marries, the children belong to the master, who sells them. The French authorities allow the master to do anything but kill slaves. The authorities will always overlook what happens inside tents in the erg. They say: slaves are necessary in this country, for without them the oases would perish. That is inaccurate. Many prosperous oases have not one slave. The only people with large contingents of slaves are the nomads and marabouts, who spend their whole lives in idleness and who rise up against us at every opportunity. Freeing their slaves would force them to work a little, which would improve them. The slaves must be liberated.[17]

And he beseeched Bishop Guérin to travel to Paris, where he could ask Denys Cochin to lay the matter before the legislators. Let Catholic members of the Assembly challenge the leftist government to live up to its convictions or simply to follow republican rules by outlawing slavery and repealing the Black Code that governed the Sahara.

His back to the wall, Bishop Guérin consulted Bishop Livinhac. The affair was close to taking a political turn that might have explosive consequences. What should they do? A scandal was going to erupt. The Church of France had pledged to the government, which remained quite anticlerical ("Little Father Combes" had recently succeeded Waldeck-Rousseau) not to interfere in African political matters. That was the only condition under which missionaries were tolerated. To act openly against the government was to risk clerical expulsion from Algiers as well as Dakar, Bamako, and Niamey.

And that is what Bishop Guérin explained to Charles on September 17, 1902, putting the hermit "on guard against his zeal". Of course, "slavery is an evil", but "it is imperative to consider carefully the circumstances and take care to see that we do not have taken from us the means through which we can do a little good as a result of making grand gestures that are

[16] CF to Henri de Castries, April 1, 1902.
[17] CF to Bishop Guérin, June 28, 1902.

useless." It was essential to "influence the masters by preaching gentleness; influence the slaves by recommending to them submission and hard work." In conclusion, "official denunciation of what happens in these countries cannot be considered."

It was hard to believe. If one did not know that the White Fathers Guérin and Livinhac were truly holy men, one might have had little hope for the future of the Church and the Republic as the century began. Why did they not consult with their founder, Cardinal Lavigerie?

Be that as it may, Charles received a specific order: Be quiet. To which he replied sharply: "It is better to obey God than men."

Next Bishop Guérin appealed to Charles in the name of "the supernatural grandeur of work". Asking him to be patient, he explained that the status of slavery had been maintained on a temporary basis through the Black Code established by General Risbourg. It would do no good to free on a massive scale people who could not at the same time be freed from poverty. What could be done with thousands of freed slaves, especially the children? Who would give them work? Who would feed them?

Again, Charles' indignation overcame his submissiveness. "The reasons you have given me so kindly and so lovingly and which have so much weight do not leave me without regrets that the representatives of Jesus are happy to defend 'with a whisper in the ear' and not 'with a shout from the rooftops' a cause which is that of justice and charity." [18]

The matter went no farther. In high places, they accused Charles de Foucauld—today denounced as a colonialist by those who have never read him—of being a dangerous revolutionary!

In the name of obedience, having said what he had to say to his superiors, he became silent, all the while continuing discreetly to appeal to his family to help put an end to "this iniquity, this abomination". His prayer and the ultimate sacrifice of his life would, he thought, be more effective than his verbal protests. But they would turn out not to have been useless. The Church would gently approach the authorities. Little by little (it would take three years) the evil was to be eradicated. On December 15, 1904, Charles would announce to de Castries that "by common accord, the chiefs attached to the oases have taken measures to abolish slavery. Not in one day, that would not be prudent, but gradually." The selling of slaves was forbidden. There were only a few mutual concessions. The owner of a slave could keep him, but he could not be resold, could not have a new master. And if he were mistreated, the chief could emancipate him.

Charles had won, though not as quickly as he had wished. And he had

---

[18] Ibid., September 30, 1902, quoted by D. and R. Barrat, *Charles de Foucauld et la fraternité* (Seuil, 1958), 90.

taken on a new dimension. In the eyes of the authorities—political, military, and religious—and of the local peoples, he became the conscience of France in Algeria. His protests were not limited to slavery. "To be freed also from the slavery of evil, vice, and error, from all that which separates man from the good and the true, from God", he wrote Bishop Guérin. And so he made his first enemies, who dreamed of slaying him, but that was the least of his concerns.

Let there be no misunderstanding: he remained a "colonialist", but in the positive sense of the word. Charles de Foucauld proclaimed the law, not of force, but of love. The French did not go to Algeria to exploit the indigenous peoples but to raise their level of civilization. And, of course, to convert them to "the true religion". He thought also in terms of integration, each group contributing its best aspects. He was a "peacemaker", devoted, convinced, patriotic. He never stopped denouncing *razzias* and slavery, but he also denounced the abuses of hard-line colonialism, such as he observed in black Africa, where "there is only cupidity and violence, with no thought for the good of the peoples", he wrote to Bishop Guérin.

From that time on, he saw his vocation with the utmost clarity. To be the brother of all, the "universal brother", was not enough. Since he could not be as holy as the Christ who was his model, he would be poorer than the poor. He wrote Marie de Bondy: "I live on bread and water. This diet costs me seven francs a month. My only capital is still what it was when I left France and comes from the words of Jesus: Seek the kingdom of God and his justice, and then all else will be given you. As a resource when you are in difficulty, strive for perfection and pray. Up to now, I have lacked nothing. I am very happy. Wretched soldiers come to me, slaves fill the little house, travelers come straight to the fraternity, the poor are all around. If I am holy enough, the harvest will be bountiful." [19]

And so he lived in complete poverty and would not accept honoraria from Notre-Dame-des-Neiges for celebrating Mass. The Trappist monastery at Staoueli dressed him, sending him a robe, two shirts, a coat, a blanket, and a few towels. But Dom Henri was on his guard. "He has just loaned me these things, so that I will not give them away", Charles said with a laugh. Moved by seeing him so poorly dressed, an officer from the redoubt gave him two sweaters. Once a month the garrison took up a collection and turned forty or fifty francs over to Charles, who was officially their chaplain.

Yes, he was completely happy, since he felt Jesus happy in him. But he was not thriving physically, thanks to his poor diet and the lack of sleep:

[19] CF to Marie de Bondy, January 31, 1902, in Gorrée, *Sur les traces*, 145.

fevers, aching joints, fatigue. Through an officer, the family learned of his condition and became worried. They begged him to stop fasting and to accept ten francs a month for a few dates to go with his bread. He was even scolded by Father Huvelin: "My dear child, sustain yourself! Be humble, patient with yourself, less concerned about overcoming sleep than about defeating your restlessness and that restless search for the best, which torments you. Stay calm to receive God's blessings, to give of yourself in peace. Take control of yourself. Do not deprive yourself too much. Eat a bit. Sleep as much as necessary to carry on your work." [20]

But to the priest who admonished him to "take the rest necessary", he replied, "I am lazy and gluttonous." [21]

Out of obedience perhaps, he now ate his fill and agreed not to rise before 4 A.M. But he was still no more "reasonable" than before, and his taste for martyrdom, which arose from a desire for union with Christ crucified, was coming to the fore. In the summer of 1902 there was a real danger that the Berâbers would attack. Charles wrote Father Huvelin: "I long to finish my miserable life, so badly begun and so empty, in that manner of which Jesus said there is no greater love than giving one's life for those one loves. I am unworthy of it, but I so long for it! Rumors of war are once again about. A state of calm in the soul. To feel so close, so on the threshold of eternity, that is a feeling of extreme sweetness and, at the same time, it is good for the soul." [22]

But he berated himself for this desire to become a martyr. It was motivated solely by love! He wrote Bishop Guérin: "Do not think that in my type of life the hope of seeing the Beloved sooner has anything to do with it. I want only to do what pleases him the most. If I love fasting and vigils, it is because Jesus loved them so. I envy his nights of prayer on the mountaintop. I would like to keep him company. Alas, I am so cold that I dare not say that I love. But I would like to love." [23]

He wrote to Father Huvelin. "I am waiting in peace. While having many desires, I try to feel them in that peace which is the measure of love." [24]

Peace, contemplation at the foot of the altar or under the starry desert night, when everything was calm in this African land parched by the sun. He wrote in his notebook: "The evenings are so calm, the nights so serene, this immense sky and these vast horizons dimly lit by the heavenly bodies are so peaceful as they silently sing the eternal, the infinite, and the beyond;

[20] Father Huvelin to CF, May 18, 1902.
[21] CF to Father Huvelin, 205.
[22] Quoted by Bazin, *Foucauld*, 228.
[23] CF to Bishop Guérin, February 27, 1903, quoted by Bazin, ibid., 247.
[24] CF to Father Huvelin, July 21, 1902, 201.

one could pass whole nights outdoors in contemplation. I cut them short, however, and go back inside to the tabernacle: nothing is anything compared to the Beloved." [25]

Alas, this contemplation and peace were going to be more and more limited. A few months after he had settled there, when he thought he could now set aside eleven hours for his spiritual exercises, he had to face the truth: he was submerged by the poor. This situation surprised the naïve Charles, as he confided to his sister: "I am astonished at seeing myself go from the contemplative life to that of the holy ministry. In spite of myself I am drawn into it because of the needs of souls." [26]

Was it not rather the needs of bodies?

"Every day the same thing", he wrote to Father Huvelin. "The poor and the sick, one after another. I berate myself for not devoting enough time to prayer. In the day, they do not stop knocking on my door. At night, which would be the right time, I fall asleep, miserable creature that I am. It is a shame and a sorrow to me, this sleep that takes a more prominent place than I would like. I do not have time for it, and it takes away from other things." [27]

"They knock at my door at least ten times a day", he wrote Bishop Guérin on September 30, 1901. "I am overrun. I have between sixty and one hundred visits a day", he told Dom Martin on February 2, 1902. He would soon have as many as two hundred! Every day, seventy poor, ten to fifteen sick, fifty children, twenty frail and elderly, thirty to forty travelers, and twenty or so slaves, and, on top of that, a few Jews from the ghetto and the military men from the garrison. "I share down to my last bite of bread with any pauper, any stranger who appears, receiving every human being as if he were a beloved brother", he wrote Henri de Castries.[28]

He himself received the poor, waited on them, washed their clothes and the area he had set aside for them, cooked and shared with them his barley gruel. For him, every guest was Christ. Not only the poor from the oasis villages, but also devout nomads drawn there by his holiness, and beggars of all sorts. Every minute of the day, someone came to the hermitage of Khaouia Carlo. And Brother Charles, interrupting his dialogue with the invisible, would appear, "his beautiful eyes radiating serenity, his hands already outstretched".[29]

And he was alone in a place that already needed two priests, a doctor, two nurses, and two cooks! By 1902, the poor were arriving as early as

[25] CF, *Carnet de Beni-Abbès* (Nouvelle Cité, 1993), September 12, 1902.
[26] CF to Marie de Blic, January 1902, in Gorrée, *Sur les traces*, 144.
[27] CF to Father Huvelin, December 15, 1902, 204.
[28] CF to Henri de Castries, June 23, 1901, in Gorrée, *Sur les traces*, 113.
[29] Bazin, *Foucauld*, 214.

4:30 A.M. He no longer had time to say his offices. And the procession would continue until nightfall. He found a little rest only at the scorching midday hour or at night, when he prayed, cutting back on what was already too little sleep. "I am so overcome with work that I do not have a minute to read and not much time to meditate", he admitted to Bishop Guérin on February 4, 1902.

And he asked himself anxiously: "Is this what Jesus wants of me?" He finally understood the practical value of monasteries, set up carefully with stability in mind: a community where each had his assigned tasks, a place where the reverence owed to the contemplation of God was reconciled with the charity owed to the world. The life of the charitable hermit in an area with a poverty-stricken population was intolerable. Impossible to be completely devoted to the poor and follow a monastic rule at the same time. Worn out, he did not always hear his alarm ring at 4 A.M., the hour for reciting Lauds. It was the poor who awakened him, and not because they wanted to be present at the offices!

In vain he tried to set up a strict schedule by cutting back on sleep and meals, "to maintain a contemplative life while being everything to everyone". But he was sacrificing meditation and reading, the two windows of the soul. He held on only because there remained the essential through which, having given all, having been consumed by the poor, "one can meet Jesus." He was burning himself out: he was heading toward disaster in the name of love.

In vain he set up his "cloister wall". At first symbolic, a line of stones, later a real wall, which was never completed. Contradiction! The monastic cloister was necessary for a well-ordered life. But since he could not leave the cloister, he was obliged to let his visitors enter, and thus he let himself be overwhelmed. Ah, if only he had a brother porter!

Observing that Charles had reached an impasse, Bishop Guérin encouraged him to become a traditional missionary: he would have his assigned tasks, God his prayers, and the poor his offerings. But he stubbornly pursued his path, all the while questioning himself. Was it God who was immersing him in this activism? Should he look for a hermitage where he really could be alone? But he rejected the latter solution, so dear to his heart, still hoping for the possible arrival of companions.

For that was the ideal solution: to obtain help. But not by way of servants, even volunteers, such as the one sent by the captain of the fort. Charles had ended up dismissing the good soldier while muttering: "Christ had no orderlies."

But he was not alone. On all sides, he was receiving encouragement and assistance. Not only from his female cousins, his sister, and Father Huvelin, but from the monasteries of Notre-Dame-des-Neiges and Staoueli, and the

Poor Clares of Palestine. The officers at the *bordj* invited him to share real meals; the military doctor fussed over him. For Christmas 1902, the Poor Clares of Jerusalem, who missed their "gardener", sent him an enormous package. Opening it, he was amazed to find saints' relics for his altar, dried flowers, a wooden spoon, a mousetrap, a piece of white wool fabric to replace his worn-out robe. But he soon gave the cloth to a young black who had nothing.

He also received the bell he had ordered from Staoueli, carefully packed inside a wine barrel that was assiduously wet down by the soldiers transporting it, who believed they were cooling off a container of fine sacramental wine! He mounted the bell in the "tower" of his chapel. And it rang for the offices, day and night, joyfully, touchingly, rousing the soldiers. One of them recalled later, "The sound would come through the air, reaching us in the redoubt, and it would seem as if we were right under the clapper. It was Brother Charles calling himself to the office!"

It was true that he had no money problems. "I have rarely had financial difficulties", he wrote Bishop Guérin. "My cousin de Bondy provides in full for the upkeep of the chapel. I have only to ask, and she pays. It is also she who paid for the land for the fraternity. My cousin de Flavigny[30] sends fifty francs a month (I have refused to accept more). From here and there I receive unexpected contributions. I find it amounts to [a total of] about fifteen hundred francs, not counting the many gifts in kind."

He ended up eating properly, it appears, thanks to a clever move on Marie's part: "My cousin sends me ten francs a month on condition I use them to feed myself . . . I have agreed. My menu: at noon, couscous or bread with canned milk. In the evening, bread and black coffee. At the garrison, the officers and the staff doctor are very kind to me and overwhelm me with attentions. Every evening, they bring black coffee and a vegetable dish. Every morning a loaf of bread. On holidays, a hundred treats."[31] Which he would distribute to the very poor, of course.

But all these "comforts" really changed nothing. He realized that if he wanted to last there, he would need companions. Besides, it was for them that he had bought and planted the twenty-two acres, "enough to provide work and food for twenty to thirty monks" and the nearby poor. And it was with these companions in mind that he put the finishing touches on his plans for the Little Brothers, which he had the pleasure of seeing approved by Bishop Guérin. He wrote to Marie de Bondy: "I have permission to found. I have been authorized to found a new religious family,

---

[30] Catherine Moitessier, older sister of Marie de Bondy. Unfortunately, her letters have been lost.

[31] CF to Bishop Guerin, quoted by G. Ganne, *Tamanrasset ou le désert fertile* (SOS, 1975), 133–34.

under the rule of Saint Augustine, under the name of the Little Brothers of the Sacred Heart of Jesus, for adoring night and day the Holy Eucharist in perpetual exposition, in the solitude of the cloister, in countries of mission, in poverty and work. I am collapsing under the weight of my blessings, of the vision of what I should be, of the vision of the good that I should do and of the good that would be done were I to be sanctified." [32]

The basics of his rule had not changed. To let Christ and charity reign, to replace hate with love, to efface oneself in a life of perfection and love, of adoration. To imitate Christ, to be his witness. Then, from the seed seemingly lost in the earth, the wheat would sprout and grow. From his radical conversion would rise countless ears of grain: the Little Brothers of Jesus!

Unfortunately, convinced that "God would do all" as far as recruitment was concerned, he did not do much to encourage brothers likely to join him. In a letter written January 5, 1902, he warned a Trappist who spoke of joining him along with three other companions, an unhoped-for offer! Charles said his life was "poor, abject, and solitary". His rule was "harsh and strict". He asked them to "be ready to have their heads cut off, to die of hunger, and to obey him in spite of his unworthiness". [33]

Even the abbot of Neiges, upon Charles' request of September 16, 1901, hesitated to send him a companion and confided his thoughts to Bishop Guérin: "I deeply respect his heroic virtue. I am only surprised that he does not perform miracles. I had never seen such holiness in this world, except in books. But I must admit I have some doubts about his prudence, about his discretion. Those ascetic practices of his, which he also insists his companions follow, are such that they would soon be too much for neophytes. Moreover, the intense mental effort he demands of himself and that he hopes to demand of his disciples seems to me so superhuman that I am afraid such concentration might drive any disciple mad before he died from excessive asceticism."

And yet Dom Martin ended his letter as follows: "If you deem we can entrust someone to him without endangering that person's mind and life, I shall accept your decision without question, and I shall go about finding him a companion as soon as possible." [34]

But could they not start by finding him an experienced Algerian Trappist? Alas! the prior of Staoueli wrote Major Lacroix: "My only regret is that I have no one I can send to assist him. His life is so ascetic that those

[32] CF to Marie de Bondy, April 28, 1902, 100.
[33] Quoted by Bazin, *Foucauld*, 242.
[34] Dom Martin to Bishop Guérin, quoted by Bazin, ibid., 243–44.

superiors of our order who have a real affection for him consider him more admirable than imitable and dread throwing into despondency the disciples the order might be able to obtain for him. Very likely he will have to live alone or recruit gradually, and right there, for his future community."[35]

But he had failed completely with his catechumens: "My big black [assistant], Paul, is not trustworthy", he wrote Bishop Guérin. "And I am not surprised at Joseph's running away. That is all that surrounds us: blacks, Arabs, *Joyeux* [African soldiers]. Seeing what is around us, one is alarmed."[36]

And at times, in despair. But he always pulled himself together, for "what is impossible for us is possible for God." And he awaited the miracle.

And he wrote to Bishop Guérin, "Whatever happens, I shall be perfectly satisfied. If I could do other than lose myself by merging with the divine will, I would prefer for myself total failure, perpetual solitude, nothing but setbacks. I do all I can in order to have companions by sanctifying myself in silence. If I had them, I would rejoice along with many worries. Not having them, I rejoice completely."[37]

Nevertheless, it is hard not to see that discouragement sometimes touched him, without defeating him, as in the letter he wrote on May 25, 1903, to Father Laurain, the priest at Saint-Sulpice. "Pray that I may be full of faith at last, that I may love and serve. That my life be nothing but obedience. Pray for this Morocco and this Sahara, which are, alas, a *sealed tomb*."

And then his obsession bursts forth: "Pray that the tiny atom that I am may do, among these millions of souls who have never heard of Jesus, the work he has sent me here to do."[38]

No recruits from outside: he discouraged them. No local catechumens: the Muslims were unapproachable and the Haratins irretrievable, "soup Christians", he called them, "listening to Christian truths only because it is in their material interest". Would his dream of "a *zaouïa* of prayer and hospitality, radiating such piety that the whole countryside would be lit and warmed by it", ever be realized? Even Bishop Guérin no longer thought so: "I fear I cannot take the responsibility of directing to you this or that seminarian or priest, as enthusiastic as he may seem."[39]

Charles countered with his unshakable determination: "If I have not companions, it is that I am not worthy of them. Pray for my conversion in

[35] Dom Henri to Major Lacroix, January 5, 1902, in ibid., 244.
[36] CF to Bishop Guérin, February 27, 1903, in ibid., 248.
[37] Ibid., September 30, 1902, 245.
[38] CF to Father Laurain, May 25, 1903, in ibid., 246.
[39] Bishop Guérin to CF, September 17, 1902, in *Cahiers Charles de Foucauld*, no. 2, 121.

order not to hinder through my faithless moments the merciful designs of God." [40]

Not only would he not abandon his austere rule, which discouraged possible companions, but he considered his own ascetic practices inadequate. "We shall have to begin there." To efface himself completely, the death of the self. But was that humanly possible, short of actual physical death?

Tamanrasset, December 1, 1916. 4 P.M.

Once again, Charles de Foucauld was drawn away from his meditation by knocking on the door of the fort. A Haratin farmer had come to return the mold for bricks he had borrowed, bringing a dozen dates in thanks. Then he discreetly slipped away, conscious of having turned the great marabout away from his dialogue with the invisible.

Shut up in the fort, Brother Charles missed the days when he used to receive in front of the hermitage. Nearly every day he would see his friends, Tuareg nomads: Dassine the poet and her husband, Aflan; Mohamed ag Mohamed; Ouksem, his adopted "son"; little Tegerit with her wide eyes. And there was deaf Meriem, who could not hear him but drank in the words from his lips. Today, all the nomads were gone, having left with Moussa and Ouksem for the wetter plains to the south, in the Adrar. Only a few elderly and infirm remained behind, and they never left their tents.

In the past, evenings under the dazzling sky of the Ahaggar had never been sad. Young people came to ask Brother Charles to teach them a few common French words. But the most beautiful evenings were spent with Dassine, who strummed her *imzad* and sang as Charles translated a fable of La Fontaine into Tamasheq.

Sometimes Dassine would bring with her one of the other women, some noble lady from the camp or village. Then the marabout would get out his stereoscope and show pictures of Algiers the White or fantastic postcards of France. The Tuareg would marvel at the rich countryside, the herds of plump cows, the huge cities. Another world, which they would never know.

The dolls sent by Marie de Bondy had also proved an enormous success. The women would pass them from hand to hand, respectfully, not daring to undress them.

Brother Charles would sometimes speak of God, but he never sought to convert. It was a kind of unspoken agreement between them. They were Muslims, he was a Christian, and things were fine that way. Dassine would

[40] CF to Bishop Guérin, September 30, 1902, in ibid., no. 29, 168.

say to him, "You love your God, I love mine." Sometimes he would suggest that there was but one God in the heavens, the same for all, but they did not comprehend, and he would stop puzzling them.

The *rezzou* of the *fellagha* was not more than ten miles from Tamanrasset. Kerzou leaned toward Beuh ag Rhabelli: "Tell me about Djanet, pearl of the Tassili, which our Senoussi brothers have taken back from the *roumis*."

"It is a fairy-tale garden in the middle of arid desert. There are lush groves of date palms. Water flows everywhere. The women are as beautiful as the moon. The flocks give the best milk, the thickest fleece."

"It is said that once, thousands of years ago, the whole Tassili was a fertile land."

"Yes, ancient cave paintings show that, in Tamrit, Sefar, Jabbaren. Elephants, rhinoceros, hippopotami, giraffes, just as in black Africa! On the high sandstone columns rising above the golden sands, our ancestors have told the story of their bountiful life."

"Today, what is left of it?"

"North of the massif, the Djerat Oued cuts its path toward the south and is soaked up by the sands. Once it was a true living river. Today a few crocodiles, the last in the Sahara, lie in muddy holes in the buried wadi, nostalgic for the old days when antelope flocked to the shore by the hundreds and drank the clear water that had come down the mountain."

"Why the death of that world? What did our ancestors do to bring down the curse of Allah?"

"The peoples of the Tassili and the Ahaggar are not cursed by Allah. On the contrary. He wants to test them because he loves them. At least that is what our holy marabouts say."

The *rezzou* proceeded through the blazing hot Koudia, the camels' pace slow and calm. Men and beasts were hungry and thirsty. The sun was descending toward the distant horizon. They soon stopped to render glory to God, as if they, the *fellagha*, were not on a mission of violence and death!

The oldest raised his hand and made his camel kneel. The thirty men dismounted and prostrated themselves, facing Mecca. They touched the sand with their noses, then with their foreheads, uttering the ritual formula: "Allah is the greatest! Let us praise his perfection!"

Then each one glanced over his left shoulder to placate the fallen angels and other *Kel essouf*, the evil spirits who came out at nightfall. Can one ever know what the Powers of Darkness may be plotting?

II

Saharan Pacification Tour

It was March 27, 1903, and two White Fathers mounted on parched horses were riding toward Beni Abbès. As they rounded a bend in the dry valley of the Saoura, between two pink dunes they spotted a green patch of oasis, a miracle of life deep in this barren desert.

"God be praised", cried Father Villard, who was perspiring under his white robe. "We shall be there in less than an hour. How is *Votre Grandeur* [Your Excellency] holding up?"

Such a term could not help but make Bishop Guérin smile. He may have been the apostolic vicar on a pastoral visit, but he did not recognize here any grandeur other than the vastness of the sands, the ever-moving dunes of the Great Western Erg, and the nighttime vastness of the stars— the grandeur of God seen through the mysteries of creation. The missionary was no more than thirty-one; worn out by asceticism and hard work, he appeared much older. Like his assistant, Father Villard, he wore the flowing robe of the White Fathers under a kind of cowl. Around his neck was a rosary with large beads, and he protected himself from the sun with a broad-brimmed trapper's hat, which made him look rather odd. His heavy black beard and his thick, trailing mustaches highlighted the features of the emaciated face, in which burned the gaze of an apostle. He murmured: "I am anxious to see Father de Foucauld again. Khaouia Carlo, the Christian marabout, as he is called by the Saharan nomads and Haratins who venerate him."

"He has been at Beni Abbès for a year and a half. What has he done, apart from redeeming a handful of slaves at a premium, thanks to the generosity of his family? Not a conversion, not a baptism, nothing! Not even a disciple. Who would want to follow him in his terrifying asceticism?"

"Yes, Father Villard. I have tried in vain to moderate him. He does not listen to me."

When it came to ascetic practices, Charles did not obey his direct superior any more than he had obeyed Father Huvelin. But the previous September 17, Guérin had sent him a strong reprimand: "Even the best things obtain their total perfection only when they are regulated through obedience. I am only asking you to be so kind as to continue being guided by obedience." [1]

"Why isn't he an African missionary like us, since obviously his is not the vocation of the monk or the hermit?" Father Villard asked.

"Yes. To make of him a good missionary like the others! That is a mystery, Father Villard. He will never be that. Our cleric of the sands does not fit any of the norms. Is he merely one of those gyrovagues incapable of settling down anywhere? Or, borne up by the Holy Spirit, is he on his way to inventing a new form of apostolate? I would certainly like to know."

"He is at a dead end. At forty-five, his life of excessive asceticism has prematurely aged him. His body is deserting him."

"He is resigned to that and has even written me: 'to see myself age and go downhill is a great joy to me. It is the beginning of a disintegration that is to our good.'"

"So, unlike the rest of us, he does not fear death?"

"He fears boredom more than anything else. Now he is bored, as always happens when he has been somewhere too long. The daily routine overwhelms him and keeps him from enjoying the consolations of the divine presence."

"Yet it is he himself who asked to be buried, as he puts it. But you are right, Reverend Father. He dreads seeing himself become an old man praying in a village where nothing ever happens. To die at Beni Abbès!"

"We shall soon know what we are dealing with. But look, Father Villard! See who is coming to greet us. On foot, wearing that impossible *sheshia* [fez] topped by a puggaree hanging down to his shoulders!"

"Yes, it is he! He has dared venture outside his cloister!"

On seeing the two horsemen and their guide, Brother Charles began to run. He stopped, winded. Bishop Guérin quickly dismounted and took him in his arms. They hugged each other, laughing, under the rather shocked gaze of Father Villard.

Half an hour later, pointing to a group of pitiful hovels, Brother Charles cried: "Here is the fraternity! Father, I receive you as a poor man receiving his dearly beloved father, that is, in great poverty!"

"I shall feel much more at ease here with you than in the comfort of an officer's room in the redoubt, where they invited me to stay."

All that day, the apostolic vicar observed Brother Charles' incredible energy. The poor milled about in the hermitage. They were all hungry, and Charles distributed to them what he had. Mothers held out their babies, and Charles gave each woman a can of milk. The sick came, asking for

[1] Archives of the Postulation.

medicine and a few words of encouragement. Laughing children, naked or in rags, crowded around him and begged three dates or a piece of wheat hardtack. A few of the poor dared enter the chapel, the door of which always stood open. They crouched on the ground and marveled at the tabernacle's little oil lamp. They felt at ease in the dwelling of Khaouia Carlo. He fed them, he listened to them, he respected them, he protected them. He loved them.

Soldiers came too, the rough French troopers of the African battalion, the *Joyeux*. One showed the latest letter from his wife. Another wanted to confess; perhaps he had committed some crime; Brother Charles was all forgiveness. Other sharpshooters came, bringing canned goods or a bottle of wine, and had their picture taken with the hermit. Then they spoke of their lives and were just as surprised as the poor of the *ksar* by seeing a holy man who listened to them in silence and did not judge them.

Brother Charles left them to go ring the bell. It was time for the office. With the two White Fathers beside him, he recited Compline:

> Lord, you have put in my heart more joy
> than on the day their wheat,
> their new wine spill forth.

Then he was lost in adoration for a very brief moment. He seemed to be recharging himself. In the distance there were muffled sounds, a caravan passing slowly by or a lone horseman. Already another indigent had knocked and was coming in.

Nightfall. A woman with multicolored veils passed by, taking home her herd of goats. The visits slowed down. In the shack set aside for them, a few wretched travelers wrapped themselves in their jellabas and fell asleep in peace.

The sweetness of evening. Above the palm grove and the distant dunes, the stars were coming out. Exhausted bodies felt the balm of a little cool air. Bishop Guérin was now alone with Brother Charles on the threshold of the hermitage. The darkness had reached the base of the cliff and was penetrating the palm grove. In the distance the Great Erg, visible through fleecy white clouds, was grazed by the setting sun. To the south rose the little golden dunes of the plain. The desert was changing from light to darkness. Not a breath of wind. No mist distorted the endless horizon of the sands. It was beautiful and impalpable, leading one to question paltry human realities and become mystical. The only reality was the boundless desert and the immensity of the starry sky. The Absolute. God.

The everyday sound of a camel bleating brought them back to harsh reality. The apostolic vicar looked the hermit over carefully: bare feet on camelskin soles, worn white robe imprinted with a heart and a cross. Under the ample folds of the garment could be glimpsed the outline of a body wasted by ascetic living. "He looks bizarre and mad", thought the prelate. But he was fascinated by Charles' expression, which was mellow, thoughtful, of a mysterious sweetness at times altered by flashes of strong emotion.

"Are you satisfied with what you have founded here, Brother Charles?"

"Yes and no, Father. Beni Abbès is both an isolated and central oasis, crossroads between Algeria, Morocco, and the Sahara. Great numbers pass through here!"

"How can what is central also be isolated? And how is it possible for a hermit to be a missionary in the usual sense of the word?"

"When Jesus takes you into himself to give you to souls, wherever you go means a life of isolation. We find that apparent contradiction in Christ, a hidden, contemplative soul who ended up giving himself to men, allowing himself to be consumed by them."

"At least you have a few conversions, some baptisms?"

"A single baptism, the elderly black blind woman you saw at the hermitage. No Muslim Berbers or Arabs. In January, some Haratins asked for instruction, but nothing will come of that. They are just soup Christians. In spite of my offer of 550 francs,[2] I was unsuccessful when I tried in February to redeem a young slave who had agreed to baptism and seemed truly sincere."

"What is the cause of this failure?"

"My lack of holiness. The apostles did good in accordance with their holiness and as long as they suffered. That is how they effaced themselves so that the Christ dwelling in them could act."

"What more can you do?"

"At first, I began with voluntary mortifications. Obviously, that was not enough. I know now that I must arrive by suffering the Cross of Jesus."

"Are you following the rule you set up?"

"No, Father. Worked out for Cheiklé and Nazareth, it is poorly suited to the realities and the terrible sluggishness of the land of Africa and its age-old culture."

"What are your plans?"

"To obey."

"But beyond that?"

"With your permission, to leave. I feel a calling to those vast territories where Jesus never prayed."

[2] About fifteen thousand in the French franc of today (about 2,460 dollars). In 1902, a slave was worth three times the price of a camel, which cost 150 francs.

"That is the vocation of a missionary, and I rejoice to hear of it. One day we shall have the support of our French authorities. I predict the hour will come when you can serve both the work of France and that of the Gospel."[3]

"Yes, except for their being slow to eradicate slavery, the army is doing good work here."

"Every French conquest in the Sahara paves the way for the work of the Gospel.[4] To pacify, to end the tribal struggles and *razzias*, which prevent progress, is a realistic policy and worthy of Christians. So you would agree to leaving Beni Abbès to spread the Holy Gospel?"

"For that, I am ready to go to the ends of the earth."

"Do you have a specific plan?"

"Yes. To go into Morocco to evangelize."

"There again, a missionary vocation. You did not want that."

"I am and shall remain a silent, hidden monk and not a preacher. I am too unworthy to proclaim the Gospel. I can only try to live it."

"It is harder to live it than preach it. Is that really your place, following after these military camps, which are nomadic for the most part?[5] What does Father Huvelin have to say?"

"He says: 'Go where the Spirit moves you.' "[6]

"How can you reconcile mission work with the monastic life?"

"The contemplative orders are always called in advance of the teaching and preaching orders, for adoration makes everything ready.[7] I have thought that all along. It is God who makes everything possible. Not man. Thus, in reaching God through prayer, we can open the way for the mission."

"But do not forget that Morocco is still closed territory. Our missionaries do not have permission to go there any more than to the Sahara."

"Last January 22, I wrote to my friend in Algiers, Major Lacroix, to request a standing authorization, kept secret, that would allow a discreet push into Morocco. He replied, 'You will be rendering a great service to France, to civilization, to the Lord, and to your old friend.' "

"So you have the backing of the army?"

"Yes, Father. The practical details still need to be worked out. I hope to contact Major Laperrine, who has become the commander of the Oases Territory after working wonders in black Africa."

Bishop Guérin began to dream aloud: "To enter the Sahara, Morocco. It

---

[3] Instruction of Bishop Guérin to CF, February 15, 1903, archives of the Postulation.
[4] Ibid., March 25, 1903.
[5] Bishop Guérin to CF, July 22, 1903, *Cahiers Charles de Foucauld*, no. 32.
[6] Father Huvelin to CF, July 15, 1903.
[7] CF, plan of January 25, 1903.

would be unprecedented for the Church. It seems obvious to me that through your whole past life as a soldier, explorer, and monk, the Lord has destined you to a mission on the borders of Morocco and in Morocco itself. I believe I see in you something more than this vocation of prayer and penance. The Lord has reserved for you a mission, which shall be enduring and is of the greatest importance.[8] Will you depart alone with a military column?"

"It would be helpful for me to have a select companion to assist in this life of poverty and to serve Mass. Without a companion, I could not celebrate Mass. This journey ought to tempt a number of souls, for it is almost glory that is offered them, because the dangers are so great!"

But no companion was forthcoming. Charles, too, began to dream: "I ask only three things of my companions: to be ready to give their blood without a struggle; to starve; to obey me despite my unworthiness."[9]

Bishop Guérin smiled. He knew that nothing would stop the apostle, even if he had to depart alone. "Under no circumstances would I want to discourage you if, after careful reflection, you think you have been called upon by God to leave here.[10] What can I do for you at the moment?"

"Pray that I am of sufficient faith![11] Like our one model . . . even following him to the Cross!"

"Brother Charles, you think about martyrdom too much. Martyrdom, that is the easy way. The ideal is to die to the self each day."

"Beloved Father, pray to Jesus that I may die to all that is not he and his will."

"The ideal way is obedience. First to Jesus, our model. To the Holy Spirit, who uplifts us. And, more prosaically, to your unworthy priest."

"Obedience is the last, the highest, and the most perfect of the levels of love. The one at which the self ceases to exist, is abolished, and we die like Jesus on the Cross."[12]

"I say it again: Do not think about martyrdom. And do not abuse fasting."

"Do not think that, in my kind of life, the hope of enjoying the sight of the Beloved sooner is behind such thoughts. I am ready to live until the Last Judgment!"

Bishop Guérin stood up. It was late, and he did not wish to take further advantage of the ascetic's short night. For a long moment he contemplated

---

[8] Bishop Guérin to CF, February 13, 1903.

[9] CF, note on mission project, 1903, in G. Gorrée, *Sur les traces de Charles de Foucauld* (Éd. de la Plus Grande France, 1936), 155.

[10] Bishop Guérin to CF, August 19, 1903.

[11] CF to Father Laurain, May 25, 1903, in Gorrée, *Sur les traces*, 161.

[12] CF to Father Jérôme, January 24, 1897, in ibid., 93.

the mysterious landscape, the moonlit dunes, and the infinite reaches of the dark desert. "How beautiful this land is!"

"It would be more beautiful were it given to Christ!"

The sky above seemed to be crying out with the glow of its billions of stars. As if it were calling the apostles to the desert!

Brother Charles, after showing the two White Fathers the modest hut where they were to spend the night, went off toward the chapel. His eyes shone with a strange brightness. It was the hour of adoration. Father Villard whispered: "Look at him, Father Guérin! It seems as though he is accompanied!"

In the letter to Rome following upon this pastoral visit, Bishop Guérin was to write:

> I have been edified more than I can say by all the virtues I admired in him: spirit of faith, zeal, charity, mortification, poverty, humility, gentleness, radiance of a celestial joy. I was pleased to observe the profound influence this veritable saint has had in the last two years on all those encountering him: Europeans, officers and soldiers, who all speak in one voice of their deeply respectful and completely religious veneration for this holy priest. On the Muslims, his influence has been no less fruitful in valuable results. For more than a hundred miles around they know the "Christian marabout", who lives so poorly and yet is so charitable toward all, especially the small and the weak, the poor and the enslaved, whom he receives, takes in, cares for, and feeds with a devotion that is not of this world.[13]

And then, looking ahead to Charles' travels into the south, he sought a dispensation on his behalf so he could say Mass without a helper: "He is likely to find himself completely isolated from Christians and catechumens, and consequently, according to the usual regulations, it would be absolutely impossible for him to celebrate the most Holy Sacrifice. I am not unaware, Your Eminence, that this is a very great favor and very rarely granted by Rome. Yet I am allowing myself to hope that in view of the truly extraordinary vocation and the very special virtues of Father Charles of Jesus, Your Most Reverend Eminence will kindly make easier for this holy hermit the conditions under which he may offer the most Holy Sacrifice." [14]

On March 6, 1903, returning from Algiers with Captain Regnault, Major Laperrine, heading toward Adrar by way of western Algeria, stopped at Beni Abbès. This officer, who would be playing a decisive role in the life of Charles de Foucauld, was already a legend in the army of Africa.

Two years younger than the hermit, Henri Laperrine de Hautpoul,

---

[13] Report of Bishop Guérin to the Vatican, August 28, 1903, archives of the Congregation of the Faith.

[14] Ibid.

related to a branch of the Foucauld family through his mother, had been in
a different class at Saint-Cyr and at Saumur. He had already met Charles at
Mascara, in January 1882, although the two were not in the same squadron
of the Chasseurs d'Afrique. The brilliant, patriotic officer, who loved Africa
deeply, had later served in Senegal, Niger, and the Sahara. In 1901, he
commanded from In Salah the Oases Territory. At one time an unruly
student with the Dominicans, Laperrine was very much a believer, although non-practicing, and initially he had been shocked by Second Lieutenant Foucauld's escapades.

"Of medium height, he had a supple, muscular build; a thin, pale face,
with fine features; a short, light-brown beard, fan-shaped; bright, mocking
eyes, stern at times. Laperrine was the prototype of the colonial cavalryman;
his rank showed in his expression, his bearing, and in his soul", René Bazin
said of him.[15]

Able to ride for ten hours under the scorching sun, he never looked
other than impeccable at the head of his men, who adored him. Because he
avoided cities and offices, they were wary of him in the ministries. Upright
and loyal, he did not forgive deceit. He was especially good with the tribal
chiefs, whom he knew how to treat honorably, never humiliating or exploiting them. The desert was his kingdom, his passion. He dreamed of
giving the Sahara to France, seeing in those limitless and seemingly sterile
expanses more than a strategic region uniting North Africa and black
Africa: an extension of France. That ideal was shared by Foucauld; the two
also had in common the quality of giving unselfishly to a noble cause.
Laperrine's officers called him "his Saharan Highness", and his personal
guard of Chaamba camel troopers was ready to die for him.

Learning of Brother Charles' plans, Dom Henri, prior of the Trappist
house at Staoueli, had told Laperrine: "You can count on him to be a
perfect instrument for pacification and moral improvement. He will do for
French influence in those regions just what the great Cardinal Lavigerie
did on a larger scale in Tunisia."[16]

The goals of the two men were not the same. Laperrine wanted to win
the Saharan people over to France. Foucauld wanted to win the Saharan
people over to Christ. But there was nothing contradictory in their views;
the two were made to understand each other.

"What are your plans?" Charles asked Laperrine.

"To pacify the mountains of the Ahaggar. To win over the tribes that are
now divided: the Taitoq, the Iforas, the Ahaggar."

"Your method?"

---

[15] R. Bazin, *Charles de Foucauld* (Plon, 1921), 234.
[16] Cardinal Lavigerie, *Bulletin des Amitiés*, no. 83, 15.

"Not to subdue them, but to tame them, through dialogue and respect."
"The opposite of the Flatters approach!"
"Lieutenant Colonel Flatters failed, may he rest in peace. He was rigid. He advanced too quickly at the head of a column ready to shoot. He aroused fear. Having chanced upon a wild tribe that had never seen a European, he felt threatened, he opened fire, and the massacre resulted. Now, contrary to the accepted idea, it is the explorer Duveyrier who was right, not Flatters. The Tuareg can be won over. Unlike the Senoussi, they are not fanatics."

The hermit qualified that: "Some Tuareg. Flatters died while on an expedition to map out possible routes for a railroad across the Sahara. In his saddlebags he carried the famous report by Duveyrier. Accused of having presented the 'natives' in too favorable a light, in 1892 my friend Duveyrier committed suicide. A shocking affair, a lumping together without distinctions. He was a defender of the Ahaggar tribe, while it was the cruel Ajjer who massacred the Flatters mission, which was made up of Chaamba camel troopers, traditionally a spurned group. Then my friend Morès-Vallombrosa was also murdered, by his own guides, Tuareg Iforas, while on an expedition heading to Rât. What a mess!"

"You are quite well informed, Father Charles. Forget these deaths. Think only of reconciliation."

"I am not forgetting these deaths. I live among the peoples who killed my friend. I shall avenge him by giving back good for evil. Morès, for whom I pray every day, helps me in this. In heaven, within the immense charity in which he is submerged, there is only prayer and love for these Muslims who have spilled his blood and will perhaps spill mine. We are working together at the same tasks of salvation and love." [17]

"Yes, let us work together. Do you wish to help me? I dream of a Tuareg confederation of the Sahara, a kind of free kingdom of Central Africa, predominantly Christian, the foundation of African colonization."

Charles was startled. "You truly believe that possible? The Muslims are so closed to our faith!"

"The Tuareg are not Arabs, and probably not Berbers either. The most ancient people of white Africa, don't they come from Egypt, driven out in the eighth century by Arab invaders? They may have been Christians. They have kept certain Christian symbols, such as the cross seen on their shields, saddle pommels, and tattoos."

"Shortly after you arrived to command the Oases, you delivered the Tuareg some harsh treatment."

---

[17] CF to the Marquis de La Roche-Thulon, March 18, 1905, quoted by J.-F. Six, *Vie de Charles de Foucauld* (Seuil, 1962), 126.

"Are you referring to the Battle of Tit? At the outset, we had to be respected. They have a false idea of us, spread by their marabouts. France is supposedly a country of pagan cannibals, worse than the savages of black Africa! In 1902, a Targui had a noblewoman beaten, claiming that she had trafficked with us. I ordered Lieutenant Cottenest to mount an operation to suppress them. He crossed the desert leading 130 mercenaries recently won over, the famous Chaamba, enemies of the Tuareg. Mohamed ag Rotman's three hundred rebels were waiting for him on May 7 at Amessera, near Tit. They were crushed, in spite of greatly outnumbering our forces: ninety-three Tuareg were killed. Ag Rotman fled, as did Attici, the chief of the Kel Ahaggar."

"And now?"

"They understood! The noble Moussa ag Amastane dreams of succeeding him as *amenokal* of the Ahaggar. He is a moderate. I hope to meet him. To that end, I plan to undertake a pacification tour through the Ahaggar. Will you accompany me?"

Charles' heart began to beat faster. "Perhaps. If Bishop Guérin grants me permission."

Once back in In Salah, Laperrine drew up the following orders for one of the officers closest to him, Lieutenant Nieger: "You will go through Beni Abbès. You will go see Foucauld. He is playing the mason. He is building himself a hermitage that he does not leave. He is not eating. He lives off public charity and still finds the means to redeem slaves coming from Morocco. He thinks only of Morocco. He is plagued by memories of his youth. There is no way we can help him with that, but he is tough. We must convince him to come and join us." [18]

Ever since his long talk with Laperrine, Foucauld had dreamed of nothing but departing, of getting to know the Tuareg, who were not only proud but at times *charitable*. In 1881, had not a beautiful noblewoman, Tarichat, taken in, nursed, and sent home the French wounded in battle, standing up to the cruel rebel Attici, who wanted them finished off?

On June 18, 1903, Charles asked Bishop Guérin for permission to leave with Laperrine. But now the apostolic vicar appeared reluctant. He feared not only the dangers of this uncertain expedition but also complications with the French authorities, who had refused to allow the sending of White Father missionaries into the Oases south of the thirtieth parallel.

But Charles was unlike the other missionaries. He persisted: "To pave the way, to begin the evangelization of the Tuareg by settling among them,

---

[18] As told by General Nieger, *Bulletin des Amitiés*, no. 102, 16.

learning their language, translating the Holy Gospels, establishing the friend-liest relations possible with them." [19]

Laperrine had agreed not only to take him along but to leave him in the midst of the central tribes, in the Tidikelt or the Ahaggar, if the risks did not seem too great. And as Bishop Guérin was taking his time about answering, Charles decided to go ahead on his own: he would depart on September 6 with the military column. Fine, but Laperrine did not even have permission from the army, the backing of Major Lacroix not being enough. Laperrine wrote to Captain Regnault, "I do not have the right to do this, but I hope, as usual, to escape with nothing more than a few insulting and threatening letters from the subdivision." [20]

In spirit Charles was already heading toward those wide open spaces. But a dramatic setback soon spoiled his plans. In southern Morocco, the funda-mentalist marabouts, supported by tribal chiefs, proclaimed holy war against the French invaders of Algeria. The chiefs could no longer stand being without their profitable *rezzous*, which had ended when the French occu-pied southern Algeria. Moreover, they feared that Morocco too would be occupied and pacified. In the nearby Algerian Sahara, the tribes rose up, making doubtful Laperrine's "pacification tour". Now was a time for pow-der, not dialogue.

On July 16, 1903, a *rezzou* of two hundred Berâber attacked a detach-ment of fifty Algerian sharpshooters from the company at Adrar, and twenty-two men were lost. Captain Regnault launched a swift counter-attack out of Beni Abbès, killing thirty rebels and putting the others to flight.

Seventy-five miles north of Beni Abbès, the palm grove of Taghit, where Captain de Susbielle was the commander, found itself under threat. Since the garrison (470 men) had no chaplain, Charles asked for permission to go there but was turned down by Regnault.

On August 17, Taghit was attacked by the sharif Mustafa's six thousand Moroccan fanatics, who had come down from Tafilalt. In his *bordj*, Susbielle, with reinforcements from Beni Abbès, defended himself successfully and carried out a sortie; the horde retreated on August 20 with one thousand disabled men, leaving three hundred naked dead on the ground. Charles was trembling with impatience. The defenders had suffered nine deaths and twenty-one wounded, and he was not there with them! Regnault still refused permission. The desert was less and less sure.

On September 2, a convoy escorted by the Legion was attacked on the heights of El Moungar and decimated. Susbielle, summoned there, saved it

[19] CF to Bishop Guérin, June 30, 1903, in J.-F. Six, *Itinéraire spirituel de Charles de Foucauld* (Seuil, 1958), 60.

[20] In *Bulletin des Amitiés*, no. 102, 18, study by General Suremain.

in extremis from total annihilation. Forty-nine wounded were transported to Taghit. When Charles heard that, he rushed to the *bordj*, asked the officer on duty for a horse, and got one, but as he was about to depart, another officer interfered: "We cannot grant the priest permission to leave without escort. He might be killed on the road."

"I shall get through", Charles said.

Just then Captain Regnault intervened: "Let him go. He will get through."

"Without an escort? Unarmed?"

"He can cross the entire rebel area unarmed. No one will lay a hand on him. Khaouia Carlo is sacred." [21]

Charles was in the saddle at 10 A.M. Halfway through his journey, he saw two horsemen coming toward him, sent by Susbielle. They were awaiting him at Taghit! All night, they rode relentlessly and reached the *bordj* at 9 A.M. Without a moment's rest, Charles celebrated Mass, then he went to the wounded legionnaires. He would stay among them for twenty-five days. Meanwhile, the Moroccan hordes had flowed back toward the Atlas. In the French Sahara, the tribal chiefs remained quiet, ready to swing toward the strongest.

When he returned to Beni Abbès, Charles found a letter from Laperrine dated August 29, 1903. He jumped for joy. The commander of the Oases had accepted him in his column, which would leave in early January 1904 to ride through the Sahara and journey right into the Ahaggar. It would perhaps go down as far as Timbuktu, in a major "pacification tour", which, after the harsh repression of the summer, would signal France's desire to integrate peacefully the peoples of the region.

After that first joyous moment when he thought only of the departure, Charles had to pull himself together and force back his old demon. Should the only priest for six hundred miles around desert Beni Abbès? "Do I waste myself in these journeys, which do no good for the soul?" he asked Father Huvelin. But the vicar of Saint-Augustin left him free to decide: "Go where the Spirit leads you."

Since there had been no answer from Bishop Guérin, Charles presented him with the fait accompli: "I am not leaving so quickly through lack of obedience to you, beloved and revered Father, but because the most perfect obedience—and this forms parts of its perfection—includes, in some cases, initiative. If I leave without hesitating, it is that I am ready to return without hesitating. As easily as I depart, I shall return." [22]

The apostolic vicar gave in. He asked Charles to take a name that would

---

[21] Bazin, *Foucauld*, 275.

[22] CF to Bishop Guérin, August 26, 1903, quoted by Quesnel, *Charles de Foucauld, les étapes d'une recherche* (Mame, 1966), 150.

allow the Tuareg to refer to him in their own language. Charles chose "Abd Issa", servant of Jesus. His mind finally free as to the approval of his superiors, he prepared for his departure.

He knew that it would not be easy to make the people accept him. Of the six major tribes of the Tuareg people, only three had surrendered to Laperrine. Among the others, the most aggressive was that in the Ahaggar, the massif in the heart of the Sahara. If Charles wanted to succeed, at some time or another he would have to leave the shelter of the army. Well, the Tuareg were not like the Arabs of northern Algeria: the latter had been won over and had even been engaged as camel troopers by the French army, one more reason for them to be hated by the still savage Tuareg and Berbers of the south.

But how not to remain dependent on the army? Charles noted in his diary: "Do without a mount, without money, without guides. Essential to have ties of dependence no longer. Make my baggage very light and get used to walking. As for money, I must get used to not needing any: go on foot, do everything for myself by making my needs very small. For guides, have friends." [23]

There remained the problem of celebrating the Eucharist without a server. Rome had rejected Bishop Guérin's plea. Their Eminences of the Vatican had given permission only for the apostle to "use any kind of candle if beeswax is not available; to celebrate even without light in regions that do not produce any olives, thus making it impossible to have fuel for lamps." [24] The fact that Paul Embarek had agreed to follow him settled the question for Charles. Although not yet baptized, the young black servant could, as a sort of catechumen, serve Mass, but he was not the ideal companion!

Departure at last, January 13, 1904. The 150 camel troopers from the Touat and Tidikelt companies (led by Lieutenants Bricogne, Nieger, and Besset) escorted the long supply caravan. They were to meet up with Laperrine to the south. Charles refused the horse offered by Captain Regnault. He did accept a female donkey to carry the heavy tent chapel, but he himself traveled on foot, like the ordinary troopers.

Doing twenty to thirty miles a day, the column descended the wide dry bed of Saoura. At the watering places, they found *ksour*, where Charles would distribute alms and medicines. Every morning at dawn, Paul raised the tent under which the priest celebrated Mass before a devout audience.

---

[23] CF, diary, August 24, 1903, in *Carnet de Beni-Abbès* (Nouvelle Cité, 1993), 82.
[24] Ibid., March 8, 1904, 92.

Then the column struck directly south, a desert without life, without vegetation, without villages. Here and there a few tents around a well, a patch of green, some lean goats browsing. A few wary nomads might approach the caravan. Their marabouts had said the French would kill them for their camels. Well, these good-humored military men proffered smiles and food. The visitors would also crowd around the strange French marabout, whose reputation had already spread beyond the desert. He soon became known to all as the *diff el Rebbi*, the guest from God.

On February 2, 1904, the column entered the Adrar Oasis, the center of the Touat. Here they were joined by Laperrine. At Akabli, for considerations of safety, the commander asked Charles to stay with the military column, which meant the hermit had to ride a dromedary.

Charles, who was seeking a site for his future fraternity, took notes. At Timissao, he envisioned "settling here in the grotto with some dates and flour, starting a little garden, a few palms, vegetables, covering the well, always leaving out for travelers some *delou* [a kind of leather well bucket] and ropes, and for the poor a few dates and a little flour: try to obtain a serious companion." [25]

On April 16, the column went into Timeïaouine, in Iforas territory in the Adrar, near the southern border of Algeria. Night was falling, and the exhausted men were happy to find themselves in the cool oasis.

Suddenly a little band of soldiers loomed up before them. Their uniforms were wrinkled, dusty. Two French officers were leading their exhausted men—twenty-five black Sudanese sharpshooters and ten Kemaya auxiliaries. Where had they come from? They had just crossed the desert, but from the south. They were from Timbuktu, the French colony of the Sudan, today Mali. The commander, as exhausted as his men, seemed in a bad way. He came up to Laperrine and introduced himself: "Captain Théveniaud, of the French forces in the Sudan."

"Delighted. As it happens, we are on our way to Timbuktu."

"The Southern Territories come under my sphere of influence. You have no business there, Major."

Laperrine was shocked by the words and the tone. "I am on a pacification tour, by order of the Minister of the Interior, who is responsible for Algeria. I have already received the surrender of the Iforas and the Ahaggar."

"I do not recognize that. The military authorities of the Sudan, who are under the Colonial Ministry, were not consulted. An officer who would accept a surrender without consulting his neighbors must be young and quite without experience in indigenous affairs."

[25] Ibid., April 6, 1904, 96.

Laperrine was shaking at this attack. The little captain, with his pathetic band, seemed overexcited. The major could disregard his words and proceed on his mission, but what a bad example to show the local peoples and the native troops! Keeping his voice under control, he asked: "What are your orders, and who sends you here?"

"I am the bearer of a letter from the lieutenant colonel who is the commander at Timbuktu. Here it is."

Laperrine studied the contents. It was clear. They were refusing to let him go to Timbuktu. The borders between the two countries had not yet been officially demarcated. Naturally, the nomadic tribes that moved all over the region paid no attention to any border, and therein lay the problem. The Tuareg Iforas of Algeria were spilling over into French West Africa. Now, the Iforas had just surrendered to Laperrine but not to the Sudanese authorities. In retaliation, when passing through their territory, Théveniaud had taken advantage of them, requisitioning camels and food without paying, according to the usual practice in unsubdued lands.

The captain was becoming increasingly aggressive. The same age as Laperrine, he seemed jealous at having one stripe less, jealous too of the reputation of the commander of the Oases. "Why do you want to go to Timbuktu? Do you have a written order?"

"No. But it is important that a French military column unite peacefully Algeria and black Africa for the first time."

"I see in that nothing but a manifestation of pride. If you insist on this mission, you will march under our escort and you will have no dealings with the natives."

"I cannot place myself under the orders of a mere captain", growled Laperrine.

"The Sudan is my territory. If you go ahead on your own, my column will see that the rights of the Sudan are respected, as per its orders, using all the means at its disposal."

Were they going to fight? The situation grew heated. Charles withdrew to keep from exploding. Wisely, Laperrine broke off the interview, "to think things over". At dawn, he ordered his troops to head back north. In exchange Théveniaud agreed not to exact anything from the tribes on his return journey.

Charles, sickened, had already gone on ahead. At their next stopping place, he scribbled angrily in his notebook. "What I see of the officers of the Sudan saddens me. They appear to be pillagers, bandits, buccaneers. I fear that this great colonial empire, which could and should give birth to so much good—moral good, true good—is presently only a cause of shame for us, that it gives us cause to blush even before the savages; that it leads them to curse the name of France and, alas, the name Christian, and that it makes these peoples, already so poor, even poorer." [26]

Charles was revolted by this incident. He recognized that there was an irreducible gulf between the two conceptions of colonialism—his, made up of generosity, the gift of self, and that of some officers, administrators, and colonists who sought only to make a career for themselves or to exploit the country while looking down on the natives.

The return across the Tanezrouft was rather dramatic. On May 7, 1904, at Ti-n-Rharo, the column found the wells nearly dry. It took them two days and nights to water their camels and to fill their goatskins with muddy water. The heat had become unbearable.

So as not to endanger his entire company, Laperrine sent two lieutenants ahead to check out nearby wells. But their guide betrayed them and disappeared in the desert. Lost in the middle of the Tanezrouft, they could not find the North Star, veiled by the blowing sands, and they proceeded with the compass, mouths dry and hearts heavy.

On May 17, Laperrine having caught up with them, they reached Tinef, on the edge of the Ahaggar. Charles was genuinely intrigued by this desolate but magnificent country, which rose as high as ten thousand feet above the scorching desert. He was determined to settle there. But where? and to do what? He noted in his diary: "To found in the heart of Tuareg country the sanctuary, the fraternity of the Sacred Heart of Jesus. . . . I offer my life for the conversion of the Tuareg, of Morocco, all the peoples of the Sahara, all the infidels." [27]

Then he asked himself, "How do I conduct myself here? Imitate Jesus in his hidden life. Be as small and poor as he. Not try, as I did at Beni Abbès, to prepare a nest or provide charity on a large scale. Build a five-by-seven-foot oratory and a shelter for Paul and me. To find work that guarantees our daily bread: farming, gardening. Pray at night, work by day, love and contemplate Jesus unceasingly with all my heart, in poverty, holiness, and love. Silently, secretly, like Jesus in Nazareth; obscurely, like him, pass unknown on earth like a voyager in the night; in poverty and toil, humbly, with charity, like him; defenseless and mute before injustice, like him; letting myself, like the lamb, be shorn and immolated without resistance or protest; imitating in everything Jesus in Nazareth and Jesus on the Cross." [28]

Once again, the contemplative life was winning out over the missionary life as lived, on occasion heroically, by the White Fathers, whose militant spirit worried the government and even Laperrine.

[26] Ibid.
[27] Ibid., April 16, 1904, 98.
[28] Ibid., May 17, 1904, 103–4.

Charles expressed himself openly to Lieutenant Besset, with whom he had become friends: "I will settle in the Ahaggar. Come with me. The Tuareg love you. Laperrine will give you a command there. One of my friends, a Trappist in Staoueli, is a physician. He will join me. He will minister to the bodies, I will take care of the souls, and you will exercise temporal power." [29]

The fantasy made Besset smile. "You're seeking martyrdom, Father Charles!"

"I am ordinarily inclined toward solitude, stability, silence. But if I believe I'm being called to something else, I obey. Love always obeys when God is its object. My task will not be to convert. I am not worthy, nor do I have the skill. And it is not yet time. This is preparatory work, the establishment of confidence, of friendship." [30]

"The region is insecure. We have to wait. The commandant will not let you go. Not yet. Theoretically, Moussa has surrendered, but he's not playing fair. He has not yet appeared in person. Pride is holding him back."

On May 26, Charles slept in Tit, only about thirty miles from Tamanrasset. Before him rose the peaks of the Ahaggar highlands, fascinating him as if they were a kind of Sinai. The region had a temperate climate. Water was plentiful, and the gardens were lush in the little hollowed-out valleys surrounded by a rocky, lunar landscape. It was in Tit in 1902 that Lieutenant Cottenest, sent by Laperrine, had harshly subdued the Kel Ahaggar, a semi-pastoral, semi-agricultural people whose archaic social structure was reminiscent of France in the Middle Ages and whose noble caste thought only of engaging in battle. In his notebook, Charles observed: "Tit seems to me the most suitable place to establish a mission, since it is really the heart of the Ahaggar. I'm asking Laperrine for permission to stay here." [31]

Already he pictured himself set up in a cave on the banks of the Tit Oued, cultivating the land nearby. He could see brothers in a Greek-style monastery with shelters carved by nature, a chapel, little nests for worship, an oratory perched high among the rocks.

But Laperrine refused permission. "Later we'll see." In fact, his decision had already been made, as he would write to Captain Cauvet: "I'm leaving Foucauld in the Sahara. He's studying Tuareg, and he has medicines and two camels. If Count [sic] de Foucauld, hussar, ex-explorer, breakaway Trappist, becomes chaplain to Moussa or someone else of that ilk, it will be no small thing." [32]

[29] Quoted by M. Castillon du Perron, *Charles de Foucauld* (Grasset, 1982), 352.
[30] CF to Henri de Castries, June 18, 1904, in Gorrée, *Sur les traces*, 179.
[31] *Carnet de Beni-Abbès*, 109.
[32] Quoted by Castillon, *Foucauld*, 354.

On June 14, 1904, Laperrine took leave of Foucauld and turned him over to Lieutenant Roussel, who was on his way from the Tidikelt plain with seventy-five Arab camel troopers. Roussel's mission: to complete the pacification tour, to contact the *amenokal* Moussa, to seek his complete and sincere surrender . . . and possibly entrust to him Father de Foucauld.

Although contacts established with the Tuareg were very good, Moussa could not be found, and the column headed back to the north. The local chiefs contacted had said no to Father de Foucauld's settling in the Ahaggar.

It would take more than that to discourage him.

In El Amra, on July 2, 1904, Brother Charles observed in his notebook: "Feast of the Visitation, the patronal feast of all the communities of Little Brothers and Little Sisters of the Heart of Jesus!" [33]

But he was still the only little brother in the world! He continued, addressing the Virgin: "Beloved Mother, convert the Tuareg, let the Little Brothers and Sisters of Jesus come into being. May they be your faithful instruments. Unworthy creature that I am, convert me. Cherished Mother, I ask you on my knees, from the depths of my misery!"

Even through the bright glow of his visions, he remained lucid and pragmatic, writing to Marie de Bondy on July 3: "The indigenous people receive us well. It is not sincere; they cede to necessity. Will they be able to distinguish between soldiers and priests and see in us universal brothers?" [34]

He did not delude himself: "My preparatory work is continuing. I am not ready to sow, and others will reap." [35]

In Tazerouk on August 3, Charles was still determined to settle in the Ahaggar. He put in a request to the local chief, Ben Otman, who refused his petition. The military authorities went the same route. The region was too insecure. They would agree to his living in the Sahara only if he were close to a garrison. There was none in the Ahaggar.

The pacification tour ended on September 20 at In Salah, where the camel troopers returned to their station. Although worn out, Charles headed north again, his only escort the indigenous soldier who served as guide. He went through the Tidikelt and Touat regions, stopping in every village to distribute medicines and alms. In El Golea, the White Fathers received him warmly.

At Metliti, a day's march from Ghardaïa, he saw Bishop Guérin coming to meet him. They embraced. The next day, November 12, Charles entered

---

[33] *Carnet de Beni-Abbès*, July 2, 1904, 143.
[34] Quoted by Bazin, *Foucauld*, 298.
[35] CF to Henri de Castries, July 15, 1904, in Gorrée, *Sur les traces*, 182.

Ghardaïa, "A poor ragged creature on foot, exhausted, leading his camel by the face, he plodded along, looking like a mendicant dervish, but his eyes were joyful, and his smile identified him." [36]

The journey during the hot season had worn him out. He was but a shadow of himself, and he bemoaned "the demands of this near-dead body", which was failing him. The eyes were sunken, the cheekbones prominent in the emaciated face, and the lines in the forehead deeply etched. He suffered from headaches and fevers. His teeth, neglected, were falling out. And so he spent more than a month in Ghardaïa, in an atmosphere of silence, solitude, and prayer, with Bishop Guérin and his missionaries providing care and friendship.

They now knew the lay of the land. The exhausting tour had been worthwhile. Charles had made great strides in his study of the Tuareg language. But founding a house was still a long way off. Bishop Guérin wanted to send White Fathers into the Ahaggar, but Laperrine was opposed. Their results in Algeria had not been good. It did not work to treat the Arabs and Berbers, solidly rooted in Islam, as if they were black fetishist tribes. Too activist, at times intolerant, the good fathers, by opposing the marabouts and other guardians of the Islamic faith, posed a threat to public order and the success of French secular pacification efforts.

Charles' method was different. No apostolic zeal, but a simple presence, that of Christ. God alone would convert, when the time was right. Charles' real problem was to keep to his life of prayer "as a restorative", at the same time devoting himself to the poor, a task that threatened to overwhelm him: "I wonder if the impossibility of combining the two things is real or merely the result of my apathy." [37]

Finally, Bishop Guérin ordered Brother Charles to return to Beni Abbès, where the garrison needed him. From there, according to what might come up, he could go to Morocco or the Ahaggar, still keeping one foot in Beni Abbès.

Disappointed, Charles obeyed. Living under the constant gaze of God, he awaited everything from him, even the worst. On December 15, he wrote his friend, Suzanne Perret, the Lyon mystic, who had offered her life for him: "In a few days I shall be going back to my cell and the solitary Tabernacle, feeling more deeply than ever that Jesus wants me to work to establish this double family [the Little Brothers and Sisters]. How? By pleading, by immolating myself, by dying, by becoming more holy, and, finally, by loving him! I beseech you to help me. Our Lord is impatient. His hidden life is not being imitated. The days we have been allotted to love, to

[36] Bazin, *Foucauld*, 301.
[37] CF to Father Huvelin, July 13, 1904.

imitate, are passing by, and we do not love him, we do not imitate him, we do not redeem." [38]

On December 26, 1904, Brother Charles de Foucauld left Ghardaïa, fêted by crowds of children and by all the Muslim notables, for whom he had become "the great white marabout who has sold this world for the other".

After a long desert journey, entirely on foot, holding his camel "by the face", constantly praying and reciting the offices, he entered Beni Abbès on January 24, 1905. Immediately, he was submerged by the flood of poor. And he gave of himself to them as he did to Christ, without reservation, without any thought of the future.

Tamanrasset, December 1, 1916, 5 P.M.

Brother Charles felt trapped in the stifling fort. The place frightened the Haratins and even the Tuareg nomads, and yet the structure had been built for them. It was as if this grim redoubt were going to attract evil. As the day ended, in spite of all the times the officers of Fort Motylinski had warned him, the hermit could not keep from venturing outside. Seated in the doorway, in front of the low bulletproof wall, he waited for his friends, who otherwise would not come in as they had used to at the hermitage.

A woman arrived to ask for needles. Another woman wanted medicine for her baby, who had a cough. The children came for milk and a little hardtack. He never refused. Miraculously, these poor people's demands were always modest, for they knew that the food reserves of the marabout were not limitless and that they must not take advantage. The village felt reassured by his presence. They knew that if there were to be a serious famine, he would give all!

There was no longer anyone around besides the poor Haratins. Before, when he had been living in his hermitage, "the Frigate", on the other side of the wadi, the nomads used to come and ask for him to serve as an arbitrator. Theft of a camel or grain, quarrel between neighbors or family members. Dispute with the military authorities. Sometimes Charles hit hard. He convinced the lieutenant to reassign a corporal who had caused the death of two camels by disrupting the water rationing arrangements; and there was the sending to prison of a soldier who had raped a young nomad woman.

He thought back to September, when Ouksem had left for the Adrar to buy millet. Reassured by the presence of the marabout, the women had been knitting little pants for their babies, following a pattern sent by Marie.

---

[38] Quoted by Gorrée, *Sur les traces*, 185.

The threat of *rezzous* seemed forgotten. The air was so pure, the nights so beautiful! Fair-skinned children had come to run in the ditches of the fort and to play war. Farmers would pass by, hoes on their shoulders. But now, with the drought, might as well hoe the rocks! Back then, Charles would sometimes go to look over the work on the In Salah road, nearing completion. When night fell, he would cross the dry bed of the wadi and sit under the lone ethel and listen to the cackle of the chickens; then he would continue to the hermitage and contemplate the landscape as he prayed. As the sun set over the peaks of the Atakor, the walls of the fort would take on tints of pink and ochre, which would blend with the violet of the sky. But on this first day of December, there were no longer any chickens, and the old ethel was nearly dead from lack of water.

To his friends in France, who worried at his being so alone, Charles would reply: "Do not worry, we are in the hands of the Beloved. That is better for us than all the soldiers in the world."

He went back inside the fort and withdrew to his chapel for the office of Vespers. "The mountains skipped like rams, and the little hills like lambs." [39]

Then he read Psalm 20, picked up his pen, and wrote an evening prayer: "How sweet they are, these hours of the night! You are there, my Creator, you are in me, around me. You fill my little cell. You envelop me. All is silent outside, all is sleeping. The darkness envelops all beings, and you permit me to stay awake at your feet, so that I alone in this death of nature am living for you. My Beloved, when all slumbers, how sweet it is to tell you that we love you, that we wish to live for you alone." [40]

"Tell me about Tam", Beuh ag Rhabelli, the Senoussi, asked El Madani.

The black man, riding beside Beuh, was not very secure on the hump of his camel. He would rather have been on foot, but the *rezzou* of the *fellagha* could not tarry. He replied: "What do you want to know, Beuh? There is nothing at Tam. Only a wretched village of stupid Haratins, about twenty households, and nearby, when there are rains, the tents of the Dag Rali and nomadic tribes. There are none there right now. Moussa and Ouksem have taken their flocks three hundred miles away or even farther, into the Aïr and the Adrar. At least, we hope so."

"Do you know a Haratin named Embarek?"

"Yes, he is the former slave of the marabout Charles, who calls him Paul. He still works for him. He is strong and dumb."

[39] Psalm 114.
[40] CF, "Méditation sur le psaume 20", *Oeuvres spirituelles* (Nouvelle Cité, 1974–1997).

"Does he live at the fort?"

"No. Since his marriage, he's been living in a *zeriba* outside the village. He has even built himself a *toub* hut."

"What time does he leave the fort?"

"At six o'clock in the evening."

"Then we'll attack after that time. But we'll have to check on the whereabouts of the black man. If he happened to be in the neighborhood, he might well alert our enemies."

"Tam is on the road connecting In Salah and Fort Motylinski. Every eighteen days or so the mail carrier passes through. There is a slight chance we might run into him. The man rides a fast camel. He could reach Moty in three to four hours."

"We'll watch for him."

12

Tamanrasset

What was going to happen now?

Humbly, once again he let the poor consume him: "The life of Nazareth can be led anywhere, even in a place whose greatest advantage is in making us ready for the next place", he wrote.[1] Basically, the location mattered little, "provided that we are where Jesus wants us".[2] For him, the ideal was to live on the outskirts of a little village, "to have at the same time the silence of retreat and the proximity of souls".[3] Which seemed impossible at Beni Abbès. Unless he could live in a community, where everyone would take turns doing the charitable tasks. Yet he was still alone, and he was doing nothing to make his lifestyle more "pleasant": "To be ready for beheading, starvation, to obey me everywhere and as my gardener", he wrote Bishop Guérin.

He did not make any concessions as far as his asceticism was concerned. He no longer ventured outside, and he stopped what he called "his ostentatious building projects". He asked to be called Brother Charles and not Father de Foucauld. He spent more and more time with the poor and the humble: "Do not fear their filth or their fleas." For all this work, he still had but one servant, the black man, Paul Embarek, who served Mass although not yet baptized, prepared bread and the grain gruel, *asida*, for Charles had lost most of his teeth. But they did not get along well. Paul could not understand the priest's ascetic life. He fantasized about a rich, generous master, with expensive tastes, who would bring him honor. Unpredictable, sometimes he would disappear for a month at a time. But he always came back. A mysterious bond united this ill-matched pair.

On January 28, 1905, four days after his return to Beni Abbès, Charles received a fortuitous visit from General Lyautey, commander of the South Oranais, who had his headquarters at Aïn Sefra. This fifty-one-year-old officer, for whom a great future was predicted, had spent his entire military career in the colonies, mostly in North Africa. Born in Nancy in 1854,

[1] Quoted by J.-F. Six, *Itinéraire spirituel de Charles de Foucauld* (Seuil, 1958), 318.
[2] CF to Father Huvelin, September 3, 1905.
[3] CF, *Carnet de Beni-Abbès*, May 15, 1904 (Nouvelle Cité, 1993).

former student at Saint-Cyr (1873), an ardent social Christian, he had not met Charles de Foucauld, whose personality intrigued him, for in his youth he too had felt drawn toward the contemplative life.

Arriving with several of the officers on his staff, Lyautey was glad to be able to question Charles about Morocco, where a grave political crisis was brewing. That country, torn asunder by its internal struggles, was ripe for the taking. France, Germany, and Spain were interested in the prospect. Since the publication of his book, Charles had been considered a resource. "We never grow tired of calling upon his documentation", Lyautey once wrote. The Foucauld concerned with social problems also interested him. In the letter announcing his visit, Lyautey had written: "I love you for the greatness of your soul, because in your priesthood you will always do good for the poor and the suffering just as you did good in the fields of the Maghreb." [4]

Having expressed reservations about an unescorted trip to Algiers planned by Charles, Lyautey was answered by Regnault: "Sir, are you not aware that Father de Foucauld never needs an escort? Alone on horseback, he can pass by all the *rezzous* without fear of rifle fire. The people he encounters on the road will prostrate themselves, kiss the hem of his burnous, asking for his blessing! Let him go."

Lyautey, in recounting this conversation, adds: "Thus I discovered the influence this man had all over the Islamic Sahara, where the Muslims thought of him as a genuine marabout." [5]

After a dinner where the wine flowed freely, Charles and the general left the *bordj* mess and retired to the hermitage for a long private talk. Both men were thinking of Morocco. The one to convert it, the other to win it for France. Charles offered to go there, but Lyautey talked him out of it. The international situation was explosive. He would have to wait.

The conversation then turned to Algeria. The anticlerical Combes government had fallen, but laws separating Church and state were still in effect, and it was out of the question to send the White Fathers into the Sahara. Charles, since his presence there was tolerated, was doing much good. Lyautey agreed with the hermit: no assimilation of the native population, an idea then popular in France but unrealistic, as the future would demonstrate. Lyautey was also against the Laperrine plan to pit the "Saharan people" against the Arabs of Algeria, but he admired the commander of the Oases and let him play his hand.

After having slept at the *bordj*, the following morning, a Sunday, Lyautey and his men heard Charles celebrate Mass in the hermitage. Lyautey com-

[4] Lyautey to CF, 1905, quoted by G. Ganne, *Tamanrasset ou le désert fertile* (SOS, 1975), 160.
[5] Quoted by M. Carrouges, *Charles de Foucauld, explorateur mystique* (Cerf, 1954), 240.

mented: "A hovel, this hermitage! His chapel, a pitiful corridor with posts and a reed roof! For the altar, a board. For decoration, a square of muslin adorned with a picture of Christ. Tin-plate candlesticks. Our feet were in the sand. Indeed, I have never heard Mass said as Father de Foucauld said it. I thought I was in the Theban desert with the early Christians. It was one of the experiences of my life that has left a very great impression." [6]

In another account, Lyautey related:

> There were a few Arabs there, come not to be converted, for the father strictly avoided exerting any direct pressure in this regard, but drawn by his holiness. And before this altar, which was only a pine table, before these vestments of coarse fabric, before these tin candlesticks, before all this poverty, but also before this priest in ecstasy offering the sacrifice with a fervor that filled the place with light and faith, we all felt a religious emotion, a sense of magnificence we had never experienced to that degree when witnessing the pomp of solemn offices in the most sumptuous cathedrals. Past the humble earthen walls, beyond the few Muslims come spontaneously to join in his prayer, there was a vision of the Saharan vastness, of that Sahara whose sands came like waves to beat at the chapel door, a Sahara where he truly ruled through the strength of that prayer. [7]

Lyautey went away from there overwhelmed. This man, who had long before ceased to practice his religion, had glimpsed through the poor hermit the greatness born of stripping away all those things with which man usually concerns himself. And he thought: "He is the most lofty spiritual figure I have ever encountered. No doubt that Foucauld will have a significant place in the order of the world." [8]

Two weeks after this visit, Charles fell seriously ill, probably the result of his travels: heavy fatigue, toothaches (he never saw a dentist), fevers, neuralgia. How to put this setback to good use? As he wrote Marie de Bondy: "God must be praised in all things. This powerlessness, this incapacity, is good. It shows us the little that we are and how little God needs our work." [9]

And if he needed nothing but our love? But Charles was thinking only of self-effacement: "This powerlessness leads us into that humility which is the truth." [10]

Worried, Marie begged him to seek medical care. She received a sharp reply: "Leave the cloister, that is what we have never done and something a

---

[6] Lyautey, *Lettres de Casablanca*, 1922.

[7] Lyautey, *Paroles d'action* (Colin, 1927), 379. For the Foucauld-Lyautey relationship, see *Bulletin des Amitiés*, nos. 107 to 109, in which Suremain corrects many misconceptions.

[8] As related by J. Benoist-Méchin, *Lyautey ou le rêve éclaté* (Perrin), 374.

[9] CF to Marie de Bondy, March 21, 1905, 134.

[10] Ibid.

good monk will never do. The cloister is our element, our homeland, while waiting for heaven. We live there, we die there, we are there well or ill, in accordance with what God wishes. We go outside the cloister in the service of God, when there is a very good reason. For reasons of health, never." [11]

And so he seemed to have settled in at Beni Abbès when, on April 15, 1905, barely recovered from his illness, he received an offer he called "sheer temptation". Lieutenant Colonel Laperrine invited him to spend the summer in the Ahaggar, accompanying another army pacification tour, led by Captain Dinaux, the commander of the Saharan Tidikelt forces. At first, he said no: his obligation to stability and the service of the poor. But his emotions were stirred. On April 18 he wrote to Father Huvelin that the Ahaggar "is a vast land at the moment shut off from all priests". And he asked him what he thought.

Naturally, he also consulted Bishop Guérin, who advised him not to accept. The matter seemed closed, the "sheer temptation" forgotten. But not long after, Bishop Guérin, in Paris, met with Father Huvelin, who led him to change his mind. Father Huvelin thought the mission, the apostolate, should take priority, since it had become quite apparent that Brother Charles could not lead a contemplative life at Beni Abbès.

This time, the expedition was to be something more than a pacification tour. Dinaux was setting off to receive the long-awaited surrender of Moussa ag Amastane and to pacify the Ahaggar. And Laperrine still thought there could be no more powerful means to their ends in the Sahara than the permanent presence of Father de Foucauld, the only person capable of enduring an isolated life among the nearly inaccessible tribes of the region.

So Bishop Guérin asked Charles to go. Charles was still hesitant, however, since he already knew that if he headed into the south, there would be no return. He wrote Father Huvelin on May 18: "I feel very weak, very cowardly. My life is the hidden life of Nazareth. Pray for me so that I may be what Jesus wishes." [12]

Finally, he gave in: "Obedience is the measure of love." [13]

On May 3, 1905, leaving his gardener, Hadj ben Ahmed, in charge of the fraternity, Charles de Foucauld once again set out into the desert in the company of Paul, his eternal catechumen. Two pack camels carried their baggage, the tent for celebrating Mass, two sacks of dried dates and roasted barley, the water supply, some small gifts. At the end of May they caught up

---

[11] Ibid., April 11, 1905, quoted by G. Gorrée, *Sur les traces de Charles de Foucauld* (Éd. de la Plus Grande France, 1936), 189.

[12] CF to Father Huvelin, May 18, 1905, 234.

[13] CF, "Retraite de 1904", *Écrits spirituels* (Gigord, 1923), 215.

with the Dinaux column at the well of Ouan Thora, in the Touat. The captain describes their meeting:

> He was walking rapidly, leading one of his pack camels by the bridle. His emaciated face, framed by a hairy beard, which he trimmed himself with great chops of his scissors, was lit up by two eyes with a serious, fervent, and penetrating gaze, and the broad smile of the toothless mouth showed in all situations the affectionate sympathy and kindness he had for everyone: humility, gentleness, spirituality, all of that was seen at once in that nervous body dominated by the will to triumph over the material. One could not help but love and respect him. He was simply clad in a white gandoura [a loose African gown] tied at the waist by a leather belt, from which hung a rosary with large black beads. On the chest was sewn a red heart and, above it, a cross. For headwear, he had a long cylindrical *sheshia* of white fabric, and a puggaree. On his badly chapped feet he wore ill-fitting camelskin sandals he himself had cut, fastening them, as did the Saharan shepherds, by a strap woven between the toes.[14]

The captain affirmed to Charles the importance of the tour. At In Salah, in February 1904, Moussa had paid lip service to peace with the French. But he had never presented himself to Laperrine in person. Would he do it this time with Dinaux? Would he grant the Christian marabout permission to settle in the Ahaggar?

"My mission consists of crossing the desert, staying a month in the Adrar of the Iforas, then going deep into the heart of the Ahaggar, where we hope to meet up with Moussa. Ordinarily, we shall do about twenty-five miles a day, the slow pace of camels laden with supplies. We must anticipate some forced day and night marches through the Tanezrouft in order to find watering places. We will make stops according to our needs, in regions where we find pasture, and always near the camps of the Tuareg, where it will be a matter of taming them with talk, camel races, and target shooting, all things of which they are fond."

The column went deeper into the desert, the men on their mounts, Charles always on foot.

Dinaux later recalled:

> The legs of our journey were for him a test of mortification. The pace of a detachment of camel troopers is considerably faster than that of a walker. The priest continued to follow us on foot to the point of exhaustion, telling his beads and reciting litanies. He forced his pace when the terrain was difficult. From five o'clock in the morning, the sun beat down mercilessly, and the temperature in the shade varied from 104 to 122 degrees. Each of us downed from eight to ten quarts of water a day, and what water, bucketed from ponds in which livestock had been splashing. And the father followed along at a rapid pace, until the moment when a windstorm began to blow

[14] General Dinaux, reported by Ganne, *Tamanrasset*, 163–65.

and one of us would say: "Father, if you do not mount, I will dismount and walk beside you." And he would resign himself to suspending his calvary, and he would smile his beautiful smile and chatter willingly.[15]

The column advanced with fingers on the trigger, dreading at night an ambush from southern Morocco or the Río de Oro. In the evening, camp would be made, in a square, and the men would stretch out on the sand, without tents, their loaded rifles at hand. Well before dawn, Charles would have the noncommissioned officer on duty awaken him. Paul would raise the tent under which the priest would say Mass. Dinaux states, "He manifested an extraordinary devotion and seemed in ecstasy. It was a revelation for us."[16]

The crossing of the Tanezrouft was punctuated by dramatic incidents. The entire column nearly died of thirst. For four days, a hot wind blew clouds of sand. Having lost its bearings, the column was obliged to halt. The thermometer rose to 130 degrees in the shade. The water soon ran out. All the wells were dry. They had to set out again or perish. Charles strode in a state of mystical euphoria. Was he going to die and join the Beloved?

On June 14, near I-n-Ziza, they found a well, alas, filled with sand. They dug for hours. Some mud appeared and, at last, water, life!

After a rest, the long march resumed, marked by contacts with caravans met on the road and visits to camps. The desert was becoming less inhuman, and little patches of green began to appear.

At I-n-Ziza, June 15, 1905, an emissary from Moussa ag Amastane left them with the hope that the *amenokal* would finally be coming; his herds were grazing a little more than a hundred miles to the south. Was this the long-awaited surrender of the chief, without which no pacification was conceivable?

As they waited, Charles was in on all the talks. He listened while Dinaux promoted the benefits of French peace: the end of banditry, the inauguration of the "rule of law", up to then unimaginable to these men, subject to the harsh primitive law of the strongest. Squatting in the sand at Dinaux's feet, Charles was improving his Tamahaq,[17] that very special language of the Tuareg, which was written in Tifinar rather than the Arabic alphabet. Then he would go into the camps and distribute medicine and a variety of objects much in demand among the women, such as thread, needles, and scissors. Collecting proverbs and verse, he was beginning to make up his dictionary.

The decisive meeting, a very formal occasion, finally took place on June 25, 1905, at the well of I-n-Ouzel. His entire face veiled, Moussa ag Amastane

[15] Ibid.
[16] Ibid.
[17] Tamasheq is a Sudanese dialect. The two terms are often used interchangeably.

was flanked by the dignitaries of his tribe, all dressed in the *saroual* (Arab trousers) fastened by a leather belt, and a long gandoura dyed blue with indigo. The blue Tuareg veil, the *litham*, covered each man's face, revealing only the eyes, for it was indecent for a noble to let his mouth be seen.[18]

Moussa was thirty-seven years old, tall and slender, long limbed, with the elongated, pale face and regular features of the pure-blooded Targui. This *amenokal*, on whom rested the fate of Charles de Foucauld's mission, was a creature of contradictions. Sincerely pious and a good Muslim, he adored honors and authority, pleasure and money. He looked back nostalgically on his days as a pillager. Already a *rezzou* leader at twenty, he had been converted by the marabout Beï. That sage opposed Abidine, the pro-independence marabout, and directed his young convert's sympathies toward France, which put Moussa at risk. In the eyes of the supporters of independence, he became a traitor, an idea that his rival, the Senoussi Attici, who had fled to Tripoli, did not fail to encourage. In 1905, the surrender of the tribes of the Sahara was far from complete. A few weeks before the meeting, France had given to the Sudan (Mali) the southern part of the Tuareg territory of the Iforas, who were vassals of Moussa. This action angered him, for the territory, soaked in summer by the Sudanese monsoon, was vital to the nomadic shepherds of the Ahaggar.

But the former *rezzou* leader knew he could not rule over the Ahaggar without French support. Intelligent, although illiterate, he recognized that there were other things in the world besides the peoples of the Sahara. Secretly, he dreamed of visiting Marseille and Paris and of being received there with military honors, like the black kings at the 1900 World's Fair; and of being proclaimed "king of the Ahaggar" by the great chief Laperrine and receiving from his hands the gold-trimmed scarlet burnous adorned with the Legion of Honor. He also seemed to concede that his country would be almost pleasant to live in if the bandits would stop stealing from the people who worked.

Actually, Moussa was playing both sides. He had been elected *amenokal* of the two noble tribes of the Ahaggar, the Kel Rela and the Taitoq, succeeding the two enemies of France, Ahitarel and Attici, who had massacred the Flatters mission. But, prior to his election, he had been secretly negotiating with Attici. If the French won out, he would be their man. If not, he would shamelessly join the cause of the Senoussi.

With great ceremony, Moussa surrendered before Captain Dinaux and

[18] There is another explanation, for women do not cover their mouths. Thus they have a reputation for being more talkative than the men, a true Tuareg male expressing himself only indirectly; he uses metaphors, what they call *tangalt* (penumbra). The masculine veil might also be a symbolic replacement for the tent (feminine privilege) of which the young male is deprived when he leaves his mother.

made amends for his past acts of violence. He promised to pay taxes and respect the laws of the French Republic. Dinaux gave him permission to collect the tribute. He would be officially invested as *amenokal* once Laperrine had ratified their agreement, Dinaux promised.

Then Dinaux introduced Charles de Foucauld to him as "the Christian marabout, servant of the one God", who loved solitude and the desert and wished to study the language and culture of the Tuareg. Moussa took him under his protection immediately and agreed that he could settle in the Ahaggar. At worst, would he not be a sort of hostage of the Tuareg and, at best, a guarantee of lasting peace? Quite aware of these calculations, Charles was seeing the realization of his dream, the creation of a hermitage deep in the Sahara, where Christ was unknown. They arranged to meet on August 1 in Abalessa, from where Moussa would take him to Tamanrasset, a village at the crossroads of several desert routes, which seemed the best place to carry out his silent apostolate and learn to know the Kel Ahaggar people. Because the high plateau stood at more than forty-nine hundred feet, he would enjoy a temperate climate. The settled population, Dag Rali and Haratins, seemed peaceable.

Charles noted in his diary: "Moussa, very proper, very intelligent, very open, very pious Muslim, wishing others well in the Muslim way, generous, but at the same time ambitious, loving money, pleasure, honors, as open minded as can be. He has agreed, my settling in the Ahaggar has been decided upon." [19]

Which Dinaux approved: "In view of Moussa's support and his solemn promise to be responsible for the safety of the priest, the latter made the final decision to settle in Tamanrasset once we are back from the Adrar of the Iforas, and I willingly granted him permission to do so." [20]

The truth is that the officer still had some doubts.

Accompanied by Moussa, the pacification tour headed south to the Sudanese border, into the Adrar of the Iforas. At Timeïaouine, the Algerian column waited in vain for the Sudanese column, which was supposed to enable Professor Gautier, an ethnologist on a research mission, to cross the southern Sahara as far as Timbuktu. Moussa then suggested the Sudanese troops be replaced by an escort of Iforas, thus showing that he bore no grudge against the French for taking this tribe from him. An enormous risk, but it was an opportunity to test the loyalty of the Tuareg. Everything proceeded smoothly. Meanwhile, the Dinaux column, still accompanied by Moussa, went back north toward Tamanrasset, where they were to drop off Father de Foucauld.

[19] CF, *Carnet de Beni-Abbès,* July 4, 1905, 178.
[20] Ibid., Ganne, *Tamanrasset,* 167.

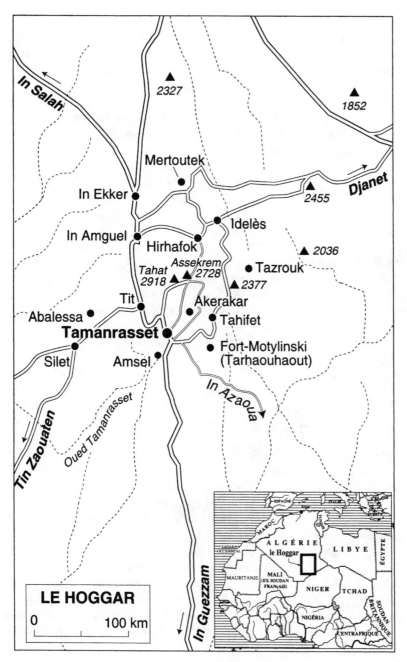

Map of the Ahaggar Region

Before returning to In Salah, Dinaux had some final doubts: "Father de Foucauld was going to find himself totally isolated, in an unfamiliar land, whose tribes were only partly subdued. Never, since his exploration of Morocco, would he have been so abandoned. No Frenchman, no Christian at his side, uncertain mail delivery, complete solitude in Muslim country."[21] And the threat from fundamentalist rebels.

But Charles was determined. From Tit, August 6, he wrote Marie de Bondy: "I am settling here with no particular plans. So many unexpected things come up, and the future is so hard to predict! In three days we shall be in Tamanrasset, and right away I shall build a hut there, and I shall live a poor and retired life, trying only to imitate the divine worker of Nazareth." [22]

After arriving in Tamanrasset August 3, he cried out, "It is here I want to live!" He was exultant and noted in his diary. "I am choosing Tamanrasset, a village of twenty households, deep in the mountains, in the heart of the Ahaggar, away from all the major centers. Principal tribe: the Dag Rali. It does not seem as if it is destined ever to have a garrison, a telegraph, or Europeans. Settle here permanently. The will of the Beloved. I am choosing this forsaken place, and I am here to stay. Taking as my only example the life of Jesus of Nazareth. May he deign to convert me. To make me such as he wishes me to be. Loving him, obeying him, imitating him." [23]

Impossible to be any more isolated. It took two weeks to reach the nearest military garrison, In Salah, more than four hundred miles to the north; two months to reach another priest, at Beni Ounif. Impossible to be any poorer. The high plateau, its altitude more than forty-nine hundred feet, was cut through by the bed of the Tamanrasset Oued, nearly always dry. Around it, on the rolling, rocky ground, grew little tufts of coarse grass nibbled by the nomads' camels and the wild rushes that the settled Haratins used to fashion their *zeribas*, miserable huts. These former black slaves, often of mixed blood, worked hard to raise a little barley and a few carrots and red peppers along the wadi, in little pockets of earth belonging to the settled Tuareg. They were essentially sharecroppers, rewarded with a share of the harvest, just enough to keep them from starving. Their lot was similar to that of domestic animals and the lowest slaves. In summer, they had to go deep to find water for irrigating the crops.

Beyond this desolate landscape, where no tree grew except for a lone ethel, rose the scattered tents of Tuareg shepherds who had come to graze their flocks of sheep and goats. How many people were there when Charles de Foucauld arrived? Sixty or so settled Haratins, former slaves in the

---

[21] Ibid., 168.

[22] CF to Marie de Bondy, August 6, 1905, 138.

[23] CF, *Carnets de Tamanrasset* (Nouvelle Cité, 1986), August 11, 1905, 48.

Sudan, their blood often mixed with that of the Tuareg; a few dozen Tuareg Imrad, settled landowners, the vassals of a handful of Tuareg nobles; a varying number of nomadic shepherds and caravan people, the latter arriving from the Tidikelt or from Timbuktu with salt, cotton fabric, and dates, which they would trade for goatskins and sheepskins.

The Ahaggar population ruled by Moussa was spread over a territory half the size of France and consisted of nine hundred families from the Kel Ahaggar tribes. Three hundred miles to the south, the Iforas of the Adrar, another region controlled by Moussa, numbered two thousand families. In the summer, when not a blade of grass grew, the Ahaggar nomads had to go as far as six hundred miles south to seek out the vegetation their flocks and camels needed for survival.

In spite of the relatively mild climate, impossible to imagine a people more poverty stricken, more forgotten. Where had they come from? Hundreds of thousands of years ago, long after the sea had retreated from the vast expanses of the Sahara, the mountain massif of the Ahaggar was an island of green, as cave paintings demonstrate. Then the tropical fauna, driven out by drought, flowed back into the Sudan. With very light skin and little resemblance to Jews or Arabs, are the Tuareg Berbers from Nubia or maybe even Hamites from Egypt, expelled by Arab invaders in the eighth century? They kept their faces veiled up to the eyes. Tall, skinny fellows, perched on their dromedaries, sword in hand, antelope skin shield on the left arm, they adopted a proud look before strangers, a scornful one before the settled blacks whom they had reduced to slavery. Until the French arrived, they had kept busy with wars between rival tribes, the *rezzous*, the pillaging of settlers and of Arab and Jewish caravans. They refused to do any manual labor, considering it beneath them. Their dream: to buy a Winchester rifle! Generally an impossible dream, unless achieved through surrender to the hated French.

Permanent housing structures were unknown among them; families lived under large sheepskin tents supported by bamboo stakes. For protection from the wind, they dug into the sand and raised around the tent windbreaks of fiber matting. No furniture. They slept on the ground, rolled up in blankets. Their only luxury was their one-stringed violin, the *imzad*, on which the women—guardians of the traditions—accompanied themselves when declaiming their poetry. The women took care of the children and did very simple cooking. Unveiled, they had relative sexual freedom from an early age until marriage. More intelligent and cultivated than the men, they held the real power and maintained the oral traditions in the Tamahaq language. Except for fighting wars and caring for the flocks, the men did nothing but talk endlessly and have saber contests. Their black slaves did the work. These Tuareg realized that the law of the French, which forbade the *razzia*, war, and slavery, was threatening their very primitive "civilization", already crushed by the Arabs.

So Tamanrasset was not a true village or an oasis. No mosque, no *zaouïa* for receiving visitors. A little agricultural center, a rest stop for caravans attracted by the watering place, a small settlement with huts and tents scattered over a bare plateau drowned in light, with a little grass growing here and there.

"Tomorrow I begin building my hut here", Charles de Foucauld wrote Marie de Bondy on August 13, 1905. Father de Foucauld's first hermitage, located not far from the wadi, was built in six days. It consisted of a hut twenty feet long and six feet wide, of rock, with clay as a mortar, the roofing a mixture of reeds and dried mud. No real windows, but little openings without glass, which could be shut with a board for protection from the blowing wind or the summer sun. The only door had a special edge at the bottom to discourage reptiles, scorpions, and spiders. This rustic dwelling with the low ceiling was divided in two by a partition. Charles ate and slept in the first room. A square of reed lattice work, raised off the floor, served as a table during the day and as a bed at night. He worked sitting on an upturned box. The chapel occupied the second room, where the priest set up his portable altar. Next to the hermitage he constructed a reed hut for visitors, about seven feet square, the structure also serving as the kitchen. Paul slept there. Other rooms were added to the hermitage later, among them a warehouse for storing grain and dates. Impossible to imagine a more rustic dwelling.

He was perfectly happy. What were his plans? He jotted down in his big notebook, on one of the large squared sheets: "Love Jesus, imitate him. Obedience will put you in the states he wants you to be in. Whatever the situation, imitate him. Outside of his imitation, there can be no perfection. Hope for the establishment of the Little Brothers and the Little Sisters. Follow the rules set up for them. Do not try to organize their establishment. Alone, live as if you were always to remain alone, removed from prayer, but given to prayer." [24]

His first contacts were disappointing. The visitors, a few poor Haratins and some of the nomad wives, came only to beg for medicines, grain, or alms. People did not even come to "chat", although the hermit had begun to master the language. Thus he found himself forced to modify his rule. Since they did not come to him, he would go to them. No cloister.

And so he gave up not only the traditional Cistercian rule, which demanded cloister, stability, and silence, but also the first version of his own

[24] Ibid., July 22, 1905, 45.

rule, which was too strict. He wrote Father Huvelin that he would hence-forth "stay put as little as possible".[25] In the imitation of Christ, but of the Tuareg nomads also, the precarious became his rule. He quickly lost his illusions about the possibility of founding a community in the near future. All he asked for was one companion, a true disciple, to participate in his spiritual and earthly adventure: "I seek someone of good will, agreeing to share my life in poverty, obscurity, with no set rule. Good will, desire to belong to Jesus, joyful acceptance of the most extreme poverty, all the perils, all the humiliations and all the strains", he wrote to Father Veyra of Nîmes.[26]

"All the perils." For the military column, which had camped at Tamanrasset for two weeks, was about to withdraw. On August 25, 1905, before sixty delegates from the tribes of the Ahaggar, Captain Dinaux granted Moussa his official investiture as *amenokal*. Then he entrusted to him Father Charles de Foucauld. Moussa solemnly promised to be respon-sible for his safety. Dinaux went off regretfully, anxiously, to the Aïr, the last region on his tour. "When I took leave of him, he had lost nothing of his serenity, and he thanked me effusively for having allowed him to realize his aspirations." [27]

"We left him on the doorstep of his little hermitage of straw and mud, alone with his piety, his goodness, and his silence!" recorded Lieutenant Dervil, adding: "In his emaciated face, framed by a short, thin beard, his eyes glowed intensely, serious, expressing gentleness but also a thoughtful firmness. For many months I had lived in the ambiance of a saint, without realizing it, I must admit. It was only now that I saw the greatness of a character so perfect that its perfection was not obvious and did not over-whelm those around him." [28]

Alone! "We are, you and I, in the hands of the Beloved", he wrote Marie de Bondy. "It is better for us to have him than to have all the soldiers in the world. Were your child to have the fate of our great-granduncle Armand,[29] would that not make you happy? Jesus said such was the greatest sign of love. I am still alone, happy, very happy to be alone with Jesus." [30]

Coming back through Tamanrasset on October 15, Dinaux had a final conversation with the hermit: "You are determined to stay?"

---

[25] CF to Father Huvelin, July 13, 1905.

[26] CF to Father Veyras, December 3, 1905, in Six, *Itinéraire*, 321.

[27] Quoted by Ganne, *Tamanrasset*, 168.

[28] Quoted by J.-F. Six, *Vie de Charles de Foucauld* (Seuil, 1962), 148.

[29] Armand de Foucauld, vicar general of Arles, was to be beatified by Pius XI in 1926. He was killed at the Carmelites' chapel in Paris during the French Revolution (in September 1792), along with his cousin Archbishop Lau.

[30] CF to Marie de Bondy, September 3, 1905, in Gorrée, *Sur les traces*, 195.

"Yes!"

Brother Charles was glowing. Dinaux and his long caravan of camel troopers rode off, this time not to return. In his report to the governor general of Algeria, the captain wrote: "And so he will stay here alone amid the Tuareg, over four hundred miles from In Salah, and will be in contact with us only through a monthly mail service, which we shall try to initiate. His reputation for holiness and the results he has already obtained in the healing of the sick are doing more for the spreading of our influence and the acceptance of our ideas than a permanent occupation of the country." [31]

Madness! What were the chances of converting these proud nomads, who had until just recently spent their time pillaging? To an impartial observer, zero. Islam was deeply rooted here and fit their primitive way of life.

Entrusting to God alone the problem of religious conversion, Charles thought up innumerable projects, which today would be labeled moralistic and sociocultural: educating the children and the women, who, fortunately were more or less equal with the men; acquainting the tribal chiefs with France so they would respect it and want to imitate it; fighting against immorality, which included not only pillaging but depraved morals and the practice of magic; encouraging and honoring work, hitherto scorned and merely endured. In order to keep the Tuareg from "stagnating in tribal tradition", he envisioned the development of stable farming communities to replace nomadic herding. To improve agricultural methods, some French farmers could come and settle there, but he would avoid attracting the exploiting colonist types. "Create a model garden in the Ahaggar with help from the government." [32] In brief, a secular program in the traditional mode, but utterly utopian here, given the isolation, the dry climate, the poor soil, and age-old habits.

And how did he plan to go about these projects? Only through Moussa could he accomplish anything. Charles was looking back to those holy individuals who had descended on barbarian Gaul: with nothing but their charisma and the working of the Holy Spirit, they had converted the local monarch, who brought with him all his people. But could Charles convert the *amenokal*?

To see him, there was no need to leave the cloister. Intrigued by the marabout, it was Moussa who came to him. Charles was a mystery. This noble French lord had left everything, honors, fortune, family, to come and lose himself in the desert to serve former slaves and nomads almost as poor. Despite his faults, Moussa did have a religious soul, and he felt a kinship

[31] Quoted by Bazin, *Foucauld*, 317 and 319.
[32] CF to Marie de Bondy, October 23, 1905.

with the hermit. "The hermit has died to the world and lives only for God and his will", he used to say in admiration, even if he had no intention of imitating Charles.

Thanks to an appendix ("Dire à Moussa")[33] to Charles de Foucauld's April 1912 diary, the first dialogue between the hermit and the *amenokal* can be reconstructed. The latter was still hesitant about siding with the French. Dinaux had advised him to go see Laperrine. But Moussa was too proud. Since he had Khaouia Carlo at hand, he preferred to ask his advice first.

"What should I do? Closer relations with the French could mean cutting myself off from my people."

"As a chief, your first duty is to give an example of perfection. Now, perfection entails putting the general interest before personal interest. In all matters you must seek what is in the interest of the Tuareg."

Moussa was flabbergasted. He had never heard such ideas. Up until then, he had acted according to his own interest, which he would then try to make coincide with that of his people, so they would be grateful to him. He tried to hedge: "But what is in the interest of the Tuareg? The French have outlawed *rezzous*, and they even want to abolish slavery, which we have practiced since time began."

"Prosperity for the Tuareg cannot be achieved at the expense of the blacks of the Sudan and the Haratin farmers who cultivate your soil."

"And why not?"

"Because God does not want that. He condemns violence and unjust force. You are a religious man; you know that the good comes from heaven. Heaven's gift is our knowing the will of God and carrying it out. You cannot love God and be loved by him without carrying out his natural law, which is the same for all men, Christian and Muslim."

"But, for me, what is the natural law, as you call it?"

"You must elevate your people and not exploit them for your own ends."

"But how do I elevate them?"

"See to the education of the children . . . and the women."

"Oh!"

"Encourage contacts with the French and with other peoples, and to that end learn Arabic and French, and travel. Promote farming and the raising of livestock, to be practiced in settled communities. The law of God should prevail everywhere. Work and family must be honored, and slaves must be allowed to lead honorable lives. All those opposed to the law of God should be removed from power and punished."

[33] Cf. *Carnets de Tamanrasset*, April 1912.

The *amenokal* was perplexed. Charles continued: "You must have good, upright folk around you. Do not keep good-for-nothings in your entourage. Reduce the number of slaves you own; they are a useless band, devouring you, making you appear ridiculous, and serving no purpose."

"But it is a question of my prestige as a chief! Who could imagine an *amenokal* without slaves?"

"Make yourself small, Moussa. Humble yourself!"

"Oh!"

"God alone is great. The man full of pride is a lunatic, for he does not know if he will go to heaven or to hell. And start by cutting down on your spending."

"A chief must spend to show his power."

"God alone is powerful. The man who thinks of himself as great does not know God."

Dialogue of the deaf. Charles then tried to talk to him about his relationships with others.

"The first duty is to love God. The second is to love all men as yourself."

"I love my tribe, my family, my wives, and our children."

"That is not enough. From this love of neighbor as yourself stems a law in three parts: the first is fraternity."

"I love my brothers."

"The second is equality."

"The slave could not possibly be the equal of the freeman, the servant the equal of the master. What is the third?"

"Freedom. When Adam delved and Eve span, where was the nobleman, where was the slave?"

"Times have changed. And were things ever like that?"

"Come and see me again, Moussa. I shall acquaint you with the prophets. I shall read you the Gospels."

"I know only the Prophet Muhammad. He never taught any of that."

"Love all men for the love of God. Even your enemies. Do unto them as you would have them do unto you."

Yes, dialogue of the deaf. Charles then tried to lead him to think about his duties as a chief. "Do not ask for gifts or accept them."

"That is our tradition. Where is the harm?"

"Gift giving is a heavy burden for a friend. And in accepting gifts from anybody, you become the slave of riffraff. If they ask you in turn to do something that is not right, how can you refuse them? If they do evil, how can you punish them?"

"The chief needs presents. How would he uphold his rank? And how could he then give gifts himself? It is our tradition."

Charles sensed his words were having no effect. So he went on to another subject: the thorny relationship with the French. "Have everyone learn French so they can become French."

"I am a Berber and a Tuareg. That is enough for me! There is nothing in the world more noble than a Tuareg!"

"Sooner or later you will all be French. Those who understand that today will forge ahead; the others will be left behind."

"I'll leave that to the Arabs of the Maghreb! What are you trying to do with my Tuareg pride?"

"You can remain a Tuareg while being French, not our subjects but our equals. Within a short time, all the soldiers and staff in the Ahaggar will be people of the region."

"So, what am I supposed to do?"

"Let Moussa be educated. Let him be *loved*. To that end, let him not proceed too fast, or harshly, but gently, softly. Let him not upset violently the established customs but overturn gradually what should be done away with. Let him be generous and reward those he employs and those who come to him."

Moussa burst out laughing. Among the Tuareg, everything ended in laughter. "But to be generous, I would have to be rich!"

"Let Moussa be strong. To that end, let him be rich, sustained and honored by the government."

"To be strong, warriors and weapons are necessary."

"You shall have them. As a recognized Tuareg chief, all the weapons will be in your hands, all the soldiers' pay. And so your influence will increase as long as honors, favors, authority, and employment are given only to virtuous and intelligent men, the others being removed."

"So be it!" shouted the *amenokal*, a bit overwhelmed by the deluge of innovations. "But I had come to talk to you about Colonel Laperrine. What should I do when with him?"

"Speak to him openly as to a friend, a brother, to earn his affection. He is a good and just man. You can trust him."

"How should I appear before him? With how many warriors?"

"The days of great ceremony are over. Go before him with your *khodja* [secretary] and just two servants. Do not go to the trouble of dressing in your finery."

"What gifts to bring him?"

"Just a fine camel. Stay with him a long while and speak openly with him, make friends with him."

"What shall I ask of him?"

"Nothing in your personal interest. Everything that will be helpful to your people. To send to the Ahaggar only the finest Frenchmen, doctors, farmers, craftsmen, who can increase the friendly feelings of the Tuareg toward us and who will not exploit them."

The *amenokal* was skeptical. He asked once more: "Marabout, why do you love me?"

"Because you are my brother."

"And the colonel? Why would he love me? He is a warrior. He does not live for God, as you do, but for France."

A gentle smile lit up the ascetic's face. "Oh! The colonel will love you because he is good."

"One more word, Khaouia Carlo. I understood what the good is. But what is the evil?"

"Stupidity!"

They laughed together. Charles walked him back to his mount. The hermit was aware of the cultural and spiritual abyss separating them. "And yet," he thought to himself, "this man is my brother, and he has been sent to me." He sought for words that could unite them. "Love God wholeheartedly, Moussa."

"Yes, indeed!"

"Say to him. 'My Lord, all that you want, I want!' "

At those words, they parted, each of them anxious, for what does God want? Did not both Christians and Muslims spend their time attributing to God intentions that were their own?

Moussa went off whispering, "Yes, what does God want?"

Charles knew but one way to deal with that question: Pray in order to ascertain God's will. Work and suffer in order to resemble the Son he had sent.

After a month of spending time with Moussa, Charles knew with whom he was dealing. Would the emblem of the Republic ever be that of the Ahaggar? To make the local population believe that the soldiers of the garrisons were friends and not an occupying force would require a century. Even in Algiers they did not believe it, and even less in the French-Spanish community that had undertaken the colonization of Algeria.

It does seem a little surprising that Foucauld went along so willingly with Laperrine's plan to domesticate the Tuareg. But what else could he have done? Charles immediately observed that the people distrusted and avoided him, in spite of Moussa's support. The latter, who had just been invested by the French, was playing for high stakes against his rival Attici. How would the tribes of the Ahaggar decide between them? It was up to Moussa to establish his authority by showing his people that the French presence was beneficial and by showing the French that he was capable of stopping the *rezzous*.

As for Charles, his position was not what it had been at Beni Abbès. There he was able to count on protection from a powerful garrison. Living in a rich and heavily populated oasis, and owning several acres of arable land, he could hope to found a community.

No good land at Tamanrasset. He was thus doomed to live from the charity of his family and the army, and it pained him that he could not sustain himself and the poor by the work of his hands. "A simple hut where, without land, without planting crops, I could live praying and crafting rope and wooden bowls, depending as little as possible on the land", he wrote Father Huvelin.[34] In his hermitage, he lived in the precarious position of a hostage always threatened by fanatics or ordinary thieves.

Naturally he found the humiliating dependence and the constant danger quite satisfying. It was what he had wished for, and now he just had to come to terms with it: "Be consumed in adoration, raise the Host each morning, sacrifice myself with Christ for the salvation of mankind. Live without power, without goods, without close contacts, the hidden life of Jesus. Diminishment of self to the point of disappearing, until the buried seed germinates."

Quite disappointed at seeing him forsake Beni Abbès, after Nazareth, Cheiklé, and Neiges, Father Huvelin once again lent his support: "Do what God inspires you to do. Follow your instinct and the assessment that only you can make of the good to be accomplished in humility, poverty, and silence." [35]

He could not have been left more free.

Was Brother Charles' happiness unclouded? No. "I lack but one thing, and that is myself. I am pleased with everything, except with myself." Indeed, he was in an impossible position. Just as at Beni Abbès, being alone, he could not devote himself fully to contemplation without neglecting charity. His way of life contained the seeds of its own destruction, at least from the human point of view. For if he wanted to "domesticate" his neighbors, he would have to be their provider, not to say their servant.

Which is what happened, little by little. First, they had avoided him. Had he not been brought by the army? Then, he ventured out, going into the nearby gardens several hundred feet from the hermitage, those pitiful squares cultivated by the Haratins. He went even farther, to the pasture lands and scattered encampments of the Tuareg nomads. First the children surrounded him, then the slaves, astonished that a Frenchman was speaking to them. Little by little, distrust gave way to curiosity, interest, then

[34] CF to Father Huvelin, September 1905, 238.
[35] Father Huvelin to CF, September 18, 1905, 239.

friendship. Since he spoke the language of the country and he adored God, they ended up loving him.

Now they would come to him for everything. To seek care for a sick child, to collect a bit of food, or simply to talk. Soon his hermitage was overrun, as it had been at Beni Abbès. And as if charity did not keep him busy enough, he planned to compile a French-Tuareg dictionary, then translate the Gospels. Large-scale endeavors that, combined with receiving visitors and gardening, would have been enough work for a community of ten monks. To evangelize, it was necessary to know the language and the customs of the country and to practice charity unstintingly. Very soon, he was to admit that the task was beyond his resources. He could only "prepare the way for the workers who would follow him".

At the end of 1905, Brother Charles would have reasons for concern. No hint of a conversion. At Maison-Carrée, the good White Fathers always thought it was enough to dispense the sacraments, to baptize, and that grace would do the rest. That was true in black Africa, but not in Algeria. It would take . . . a miracle. Did he believe in it? On the endpaper of his notebook he had copied Teresa of Avila's famous poem:

> Let nothing disturb you,
> Let nothing afright you.
> All things are passing.
> God never changes.
> Patient endurance
> Attains all it strives for.
> With God as your portion
> Nothing is wanting:
> God alone suffices.

God alone suffices. "Consider me dead and buried here with Christ in his life of Nazareth." [36]

And was that the secret of Charles de Foucauld: to live the gospel to perfection without worrying about the results?

Tamanrasset, December 1, 1916. 5:30 P.M.

At "Tam" the proud Tuareg nomads had once settled their differences with the sword. The French authorities tried in vain to stop such violent practices, and Moussa ag Amastane had named a *kadi*, or civil judge. But because of family ties, the judge was too involved to render justice impartially. And too poor to resist the usual corruption.

And so the French marabout became the real *kadi*, whom people came

---

[36] CF to Father Huvelin, October 26, 1905, 241.

to consult in every serious matter. That day of course nearly all the nomads were gone, grazing their flocks in the Adrar, but Charles remembered vividly one particular dispute:

Two huge Tuareg dressed in black, their faces veiled by the blue *litham*, have sought his mediation. They are agitated and ready to fight. They carry their battle gear, sword hanging at the side, dagger on the left arm, spear in the right hand. They are followed by other Tuareg noisily taking sides. These uncouth, proud fellows sound as if they would not be averse to watching a bloody duel to break up the monotony of their days. The marabout is the last resort before bloodshed. Whatever the means, God will be the judge.

Father de Foucauld stands tall before the door of his hermitage. "My friends, may peace be with you! God alone is great!"

"*Allah akbar!*"

The men sit in a circle on the dusty ground.

"I am listening to you", the priest says.

It is a serious matter. The complainant accuses his adversary of trying to steal his camel. The accused denies it. The priest asks the witnesses to speak. There is only one, a black slave, the victim's herdsman. He has been mistreated and bears the marks on his face. The testimony seems to settle the matter, but the accused challenges its validity, essentially because the witness is a slave. But the priest says that the black man's statement has the same value as that of a freeman, which shocks the listeners. The priest does concede, however, that the testimony of a man in the complainant's power may be challenged. They are at an impasse.

Charles then says: "Bring the Koran."

They go get the Book. It is placed on the ground, respectfully. The company has become silent. Charles turns to the complainant: "Swear! Swear that you are telling the truth!"

Without hesitation, the man swears. Then the priest addresses the accused: "It is your turn. Swear!"

The man hesitates. Then he shouts angrily: "Yes, I tried to take the camel. But it was not a theft. He owes me money."

"Swear."

The man swears. Now it is the complainant who loses his self-assurance. He admits the debt, but no repayment date had been agreed on.

"You shall pay the interest. And you shall repay him at the next moon." They depart, reconciled.[37]

Night had fallen over the Ahaggar Massif. Guided by Kerzou, the *fellagha rezzou* was proceeding slowly along the dry bed of a wadi dotted here and

[37] As told by Doctor Hérisson, in Bazin, *Foucauld*, 381–83.

there with an acacia. From now on, night would hide the plotters. Their throats were dry from thirst and anxiety.

Beuh ag Rhabelli rode up to Kerzou. The Senoussi found it hard to believe that this Targui from the Ait Lohen tribe could have been a non-commissioned officer under the Franks, that he could have commanded Arab camel troopers! He asked: "You were acquainted with Khaouia Carlo, the marabout? Tell me about him."

"A strange man, definitely dangerous, despite his humble appearance. He is a marabout, a kind of White Father. Yet he does not preach, he does not take up collections. On the contrary, he shares everything he has, which entire caravans bring him from Algiers and Paris. They say that he makes gold multiply with magic in a ceremony called 'transubstantiation', but I don't believe it. The gold is supplied by his family and by the French military leaders from In Salah . . . along with weapons."

"Why does he stay in these desert mountains, instead of living comfortably in Algiers, or Paris, or some other large city? Is it because of a liking for solitude?"

"No. He would have more solitude for prayer in one of the monasteries of his sect, such as they have at Maison-Carrée and Staoueli. At Tam he is constantly disturbed by the poor and the lazy harassing him, and by the sick too, for he is also a skilled healer. The nomad women ask him for needles and remedies, the poor for barley. They say he is beginning to regret feeding them. That encourages them to be lazy. Now he prefers to give them work, even if what they are doing, such as constructing roads, serves no useful purpose!"

"All this is incomprehensible!" said the Senoussi.

"Soon you will be able to question him yourself."

Beuh recoiled. "No, he could cast a spell on me!"

Behind the cirque, the last bit of daylight lingered in the sky, lighting up the great jagged peaks of the Koudia. A silent fire seemed to be consuming the huge masses of basalt. Kerzou shuddered. The men of old had refused to venture into the massif, saying it was haunted by evil spirits.

13

Hermit of the Tuareg

The year 1905 was not good. Isolated, little contact with his compatriots (the mail took a month), Brother Charles sank into a state of gloom, happily interrupted by mystical moments through prayer and the celebration of the Eucharist. He had not yet been truly accepted by the Tuareg, who tolerated him only in obedience to Moussa. As for the poor Haratins, those uncouth creatures came only to beg. Charles was living with Paul Embarek, who was now twenty. The hermit kept him on because he could not do without him: this "catechumen" who could not bring himself to receive baptism served Mass. Without him, no Mass. "Pathetic catechumen", Charles confided to Father Huvelin. "Quite a pathetic fellow. Unless his faults become close to criminal, I shall keep him with me, remembering that Jesus kept Judas." [1] "It is almost as if I have been handed over to him."[2]

Obviously, a priest as companion would have been ideal. To that end, Charles began writing more letters to France after he had in vain solicited the help of Bishop Guérin in Ghardaïa. On the other hand, "I am so cowardly that I cannot without trepidation picture having a brother in my solitude. For me, it is so much better to be alone." [3]

Father Huvelin agreed, frightened by Charles' asceticism. He had advised the hermit to make a trip to France, which would provide Moussa the opportunity to visit that country. But Charles, fearing the temptation to see Marie again, answered him: "I am always that weak child you know so well. My heart has not changed. Under the circumstances, I think I should never come back to Paris, and not even to France. For the reason you know so well." [4]

His depression was not the result of isolation but of a feeling of uselessness. At Beni Abbès, he had at least been of use to the Christian soldiers. In Tamanrasset, he was hitting his head against a stone wall. Whether it was the Tuareg or the blacks, "there is no point in talking to them directly of our

[1] CF to Father Huvelin, December 1905, 243.
[2] CF to Marie de Bondy, December 16, 1905, in G. Gorrée, *Sur les traces de Charles de Foucauld* (Éd. de la Plus Grande France, 1936), 199.
[3] CF to Father Huvelin, December 14, 1905, 250.
[4] Ibid., 246.

Lord, for that would make them flee", he wrote to Marie de Bondy.[5] Then what was to be done? Prepare for the future, "putting them at ease, making friends with them, helping them in small ways, giving them good advice, exhorting them quietly to follow natural religion, proving to them that Christians love them." [6]

These people were so poor that they thought foremost of survival. Eternal life? "The little they know of it is contaminated by the error that having faith in God and his prophet are enough to guarantee heaven." [7]

And what if that were true? Knowing he would obtain nothing just from his own efforts, he decided to give himself up to God. "Total oblivion of self. Presence of the Blessed Sacrament, oblation of the Holy Sacrifice. Prayer, penance. Good example, kindness, personal sanctification", [8] he wrote Father Huvelin.

But he realized that the life of the hermit was at times unbearable and solitary adoration difficult. He missed "the cozy little nest of Nazareth", where, humble gardener, he used to pray in the shadow of the Poor Clares' chapel. He sank into depression. Even reading did not do much for him, although he had brought along some treasures: The Bible, *The Imitation*, the breviary, and, "to rekindle my enthusiasm, a few good treatises of dogmatic theology": Saint Thomas Aquinas, Saint John Chrysostom, and the indescribable Teresa of Avila.

"I am cowardly and cold", he told Father Huvelin once again. The letter continues, "Very halfhearted in my prayers. My life is very prosaic, lukewarm, and empty. Prayer is difficult for me. Barely have I begun than I must do battle with sleep or with unbearable thoughts. This difficulty is constant. I see that I am lacking one thing: my conversion. Pray for me, beloved father, so that I may finally be what I should be." [9]

All that sustained him was the celebration of the Eucharist and the adoration of the Blessed Sacrament exposed. And even that was to be taken from him. "Paul is going from bad to worse", he wrote Bishop Guérin on April 2. "If I were forced to part from him, or if he left me, could I say Mass every two weeks, alone, to renew the holy species? Could I offer myself Communion every day, as do imprisoned priests?" [10]

He knew he could not. The divine sacrifice is a community liturgy, a sharing of bread and wine. And his whole life was undermined. He was there to let the living Jesus come to the Ahaggar. Without Christ, without

[5] CF to Marie de Bondy, December 16, 1905, in Gorrée, *Sur les traces*, 199.
[6] Ibid.
[7] CF to Father Huvelin, June 14, 1909, 289.
[8] Ibid., December 1, 1905, 247.
[9] Ibid., April 6, 1906, 258.
[10] CF to Bishop Guérin, April 2, 1906, in R. Bazin, *Charles de Foucauld* (Plon, 1921), 328.

Communion and the adoration of the Blessed Sacrament exposed, Charles was no longer anything. Less than one of those slaves he saw loitering around his hermitage, begging a bowl of grain.

With the back of his hand he tried to sweep away his concern over Paul's inevitable departure. But if Paul went away, even if he replaced him—he could always buy another slave and have him serve Mass—that would not help him much as long as he was alone. "I should like the good to be done, to be spread, to be propagated." It was obvious and devastating: he could not be saved alone.

Once again, he swept away his doubts. He gave himself up to God: "Not my will, Lord, but yours!" Then he practiced what was to become popular in the coming years, autosuggestion, so effective: "I am the happiest of men. My soul is at peace. There is nothing tormenting me. I remain happy and serene at the feet of the Beloved!" [11]

In his diary on May 17, 1906, Charles noted: "This morning Paul leaves the fraternity. Dear Lord, may I be able to continue celebrating the Holy Sacrifice. Do not let this soul be lost. Save it!" [12]

And so Paul was sent away for disgraceful behavior: thievery, vice, lying, laziness? Charles did not specify. He replaced him with two Haratins, Khali Barka and Bimbi, who, as professed Muslims, could not serve Mass. Fortunately, Charles was awaiting Motylinski, a former officer and interpreter, whom he had known years before in the South Oranais. Retired from active duty since 1897, "Moty" taught Arabic at the university in Constantine, and Charles had invited him to study the Tuareg language with him. And on June 3 the guest arrived. He would make a good Mass assistant. What a relief!

Motylinski's arrival turned out to be doubly providential. On August 11, 1906, right outside the hermitage, Charles was bitten on the foot by a horned viper, a desert snake whose venom is nearly always fatal. Charles lost consciousness. Motylinski immediately called Mohamed ben Hamida, the native soldier serving as his guide. The man employed drastic measures: red iron on the wound and three bleedings to keep the poison from invading the body. Charles was saved, but he was not in good condition! Then, the miracle so long awaited occurred. The nomads, until then distant and indifferent, mobilized. They surrounded him, comforted him. They were finally aware that this bizarre hermit had given all for them.

Father Huvelin had advised Charles to travel: to spend the summer in Tamanrasset and the winter at Beni Abbès. Although that broke his rule of

---

[11] Ibid.
[12] *Carnets de Tamanrasset* (Nouvelle Cité, 1986), 65.

stability, he set out on September 12, 1906, for the long trip would mean contacts with other Tuareg. He also planned to visit Maison-Carrée to obtain a companion. He parted from Motylinski, who returned to Constantine.

Charles received an enthusiastic welcome at Beni Abbès, with tears of joy from Mama Hakem, the elderly mulatto woman, blind and poor, who was his only convert. The soldiers of the redoubt also fêted his return. There was a certain temptation to stay at the oasis. There, he had security, the warmth of his compatriots, the assurance of servers for Mass, a doctor, no lack of supplies, and regular mail delivery from France. But he felt that relative comfort in the shadow of the army did not correspond to his vocation, and he wrote Father Huvelin on November 7: "I am quite miserable; only my intentions and wishes follow the right path, while I get lost in a mass of petty things, not finding any time for reflection in this exterior life." [13]

At Maison-Carrée, where he passed some days of peace, Charles had long conversations with Bishop Guérin and the White Fathers. He headed back to Beni Abbès on December 10. Miracle, he finally had a companion: a young lay novice of the White Fathers, Brother Gilles (Jean-Marie Goyat), aged twenty-three. This son of a Breton fisherman had been attracted to the missionary life after three years spent in a Zouave regiment in Africa. The heroic and romantic life of Father de Foucauld had intrigued him. Bishop Livinhac did not have to be begged to give him up. The boy burned with an ardent faith, but he was unstable, and the White Fathers could not picture him in the cassock of the traditional missionary.

With deep emotion, Charles received his first "Little Brother" postulant and named him Brother Michel.

The train took them to the headquarters of the military subdivision, Aïn Sefra, a large Arab village in the middle of dunes and palms. To his embarrassment, Charles found himself being welcomed by Lyautey in person, as a friend, along with his staff. The general later recounted the meeting to René Bazin: "I found him poor and unkempt, he once so refined. And that was intentional. There was nothing left of the old Foucauld. Oh, yes, the eyes, which were beautiful, shining. The officers adored him. He rode with them, his feet bare. I had given him a room. He slept on the tile floor." [14]

Of course, they talked of Morocco, still in the grips of its divisions. It was too soon to go there. Lyautey wanted Charles to stay put at Tamanrasset, where he exerted a pacifying influence through Moussa, in that vast territory not yet occupied by the army, except for the eastern region (the Ajjer),

---

[13] CF to Father Huvelin, November 7, 1906, 265.
[14] Bazin, *Foucauld*, 331.

where Laperrine was building Fort Polignac to counter the threat from Tripoli.

Father Charles arrived back at Beni Abbès on December 20, 1906, and showed his new disciple around the hermitage. The young man could not hide his disappointment: "It was a very modest convent of earth and wood, built like all the huts of that country. The cells for future monks were so low that a man of average height could raise his hand a little and touch the ceiling, so narrow that you could stretch out your arms and touch the walls. No bed, no chairs, no table, no prie-dieu. You were supposed to sleep fully dressed on a palm mat spread on the floor. The chapel, also built of wood and earth, contained only an altar and two prie-dieux. Thus, during long offices of the day and night you had to remain standing, go down on your knees, or else sit on mats." [15]

They spent a week at Beni Abbès, where, for the first time, Charles tried to apply in community—albeit a modest one, limited to two people—his rule for the Little Brothers of Jesus.

As an economy measure, daylight regulated their life. Charles himself would awaken his companion before dawn. They would speedily wash and dress. Angelus at the ringing of the bell. The Mass of adoration lasted two hours. The only attendees, a few soldiers passing by and old Marie. The thanksgiving, orison, breviary, in Latin. At 9 A.M., to work. Seated in front of a box that served as his table, Brother Charles would pursue the compiling of his dictionary or write letters. In his cell, also used as the kitchen and the refectory, Brother Michel would do his *lectio*, then he ground wheat between two stones, crushed dates, and baked hardtack in the fireplace, under the hot ashes. He already missed the comfortable, reassuring house of the White Fathers, and their meals, not elegant, but balanced.

They would meet again at 11 A.M. Examination of conscience, reading of the lesson for the day, then the *Imitation*. At 11:30, with the black servant they would silently take their places on a mat on the ground, around a pot just come off the fire: rice with carrots and turnips, or a wheat-flour mush. A few crushed dates. No plate, no knife, no fork, no tablecloth, no napkins. Each one dipped into the mixture with his spoon. They drank water from the same jug. This light meal took only a few minutes.

Then they would go to the chapel. *Miserere, lectio.* Work again, from 2 to 6 P.M. Then a quick supper, as frugal as the noon dinner. At 6:30, prayers in the chapel. Then the father would bless his disciple and send him to bed. He himself would go on working and praying. Such an austere and

---

[15] Brother Michel's account, which is in the archives of the Postulation, has been published in part by Bazin, ibid., 333–42.

monotonous life is bearable only if there underlies it a continual adoration, involving the Real Presence of the Beloved.

That Christmas 1906, one hundred soldiers, deeply moved, were present at Father de Foucauld's midnight Mass. Then they withdrew to celebrate, while the hermit and his disciple spent the night in prayer, prostrate on the ground in the little chapel. To economize, they had blown out the candles after the service. Brother Michel held out only for an hour. He gave in and fell asleep. In the morning, he arose and saw Brother Charles still praying, kneeling on the sand.

"How could you stay awake so long in complete darkness?"

"One does not need to see to speak to him who is the sun of justice and the light of the world!"

Brother Michel remained amazed by Charles' devotion. Later, he would say: "He loved Jesus Christ passionately, and his great happiness was in conversing with the prisoner of love, really present in the tabernacle. Prayer was his delight. It was truly his life and the breath of his soul. He spent the greater part of his days and his nights kneeling before the Blessed Sacrament, adoring, pleading, thanking, atoning. To the end of my life I shall remember the Mass of Father Charles, which I had the good fortune to serve."

His faith in the Real Presence was absolute.

On December 27 they started out on the desert road again, heading south, Charles on foot as he led his camel by the halter. Brother Michel notes, "He always walks, feet bare and chapped from the cold, in crude sandals. He wears a robe of unbleached cotton, always too short, often stained and torn. He cuts his own hair and beard, without a mirror. Provided that he pleases God, he cares not about the judgment of men."

And it gets worse. He seemed to work at provoking a reaction: "He likes humiliation, scorn, insults, and he asks for them by making an effort to look eccentric."

These little excesses did not undermine his exemplary humility: "I never heard him saying anything to show himself in a favorable light. He would call himself 'a useless servant'." He was constantly seeking martyrdom and saw in it the greatest proof of love "that a friend can give to a friend by dying for him as he had died for us".

"He was always a magnificent example for me: devotion, ardent zeal for souls, charity toward one's neighbor, strong faith, unwavering hope, complete detachment from the things of this world, deep humility, unshakable patience in times of trial. And especially in his terrifying mortification. One fault: once in a while, when things were not going as he would like, he would let his impatience show, but then just as quickly he would repress it."

Terrifying mortification . . . The desert nights were cold and the wind howled. With their hands they would dig a hole in the sand to sleep in, not lighting a fire. Their one piece of canvas was reserved for the Blessed Sacrifice. Charles always walked, refusing to ride. Shivering at night, he gave his burnous to Michel. His poverty was not an act. "At Beni Abbès, I never saw him drink wine or liqueurs. He never ate meat, except to keep from offending a host. He never smoked."

All the money he received from his family went to the poor. When his robe fell to pieces, he would make it into towels. He turned over envelopes and used them for rough drafts and notes. And his generosity bordered on recklessness. "He gave without counting", says Michel. In 1906, his reputation for holiness had already spread through the desert. His arrival in a village would give rise to a scene that astonished the Europeans. The inhabitants would come out to meet him, led by their *kaid*. They would greet him reverently, kissing his hand or the hem of his robe. They would address him as "Sidi Marabout", and the beggars would crowd around him.

Brother Michel adds, "No unoccupied moments in his days. In the desert, during our stops, instead of resting, even if worn out by a long march in the sun, he would work on his dictionary. He never took any recreation. To rest, after prayer and study, he would make little wooden crosses, do paintings and sketches for decorating the cells and the chapel. He would write out in a fine round hand edifying sayings of the Desert Fathers and maxims of the saints suitable for inspiring a spirit of sacrifice, and he would mount them on all the walls. He practiced the Christian virtues to a heroic degree."

Thus ends the eyewitness account by his first and last disciple, who asked God to let him "be his imitator as far as his strength would allow".

Unfortunately, his strength was going to fail him. Upon their arrival in early February 1906 at In Salah, where Laperrine resided, Michel's fine enthusiasm was only a memory; it was a somewhat rebellious youngster, sick with dysentery and exhaustion, who went to see the garrison doctor. He was declared medically unfit to continue the journey.

Charles then decided to spend a month at In Salah, hoping that Michel would regain his strength. For six hundred francs he bought a little house in Ksar el Arab, the native quarter, and transformed it into a hermitage.

While there he learned the terrible news from Laperrine: his friend Motylinski had died in Constantine, felled by typhus. His exhausted organism had no resistance when the epidemic broke out.

Following upon Michel's collapse, that should have served as an additional warning to Charles. But he took no account. Yet, feeling in some small way responsible for the officer-interpreter's death, he agreed to get hold of his research and pursue without him the work on the Tuareg dictionary. He devoted himself to that task in In Salah with the help of an astonishing, very learned person, Mohamed ben Messis, who was scorned by the Ahaggar because he had a Tuareg mother and an Arab father. When the tribe had his wife beaten, he adopted the French cause and became the army's best informer. It was he who was responsible for the arrest of the killers of the Marquis de Morès. It was also he who had in 1902 guided Lieutenant Cottenest, making possible his victory at Tit, prelude to the pacification of the Ahaggar.

Charles had a strong need to immerse himself in this overwhelming project in order to forget his disappointments. For Brother Michel, the adventure was over. He gave up. In his diary, Brother Charles merely noted, on March 2, 1907: "Sent Michel back to El Golea. Extremely weak in body and spirit, soul and virtues." Writing to Bishop Guérin, he was less vague: "Lack of judgment, humility, and obedience."

For Brother Michel, too, it was the end of a great dream. Tears in his eyes, leading his camel by its thong, he turned around one last time to gaze at the ascetic silhouette of Father de Foucauld, which stood out against the dune: "Like Moses, I was only to see the Promised Land from afar." Tamanrasset! [16]

A few days later, Charles de Foucauld set out again to follow the desert road, heading for Tamanrasset. Alone!

Alone, no. Not yet. For this long trek, he had connected once again with his faithful friend Captain Dinaux, who was leading a company of eighty camel troopers. He had invited Charles to accompany him on a new "pacification tour" among the Tuareg Iforas, along with the Arnaud-Cortier mission, which was on its way to Timbuktu. Charles accepted joyfully, for this would allow him to collect the Tuareg poetry that was to round out his dictionary, providing living illustrations of the language.

And indeed, still in the company of Ben Messis, he gathered much traditional material about to disappear. Since he paid a sou for each line, the poetry poured in. Songs of love, songs of war, anything was good. The black man Chernach, Moussa's courier, was an inexhaustible source. Lieutenant Cottier remembered: "Inside the cramped tent, until an advanced hour of the night, all three of us worked by candlelight, hermetically sealed in our canvas shelter, while outdoors the wind raged." [17]

But day was already breaking in the east, beyond the white sands of the

[16] Brother Michel was not lacking in virtue or moral fiber. He would take vows as a Carthusian, entering their house at Valsainte, in Switzerland, where he was to remain faithfully. The Carthusians are the strictest of orders, each monk living isolated in his cell.

[17] Narrative taken down by Antoine Chatelard, in G. Ganne, *Tamanrasset ou le désert fertile* (SOS, 1975), 192.

Tidikelt. It was the sacred hour of the Eucharist: "Long before dawn, we would crouch on the sand in the rear of the little tent. The canvas doors had been shut, and the effect was not lacking in the picturesque, this ceremony deep in the desert, in this frail shelter, by the trembling light of two candles."

Thanks to his incessant labors, Charles' work was progressing, but he kept his part in it invisible: "I asked Laperrine to have this published by whomever he would like, as something belonging to him, the grammar, the lexicon, the poetry, on the one condition that my name not appear, that I remain unknown, obscure."[18]

He himself wanted only "poverty, abjection, humiliation, abandonment, persecution, suffering, cross".[19]

It is easy to understand why he did not attract disciples!

Brother Charles finally arrived back in Tamanrasset on July 6 and found there terrible misery and famine, result of the extended drought. For seventeen months it had not rained. No milk. The nomads had led their flocks to less unfortunate areas. Only a few goats remained, "as dry as the ground, and the people like the goats", he wrote Marie de Bondy. "I have resumed my orderly monastic life with delight", he added.[20]

He was not being entirely truthful. He confessed in his diary, "No Mass, for I am alone."[21] At Maison-Carrée, Bishop Guérin had confirmed what Charles already knew: Rome would not grant him a dispensation. He would not be allowed to celebrate Mass without a server. He had been counting on a young White Father he had met at Maison-Carrée, Father de Chatouville. After Brother Michel's defection, either he changed his mind or his superiors forbade his joining Brother Charles. It was not just the excessive rule and the ascetic life. The founder of the Little Brothers of Jesus offered his postulants no monastic structure, no community. Saint Benedict, Saint Bernard, and Saint Francis had, in their wisdom, established a minimum of twelve monks for the formation of a community.

Charles attributed his failures to his unworthiness and continued to follow his heroic rule. He thought he had given all. But now he would have to renounce the essential: the Eucharist. His life. His nourishment. He was afraid. He did not yet know that Rome had also decided to take away his last support! The consecrated Host, the reserve that he kept in his tabernacle for adoration. It could be said of Charles de Foucauld, as of the

---

[18] CF to Bishop Guérin, May 31, 1907, quoted by Bazin, *Foucauld*, 345.

[19] Ibid., December 25, 1907, 346.

[20] CF to Marie de Bondy, July 11, 1907, in Gorrée, *Sur les traces*, 213.

[21] *Carnets de Tamanrasset*, 86.

Canadian martyr Jean de Brébeuf, that "his soul was glued to the Blessed Sacrament."

His letters to Father Huvelin were a series of appeals, but for twenty months, Huvelin, seriously ill, had not replied. Yet Charles continued to write him. These letters of pathetic confession, in which he painstakingly reviewed his every action, were a necessity for him: "Deep-seated pride. I do not sufficiently keep the presence of God. I get absorbed in what I am doing and in distractions, reveries. I do not look enough upon Jesus, who is here. I do not see enough in all human beings. I am not supernatural enough with them. Not sufficiently gentle or humble, not careful to do them good whenever I can. All my pious exercises leave something to be desired. They are always halfhearted, sometimes too short or too fast, full of distractions. At times sleep overtakes me, at other times I put them off from hour to hour. So halfhearted about suffering and humility. I leave out the minor penances, I take too much care of my body. Instead of having a love of disdain, I take pleasure in kindnesses." [22]

And what kindnesses does he mean? Gestures of gratitude from the poor blacks whose misery he was alleviating? Veneration he judged excessive?

Famine hung over the Ahaggar throughout the summer and fall of 1907. The settled nomads survived only because they had milk from their goats. The goats were starving; there was no longer a blade of grass or a leaf to be seen. The Haratins despaired when they looked at their dried-up vegetable patches. Charles distributed his stock of wheat, which, miracle of respect, had not been rifled during his long absence. To be sure that the smallest had their share, he arranged dinners for the children, where he would serve them and forget to serve himself. Laperrine notes, "Seeing all those little jaws chewing so merrily, he did not have the heart to save a portion for himself."

Relayed to Charles by a distressed Bishop Guérin, the Vatican's order not to keep the consecrated Host in the tabernacle as long as he remained alone served as the final blow. What was the point of staying since he could no longer celebrate Mass or adore, and if there were not even any Tuareg there? All those with any resources had already departed. Why did he turn down Bishop Guérin's suggestion to rejoin "civilization"? He would always opt for the most heroic solution. Come what may, he would stay there, with the poorest, the most neglected, "leaving it to God to give me the means to celebrate". Once again, he was attempting the impossible, at the risk of destroying himself. With a choice between the blessed mystical life and the charitable life of helping the poor, he chose charity. He stayed, "so that

[22] CF to Father Huvelin, September 17, 1907, 270.

between Timbuktu and El Golea there would be at least one soul who adored Jesus and prayed to him".[23]

"Monastic life, prayers, reading, work", he wrote Marie de Bondy. "Like the brother porter in a monastery, I am at times interrupted by someone calling to me from the outside. It is one of the poor. I hardly have any other visitors. Everyone with any resources is two hundred, three hundred, four hundred miles away in places where it has rained. The poor, alone, without camels for traveling, are confined to the immediate area. I can help out a little these poor hungry folk."[24]

But for how long? His reserves were dwindling, and he dared not seek more help from his friends. Two years since Father Huvelin had answered him! Even Marie no longer replied to his letters, she who used to write every two weeks. For five months he had received no word from her. With all his heart he reaffirmed the offering made at the time of their separation: they had not seen each other for eighteen years! And the wound was as open as it had been the first day.

Had he given all? He still had his miserable life, his worn-out body. Day by day he became more anemic, and this time it was not from voluntary asceticism. He had severe dietary deficiencies and was suffering from scurvy: no meat, no raw vegetables. Why did he not request a bare minimum from Laperrine or Bishop Guérin, who could have sent him supplies? Because of his rule, sublime and absurd: "Do not concern yourself with the body any more than the tree concerns itself with the leaf that falls", he once wrote from Nazareth. "God will provide." But had not God abandoned him?

Now assisted by Ba Hammou—Moussa's secretary and son of the *kaid* of Rhat—he was still stubbornly working on his dictionary, eleven hours a day, as if, having failed at everything else, he wanted at least to leave this tool of conversion, which would be useful to the missionaries who came after him, when God wished, if God wished. He was not eating, he barely slept, and he grew weaker. But he persisted in his madness: "I am happy to be and do what Jesus wishes. Happy with the infinite goodness of God. If there were not this inexhaustible source of happiness and peace, the evil seen all around would lead to sadness."

When he wrote to Bishop Guérin, however, the same old complaint would always be repeated: "No Mass, since I am alone." And yet the apostolic vicar had managed to win a concession from Rome. On November 22, 1907, Charles received permission to say Mass without a server, but on condition there be at least one Christian present. Well, there was none around. Who was going to come to this sun-scorched desert except for a

[23] CF to R. de Blic, December 9, 1907, in Bazin, *Foucauld*, 350.
[24] CF to Marie de Bondy, July 22, 1907, in Gorrée, *Sur les traces*, 213.

few soldiers on patrol, who passed through every two or three months? He
did take advantage of these brief visits to renew the Sacred Species. But he
did not have permission to receive Communion alone or to keep the Host
in the tabernacle.

Once again he was plunged into the dark night of the spirit. His solitude
and his "uselessness" overpowered him. "Jesus cannot be in a place without
his light shining forth." No more contacts. Even the poor Haratins established there, the forty or so who had been not killed or driven away by the
drought, no longer ventured out. He had nothing more to give them. Go to
see them? He wanted to respect the principle of the cloister, to which he
was adhering once again. "I keep my cloister, I am still a monk."

On December 25, 1907, he reached the depths of despair. Christmas
without the Eucharist! "That night, no Mass, for the first time in twenty-
one years", he wrote Marie de Bondy. "Up to the last minute, I hoped
someone would come. But nothing came, no Christian traveler, no soldier,
no permission to celebrate alone! For three months, more than three
months, I have received no letters. May the will of the Beloved be praised
in everything." [25]

He felt the end coming. No rebellion roused him. Astonishing that at the
hour he reached the bottom, his faith and his love of Christ remained
intact. He quoted Saint John of the Cross: "It is precisely at the hour of the
greatest prostration of the spirit that the Savior discharges fully the debt of
depraved man and effects our redemption." [26]

Three months without a letter! What were his relatives thinking, those in
Paris, in the Périgord, in Alsace? With the exception of Marie de Bondy, his
old aunt Marie de la Touche, and Mimi, they judged him harshly: "Pity
tinged with scorn" (Castillon). "A lunatic, a real lunatic" (his cousin General
de Morlaincourt).

Even the three who loved him unconditionally, the three Maries,
wanted him to come back to France. He had failed, that was obvious. No
one could understand his desire to depart (or flee?) when he had barely
gotten settled somewhere. He was still the unstable child, traumatized by
the tragic death of his parents. The peace of which he spoke, where was it?
In the family country estates and in the monasteries, not in his miserable
hermitages doomed to oblivion and dust, battered by the floodtide of the
poor.

He was alone. He was cold. He was hungry, not just for bread but for the
Host. He was weak, worn out, to the point where he would lose consciousness and lie there on the sand, abandoned, like a dog without a master. Even

[25] Ibid., December 25, 1907, 215.
[26] Quoted by M. Castillon du Perron, *Charles de Foucauld* (Grasset, 1982), 397.

God did not have the pity to allow him to die. Nobody came to see him. He did not dare go out himself, not because of cloister but because he was afraid of collapsing on the road, although it was only a few hundred feet to the huts of the village. Only yesterday he had been able to cover twenty-five miles a day on foot!

New Year's Day, 1908. "No Mass, since I am alone", he notes in his diary. This year, he was fifty, and he wrote to Father Huvelin: "I have almost become an old man. I puff like a broken-winded old horse. My work gets slower and slower. It is the work of a tired man."

He was nearly toothless, and he was losing his hair. Frightfully thin, he walked with a stoop. Even the indomitable light in his eyes had disappeared. He was hungry. His last sack of wheat had been distributed to the poor. He was using the strength he had left to write, to cry out in the wilderness, not for himself but for others, his disdained black and mulatto brothers. But who would hear him? "I live amid infinite poverty and suffering, for which the world does nothing and wants to do nothing. What the natives see of us—Christians professing a religion of love—is neglect, or ambition, or greed, and in most of us, indifference, dislike, and harshness." [27]

He had reached fifty. He was through. What had he done with his life since becoming a monk eighteen years before? "What a harvest I should have had! Instead of that, misery, destitution, and not the least good toward others. A tree is known by its fruit, and mine shows what I am, a useless servant." [28]

There was nothing more but to offer his life, that poor emaciated body, which, belying its appearance, hung on fiercely.

On January 7, he finally had a life-preserving reaction. He wrote Laperrine and Bishop Guérin to ask for a "bit of milk and wine"! But it was late. Laperrine would not receive his appeal for two weeks, and it would take a month to deliver the supplies. Moreover, writing to Marie de Bondy, Brother Charles immediately regretted his distress calls: "My letter to Henri [Laperrine] is unworthy of a hermit."

Was he going to die? On January 20, 1908, in a trembling hand he wrote in his notebook: "Am sick, forced to interrupt my work. Jesus, Mary, Joseph, I give you my soul, my spirit, and my life." [29]

Was he going to die alone? No. One morning he awakened surprised and disappointed to be still of this world. "I thought it was the end, but the Lord had not so willed", he wrote Marie de Bondy.[30]

---

[27] CF to Father Huvelin, January 1, 1908, 279.
[28] Ibid., 280.
[29] *Carnets de Tamanrasset*, 87.
[30] CF to Marie de Bondy, January 26, 1908, in Gorrée, *Sur les traces*, 215.

Miracle, there was someone with him! A Targui was smiling at him, worried at seeing him so unwell. He had even thought he might be dead. The man held out a bowl of goat's milk, whispering with affection and respect: "Sidi Marabout!" Then he added fervently: "Khaouia Carlo!"

Brother Charles sat up with some help and greedily drank the sour-tasting liquid. Then he collapsed back onto his bed. He was happy. This time, once again, they had come to him. Just what had happened?

Ba Hammou, frightened at seeing him so emaciated, had alerted Moussa, far away to the south. Learning that Brother Charles was seriously ill, the proud *amenokal*, very upset, had sent a messenger riding at full speed. Not to let the foreign guest die alone, that was a matter of honor for a Targui! More than that. Moussa and his people, as with the snakebite incident, were truly moved. For this man who was dying of hunger in their land had given everything for them. Until then they had not thought of him as genuinely poor, and thus their brother in poverty, since he had so many things to give away. The goods that he received were from abroad or from the army and thus were regarded with suspicion. Alms! This time, he was giving his very flesh, and he would die of his sacrifice. And it was precisely when he had been reduced to powerlessness that the Tuareg people finally felt solidarity with him and responsibility toward him, and they could finally enter into his life and share with him the little they had in this year of famine.

Actually, he was to be saved by Dassine, the poetess of the Ahaggar, who would give him intelligent care, after sending away the medicine men with their dangerous practices.

Having come back to life, he wrote Marie de Bondy, January 26: "I have been rather ill, something to do with the heart. The slightest motion made me so breathless that I was ready to faint. One or two days, I thought it was the end. But God has not so willed. I am staying completely quiet, total rest, I have to break off my work for a month." [31]

A few weeks later, Charles received the food supplies from Bishop Guérin, with orders to "rest and overeat". But the apostolic vicar was not hopeful. Not that the pillagers were going to rob the caravan. "I fear you more, my dear friend, than I do the Tuareg. Thus I ask you very insistently to make use of these supplies *for yourself* and not just to distribute them to others." In reality, it was not the food that saved him, but the news from Laperrine, January 31, 1908, that he could celebrate alone. It was a resurrection: "*Deo gratias!* Today I received a letter from Laperrine announcing that the pope has granted me authorization to celebrate the Holy Mass com-

[31] Ibid.

pletely alone, without a server or an attendee. So tomorrow, I shall be able to celebrate. Christmas! Christmas! Thanks to God!" [32]

The pope! So what had happened? Bishop Guérin had already written the pope: "For ten years, this very holy priest has continued to lead a most heroic and admirable life. He finds himself alone in the midst of the savage Tuareg tribes, whom he has succeeded in taming and for whom he does the greatest of good by the example of his life of extreme poverty, inexhaustible charity, continual prayer. The apostolic prefect of Ghardaïa thus humbly beseeches Your Holiness to grant him. . . ." [33]

But the petition had not been submitted to the pope.

In January 1908, Father Burtin, procurator general of the White Fathers, met with the pope and forthwith obtained the requested authorization.

For his part, Laperrine had done quite well with providing earthly nourishment. He had sent Charles two camels carrying grain and canned milk, which Charles received in early March. The outraged colonel wrote Bishop Guérin: "He feels 'tired'. For him to admit that he is tired, he has to be really ill. He probably tried to overdo the fasting and penance, but anyone's strength has its limits. I am going to say some foolish things to him and also invoke your authority to inform him that penance verging on gradual suicide is not permitted. I believe it essential that on his next trip north you get him in your clutches and keep him a month or two in Ghardaïa to grow back his hump." [34]

A few weeks later, Laperrine would revise his judgment: "I made a gross blunder in blaming his asceticism for the extreme deprivation that nearly caused his death. It is his charity that should be considered the major culprit." [35]

But Charles did not dream of leaving Tamanrasset. First he needed to recover, to rest. He did nothing. He did everything: he prayed. He celebrated the Eucharist, what happiness! Then he took up his pen. To Father Huvelin: "Great happiness. Every day I say Mass, it is a new life for me and an infinite grace for this poor country. . . . Alone at the foot of the tabernacle with Jesus so near me day and night, and now being able to celebrate each morning, I lack nothing." [36]

"God alone suffices", his dear Teresa of Avila had written.

[32] *Carnets de Tamanrasset*, 87.

[33] Bazin, *Foucauld*, 352.

[34] Laperrine to Bishop Guérin, February 3 and 11, 1908, in ibid., 356.

[35] Quoted by M. Carrouges, *Charles de Foucauld, explorateur mystique* (Cerf, 1954), 311.

[36] CF to Father Huvelin, February 9, 1908, 283 and 285.

Tamanrasset, December 1, 1916, 6 P.M.

Three knocks on the door of the fort. Paul Embarek. The Haratin had come to prepare the father's supper. Charles could have done it himself, but he liked to justify the salary, small as it was, that he paid the black man, from whom, as ever, he did not want to break away.

Tonight's "supper" consisted of nothing but *tarrouaït*, the thick gruel of sour milk mixed with local flour. It had a sourish taste, and bits of grain scratched the tongue and the throat. Yesterday it was a *couscoussou* without a scrap of meat. Charles had promised Marie de Bondy that he would vary his menus, if they could be called that.

Supper over, the father said grace. It was only 6:15, and night was closing in around the fort.

The father sent Paul on his way with a measure of wheat, his pay. He allowed himself an hour of recreation before Compline, the evening office. He walked round and round the narrow courtyard of his fort. It would not have been wise to venture outdoors at that hour. He missed the happy days when he could leave his hermitage, "the Frigate", and walk along the esplanade, enjoying friendly chats with visitors and sharing his memories. On those occasions, he was very cheerful and laughed often, revealing his toothless gums.

Then he would question the visitor, and unless he was some important figure, the talk would invariably come around to the examining of con-science. The father often asked the young aide-de-camp or lieutenant how he had spent his day. If he had carried out all his duties, and more. The French had a duty to learn Tamahaq to be closer to the Tuareg. Foucauld was anxious to learn the origins of this people. He would make use of any anecdotal information whatever to support this or that theory, for example, that of Egyptian origin. He was fascinated by the idea that the Egyptians had been driven from their homeland and into the desert, like the Jewish people. He saw in that a sort of purification following upon centuries of decadence.

After pillaging the Amsel agricultural center and rifling their stock of grain, the *rezzou* of the *fellagha* stopped in the desert for a brief rest. The night was black. They were but a few miles from Tamanrasset.

Not feeling very reassured, Beuh ag Rhabelli asked Kerzou: "The marabout Charles is certainly on the alert, especially at night. After the failed Amsel plot, how could he sleep in peace? And if he has had arms brought into the fort again, he must intend to use them!"

"That is mysterious. If he has weapons, they are for defending the Haratin village and his food stocks. But keeping weapons is dangerous. Right now in the Ahaggar, arms are more valuable than food or gold. Why is he provoking the *rezzou* like this?"

"Do you mean that any kind of surprise is possible?"

"Yes, any kind. Who knows if the *goum* from Fort Moty, those hateful Shaamba Arabs, are not lying in wait in the fort? A few determined men hidden in the towers would be enough to keep us from getting close. And the door is impregnable. It would take a cannon!"

"We have no choice. Our orders must be carried out. The marabout is the last obstacle keeping the people of the Ahaggar from swinging over to the side of the rebellion. Despite Moussa, all the tribal chiefs long to drive the French out of the Sahara. The Ajjer have risen up. And soon it will be the same with the Kel Ahaggar, the Taitoq, the Iforas, and the Tidikelt. Even the blacks and the mulattos long for the old order, that of our ancestors."

The dromedaries appeared to be settling down for the night. This was not the time to let up. Beuh issued an order: "Mount. Off we go, and may Allah keep us!"

They were not so sure about that. The Koran forbade touching a hair of the head of a holy hermit, even if he might be a Christian or Jew!

"*Ya Allah! Nemshou!*"

The beasts rose slowly and bleated. Then they moved off, to the sound of a hail of pebbles kicked up by their hooves. They lengthened their stride, their long necks undulating, while each warrior sought a secure perch, merging with the hump of his mount.

14

"Still Alone"

It was spring of 1908, the Ahaggar still desperately dry. Charles felt the need to take stock in an effort to understand the reasons for his double failure: no conversions, no disciples. He opened his heart to Marie de Bondy: "Amid an ocean of evils, the lack of training and education [of the tribes]. The degree of ignorance is such that they are incapable of distinguishing truth from falsehood and, often, good from evil. Great moral laxity." [1] "They shall probably have to be taught first, then converted. They cannot be made Christians first and civilized afterward." [2]

Writing to Bishop Guérin, he wondered about his mission: "Is the Sahara worth so many sacrifices for a few wandering tribes who are not asking to be converted?" [3] The answer was clear: Jesus died for the whole world and especially for the poor. For any Christian nation with colonies, conversion is an absolute duty. His anguish in this regard came from the certainty that "these souls are lost and will remain in that state if we do not take measures to influence them." [4]

But how to influence them? There again, he had failed. He had tried to found a new order, the Little Brothers of Jesus, whose apostolate would consist wholly of adoration and of presence, the gift of the living Christ in the Eucharist, which the brothers would take where it was absent, preferably among the poor, while remaining poor themselves. But no one had come. He was still alone. As with conversion, he recognized his failure. But that did not mean he was about to give up. Christ, too, had failed during his lifetime, converting neither the Jews nor the Romans. Yet "what is impossible for man is possible for God", Charles never tired of repeating. Now he thought it would take centuries to bring the world around to a genuine practicing of Christian virtues.

Ultimately, the method of evangelization he offered was none other than the one that had converted him: the example of Marie de Bondy,

[1] CF to Marie de Bondy, March 25, 1908, in G. Gorrée, *Sur les traces de Charles de Foucauld* (Éd. de la Plus Grande France, 1936), 217.
[2] Ibid., June 4, 1908.
[3] CF to Bishop Guérin, June 1, 1908, in R. Bazin, *Charles de Foucauld* (Plon, 1921), 358.
[4] Ibid.

silent, welcoming, and good. Love and make oneself loved. "When they are at the point of performing actions of perfect love and asking God for the light, they shall be ready for conversion", he wrote his friend J. Hours.[5]

Had he at least succeeded with Moussa ag Amastane? He had "tamed" him. Laperrine was satisfied on that score. With the help of the *amenokal*, the Ahaggar had become peaceful. Moussa himself had adopted the settled life. He had a house built in Tamanrasset and planted crops there. He was assessing the tax fairly, and he levied warriors, using them to maintain the order without which the colony could not prosper. The army supplied him with light arms and ammunition. It was a victory.

But not for Brother Charles. Not only had he not converted Moussa, but the *amenokal* now dreamed of strengthening the Muslim faith of the Tuareg, who until then had been rather indifferent. He even envisaged building a mosque and an Islamic school in Tamanrasset. Apparently that was his way of pledging friendship to the fundamentalist marabouts and anti-French Tuareg. He was hedging his bets.

Moussa was indeed under the influence of marabouts hostile to France, who came from the Touat or the Tidikelt, traditionally rebel regions. The *amenokal* set up one of these holy men in Tamanrasset, his mission the construction of a mosque and a *zaouïa* in order to bring back Muslim law and teach the Koran, so little heeded by those former slaves, the Haratin mulattos and blacks. But unlike Charles, whose capital came in from outside, this marabout made himself hated by trying to extract the tithe stipulated in the Koran. He was driven out, and there was no more talk of a mosque.

Charles saw in these efforts "the spirit of Evil counteracting his work". And he wondered about the wisdom of choosing Tamanrasset. Would it not be better four hundred miles to the south, more productive? And even better in Morocco? General Lyautey had just begun punitive expeditions there, his main goal to halt the *rezzous* on the Algerian border while preparing Morocco for a French protectorate. But Lyautey, in spite of some rather vague exchanges, had issued no invitation to Charles, who felt disappointed. Loyal to the Republic with its secular views, Lyautey proved somewhat hostile to Christian missionaries working in Islamic lands. He would rather the Muslims retain their religion, which was intertwined with their culture.

And if Lyautey was right? Charles wondered. Suddenly, he had a flash of insight, realizing why he had not been well received. He had arrived on a camel belonging to an army imposing its force on the country. He was and

[5] CF to J. Hours, November 25, 1911, quoted by J.-F. Six, *Itinéraire spirituel de Charles de Foucauld* (Seuil, 1958), 351.

remained a foreigner, one of the hated occupiers. And he was doubly a foreigner, for he professed a different religion. Was there not a danger that he would take their souls, the little they possessed, their age-old culture? The proud Tuareg did not wish to be "tamed" as the first step toward being "assimilated" by this conquering people. They would rather stay poor. Only the mulatto Haratins and the black slaves might accept new ways, for they had nothing to lose, their primitive culture having already been taken from them.

And Charles was not really one of the poor, since he gave alms. Certainly, he was isolated and unarmed, but the army watched over him, and he had only to say the word if he needed protection. Even if he said nothing, "his Saharan Highness" (Laperrine) would not stand for anyone touching a hair of his friend's head. Powerful in spite of himself, the marabout was also learned. Priest, basically he thought only of converting, like other missionaries. Strong through his learning, his experience, and, most important, his Christ, Charles had come there as a conqueror. Of course he sought only the good of the tribes, but he was acting like a conqueror. He had proclaimed their salvation just as Laperrine had proclaimed security under the protection of the army, and the governor general in his turn had promised prosperity through French economic development.

Yes, therein lay the cause of his failure. Deep down, he knew very well that "to love is enough". To love is not to convert; it is first of all to listen, to learn to know these men and women from a different civilization and a different religion, as he had done in Morocco.

Now he realized the importance of the work on the dictionary and the anthology of poetry. Not only for translating the Gospels and paving the way for future missionaries, but above all for listening, the first step in sharing. Thus, henceforth he was to have a new approach, surprisingly "modern"; at the same time, he would continue to provide his own example of brotherhood, if not of holiness, since he felt incapable of that. The real conversion of the Tuareg could be carried out only through the will of God.

"The more I go about here, the more I think it not necessary at this time to seek isolated conversions." For him that was a reversal. He told Doctor Dhauteville, a Protestant: "I am here, not to convert the Tuareg in a single stroke, but to try to understand them and improve them. I am certain the Lord will welcome in heaven those who led good and upright lives, without their having to be Roman Catholics." [6]

At last, Charles de Foucauld was allowing himself to be "tamed"! He was also less wrapped up in himself, in his own search. He was discarding plans

---

[6] L. Lehureau, *Au Sahara avec le père de Foucauld* (Algiers: Baconnier, 1944), 115.

that were too elaborate, too ambitious. He was becoming more human, sleeping and eating like everybody else. He was coming to accept others with their religion and their weaknesses, turning into a spokesman for the very poor without trying to convert them.

Life at the hermitage slowly picked up for Charles. On June 9, 1908, Laperrine received from the army the funds to build a mighty fort, a *bordj*, at Tarhaouhaout in the heart of the Ahaggar, for housing a permanent garrison of troops from the Saharan Tidikelt forces. The site was no more than thirty-five miles from Tamanrasset, or a few hours' journey for a fast camel. An event for Charles, who, along with being less isolated if not more secure, would receive mail on a regular basis.

The construction proceeded rapidly. When summer arrived, the garrison moved in: two officers and more than forty men. Laperrine wanted to name the place Fort Foucauld, but naturally the hermit objected. They opted for Fort Motylinski. Laperrine was happy. With the Ahaggar he was completing the pacification of the Sahara, and it had been done discreetly.

On July 16 he took advantage of an inspection of Fort Moty to pay Charles a visit. He stayed with him four days and sent news of him to Bishop Guérin: "He is very well. He is glowing with health and good cheer. He arrived at my camp June 29 galloping like a second lieutenant, at the head of a group of Tuareg horsemen. He is more popular than ever with them, and they appreciate him more and more. On the other hand, he has little respect for the blacks settled here, who are simply lazy people, having only the basest of feelings." [7]

In a later article, published in the *Revue de cavalerie* in 1913, Laperrine offers the following portrait of Father de Foucauld: "He does not make a display of his asceticism, and [when a guest] he eats like everyone else. One would almost have to spy on him to be aware of the strict diet he imposes on his poor body, probably to atone for all the fine dinners at Saumur. His influence is very great. The *amenokal* Moussa makes no important decision without first consulting him." [8]

Unfortunately, a letter from Charles to Marie de Bondy, written September 20, 1908, contradicts Laperrine's view of the hermit's health: "Solitude is so sweet to me, but how many things could be done were I not alone. I am well, but I feel I am getting old. My work gets slower and slower and is that of a tired man. I have just reached my fiftieth year. I feel

---

[7] Laperrine to Bishop Guérin, July 22, 1908, in Bazin, *Foucauld*, 360. Foucauld often repeated this harsh judgment. At his most moderate, he wrote (in a 1908 letter to his sister): "I live alone among savages" (quoted by Bazin, *Foucauld*, 361). But that gave him an additional reason for loving them.

[8] Laperrine, "Les Étapes de la conversion d'un houzard", *Revue de cavalerie*, October 1913.

it, and I would like to have around me others who could take my place when I am gone." [9]

During his stay in Tamanrasset, Laperrine managed to observe the hermit's leisure time activities and came away puzzled: "I have often been asked just what could Foucauld find to do to kill time. It is a godsend for him when he can get hold of a few elderly ladies of the Tuareg nobility, for it is they who are the most well versed in the tribal traditions. On those occasions, there is nothing more entertaining than to watch him holding court, pencil in hand, in the middle of an elite assembly of old dowagers sitting on the ground, chatting about everything while sipping their tea and smoking a pipe." [10]

Brother Charles took this work very seriously. Grabbing the large pencil attached to his belt by a string, he would take notes on a fat notepad he had made out of the envelopes from his mail. Back at the hermitage, he would carefully copy everything into a student notebook.

Near the end of 1908, Brother Charles, at the insistence of his sister and with the approval of Bishop Guérin and Father Huvelin, decided to undertake a trip to France, the first since he had left his homeland eight years before. He intended to set up a lay association there to help him realize his plan to found an order. He left Tamanrasset on December 25, met with Bishop Guérin in Ghardaïa, then with Bishop Livinhac at Maison-Carrée on February 13. What he had to say amazed them: "Preaching Jesus to the Tuareg, I do not believe Jesus wants that, not from me, not from anyone. We must proceed very cautiously there, gently, get to know them, make friends with them.[11] All that to lead them to Christianity in God's good time, maybe in centuries." [12]

What a great change for the apostle of the Sahara! It is not hard to imagine the White Fathers asking anxiously: "Then what is the mission?"

"To regard every human being as a beloved brother. To banish from our midst the spirit of militancy. Jesus has taught us to go like lambs among wolves, not to take up arms." [13]

On February 16, he sailed from Algiers and, upon landing in Marseille, immediately went north to Paris. He stayed only five days; with deep feeling, he celebrated Mass at Saint-Augustin's.

His first visit was to Father Huvelin, whose health remained delicate. He

---

[9] CF to Marie de Bondy, September 20, 1908, 172.

[10] Laperrine, "Les Étapes".

[11] CF to Bishop Guérin, quoted by J.-F. Six, *L'Aventure de l'amour de Dieu* (Seuil, 1993), 37.

[12] CF to Bishop Livinhac, ibid., 37.

[13] CF to J. Hours, January 9, 1912, ibid., 37.

presented to him his revised plan for the Union of the Brothers and Sisters of the Sacred Heart of Jesus, which had been approved by Bishop Guérin. A kind of third order, prefiguring the great lay movements of this century, such as the Focolari. No unworkable ascetic regulations, but personal conversion through identification with the poor, hidden, humiliated Christ, followed by patient imitation. Self-effacement, sacrifice, the giving of all, these were acceptable to Father Huvelin, he who had already given all and was nearing the end of his earthly life. He merely toned down parts in the document he thought too constraining: "Ahead of everything, let grace do its work."

Then, at the priest's insistence, and in spite of his promise never to see her again, Charles met with Marie de Bondy in her residence on rue Percier. Their emotion can be imagined: "Now that I have seen you, it seems as if this long separation never existed." [14] Marie was no less moved. Eighteen years since they had seen each other!

She was fifty-nine and had aged early, but he saw only the jet eyes, unchanged, which revealed a soul devoted to the absolute. Still very hard on herself, a perfectionist, she lived a secluded life, liking only the silence of her hushed drawing room, going out only to attend morning Mass at nearby Saint-Augustin's. In spite of her wealth and her "divine consolations", her life was agony, because of three men she had loved: her cousin Charles, who had left; her husband, Olivier, who had died in 1895; her oldest son, François, who had turned out badly, corrupted by life in high society, money, and sensuality. Corrupted as Charles had been at twenty. But François had not found the path of Christ. The beneficial mediation that Marie had effected for her cousin was not to be repeated with her son. Being an amoral person, François never let up with his unscrupulous behavior. Ruined by gambling, racing, women, and deeply in debt, he was ruining his loved ones. His father had disinherited him, but his mother paid his debts to save the family honor. He reacted to that only with hate, and they no longer saw each other. Marie was worn out, at her wits' end. The woman whom a dismayed Charles embraced was completely finished. At least he brought her, for the few days he stayed in her house, the unalloyed joy of his presence. He was indeed her true spiritual son!

The sight of these two creatures who had counted for so much in his life and were now almost destroyed did nothing to raise Charles' spirits. Fortunately, while in France, he also met a shining light, in whom he was to place all his hopes.

It was in October 1906 that twenty-three-year-old Louis Massignon, at the suggestion of Henri de Castries, had first written to Charles de Foucauld,

---

[14] CF to Marie de Bondy, December 4, 1909, 187.

sending him his study of the guilds of sixth-century Fez. This gifted and enthusiastic young student, who hoped to become a professor, had explored Morocco, writing his thesis on that country. He was all the more intrigued by Charles because he himself had lost his faith at the age of fourteen. Charles had replied with these words: "I am offering to God on your behalf my poor and unworthy prayers, asking him to bless you, to bless your work and your entire life." [15]

Who can measure the efficacy of prayer? In 1907 Massignon was in Cairo working on a dissertation on the tenth-century Sufi mystic Al Hallaj, crucified in Baghdad for his nonconformist approach to loving God. Like Jesus, he had dared to say: "The Father and I, we are one." The following year, doing archaeological work in the Baghdad area, Massignon had been kidnapped by Turkish fanatics, who, thinking he was a spy, had threatened to kill him. Still an unbeliever, he was thinking of suicide to escape torture, when suddenly he was overwhelmed by "an ecstasy of fire and light, the certainty of the existence of God and Love". According to his own account: "Try at suicide out of incredible self-loathing; eyes closed and a sudden feeling of reverence before an inner fire judging me and consuming my heart, the certainty of a pure, ineffable, creative Presence suspending my sentence at the prayers of beings, invisible visitors to my prison, whose names suddenly burst upon me: Al Hallaj, Huysmans, *Foucauld*." [16]

Not long afterward, he was released without explanation and even taken under the wing of the Muslims. For three weeks he remained, "besieged by grace". Then he was converted, totally committing himself to the religion of his childhood. Writing to Charles de Foucauld to tell him of his adventures, he ended his letter, "How I suffered when God converted me! It is my entire life that he wished to make his!" [17]

From their long talk at his quarters on rue Monsieur, Massignon recalls Charles' consuming concern: "Hallaj and Gandhi in fact gave God their lives and their deaths for the most forsaken of mankind, respecting in them an image of God more clearly visible than that found in those rich in intelligence, power, and fortune. As long as we do not respect the human being in the non-Christian believers we are trying to 'convert', we are betraying God. Conversion is not a shipping permit we attach to the conscience of others. It is a deepening of what is best in their present religious loyalty." [18]

Marveling at the faith of the young convert, Charles thought to make him his spiritual heir and in the meantime the longed-for companion who

---

[15] *Bulletin des Amitiés*, no. 73, 11.

[16] L. Massignon, *Parole donnée* (Seuil, 1983).

[17] Quoted by M. Castillon du Perron, *Charles de Foucauld* (Grasset, 1982), 416.

[18] Massignon, quoted by *Bulletin des Amitiés*, no. 73, 17.

would assist him in Tamanrasset. He introduced him to Father Huvelin. Then he took him to the basilica of Montmartre for a night of prayer, a night of adoration for Charles. A "slow, dark, bare night, without consolation, in that glacial, lofty tomb", Massignon would admit,[19] on this occasion feeling strangely distant from the tenderness of Christ found in the basilica by those able to efface themselves.

He remained intrigued by Charles de Foucauld, who invited him to follow him to Tamanrasset. Although tempted, the younger man hesitated. For the hermit had not hidden what awaited him: total renunciation of self. He would be sharing Charles' life of absolute poverty in Tamanrasset, his own stays there to be broken up by voyages of exploration in the Sahara, a whole life's work, for which Charles no longer had the strength. Possibly, Charles would train him for the priesthood. Above all, he would be the desired companion, long awaited, the second Little Brother of Jesus!

But family pressures came into play, countering these noble plans. Louis' mother wanted him to marry. His father, an atheist, could not understand his conversion, and still less his going to the Ahaggar. Even his spiritual adviser discouraged him, considering Father de Foucauld unstable and lacking a well-defined place in the Church, since his plan for foundation had not yet been approved by Rome. Charles and Louis said good-bye, promising to write each other.

Charles had promised Marie he would see her son before leaving Paris. They had last met in 1891, when François was a boy of fourteen whose already difficult personality portended a troubled future. He was now thirty-two.

The two met on February 25, 1909, in Paris, at the home of François, who has left a lengthy account of the visit from this legendary cousin about whom his mother always spoke with a catch in her throat. It is one of the most realistic and moving portraits we have of him and was published in *L'Appel du Hoggar*:

> The wind was howling. It was cold and nasty. The snow was melting on the streets. I saw the black outline of a funny little priest. He entered the room and peace entered with him.
>
> The glow of his eyes and especially that very humble smile had taken over his whole person. Aside from that intelligent, searching look, tempered if not belied by the determined self-effacement so etched into his face, nothing remained of the Charles de Foucauld whom I remembered. There stood before me a puny model of the secular priest, owing to the pathetic black quilted overcoat, which hid almost completely his missionary robe. It was only on his chest that I could see something of the coarse white fabric, on which stood out the cross and the cherry-red heart. In his hand he held a

---

[19] Ibid.

pitiful clerical hat, which must have rolled in the mud, for it was streaked with dirt. And I looked at that emaciated head, the face of the anchorite through the ages, without any age itself, lined and weathered, the scanty little salt-and-pepper beard, the short-cropped hair and the gray skull.

"I know that you have written a novel. If you can give me a copy, I shall be happy to read it."

"But it is not at all the kind of work you would like!"

"Why not? I know the world. I too have lived. It must be very fine."

Such benevolence made me ashamed of myself, embarrassed at having, in face of the course so pure and so hard chosen by Charles, nothing but pleasures, foolish actions, or at any rate frivolous ones, to present to him, everything that he was likely to consider an unending trail of sins. So that, without his prompting me to do so, I berated myself for not leading a life in accordance with the one I might have originally envisioned, for being unceasingly prey to uncontrollable laziness and weakness. Contrary to what I had imagined, it was I who was reproaching myself and he who found excuses for me, with his kindness and his humble gentleness.

After he was gone, I remained intrigued by this unusual visitor. A blessing was on him in the room, and there still floated around me something sweet and infinitely peaceful. He had said nothing of a nature to upset me. There was an incredible joy emanating from him who had given all, showing me the superiority of that which constituted his essence—stability, continuity. Having tasted "the pleasures of life" and able to entertain the hope of not having to leave the table for a good while, I, upon seeing that my whole sum of satisfactions did not weigh more than a tiny feather in comparison with the complete happiness of the ascetic, found rising in me a strange feeling, not of envy, but of respect.

Why should he have over my mind this mysterious power? He made no attempt to lecture me any more than he endeavored to convert Muslims. Perhaps he loved in me what he himself knew of enthusiasm—even though mine was directed toward everything counter to his ideals—because, in the wild extremes of my restless nature, at times I must have been close to feeling what he felt in that unbridled heart, which never beat with the reliable, restrained rhythm of the peaceful heart.

For the duration of that visit I had seen Charles surrounded by a radiance, neither luminous nor visible, but perceivable to some sense that we have not yet come to identify. So much faith, hope, and charity placed around him that nimbus which painters, who can appeal only to the eye, depict as rays of gold. Silent music, beneficial waves, bringing beatitude and dreams. [Thus] the minute with Charles is engraved in me, eternal.[20]

Leaving Paris, Charles traveled to Notre-Dame-des-Neiges, then on to Viviers on February 28 to seek Bishop Bonnet's approval for the statutes of his association, a "pious union" of laypersons, which would be directed by a priest from Saint-Sulpice, Father Laurain. The bishop gave his approval, but that did not mean the founder could bypass Rome: "Yes, I approve your

[20] F. de Bondy, *L'Appel du Hoggar*, no. 10 (1954), 4.

plan, and I wish it complete success. But if God wants it to be realized, how many difficulties it is going to encounter and how much suffering will be required before it wins a place in the sun of the holy Church! But that is no reason to back down. On the contrary, that should be an incentive to begin working valiantly. I shall help you with my poor prayers. The work is worth devoting to it everything in one's power." [21]

On March 1 in Grasse, Charles saw his beloved sister, Marie de Blic, Mimi, at Villa Fragonard, which belonged to her brother-in-law, Eugène de Blic. The young woman he had left in 1901, a delicate and nervous creature unprepared for her heavy family and domestic responsibilities—she had given birth to six children—was now physically changed. Her body had grown fleshy, but her spirit remained fragile, anxious, and scrupulous. She assumed her responsibilities courageously but without pleasure, finding happiness only in her religion and in the escape offered by reading. Charles was in no position to criticize her for the mortifications she imposed on herself. Like him, she was paying for the tragedies of their childhood.

Together, they went to Toulon on March 2 to visit her twenty-two-year-old son, Charles de Blic, the godson of the hermit, who had fervently hoped the boy would become a priest and missionary. Having graduated from the Naval School, he was serving aboard a warship.

Charles was back in Algiers on March 8, 1909, feeling little fatigue after this journey so rich in emotion. Staying in Algiers only four days, he set out for Beni Abbès, where he remained for a month. He noted in his diary on April 4: "I have instituted a rosary with seven steps, called the rosary of love, for Christians and Muslims." A medal had replaced the cross. Among the invocations: "Lord, I love you with all my heart. All that you wish, I wish, and I love my neighbor as myself for the love of you."

On May 11 he stopped at In Salah, where he deeply moved the garrison during the ceremony of the colors, "dominating the horizon with the fine posture of a one-time cavalryman, reciting aloud the Our Father as no one has ever recited it", relates the military doctor Dautheville.[22] Leaving In Salah, he set out on the road home, walking across the vast desert. Entering the Ahaggar on June 8, he scribbled a few words to Marie de Bondy: "It has just rained for the first time in three and a half years. The suffering was extreme. If people could emerge from death the way plants do . . ." [23]

On June 11 he was once again in Tamanrasset, at his beloved hermitage, "the Frigate", as Laperrine called it. None of his problems had been solved, but he confidently abandoned himself to whatever God's will might be.

---

[21] Bishop Bonnet to CF, March 6, 1909, in Gorrée, *Sur les traces*, 236.

[22] *Bulletin des Amitiés*, no. 111, 3.

[23] CF to Marie de Bondy, June 8, 1909, 182.

He stayed in Tamanrasset only a month and a half. On August 31, 1909, he was once again walking desert trails, this time in the company of Colonel Laperrine, who had asked him to serve as interpreter on a new pacification tour in the Ahaggar.

Mission accomplished, Charles parted from Laperrine on September 10. Then he was off again, a guide his only escort, this time to scale the massif of Atakor and reach Assekrem, in the heart of the Ahaggar, where he planned to established a summer hermitage thirty-five miles from Tamanrasset. He had not yet gone deep into this massif, which Motylinski had described in glowing terms back in 1906, vaunting its extraordinary beauty and the pleasant green pastures that stretched out beneath the peaks. Indeed, the year of that visit it had rained in the area, and the nomads had hurried there to look for *tawit*, the plant whose tiny seeds were a favorite with their flocks. But what did it have to offer in other years?

Most important, Assekrem was a natural fortress where the Tuareg sought refuge when under attack. It could be reached from Tamanrasset using relatively passable trails interrupted in places by gigantic piles of fallen red and black rock. Walking four days along the rocky ground of a labyrinth, crossing steep cliffs on vertiginous goat paths, a traveler would finally reach the narrow barren plateau 8,900 feet above sea level and nearly ten thousand feet long, a landscape battered by winds, with no water and no vegetation, unfit for life, unless it was spiritual.

On September 15, 1909, a dazzled Charles looked out over the Ahaggar Massif rising above the sands, its most prominent peaks Mount Tahat (9,500 feet) and Mount Ilamane (8,980 feet).

The sober, savage grandeur of the scene enchanted him, that romantic jumble of bare peaks reminiscent of a fairy-tale stronghold, sometimes snow covered, in the middle of the scorching desert. He made up his mind to build a rustic summer hermitage in that spot.

Once back in Tamanrasset, he obtained permission from Bishop Guérin and a promise of financial aid from Father Huvelin and Marie de Bondy. Then he sought the support of Laperrine. More prudent than the others, the colonel advised him not only to give up the idea but also suggested he leave Tamanrasset and settle in Tarhaouhaout, under the protection of the new fort, Motylinski, which was nearly completed.

And, in fact, the situation was deteriorating. A *rezzou* of rebel Tuareg Ajjer threatened Tamanrasset, taking advantage of the absence of Moussa, who was participating in an operation to the south with native troops loyal to the French. Camel troopers gathered the people of Tamanrasset who wanted to take shelter in the *bordj*. When it was time to go, Charles refused to join the group. Doctor Hérisson ends his account of the incident as follows: "I realize that he is determined to die murdered. That is the end he foresees and longs for. He will remain alone in his quarters, unarmed, unguarded, under the sole protection of God." [24]

Brother Charles did not want to live at Fort Motylinski, under the wing of the garrison, as he had at Beni Abbès. Doing so would make the people suspicious of him. As for Assekrem, he held firm on that idea because of the solitude. No crowds in that place, since the high, barren plateau was off the caravan routes and water had to be fetched from sixteen hundred feet below.

Once the danger was over, Laperrine finally gave in and even offered his French masons upon completion of the Motylinski fort.

While waiting to carry out this project the following summer, Charles reestablished his Tamanrasset routine. Because of the rain, the nomads were returning, and he found himself once again swamped with visitors. On October 31, 1909, he wrote Marie de Bondy: "Seeing worse and worse, tiring more and more easily, having to do an amount of work that surpasses my strength, I feel more and more often unequal to my task. I am going to remake my hermitage to accommodate a companion. The companion is not appearing! I feel overburdened. So many things to do, and I am less and less able to do them all myself, with age weighing on me." [25]

All his hopes centered on young Louis Massignon. Would he come to join him? Would he be able to pull away from his family? In vain Charles kept after him. As did Paul Claudel, the famous Catholic writer, diplomat, poet, and dramatist, made famous by Le Partage de midi. Converted at Notre-Dame-de-Paris on Christmas 1886, two months after Foucauld. "Rarely have I seen a man your age with a personality so fully formed", Claudel wrote Massignon in December. "What a soldier of God you could make!" [26] "Why not toss aside all your books and go put yourself at the feet of Father de Foucauld, who, you told me, was calling you to join him?" [27]

Massignon could not decide. "My old desire to be a hermit won't leave me in peace", he wrote his friend Maspéro. "As soon as possible, I shall try to make haste and go to the Ahaggar." [28]

But he made haste slowly, and he finished his dissertation. He replied to Claudel on January 7, 1910, invoking "the withering of grace": "I should like to be at last consumed in oneness, stabilized, reposed in God, where he wants me. I am more weary of having disobeyed than I am passionate about obeying. Besides, all my friends who have taken holy orders are

[24] Quoted by J.-F. Six, Vie de Charles de Foucauld (Seuil, 1962), 203.
[25] CF to Marie de Bondy, October 31, 1909, 186.
[26] Paul Claudel, Louis Massignon (1908–1914): Correspondance (DDB, 1973), 74.
[27] Ibid., 79.
[28] Bulletin des Amitiés, no. 79, 14.

persuading me not to study to that end, and I find myself thrown back into the uncertainty of a secular life." [29]

That referred to marriage, which his family wanted and which Claudel advised against.

Massignon wrote him from Cairo on February 9, 1910: "I would like to escape from my books, but I do not have the strength. Father de Foucauld is the only one who believes me capable of renunciation, not merely in word, but in deed." [30]

Claudel replied immediately: "The opinion of a saint carries more weight than an abundance of empty words. What a unique opportunity for you, to be able to live under the wing of such a man! Why not chance this marvelous adventure? By an incredible miracle God has plucked you from the death of the body and that of the soul. You must resign yourself to the inevitable; you are his thing and no longer your own. Ah! If you could become one of those saints for whom the world thirsts!" [31]

Massignon appeared convinced: "You are right. God alone can fulfill. Now, may he give me the strength, the means, and the order." [32]

The order? Claudel answered on Good Friday 1910: "Do not wait for God to come and take you by the hand and lead you where he wants you to go. That is the kind of miracle reserved for the dead, and you are now living. You must collaborate with grace. Every man living should always try to do the best thing he sees." [33]

Edifying words! But the poet-diplomat himself had remained in the world and had married, despite his lightning-swift conversion. Contrary to what he wrote Massignon, marriage was not necessarily "that mediocre path on which we all flounder". It was also possible to flounder inside the cloister or deep in the desert, and that was worse!

That winter Charles received a visit from Doctor Hérisson, Fort Motylinski's medical officer. He had been sent by Laperrine to get some advice from the hermit.

"How do we approach the Tuareg?"

"Be straightforward, pleasant, and kind. You have to love them to be loved in return. Be human, generous, and always cheerful. In their company, you must always laugh. I myself always laugh and show them my awful teeth. Let them get to know you. The story is that we eat babies and that by night we turn into beasts. Help them understand that the life of the French is peaceful and virtuous, that we work hard and are productive.

[29] *Paul Claudel*, 78.
[30] Ibid., February 9, 1910, 79.
[31] Ibid., February 19, 1910, 80.
[32] Ibid., March 11, 1910, 80.
[33] Ibid., April 1910, 81.

Show them that basically the life of our peasants is much like theirs, that we are similar to them." [34]

A second visitor was Lieutenant Nieger, commander of the little garrison at Fort Motylinski.

"I extend my hospitality", said Charles, with a laugh. "In your honor I promise to deviate a little from my diet."

He showed the lieutenant around the hermitage. Laperrine had not been exaggerating: The long rectangular building with its flat roof was "a mixture of holes and humps". Tracing paper that shook in the slightest breeze substituted for windows.

"You can see, it's very comfortable. I've been terribly spoiled. There is room in the chapel; you may sleep there. The altar step will be your pillow. I'm sorry to have to ask you to get up early. I say Mass at 5 A.M."

Thus, well before dawn the officer was asked to leave his spot. He was shivering with cold.

"Would you like to assist with the office? Afterward we'll go outside. It has snowed, and we shall have a splendid sunrise."

At noon, an elderly black man served a *kresra*, a flat cake made of wheat flour and baked in the sand, four raw tomatoes, and in an old pot some dates cooked up in water and seasoned with roasted barley, for the officer a revolting gruel, for Charles a treat verging on the sin of gluttony.

"Delicious, don't you think?"

Nieger later commented:

He had a will of iron, and it kept his impatience under control. He barely raised his voice when expressing an opinion. It was only in moments of crisis that his cavalry officer reflexes surfaced. Then, energy and decisiveness in his gestures, his voice, and his plans formed a surprising contrast with his usual gentleness.

He sought contact with us only when it was useful to the cause. His kindness could not hide his impatience at putting up with purposeless visits. His indulgence and patience came in different doses: unbelievably large for children and ordinary folk, then smaller and smaller according to the intellectual level of his interlocutor.

He had a very strict daily schedule. It was quite difficult to get him to change it. The people said, "The marabout is *ouar*": harsh, exacting, hard to please. One evening, as he strolled outside his pathetic hovel, he observed: "I have a horror of the world and its hypocrisy." He was speaking of our world. I cannot believe he attributed to the Tuareg, whose faults and vices he knew so well, a moral level superior to ours. Yet he lived for them and seemed happy in their midst. [35]

---

[34] As told by Doctor Hérisson to R. Bazin, in Bazin, *Foucauld*, 379.
[35] General Nieger, in *Construire*, no. 13 (1943).

In May 1910, after accompanying Laperrine on his last pacification tour, Brother Charles began to put up his modest Assekrem hermitage, a rectangular building of stone with clay mortar, hardly more than a shepherd's shelter, but sturdy enough to resist storms.

In spite of help from the army, he spent an enormous sum, more than eighteen hundred francs, instead of the planned five hundred, and Marie de Bondy paid the extra without batting an eyelid. Lieutenant Sigonney supervised the work. Water had to be fetched from sixteen hundred feet below, an hour's walk. Charles would realize, but too late, that Assekrem was rarely visited other than during rainy spells, which came only once every two years. He had counted on the presence of nomadic Tuareg shepherds, who left Tamanrasset during the summer. But they were scattered over a thirty-mile radius and hardly ever made the climb to barren Assekrem. The only justification left was that he needed solitude for the contemplative life, "the marvelous view, a beautiful place for adoring the Creator",[36] he wrote. And also for escaping the sweltering summer heat of Tamanrasset.

So, Assekrem, a summer residence for Charles de Foucauld? In making it possible for him to build there, his friends had only been responding affectionately to his secret wish for solitude in a place of spectacular beauty. Even saints have their weaknesses.

In September 1910, Lieutenant Nieger took Moussa ag Amastane to France for an official visit. Busy at Assekrem, Charles did not go along but recommended him warmly to his family. The French government's purpose was to make known to the Tuareg that there existed something in the world besides the Sahara. Convinced that they were the superior race, with no equal, these tribes saw the French as barbaric invaders who practiced magic and lived in boreal isles. The French wanted in particular to show their country's military might, thus discouraging any tendencies toward rebellion. Colonized peoples had to blend in or they would disappear. As for Charles, he hoped that Moussa would observe, through the Foucauld family, the moral quality of the French, so he might be led toward conversion.

Thus Moussa went to France. No pains were spared to impress him: demonstrations of artillery fire—with the famous 75-mm cannon—and bayonet charges. Moussa had too much of a warrior's soul not to appreciate these weapons. But when asked what he thought, he answered: "People with such means of destruction are crazy if they go to war against each other."

[36] CF to Marie de Bondy, July 16, 1910, in Gorrée, *Sur les traces*, 248.

Other surprises were in store for him: visits to national stud farms, model factories, and cities of course, Paris in particular, a place inconceivable to a man of the desert. All the palaces and monuments, and all the automobiles driving about among the fiacres! They also showed him the capital's frivolous specialties, such as the Moulin Rouge in Montmartre, which aroused the anger of pious René Bazin toward "these governments that do not have a feeling for the paternity of power".

But three things were to affect deeply the *amenokal* from the Ahaggar: not the Legion of Honor that a general pinned on his burnous during the military parade at Longchamp, but the sight of a waterfall (all that water going to waste!), the vast flocks in the green French countryside, and most of all the reception he received at Barbirey, the estate in Côte-d'Or belonging to Raymond and Marie de Blic.

"I saw your sister and spent two days at her home", Moussa wrote Foucauld. "I saw your brother-in-law. I visited their grounds and their château. And you, you live in Tamanrasset as if you were poor!"

Obviously, he did not understand.

For Charles, 1910 ended in great sadness. Laperrine was leaving, transferred at his own request to lead the Eighteenth Chasseurs in Lunéville. Charles noted, "He found with reason that one must not appear to cling to one's post. It is he who gave the Sahara to France, *in spite of herself*, risking his career to do so." [37]

Bishop Guérin, first apostolic prefect in the Sahara, had also departed that year, in the spring, but for a better world, dead of exhaustion and asceticism after sharing the sufferings of the Tuareg people. He was only thirty-eight. "I had never dreamed of the possibility that he might not survive me, and I depended on his friendship as if it could never leave me", Charles wrote Father Villard, his confessor in Ghardaïa. "You sense the void that his departure leaves me. Jesus remains, may he be praised for all things!" [38]

He was grief stricken: "Holy person, kind, perfect, delightful, with the most affectionate, paternal kindness toward me", he had written to Father Huvelin. [39] And to Marie de Bondy: "It is a great loss for me, but it is justice for saints to receive their reward. His was an admirable soul, cast in charity and humility. This leaves me a great void." [40]

Then there was the death of his old friend Major Lacroix, head of the Office of Indigenous Affairs in Algiers. "All these voids leave me to face a

---

[37] Quoted by Bazin, *Foucauld*, 390.
[38] Ibid., 388.
[39] CF to Father Huvelin, September 17, 1907, 273.
[40] CF to Marie de Bondy, May 16, 1910.

future that may offer obstacles of many kinds", he wrote to Marie once again. "But he who can do all is always there, and we shall never be without him." [41]

The final blow came on August 15, when he learned of the death of Father Huvelin on July 10, after years of terrible suffering. "Jesus does not forbid tears", Charles wrote Marie de Bondy. "He gives us the example. It is a heartbreaking loss for me as it is for you. May Jesus be thanked for everything! For having given him to us, for having let us have him for so long, and for having let him enter into his eternal glory." [42]

Like him, Marie was distraught. Charles felt "like the olive left by itself on the branch, forgotten at the harvest". [43] But his cry of distress ended with a declaration of faith: "We are not to be pitied; we are not alone; we are not forgotten; Jesus is still here!" [44] "Yes, Jesus is enough. Where he is, nothing is lacking. It is he who remains All." [45] Where he is now, the cherished priest "can do more than he did before, but we no longer feel the strength and gentleness of what he does". [46]

Then he told himself that he, too, was to depart. Probably soon. At fifty-two, he felt completely worn out! Like Bishop Guérin, the desert had prematurely aged him, along with serving the poor. Thus, writing to Father Villard, he thought of those who would succeed him, for that was becoming an obsession: "This unexpected departure [of Bishop Guérin] makes me desire more strongly than ever the company of a priest to continue the work, so far very little, begun here. He could live near me, living my life or choosing not to. I do not ask to be his superior, but his friend, ready to leave him on his own once he is up on things." [47]

But who would want to disappear into the solitary heights of Assekrem or the poverty of Tamanrasset? Massignon? In vain Charles extolled to him "the beautiful solitude of Assekrem, where one can adore God while gazing upon the summits of his creation". [48]

Massignon, however, had not yet given up the world. Paul Claudel, then writing L'Annonce faite à Marie, continued to encourage him: "All shall be returned to you by the life itself, a hundredfold. They say youth is the age of passions, but that is not true: it is the age of heroism." [49]

---

[41] Ibid., 188.
[42] Ibid., August 15, 1910, 191.
[43] Ibid., September 1, 1910, 192.
[44] Ibid.
[45] CF to a White Father of Ghardaïa, in Bazin, Foucauld, 389.
[46] CF to Marie de Bondy, October 1, 1910, 193.
[47] CF to Father Villard, in Bazin, Foucauld, 388.
[48] CF to Massignon, May 15, 1910, in Six, L'Aventure, 78.
[49] Paul Claudel, 103.

Massignon replied: "I am almost homesick for the desert, that perfect, serene sea. It is there I was truly born, summoned by name by the Voice that cries out in the wilderness. When I have finished with my books, I intend to go to clarify my doubts in its great light, in the Ahaggar, with Father de Foucauld, who is rather expecting me, I believe. . . ." [50]

But he was still hesitant: "It's no good my remembering the unhoped-for divine favor and my first enthusiasm, for I lack heroism in patience, and becoming blind again is a terrible thing for one who was born blind and then cured." [51]

Heroism in patience—henceforth the cardinal virtue of Charles de Foucauld.

Tamanrasset, December 1, 1916, 6:20 P.M.

The massive door of the fort closed behind Paul Embarek, who was now heading back to his clay hut. Charles fastened the giant bolt. Once more he could enjoy the silence of the night. How was he going to use this hour of "recreation" that his rule allowed him to take before going to bed?

He had an irresistible urge to read and remembered back to his early years when he would spend whole nights with his favorite Greek authors. Today, the authors had changed, but the craving was still there. Should he read the *Life* of his dear Teresa of Avila or her *Interior Castle*? No, he would save those major works for morning reading. At the end of the day, he could allow himself some recreation.

He looked over his "library": two six-foot boards placed on the floor, containing his treasures, more than a hundred and fifty books. Paul Bourget, Henri de Régnier. He paused over René Bazin's *Les Oberlé*, then Paul Claudel's *Le Père humilié*, rejected them, and picked up *Le Voyage du centurion*, by Psichari, removing a scorpion's nest from the volume.

He felt a close kinship with the writer: a lieutenant in the African Army, converted by the desert as Charles had been, in 1914 Psichari had lost his life on the Belgian front. Grandson of Renan, friend of Péguy . . . The front, the war. Charles felt close to his countrymen: Psichari, Laperrine, Massignon, those now fighting to defend the homeland. He himself was useless. "I can only pray. The Church does allow priests to serve in the army when they are called up by national law, but it does not allow them to join up as volunteers. My fifty-seven and a half years, though, keep me from being called up, for indeed it has been twenty-five years since I resigned my commission as a reserve officer. I would still have enough strength to serve,

[50] Ibid., December 26, 1910, 100.
[51] Ibid., February 7, 1910, 99.

however. My health stays good, even though I look old: no teeth, no hair, very gray beard, countless wrinkles." [52]

Charles opened *Le Voyage du centurion*. By the wavering light of the paraffin candle, he read: "Christians, what have we besides our faith? The consciousness of our worthiness and our unworthiness. The knowledge that we are valuable and that we are naught but refuse. The sense of our power and of our impotence, the awareness of our inner strength and our inner weakness, of our dependence and our independence, but all is harmonized through grace, the feeling of our freedom and of our servitude." [53]

The words grew blurry. The one candle stuck to the table was no longer enough for his bad eyes. He returned the book to the shelf. Holding the taper, he went to the chapel and gazed upon the exposed Host. His knees buckled and soon rested on the sand. An inner light rose within him. The Beloved was there.

The *rezzou* of the *fellagha* was but a few miles from Tamanrasset; they would be there in less than an hour. It was now completely dark. The stars shone in the Ahaggar sky. A half-moon was setting behind the cirque of the mountains.

More and more anxious the closer they were to their destination and violent action, the Senoussi Beuh ag Rhabelli questioned Kerzou and El Madani.

"What is around the fort? How do we carry out the final approach?"

"There is nothing", Kerzou said. "A carefully cleared area. The marabout is experienced in defense."

"And the ditch? All the forts have a ditch, which makes their walls that much higher."

"It will have to be crossed. At the front, there is a narrow bridge leading to a low door protected by a parapet."

"Why a parapet?"

"An armed man can be sheltered there and fire all around him."

"What is behind the door?"

"It opens onto a sunken courtyard", said El Madani. "And the corridor is blocked by a low interior wall that has to be stepped over by bending in half, because of a beam. Farther on a second door closes off the corridor."

"Yes", put in Kerzou, "this entrance is a real trap."

"And if the door does not open, the *bordj* will have to be scaled."

[52] CF to Doctor L. S. de Balthasar, March 7, 1916, in *Bulletin des Amitiés*, no. 97, 14.
[53] E. Psichari, *Le Voyage du centurion* (Livre de poche chrétien), 174.

"Impossible", groaned the black man. "You will all be killed before landing in the courtyard."

"Well, then, we'll have to get in through trickery! That will be up to you, El Madani."

15

Solitude on Assekrem

Brother Charles used the winter of 1910–1911 to enlarge his Tamanrasset hermitage. He brought back Paul Embarek, who had settled down and had taken up masonry. Paul had built himself a hut in the Haratin village and was planning to get married. Following Charles' example, there was a general building boom, with clay-brick houses going up. The Haratins were deserting their mud and rush shacks, and the settled Tuareg were building near their gardens. Even Moussa had built a house, making fashionable the settled lifestyle the French hoped to encourage.

But no rest for Brother Charles! At the end of January 1911 he was once again trekking through the desert. On February 17 he landed in Marseille, heading for Paris to stay with Marie de Bondy on rue Percier, following visits to Viviers and Notre-Dame-des-Neiges. With deep feeling he celebrated a Mass at Saint-Augustin's in memory of his beloved Father Huvelin. Won over by the desert hermit's charisma, the curate, Father Jouin, had taken up a collection on his behalf, bringing in the tidy sum of five hundred francs. Charles had two overriding concerns: creating the lay association that was to bring into being the future fraternity and finding someone to succeed him in Tamanrasset.

Of course he met with Louis Massignon. Once again the hermit's charisma did its work. Massignon declared himself ready to follow Charles, at least for a trial stay. When Paul Claudel found out, he congratulated the young man: "The greatest human happiness and the easiest path to perfection, the one that follows most closely the heart of God, is assuredly the company of a saint." [1]

After visiting Laperrine in Lunéville, Marie de Blic at Barbirey, various members of his family, Father Crozier in Lyon, and paying a second visit to Bishop Bonnet in Viviers, Charles was back in Africa March 16. After a brief stay at Beni Abbès, he was walking desert roads again, on his way to Tamanrasset.

At the post of Aoulef, he met Captain Lehureau, future commander of the Southern Territories. They traveled together to In Salah, a journey

---

[1] *Paul Claudel, Louis Massignon 1908–1914: Correspondance* (DDB, 1973), 113.

resulting in this portrait: "Charles de Foucauld was courtesy itself. His affability, his gentleness were equaled only by his extreme humility before everyone, from the most mature to the youngest. This humility made us uncomfortable, for we were aware of his glorious past, and we knew that, if he had so wished, he could have been our great leader. His frugality was extraordinary. A few dates, a piece of Arab hardtack soaked in black coffee sufficed for his dinner. This harsh diet explained his striking thinness and the emaciated features, which a thin, shaggy beard could not conceal." [2]

At In Salah Charles saw again "his microscopic earthen house". Captain Charlet, who had succeeded Nieger as head of the Saharan Tidikelt company, which was in charge of the Ahaggar, welcomed him warmly.

After twenty-one days on camel paths, Charles was finally back in Tamanrasset. He had planned to get down to work on his Tuareg dictionary, but, as at Beni Abbès, he found himself overwhelmed by the poor.

Happily, a letter from Massignon confirmed that he would be coming the following summer. That aroused great hope. Charles would take him to Assekrem, and there, God and the spectacular beauty of the Ahaggar would do the rest! He wrote back: "Whenever you arrive, you will be received with open arms as a cherished brother."[3]

This beautiful hope crumbled. The family pressures were too strong. Massignon's father ordered him to apply for a chair in history at the university in Lyon. He dared not disobey by making the liberating gesture that would propel him toward the desert and spiritual adventure. He came crashing down from dream to reality. He wrote Claudel: "Where is the transfiguring fire of Truth, which sublimated me as it burned me? Left are the ashes growing cold in the night, without the slightest spark to rekindle them." [4] But nothing was played out as yet. Massignon had obediently stood for the post in the faculty of letters at Lyon. The rector rejected him because of his strongly held religious convictions. "Unless you declare on your word of honor that you will never attend High Mass [sic]." Presented with that ukase, Massignon was enraged and replied with an indignant refusal: "I am a free man!" [5]

And so all things were still possible. He wrote Charles that perhaps he was going to come. And Charles went on hoping . . .

[2] L. Lehureau, *Au Sahara avec le père de Foucauld* (Algiers: Baconnier, 1944), 17.
[3] CF to Massignon, April 11, 1911, in J.-F. Six, *L'Aventure de l'amour de Dieu* (Seuil, 1993), 98.
[4] Massignon to Claudel, June 23, 1911, 121.
[5] Remarks by Daniel Massignon about his father, from an article quoted by J.-F. Six, *Itinéraire spirituel de Charles de Foucauld* (Seuil, 1958), 105.

In early July 1911, the hermit, accompanied by his "Tuareg informant" Ba
Hammou, climbed up to Assekrem, determined to stay there until the
snows drove them out. At 8,900 feet, he was living at a higher point than
any Christian hermit in history. It took them three days to get there. Their
mount, which they led by its halter, was carrying what they needed for
survival: flour, couscous, dates, sugar, tea, and dehydrated soups sent by
Marie. Charles was, in his own words, "like someone on an ocean voyage
unable to put in at any port".

But once at the summit, which was protected by a steep cliff over three
hundred feet high, what a reward! He was overjoyed to see once again this
fantastic landscape with the bare peaks constantly eroded by the sand-
blowing winds of the desert, which wore away the crumbly rock, leaving
only the hardest stone. From the center of the Ahaggar, the Koudia (fortress), the view stretched out, glorious in the clear air. The peak called
Ilamane dominated the little rocky plateau battered by ceaseless winds. To
the north and the south the vast desert stretched as far as the horizon. To
find life meant going back down more than three hundred feet, at least a
half hour's walk. There, in the ravines, grew a fairly dense grass. Charles
wrote to G. Tourdes, "As soon as it rains the ravines are covered with a
fragrant grass, and immediately the Tuareg pitch their tents to drink the
good milk of the mountains." [6]

Unfortunately, it hardly ever rained!

At least there was always pure water, which they drew from a spring.
Charles met up with a little nomad encampment, four tents sheltering the
Akroud family from Tamanrasset. To see other nomads meant a ninety-
minute walk to the Igebat camp.

Charles got along well with everyone. "They are comforting and gentle",
he wrote Marie de Bondy. But he could not hope to replenish his supplies
at their camps, for the milk and meat from their goats were barely enough
to feed themselves.

The two men took possession of the hermitage, a rectangular structure
sixteen feet long and six and a half feet wide, built of rocks with clay as
mortar. A small entryway packed with supplies, a chapel, a bedroom containing books. They slept on boards laid out on the floor. It is hard to
imagine two men living and working there for five months, the light
filtering in through the narrow, windowless openings blocked by oilcloth
that flapped in the wind. Charles, however, wrote Marie de Bondy: "The
hermitage could not be any more comfortable. The chapel is very nice,
quite conducive to meditation. The bedroom is light and rather large, thus
fine for two, and, with a little crowding, for three. I arrived here in rain,

[6] CF to Gabriel Tourdes, June 16, 1911, 174.

thunder, and lightning. It was quite beautiful. Sixty degrees here at noon! I find it hard to believe that it is July in the Sahara."[7]

It is pleasant to imagine his enthusiasm. He wrote to General Mazel: "Fantastic peaks and rocky needles stand up like bristles all around, an opera set, a witches' Sabbath, it is marvelously beautiful."[8]

The beauty of a pristine nature, with solitude guaranteed. "The sweetness of solitude is something I have felt since the age of twenty. I used to love solitude amid the beauty of nature, with books, and appreciate it even more now, when the invisible world has become so sweet that it keeps one from ever being alone in one's solitude. This is a beautiful place to adore the Creator."[9]

On August 14, 1911, the donkeys arrived, laden with food and some mementos left to him by Father Huvelin, most notably a little altar of dark wood, which Charles immediately, enthusiastically, set up in the chapel, exclaiming: "I hope they will say Mass here long after my death!"[10]

And life took on a routine. A life of prayer, nights at the foot of the altar, meditation before the spectacular landscape, exhausting linguistic work with Ba Hammou. On the crate that served as a makeshift table were piled hundreds of sheets, which he never stopped going over as he heard more about the oral tradition from his companion and the occasional nomad visitor.

In the nearby Tinseghin Ravine, where he had found some soil, he planted a vegetable garden and surrounded it with rocks. Water was a major problem, for he had to fetch it from below at quite a distance. He watered sparingly with his teakettle, but he was never to have any vegetables!

Once a week he would receive the Tuareg. Some had walked for two days to visit the Christian marabout, the madman of God who lived on this barren summit in the middle of the sky, in the middle of the absolute! He would share with them his frugal meals.

And he was still awaiting Massignon, to whom he had written August 18: "Seven or eight months spent in the desert, in a fantastically beautiful spot, on a summit overlooking a chaos of mountains, at the foot of the

[7] CF to Marie de Bondy, July 9, 1911, in G. Gorrée, *Sur les traces de Charles de Foucauld* (Éd. de la Plus Grande France, 1936), 256.

[8] CF to General Mazel, July 1911, in G. Ganne, *Tamanrasset ou le désert fertile* (SOS, 1975), 207.

[9] Quoted by R. Bazin, *Charles de Foucauld* (Plon, 1921), 395.

[10] After the hermit's death in 1916, a Mass would not be celebrated there until 1935, by White Father Joyeux. The hermitage, fallen into ruin, would be restored in 1939, then rebuilt in 1954, making it possible for the Little Brothers of Foucauld (Jean-Marie and Antoine) to establish, with others, a religious presence on the summit, until the Algerian government ordered their withdrawal in August 1996, following the murders of the Trappists of the Atlas and Bishop Claverie of Oran.

Blessed Sacramment, could do you nothing but good. Do not worry about the question of food at the hermitage, I have a goodly supply that should do for the two of us. We shall live together in the holy poverty of Nazareth!" [11]

But Massignon still hesitated, using the excuse that he had to finish his dissertation before the journey. Claudel himself began having doubts and on August 13 wrote him: "Have you given up on seeing Father de Foucauld? I do not think you will remain with him permanently. But staying for a few months in the middle of the desert with a saint would be a beautiful thing!" [12]

The months went by, however, and Massignon did not come, in spite of a final plea from Claudel: "This journey is a decisive opportunity in your life." [13] It is touching to read of the hermit's wait. He would rise at night to sing aloud the *Veni Creator* in the starry solitude of Assekrem, on Massignon's behalf. In vain. "And so your loved ones will not be anxious over a summer spent in the Sahara", Charles sent him a chart of the temperatures he had recorded for July, showing it was cooler on Assekrem than in Paris.

And he extolled the life awaiting Louis by his side in the Ahaggar: "With some books you can carry out your theological studies here, piously, slowly, and in prayer and lead a true monastic life. At the same time, you will become acquainted with the population; you will make them love you. Furthermore, the study of Berber dialects and customs, the excavating of prehistoric monuments, those are tasks that will open for you the doors of the Institute." In short, "a life both religious and scholarly. After a period of time, when God so wishes, your adviser will see what Jesus is asking of you, and you will find yourself equally ready for the priesthood or for a pious and scholarly life within marriage."

And he finished in that practical way of his, which was so charming: "To make the Tuareg love you, you might bring two hundred sewing needles, fifty safety pins, ten thimbles, four pairs of manicure scissors, the 'au Bon Marché' brand. I recommend 'Y' needles and am including a sample." [14]

The weeks went by, and Massignon did not come. October brought the first cold weather, the fierce winds. Ba Hammou, worn out by the short rations and the work, began to grow impatient, in spite of his comfortable salary (one hundred francs a month). It is hard to imagine this couple with so little in common living together, the hermit overactive and thin, the Targui "big and chubby like a monk from a Balzac story, very intelligent

[11] CF to Massignon, August 18, 1911, in Six, *L'Aventure*, 107.
[12] *Paul Claudel*, 131.
[13] Ibid., 132.
[14] CF to Massignon, September 19, 1911, in Six, *L'Aventure*, 109–11.

but a lazybones, and as gluttonous as he was slothful" (Laperrine). Soon they would have to think about heading back to Tamanrasset. But Charles, in spite of poor health from the lack of fresh food, wanted to stay until winter, in the hope that a little moisture might attract the nomads. The summer of 1911 had been very dry, and thus there was no one within a radius of twenty miles. Charles had seen only a dozen or so nomads, fewer than in an entire day in Tamanrasset. A situation favorable to prayer but not to linguistic work or to the missionary work that was his major concern.

November arrived with its cold weather, its icy winds, its interminable nights, when the thermometer went down to thirty-two degrees. Impossible to heat the hermitage, for lack of wood. Charles fell ill. Ba Hammou wanted to leave, but he did not dare leave the hermit alone in that wilderness, and all the nomads had departed. They could not even enjoy the beauty of the landscape, for Assekrem was covered with mist.

He would hold out to the bitter end. While waiting for the mounts he had requested, he drew up his will: "I wish to be buried in the same place I die and rest there until the resurrection. I forbid their taking my body from the place where the Lord is to have me finish my pilgrimage." [15]

They left Assekrem on December 11, 1911, Charles once more convinced that God alone could fulfill man in solitude and silence.

He found the population of Tamanrasset in a frightening state of poverty. The drought, which had been going on for twenty months, had dried up the country's meager resources: milk, butter, and meat from their livestock. The two grain harvests had produced almost nothing. People did not even have much to wear anymore, because they had been unable to acquire new clothes by trading grain or livestock products. Those better off, who had a vegetable garden, made do with one meal a day; the rest ate wild roots. Only the wretched Haratin farmers remained in Tamanrasset. The ablebodied nomads had taken their flocks to graze four hundred miles away; some had gone to the Sudan (Mali) to buy millet.

Moreover, political agitation was cropping up again among the tribes in the wake of an Italian-Turkish conflict that had broken out in November 1911. The Turks were preaching holy war through the Senoussi leaders, those Ahaggar rebels who had been driven back to Tripoli, such as Attici and the Muslim marabouts who had never accepted Christian occupation.

From Tripolitania (southern Libya), which had been abandoned by the Italians, the hotbed of subversion had traveled to the southwest edge of the French Sahara. Captain Charlet occupied the Djanet Oasis, capital of the Ajjer, which the French had conquered in 1904, then lost. The majority

---

[15] Quoted by Ganne, *Tamanrasset*, 209.

of the Tuareg laughed at the "holy war", but some were delighted to use it as a pretext for starting up the *rezzous* again, their traditional piracy.

For the moment, Moussa remained faithful to his promises. But it could be sensed that he was agitated, and his savage instinct was reawakening. As long as France was strong in the Sahara, the Ahaggar would not budge. But what if there were a European war and France were forced to withdraw her troops from Africa? Yes, Moussa himself would be delighted to start up his *razzias* again. His income had fallen drastically, and the indemnity paid him by France did not make up for the loss. Proud and idle, he refused to live more modestly and had gone into debt, which was weakening his power. The Laperrine system—a strong *amenokal* holding the Ahaggar—was threatened.

After reassuring his loved ones, Charles resumed his charitable life of poverty. He distributed all his supplies, which he replenished thanks to gifts from his family. He was no longer hoping for conversions, contenting himself with preparing the ground for the missionaries who he hoped would come after him, if God so willed. Close contact with the local peoples and the perfect life were now his sole objectives. These were not to change. As he wrote to the Duke de Fitz-James: "I do not desire there be Christians among them for a few years yet. Before talking religion to them, we have to gain their trust and friendship. We have to show them our religion by practicing its virtues, instead of using words. Unless there is a miracle of grace, they can change religions only if we inspire in them much more trust and respect than anything they have known up until now." [16]

Charles was well aware that Africa was changing rapidly under the impetus of the West. The telegraph had come in. An aviator had crossed the Sahara. Captain Nieger was investigating a route for the future Transsaharan railroad, which was to connect Oran to Chad, going through Beni Abbès, the Touat, and Silet, forty miles from Tamanrasset. Charles rejoiced over that prospect: "The railroad is a powerful means for spreading civilization, and civilization aids Christianization. Savages cannot be Christians. Thus it is a necessity for preserving our African empire and for enabling us to transport to the Rhine, if need be, as many troops as possible." [17]

Really, he thought about everything! "Natural morality" concerned him also. He wrote to Bishop Livinhac: "There is a scourge in the Ahaggar! The number of infanticides is incredible, maybe a quarter, maybe a third of babies perish at birth. Morals are very loose here, that is allowed by custom. But custom does not allow births out of wedlock." [18]

[16] CF to Fitz-James, December 11, 1912, in Gorrée, *Sur les traces*, 266.

[17] Quoted by Bazin, *Foucauld*, 400.

[18] CF to Bishop Livinhac, December 7, 1911, quoted by J.-F. Six, *Vie de Charles de Foucauld* (Seuil, 1962), 224.

And he sought to have White Sisters sent to the Ahaggar to found orphanages.

Yes, Africa was changing. On March 30, 1912, the sultan of Morocco, released by the Germans, agreed to the French protectorate. On April 12, Lyautey became the resident general there and, with Gouraud, deployed his troops as far as Marrakech to put down the Berbers opposed to the sultan. He did not send for Charles, who had offered his services. Their views were very different. Charles would have liked annexation rather than a protectorate. Lyautey, who did not believe in converting the Muslims, preferred to depend on the traditional religious chiefs.

Naturally, in Charles' mind, it was not a matter of promoting colonization of the brutal, exploiting kind. As he wrote to Captain Pariel: "Algeria, Tunisia, Morocco, the Sudan, the Sahara, what a beautiful empire! Providing that we civilize it, Frenchify it, and do not content ourselves with exploiting it. If we seek to civilize these peoples and to raise them to our level, in fifty years this empire will be an admirable extension of France. If, neglectful of the love of our neighbor ordered by God, and of the fraternity written on our walls, we treat these peoples, not as children, but as material for exploitation, the union we are giving them will turn against us, and they will cast us into the sea at the first European difficulty." [19]

And he wrote to Marie de Bondy in the same vein: "In the eighty years since Algiers has been ours, there has been so little attention to saving Muslim souls that it could be said there has been no attention. Or to governing them well, or to civilizing them. They have been kept subjugated and nothing more. If the Christians of France do not understand that it is part of their duty to evangelize their colonies, it is an error for which they will be accountable, and it will be the cause of losing a great number of souls that could have been saved. If France does not govern her colony better, she will lose it, and these people will slip back into barbarism and the hope of Christianizing them will be lost for a very long time." [20]

He went even farther when he wrote to Fitz-James, asking him to alert Albert de Mun: "In fifty years, France's North African colonial empire, with sixty million inhabitants, will be in an advanced state of material progress, crisscrossed with rail lines, populated by inhabitants accustomed to handling our weapons, and whose elite will have been educated in our schools. If we have not learned by then how to hold these people to us, they will drive us out. Not only will we lose our entire African empire, but

[19] Quoted by M. Castillon du Perron, *Charles de Foucauld* (Grasset, 1982), 455.
[20] CF to Marie de Bondy, September 21, 1912, in Gorrée, *Sur les traces*, 265.

it will become, only a few hours away by sea, on the other shore of the Mediterranean, a hostile neighbor, fearsome and barbaric."

And he asked that "these younger brothers become brothers equal to us, like us." [21]

The blacks, maybe. They dreamed of being "like us", that is, as rich, as well fed, as white . . . But the Muslims? How to go about converting them, and, more basically, how to get them to espouse our morals, what Charles called "natural morality", which came out of the Bible. What was clear to him was not to them. In their eyes, violence was a lesser evil. The law of the strongest still reigned. And what Charles called looseness of morals consti- tuted age-old customs. Besides, were things that much better in Europe, where fearsome conflicts were brewing?

The year of 1912 ended, and Massignon had not yet made up his mind about joining Charles, in spite of renewed encouragement from Paul Claudel. King Fouad of Egypt had invited the young scholar to deliver lectures at the new Muslim university in Cairo. Massignon's spiritual ad- viser, Father Fontaine, advised him to accept and forget the Ahaggar, along with its unkempt hermit. Distraught, harassed by a family urging him to marry, Massignon turned once again to Claudel, who, abruptly, doubting his priestly vocation, went in the opposite direction and advised him to give up the thought of joining the apostle of the Sahara: "The idea of Father de Foucauld was probably too romantic and too ambitious. It is better to seek humble ways, hidden, ordinary." [22]

Claudel was thinking primarily of the Franciscans. Charles' invitation, however, suggested nothing more than "six months of evangelical life, spent in humble manual work, prayer, adoration, and poverty, with the great repose of spirit offered by this life tied to solitude". [23]

In the end, Massignon accepted the king's offer and left for Cairo, suffer- ing inside, to consume "this bitter-tasting bread baked in the ashes of sadness". [24]

On February 27, 1913, young Ouksem, coming from faraway pastures, ar- rived in Tamanrasset. He was twenty-two, the son of Brother Charles' friend Shikat. The hermit took an interest in this young nomad of good family, "intelligent, upright, serious. I treat him like my child, and he shows me a most affectionate devotion", he wrote to Laperrine. [25] And in a letter

---

[21] CF to Fitz-James, December 11, 1911, in ibid., 266.
[22] Claudel to Massignon, January 21, 1913, 204.
[23] CF to Massignon, March 10, 1912, in Six, *L'Aventure*, 122 and 123.
[24] Massignon to Claudel, August 10, 1912.
[25] CF to Laperrine, quoted by Gorrée, *Sur les traces*, 339.

to Marie de Bondy, "He is unusually fine. We can expect him to make great progress."

Ouksem had been named to succeed a relative as chief of the Dag Rali, settled Tuareg landowners. Accordingly, Charles thought it his duty to educate the young man, first introducing him to France. Not an official visit, as Moussa's had been, but a family tour. "To have him share the gentleness and the loving atmosphere of family life in Christian circles and show him how religion penetrates every aspect of life", he wrote.[26] Secretly he hoped to convert him one day.

Ouksem married pretty Kambeshisha on April 3, but her accompanying him to France was out of the question. Charles left with Ouksem on April 28, 1913, feeling reassured about the threat of rebellion. Lieutenant Gardel, at the head of forty *spahi* camel troopers, had just decimated a group of three hundred Kel Ajjer rebels at Esseyen, near Djanet. The enemy, driven back by a bayonet counterattack, had retreated, leaving fifty-six dead on the field, with Gardel reporting only two dead and seven wounded.

Spending May 13 at In Salah, Brother Charles found his little hermitage almost buried under the sand, but that did not bother him. They made a stop at Maison-Carrée on June 8. Charles was asked to recount his life story to the novitiate of the White Sisters of Birmandriéis. He made good use of the opportunity: it was an old dream of his, taking sisters to Tamanrasset. Thus he finished his talk with a ringing appeal: "Who among you, my sisters, would like to sacrifice herself for the Tuareg?"

They all stood up at once.[27]

But their superiors would not agree to it; neither would the army. Charles sailed from Algiers with a little twinge of regret.

Ouksem's tour of France began on June 13 with an appropriate way to astound the young nomad—a visit to the battleship *Condorcet* at Toulon. Conducting the two travelers through the naval shipyard was Ensign Charles de Blic, the hermit's nephew and godson. The officer entertained them at lunch on his ship, the torpedo boat *La Cognée*. Then they visited the naval secondary school at La Seyne, where another of Mimi's sons, Édouard de Blic, was preparing for the École Navale.[28] The next morning, Charles celebrated the Eucharist at the grotto of Saint-Baume, a "torrid" Mass, as they used to say in the Navy, with his nephew as server.

[26] Quoted by Bazin, *Foucauld*, 407.

[27] Ibid.

[28] Édouard de Blic, who, like his brother, became a naval officer, met a tragic death on December 3, 1916, off Funchal, on board his torpedo boat, *La Surprise*, sunk with all hands by a U-boat. Charles de Blic was to have a brilliant career, becoming an admiral. His widow, one hundred years old, spoke with us about him just recently.

Stopping briefly in Lyon, Charles paid a visit to his old friend Laperrine, who, promoted to general, now commanded the Sixth Dragoons.

This stay in France was to last three-and-a-half months; mostly, they made the rounds of the châteaux, where Ouksem was warmly received: two stays with the Blics at Barbirey, and stays at Bridoire in Périgord, at La Renaudie, La Barre, Saint-Jean-de-Luz, not to mention time spent with the bishop of Viviers. Duke, count, viscount, marquis, generals, a bishop—an incredible journey among the nobility, with the young "savage" (for they still used that term in those days) astounded by this display of titles and wealth. All the more surprising to him because Brother Charles never stopped preaching and embracing poverty. Might Ouksem not have felt more at home with a family of French peasants?

But Charles remained true to himself. To his sister, Mimi, he appeared old, worn out by asceticism. Of course, in France, he ate what they served him—off silver dishes even, in the châteaux—so as not to upset anyone, but he spent his nights praying.

And then Charles was in Paris, where the newspaper *La Croix* presented him as "the man who left the world after having completed the most extraordinary, the most marvelous voyage of exploration into the wildest parts of Morocco", and who had subsequently shut himself away "in a mysterious retreat".

In Paris, Charles was determined to see Massignon, who had finished his contract in Cairo. Their first meeting was on June 22, 1913. The young scholar seemed more tormented than ever.

Massignon wrote Claudel: "I can no longer wholeheartedly love human beings for themselves, and I cannot for myself invent the Love that God, on some occasions, has inspired within me. I am empty, like a seashell emptied, and I lie paralyzed, in horror of myself and in my inability to love others purely." [29]

Charles made him a last offer: "If you have finished your doctorate by September, you could leave with me. It is likely that, once in that retreat, God would give you light and peace." [30]

Massignon's response was still cautious, noncommittal. This vocation manqué has been much discussed. It is undeniable that the young writer had been marked by grace. Why did he hesitate to "give all"? Scrupulous, he allowed himself to be devoured by remorse for his sins. Sins of the flesh, he humbly confessed to Charles. The latter knew the problem only too well. Was he not an example of someone who had succeeded in transcending the flesh?

[29] *Paul Claudel,* 205.
[30] CF to Massignon, November 14, 1912, in Six, *L'Aventure,* 133.

He advised Massignon: "Do not cast blame on yourself. The miseries of our souls are as mire in which we must humiliate ourselves often, but it is not necessary to have our gaze fixed on these miseries at all times." [31]

Easy to say, thought Massignon, still devoured by desires of the flesh and other fantasies. Under the circumstances, how could he consider priestly celibacy, a monastic life in the wilderness? He cried out in despair: "There's nothing left but to bury myself in marriage!"

How could Charles respond to that? He knew only too well that there was nothing worse than a hermit who brought his fantasies with him to the desert, where he would be a monk in a cell.

He contacted Massignon's spiritual advisor, the famous Father Fontaine, curate at Clichy, who was also advisor to Claudel and Huysmans! There was a meeting with the priest at Clichy on September 1. But they talked of something else. The Union of Prayer that Charles was setting up in France, the embryo of his lay association. On that subject, he proved convincing, for Father Fontaine, in giving him his support, exclaimed: "Father de Foucauld's idea is divine. Now we must reach out to put it into practice. A current of holy convictions that must first be spread into the monasteries of the contemplative orders." [32]

Massignon's vocation had not been brought up. The next day, September 2, Charles was to celebrate Mass in the crypt at the Carmelite monastery in memory of his great-granduncle, Armand de Foucauld, vicar general of the diocese of Arles, who had died a martyr during the Terror. But something very bizarre happened. Charles was an hour late. In the church, Massignon, there to serve the Mass, grew impatient. Suddenly, an unfamiliar priest came out of the sacristy and asked him if he would be willing to serve his Mass. Oddly, Massignon accepted. When Charles arrived, he was upset and saw in Massignon's action a sign. Massignon did too, for he would say later: "A strange sign from God has passed between us like a sword." [33]

It was over. They would not see each other again. A few days later, at La Barre, Charles received a letter from Massignon announcing his coming engagement. The family had won. For Charles, it was the end of a hope. A good sport, he replied: "I too advise you to accept this marriage. God wants many souls to sanctify themselves thus. How great and beautiful, the mission of husband and wife!" [34]

Then, on September 30: "If God wants marriage for you, do not accept it

[31] Quoted by Castillon, *Foucauld*, 470.
[32] Father Fontaine, quoted by Castillon, ibid., 469.
[33] Six, *L'Aventure*, 147.
[34] CF to Massignon, September 16, 1913, in ibid., 150.

as expiation but as the state in which he has saved for you the greatest graces." [35]

During his stay in France, Charles was affected by the controversy over General Lyautey's peaceful policies in Morocco, questioned in some military and political circles, which wanted to "pacify" the country by force. But Lyautey put matters in perspective: "I have not come here to reign over a desert, or to annex lands, but to rally souls. Being colonial means making friends." [36] That position won him Charles' unqualified approval. Knowing the general was threatened and ready to resign, the hermit took advantage of being in Paris to employ his influence, which was considerable when it came to North African affairs. He spoke with his friend General Beaudemoulin, whom he had met during the 1881 campaign and who was now the head of President Raymond Poincaré's military cabinet. The general asked him to state in writing his approval of Lyautey's actions in Morocco, which Charles did at once, emphasizing his "spirit of justice and gentleness, his high-minded vision, his moderation, his honesty". [37]

A few days earlier, Charles had written Lyautey a ringing letter asking him not to resign: "How ardently I desire that, out of devotion to the public good, you remain in charge in Morocco for a long time, in spite of the difficulties they are causing you. I desire it for France, for its security, its honor, its greatness. I desire it for the Moroccan people, for their moral, intellectual, and material progress. I desire it for all of our North Africa, where the Moroccans will soon take the lead. I understand your moments of sadness at the thought of the good you could do if France were to carry out her duty toward you, and that you cannot do because she does not carry out that duty. But no one else could do as much as you are doing. Who more than you wishes the public good, who is better able to procure it? *You must stay.*" [38]

Charles de Foucauld would have his wish granted. Lyautey would remain in Morocco with full powers, to the great good of that country and of France.

After five months away, it was time to think of returning. In Viviers,

[35] Ibid., September 30, 1913, 153. Massignon married Marcelle Dansaert on January 27, 1914. The marriage brought these sarcastic comments from Claudel: "Here you are, once again captivated by trifles. I greet with pity your little household. You are no longer romantic and interesting, Massignon, but it is certainly a fine thing to be neither one nor the other!" (*Paul Claudel*, 217). The couple headed for Tamanrasset on their honeymoon, but the army stopped them at Toggourt for security reasons.

[36] Letter to Albert de Mun, 1912, *Bulletin des Amitiés*, no. 110, 16.

[37] CF to General Beaudemoulin, September 7, 1913, ibid., 17.

[38] CF to Lyautey, August 28, 1913, in Gorrée, *Sur les traces*, 272.

Charles saw his Union of Prayer approved by Bishop Bonnet. He sailed from Marseille with Ouksem on September 28, 1913, after he had celebrated the Eucharist at the main altar of Notre-Dame-de-la-Garde, a Mass served again by his faithful nephew Charles de Blic.

The results of this exhausting voyage were mixed. The Union of Prayer[39] had not aroused the enthusiasm of Cardinal Archbishop Amette, to whom Father Laurin had introduced Charles on September 5 in Paris. His Eminence was not interested[40] . . . Charles had found only a few dozen supporters.[41] However, there would have to be at least forty before Bishop Bonnet would agree to present the cause to Rome. In Lyon, Father Crozier gave him twenty-six more. Charles would soon reach the figure of forty-eight with another supporter . . . Massignon, who also sent the one-franc dues. A franc, even a Poincaré franc, was very little when one had been expecting the gift of a whole person.

So, with Massignon it had been failure. And with Ouksem too. Of course, the young Tuareg went home changed. He swore only by France. Seeing Africa again, he was to express his disenchantment: "Here lots sun, lots sand, lots rock. Road not lots pretty." [42] But soon he would be taken in hand by the family and sent six hundred miles away into the Adrar to watch over the flocks. Not a shred of hope for a conversion. Naïvely, Charles was surprised, writing to Marie de Bondy: "When will his soul come around completely? He, his father, his father-in-law, his mother, and still others are folk of good will. But to stop believing what one has always believed, what one has always seen believed around one, what those whom one loves and respects believe, that is indeed difficult. All the more so when one's body of belief is admissible and reasonable and when it is impossible for one to analyze its basis." [43]

Reaching Tamanrasset November 22, 1913, Charles de Foucauld had come home to his hermitage and the everlasting problems of the extreme drought and poverty, which meant bare survival. The year of misfortune, 1914, was about to dawn over Europe, as well as over the peaks of the Ahaggar and the parched plateau of Tamanrasset. Did Foucauld know his days were num-

---

[39] Association rules drawn up in 1901; the Union, created in 1913, was first called the Catholic Colonial Union, which certainly shows the founder's desire to convert colonized peoples. In 1914, it would take the name Universal Apostolic Union.

[40] In 1919, however, Cardinal Amette would support the rebirth of the Union of the Brothers and Sisters of the Sacred Heart.

[41] In a letter to Jacques Maritain on February 9, 1914, Ernest Psichari wonders about joining the Union of Prayer he has heard about.

[42] CF to Louis de Foucauld, October 13, 1913, ibid., 275.

[43] CF to Marie de Bondy, January 1, 1914, 226.

bered? His health was deteriorating. but he still needed five years to finish the work on his dictionaries, grammar, and anthologies.[44] "Will the Lord give them to me?" Charles was apparently not sure, for on December 13, 1913, he updated his will:"I wish to be buried in the very place where I die. A very simple burial, without a casket, a very simple grave, no monument, just a wooden cross."[45]

Totally submissive to God, he in no way modified the rule he had established for himself. Let us now follow him day by day, through his diary and his correspondence.

On January 20, 1914, he received a visit from Major Meynier, who in December had succeeded Commander Payn as head of the Southern Territories. The officer was accompanied by Lefranc, a journalist from Le Temps, and by Doctor Vermale, a military doctor who had come to study the tribes. Charles entertained them at "the Frigate". His gramophone, bought in 1913, enchanted the Tuareg, men and women, who had come to greet the French.

Rumors of war in Europe had not yet come to the Ahaggar; instead, as Charles wrote Marie de Blic, "There is much talk about a Transsaharan railroad. There is also talk of roads and the wireless telegraph.[46] In the general interest, I sincerely hope that all these things are accomplished."[47]

Charles was also rejoicing over Lyautey's pacification of Morocco. It was now possible to cross that country without being relieved of one's possessions and slaughtered. "So now our North Africa is becoming one, from Tunis to the Atlantic. It is a great joy for me", Charles wrote Raymond de Blic.[48]

A Parisian journalist, P. Bourdarie, who had praised "the political, scientific, and social work" of Charles de Foucauld in Morocco, suggesting he be awarded the Legion of Honor, received a letter from the hermit: "All the credit should go to Lyautey. I prefer to remain in that last place of which our Lord has given the example. I prefer to remain as small as possible."[49]

[44] The abridged Tuareg-French lexicon was finished in February 1914 and was going to be published. He hoped to finish the big dictionary in 1914, along with the dictionary of proper names. He was still working on the anthology of poetry and proverbs as well as the prose selections and the grammar.

[45] Quoted by Gorrée, Sur les traces, 279.

[46] General Bailloud, on February 11, 1913, had tested in Tamanrasset a portable transmitter-receiver designed to communicate with the one on the Eiffel Tower. The experiment was a success but had no immediate results, for Charles was to write on March 6, 1916, "In a year, Fort Moty will have a wireless telegraphy station." Nothing was said about Tamanrasset.

[47] CF to Marie de Blic, April 24, 1914, in Gorrée, Sur les traces, 281.

[48] CF to Raymond de Blic, April 16, 1914, in ibid., 282.

[49] CF to P. Bourdarie, July 22, 1914, in ibid., 285.

On July 3, 1914, Brother Charles climbed to Assekrem, in the company of Major Lehureau, Saint-Léger, Vermale, and Ben Messis, to retrieve his tabernacle. Living up there was now out of the question, for the drought had turned the massif into a desert. The major recounts the visit: "We found the house in a rather pitiful state, the walls crumbling but still standing. He celebrated Mass in that dilapidated chapel, which the raging elements caused to quake on its fragile foundations and threatened to carry off into space."[50]

Three days later they went back down to Tamanrasset. And that ended his dream of beauty and solitude. He was deeply shaken. On July 20 he wrote Marie de Bondy: "I cannot say that I desire death. In the past, I wished for it. Now, I see so much good to be done that I would like, above all, to do a little good."[51]

Germany declared war on France on August 3, 1914, but Charles did not find out until September 3, noting in his diary: "At 5 A.M. received fast-riding courier from Fort Motylinski informing me that Germany has declared war on France and invaded Belgium and that the Germans are attacking Liège."

Writing to his friend Lutowlaski, he commented: "My thoughts, my heart, and my prayers are on the French border and the Polish border."[52]

On September 11 he noted in his diary: "At noon received the courier from In Salah. Captain de Saint-Léger is ordering La Roche to stay in the Ahaggar with the entire group. Bad news. We retreat along the border. Lunéville is occupied by the Germans. We are retreating everywhere before superior forces. We are not coming to the aid of Belgium. Germans occupy Brussels."

How would the Africans react to a European war that was destabilizing the world powers? Mobilization in Algeria, like that in all parts of Africa under French or British authority, had gone very well, but a silent threat hung over the Oases Territory.

On September 9, the army had entrusted to Charles "fifteen hundred cartridges, model 1874, for Moussa" (diary). On September 12, Charles added this note: "Tonight, I'm handing over to Afeggag the fifteen hundred cartridges with a letter to Moussa telling him that he is responsible for them, that they are to be fired only at the enemy; any that are not fired at the enemy must be sent back to the office [the military post at In Salah]."

Charles wrote Marie de Bondy September 15, "There are already indications that the marabouts are inciting to violence in the Sudan and

[50] L. Lehureau, *Au Sahara*.
[51] CF to Marie de Bondy, July 20, 1914, in Gorrée, *Sur les traces*, 284.
[52] CF to Lutowlaski, in *Bulletin des Amitiés*, no. 66, 10.

Tripolitania, instigated by the Turks. Here, calm reigns. The Tuareg know nothing of Germany, not even the name. You realize how it pains me to be so far from our soldiers. But my duty is to remain here to help and to keep the people calm. I shall not leave Tamanrasset until the war is over. My place is here to help maintain peace of mind. The Tuareg will remain in their usual calm state, unaware of the storm brewing around us, unless agitation and violence come from Algeria, the Sudan, or Tripolitania." [53]

There were indications that the European conflict would spread beyond the frontier of the Rhine. The Trappists of Cheiklé had to leave, and Charles' beloved Poor Clares of Nazareth had to take refuge on Malta. "How many souls are appearing suddenly before God and perhaps very little prepared!" he wrote their abbess, Mother Saint-Michel. "May God protect France from this war, which will end with Europe either independent or subjugated! May God have pity on all these souls! May he let good come out of this great evil!" [54]

He would anxiously await the arrival of the mail. The battle was being played out around and for the province of his birth. "The First and Second Armies are engaged in daily battles, neither advancing nor retreating", he noted in his diary on September 24. "The line between the two armies seems to be Belfort. Lunéville, Pont-à-Mousson, Longwy, occupied by the enemy. The Second Army between Sambre and Meuse (Commander in Chief Joffre) gradually retreating. The Prussian Army reaches the Compiègne Forest. On the twenty-sixth, the ministry resigns. Is replaced by Viviani, Briand, Delcassé, Millerand. The seat of government now Bordeaux; Paris is in danger. General Gallieni defends the capital." [55]

His anguish reached a peak October 20: "The great Franco-British army engaging in battle after battle. Left flank penetrates, then is driven back. Many German planes fly over Paris." [56]

But on October 12, some relief: "Dispatches of September 7 to 14. General battle on the Marne. Victory along the whole line! The Prussians in a hurried retreat. Our troops in relentless pursuit." [57]

At the same time, things were getting worse in the Ahaggar. Besides the drought, which had led to famine, there was now malaria. Moussa was keeping his men and flocks four hundred miles away to the south. But another danger was lying in wait. On October 16 Charles noted: "Two letters from Moussa from Tin-Zaouaten. Thirty Oulad Djerrir [rebels] are

[53] CF to Marie de Bondy, September 15, 1914, in Gorrée, *Sur les traces*, 287.

[54] CF to Mother Saint-Michel, September 15, 1914, *Bulletin des Amitiés*, no. 82, 21.

[55] *Carnets de Tamanrasset* (Nouvelle Cité, 1986), September 24, 1914, 315.

[56] Ibid., October 2, 1914, 317.

[57] Ibid., October 12, 1914, 320.

at Tin-Zaouaten. Their bullets are red copper (therefore German?). They are camped in a circle, surrounding their camp with thorny branches. They told the courier's sister they wanted to destroy the *beilik*'s house and take Moussa captive. He was close by, with only four men. Other news: Djafar, his wife, and daughters have all *died of thirst*. Old Aklessou has died of malaria." [58]

And indeed, a group of around sixty Moroccan pillagers from Timetrin, after a very long ride, had succeeding in surprising Moussa, who only just escaped in the depths of night. He then regrouped his men and pursued the Moroccans. Determined and unscrupulous, these pillagers had stolen four hundred camels and kidnapped ten Tuareg. On November 9, Moussa counterattacked in the Erg Chech. He decimated the enemy. There were eleven deaths, counting the fallen on both sides. This bloody affair showed that it took only a few aggressors out of Morocco or Tripolitania to threaten order, once the army, called back to France, was no longer patrolling the country.

The danger was no less great in the Ahaggar. On his own authority, Foucauld advised and even gave orders. The little garrison at Fort Motylinski, last fragile rampart against the subversion threatening the Ahaggar, was without French officers, their having been called to the French front (Warrant Officer Constant was in charge at the fort). Charles' diary of November 27 supplies some details: "Saw Aflan. *I gave him the order* to call to Fort Moty fifty native troopers to replace those gone to fight." Able to resist an assault by pillagers, Fort Motylinski, lacking a good well, could not withstand a genuine siege.

Just as he had given munitions from the army to Moussa, Charles passed out foodstuffs and quinine from the army among the starving, fever-stricken people of Tamanrasset: "Gave instructions to Ouksem [chief of the Dag Rali] about the four thousand pounds of dates that are to be given out as follows", and so on. [59]

The mere presence of the marabout maintained a precarious order, but anything could happen. On November 21, two stores of grain were raided in Tamanrasset.

And yet, because of his presence, there were not—not yet, anyway—*rezzous* or organized rebellions in the Ahaggar. The Tripolitanian disease had not yet spread into the region. In Tamanrasset, the many other evils were already enough to handle: "Now it's five years since we have had rain", Charles wrote Marie de Bondy November 24. Elsewhere, he pointed out that, in the ten years he had been living in Tamanrasset, it had rained

---

[58] Ibid., October 16, 1914, 321.
[59] Ibid., November 27, 1914, 330.

only twice. Four-fifths of the goats and sheep had perished, and half the camels. The surviving goats no longer gave milk. The camels were so weak they could not be used for caravans. In addition, in September five waves of grasshoppers had come through, devastating the meager crop of grain and garden vegetables.

By December 1914, Charles was only a shadow of himself, "reduced to a skeleton, with a bad case of scurvy from being underfed", according to Doctor Vermale. On December 14, the hermit wrote to General Laperrine, fighting on the front lines in France: "Wouldn't I be more useful on the front, as a chaplain or a stretcher bearer? If you tell me to come, I shall leave at once and hasten there." [60]

"Stay in Tamanrasset", was Laperrine's response.

On December 31, Charles de Foucauld finished the eleven-hundredth page of his Tuareg dictionary, which was to have two thousand pages.

Tamanrasset, inside the fort, December 1, 1916, 6:30 P.M.

The candle had gone out. At the foot of the altar Brother Charles knelt in contemplation on the chapel's golden sand. By the feeble light of the tiny oil lamp, he gazed at the Christ he himself had drawn on a piece of fabric. On the pine altar glowed the Host in its monstrance. He was think-ing of Christ crucified and his seeming failure.

His own failure was no less apparent. He had not converted a single one of those proud nomads his countrymen asserted they had "tamed". They were tame now but were only awaiting France's defeat so they could take up arms again and go off on *rezzous*!

In his whole useless life, he had baptized only two people: Marie, the elderly blind mulatto from Beni Abbès, and Abd Jesus, the little black slave he had redeemed. All his endeavors had failed. Though he had been an officer trained at a prestigious military school, he had resigned. Though he had been a Cistercian monk, he had left two Trappist houses, Neiges and Cheiklé. Useless as a gardener for the Poor Clares, he had refused to be-come their chaplain. Though he finally became a priest, he had not wanted to become a traditional missionary. His hermitages at Beni Abbès, Taman-rasset, and In Salah—all abandoned and invaded by the sands! The one on Assekrem, in ruins, left to the furious desert winds, would soon be a pile of rocks upon rock.

Who would ever read his writings, his modest meditations on the Gos-pels and the lives of saints, the "directories" intended for his imaginary disciples? Who would open his dictionary or grammar of Tamasheq, a dying

---

[60] CF to Laperrine, quoted by Bazin, *Foucauld*, 428.

language? Who would still have any interest in his *Reconnaissance du Maroc*, other than a few French veterans of North Africa or a few officers dealing with indigenous affairs?

"I see myself in the evening of this pitiful life, having produced so little fruit, like a grain of wheat that will not die." [61]

"My solitude is growing. I feel more and more alone in the world. Some have left for the homeland; others have lives more and more apart from ours. I feel like the olive left alone on the end of the branch, forgotten after the harvest." [62]

The little Host, both fragile and eternal, seemed to throb in the monstrance. Abruptly, without knowing why, Charles felt this treasure threatened.

The *rezzou* of the *fellagha* was approaching Tamanrasset under the cloak of night. At the head, on one of the extra camels, the black Haratin El Madani. Behind him, Kerzou, the Tuareg, did not take his eyes off him. By his side rode the Senoussi Beuh ag Rhabelli, who felt his anxiety rising. Of course, their band was large. A surprise attack by the native troops from Fort Moty seemed unlikely, since the French and their Arab soldiers were shut in behind the thick walls. There was only the risk of running into a caravan with a powerful escort in Tamanrasset. Or of encountering a messenger, of whom they could easily rid themselves.

The *rezzou* was now proceeding along the dry bed of the Tamanrasset Oued. Pebbles rolled under the dromedaries' shoes, and the sound awakened a bearded vulture asleep in an ethel. Before he flew off, his ominous cry echoed in the night.

The light of the stars and the quarter moon lit up the desolate countryside. Suddenly, El Madani raised his arm. The column stopped. Through the darkness could be made out ochre cubes, the brick huts of Tamanrasset, the Haratin village, and here and there, a few *zeribas* made of rushes.

Turning toward the men, Kerzou put his hand over his mouth, invisible under the blue *litham*. They had arrived. Complete silence was necessary.

Beuh, more and more uneasy, opened his eyes wide. Suddenly, beyond the village he could make out, silhouetted against the starry sky, the enormous mass of the fort, the Saharan donjon! The hideaway of the great white marabout!

Led by Kerzou, they drew up their mounts near the fig trees of the Konali *Foggara* (a well system) and had them kneel down silently. Then, like shadows in the night, they spread out toward the fortress, weapons in hand.

[61] CF, *Oeuvres spirituelles* (Nouvelle Cité, 1974–1997), September 1907.
[62] Ibid., September 1910.

16

Threat from the East

As 1915 began, anxiety was in the air. What would be the outcome of the battle for France? Brother Charles' patriotism never wavered. To him, the Germans were barbarians. They had annexed his native city and driven out his family. News from the front was rare and always outdated. A letter from France took a month to arrive. Twice a month, a military courier brought bags of mail from In Salah to Fort Motylinski, stopping in Tamanrasset. Marie de Bondy had given Charles subscriptions to *L'Écho de Paris* and *La Dépêche algérienne*. In emergencies, Fort Motylinski (which still did not have a radio) would receive messages carried by a camel trooper.

In spite of the great poverty brought on by the drought, Tamanrasset had grown. *Zeribas*, those huts built with rushes, were rarely seen now, thanks to Brother Charles. The regular inhabitants had built small houses with the clay bricks known as *toub*. Some of the Dag Rali landowners and a few of the nomadic Tuareg nobles had even given up their uncomfortable tents to live in small European-style houses with terraces and grounds cared for by slaves. Moussa's house and that of his cousin Dassine were among the largest. Tamanrasset now boasted eighty houses.

Charles was encouraging the nomads to work the soil and gradually abandon the pastoral nomadism that meant bare subsistence. But was the land any more profitable, with the continuing drought? The proud Tuareg seemed to miss the days of the *rezzous*. Young Ouksem was not to be relied on. His friendship with the marabout was genuine, but he maintained secret contacts with the Ajjer rebels. It would not take much for him to go over to their side. A French defeat in Europe would be enough. Moussa, too, felt loyalty to France, but, when necessary, he could play both sides. His own secretary, Ba Hammou (who was giving Charles Tamasheq lessons), kept in touch with the Adrar rebels' sultan, Ahmoud. Moussa himself was beginning to have doubts about the French, who did not pay him many benefits for being *amenokal*; they also requisitioned his camels and supplied him with inferior cartridges.

Recently, Ouksem had told Charles a story that made his hair stand on end. A few years before, when Laperrine had crossed the Sahara, escorted by a still wavering Moussa, a tribal chief named Fihroun suggested the *amenokal* kill the major and his escort and make off with the weapons and camels. After weighing the pros and cons, Moussa had refused. An argument followed:

"You lack courage, Moussa!"

"You follow your path, Fihroun, and I'll follow mine. In a few years we shall see which was the better one."

As for the present, who could say who would win the European war, France or Germany?

Rebel pressure was being felt to the southwest too, coming out of southern Morocco in the form of Berber *rezzous* that had evaded sharifian authority. Through the efforts of Lyautey, since 1912 the resident general in Morocco, there was hope that the marauders would soon be overcome, leaving only the possibility of an occasional surprise. The northwestern area was much more dangerous. By withdrawing troops from Tripolitania to reinforce their defenses at home, the Italians had created a vacuum between Algeria and Tunisia, which the Tripolitanian and Senoussi rebels—around two thousand men armed by the Germans and Turks—used to their advantage. They occupied the Fezzan in 1914, making it an independent state, thereby threatening the French Sahara, which had few troops left. There were only three hundred soldiers, Arabs under the command of a handful of commissioned and noncommissioned officers from France. The majority were stationed at border posts, mainly Djanet.

In February 1915, Fort Motylinski had only six native soldiers, commanded by Warrant Officer Constant. Captain de La Roche had taken most of the men to the Adrar, over four hundred miles to the south, where they were protecting the pastures on which the flocks of the Ahaggar depended for survival. The most significant military post was In Salah, which had been under commander Captain de Saint-Léger until Captain Duclos replaced him in April 1915. Brother Charles got along well with the latter and sent him regular reports on the situation in the Ahaggar.

On one occasion he wrote: "As you can see, things have changed greatly. The roads are no longer safe. The Adrar is periodically plundered. The son of Abidin has told his prisoners: 'Soon there will be nothing left in the Adrar. We will have to go *razzia* in the Ahaggar.' Three things are absolutely imperative: the presence of a mobile force in the Adrar; a little fort guarded by fifteen or so men, which would serve as a supply center for the mobile force; and a force in the Ahnet, at Aoulef." [1]

A fort . . . a *bordj*. Charles was also beginning to think seriously of one in Tamanrasset. Not for him; his life had little value. But to protect the resi-

---

[1] CF to Captain Duclos, May 4, 1915, in G. Gorrée, *Sur les traces de Charles de Foucauld* (Éd. de la Plus Grande France, 1936), 296.

dent population, in danger because at best the nearest mobile French force was two or three days' march from there. An ordinary *rezzou* of ten to twenty rebels armed with rifles, arriving on swift camels, would be enough to create a reign of terror.

In April 1915, events began moving faster. A massive thrust by a thousand Senoussi led to the fall of the key fort, Djanet, France's strategic border post. The fifty men holding it were overwhelmed, most of them dying or becoming prisoners. Very few escaped. The road was now open for the Senoussi to invade the Ahaggar. Between Djanet and Tamanrasset stood nothing but insignificant Fort Motylinski, which Constant, now a second lieutenant, held with three French soldiers and thirty or so Arab troopers.

An untenable situation, Foucauld judged, and he advised evacuation, with the soldiers retreating into the narrow mountain gorges. "If the fort is attacked, I shall join you. We are all in the hands of God." [2] But not long after, Djanet was recaptured, although the threat remained.

With no help from the army, on June 9, 1915, Charles began the construction of his fort, following the classic design of the native *bordjs* of southern Morocco.[3] Paul Embarek and another mason laid the thousands of bricks cast all day long by his wife, his mother-in-law, Salah, and three other Haratin, everyone being paid in grain. It had rained a little—not enough—and the people grew hopeful.

Summer went by peacefully in the Ahaggar. On July 25, Charles finished his dictionary, which came to 2,028 pages.

On the French front, the situation was still uncertain, but Charles did not doubt victory would come. He wrote to his sister: "Total victory is absolutely necessary; otherwise it will start all over again in a few years and probably under less favorable conditions."[4]

The war was exacting a heavy toll: tens of thousands of dead! Several of his old comrades from Saint-Cyr had been killed or wounded. And the slaughter of the African troops could not be ignored: Black, Arab, and Berber, they were sent into the front lines to become mincemeat. In his correspondence, Charles, who up to then had spoken of "the maternal duty of France toward native peoples", now spoke of "the duty of gratitude resulting from all these deaths",[5] "so many of our infidel subjects giving

---

[2] CF to Laperrine, April 11, 1915, quoted by R. Bazin, *Charles de Foucauld* (Plon, 1921), 436.

[3] The word *bordj* would not be used during Brother Charles' lifetime. In Saint-Augustin's in Paris there is a remarkable model of the fort, to be found on the right side of the chapel, where Charles' conversion took place.

[4] CF to Marie de Blic, May 15, 1915, in G. Gorrée, *Sur les traces*, 438.

[5] CF to Massignon, June 29, 1915, quoted by J.-F. Six, *L'Aventure de l'amour de Dieu* (Seuil, 1993), 193.

their blood for us".[6] "Fighting on our soil in great numbers, they are learning to know us. Their loyal devotion will arouse the French to take more interest in them than previously, to govern them better." [7]

Naturally, Foucauld burned with a desire to serve on the French front. On August 2, he learned that Father Rivet, a Jesuit theologian and former officer, had "died facing the enemy" while leading his section on an attack, nothing but a stick in his hand, since by Church law a priest was forbidden to shed blood. This loss inspired him to write to Laperrine, who enjoined him to stay in Tamanrasset, where he was using his powers to the fullest.

The debate was not new. In his faithfully maintained correspondence with Massignon, Charles praised his friend's decision to fight in the Dardanelles as a volunteer noncommissioned officer after stubbornly refusing the post at the Foreign Ministry in Paris suggested by his family and Claudel: "A Christian must do his best to carry out all his duties, give an example of perfection in everything, be in the first rank in the sacrifices made for his neighbor, for his country." [8]

In Tamanrasset, the summer had gone by without rain, except for showers of grasshoppers. To the south, Moroccan pillagers were still threatening Moussa and Ouksem's flocks. To the northeast, on the border between Tunisia and Tripolitania, Khalif Ben Asker, head of the Libyan rebels, with the aid of Turkish and German officers hounded the few remaining French troops. With three thousand fanatical soldiers, on October 2, 1915, he attacked the French post of Oum-Souig, where Captain Bermond and his four hundred men had dug in; the captain died, along with nearly half his troops. Dehibat Oasis endured eleven assaults by the Senoussi. On November 10, the Tripolitanians carried out their first raid on the Ahaggar frontier, in the territory of the friendly Ajjer.

On December 25, 1915, Brother Charles celebrated Christmas Mass in his hermitage, alone. Less than a mile away, on the other side of the wadi, the Haratins were still raising the fort. Would this exhausting task be finished in time?

In January 1916, in the Adrar, over three hundred miles from Tamanrasset, Moussa and Ouksem's nomads fought a battle against Moroccan pillagers, which resulted in a number of dead and wounded.

But it was not only the "natives" who were being slaughtered. In France, the Battle of Verdun had begun, the greatest massacre in human history. Colonel Driant, a cadet senior to Foucauld at Saint-Cyr, was killed. Charles

[6] Correspondence of March 12, 1915, quoted by Bazin, *Foucauld*, 431.
[7] Ibid.
[8] CF to Massignon, September 9, 1915, quoted by Six, *L'Aventure*, 189.

could be proud of his class, which distinguished itself in the struggle: Pétain, Mazel, d'Urbal. And the one preceding his: Maud'huy, Sarrail, to name only the generals.

In the Sahara, the rebels took advantage of France's weakened presence to attack to the northwest, on the Tripolitanian frontier. Besieged on March 6 by a thousand Senoussi armed with a cannon and machine guns, Djanet fell on March 24, after heroic resistance from Sergeant Lapierre's fifty men.

"The way is clear for the Senoussi to come here", Charles wrote Marie de Bondy on April 11. "Nothing can stop them, except the Lord. There are only twenty-five soldiers in the area, not in Tamanrasset, where I am alone, but at Fort Motylinski. I have advised them to retreat with all their arms and supplies to an impregnable location that has water from the mountains and where they can hold out indefinitely because it is out of reach of any cannon. If they do not follow my advice and are attacked, God knows what will happen. Moussa remains loyal, and the people are perfect." [9]

Be that as it may, the Tuareg in the Djanet region had now rallied to the Senoussi cause. On April 12, Charles suggested to the native troops at Fort Motylinski that they establish a line of defense four miles from the fort. But, manpower lacking, it could not be done. Major Meynier, head of the Southern Territories, managed to retake Djanet May 16. Tenuous victory. They barricaded themselves, the Fort Moty and Djanet soldiers, as well as Brother Charles, for by the end of June the major work on his little fort had been completed. On August 11, Constant sent him thirty rifles with six boxes of cartridges, a supply of wheat and dates, all brought by a caravan of nine camels.

"We are establishing our defensive position", Charles wrote Marie de Bondy. "Moussa has proved his loyalty. Our troops on the Tripolitanian border have moved back somewhat. The natives have interpreted this withdrawal as a defeat. The situation remains threatening, and if our troops had a setback or if the surveillance were inadequate, the effects would be felt here." [10]

On September 1, 1916, Charles wrote to his old classmate General Mazel, commander of the Fifth Army and Laperrine's superior: "Our Tuareg here are loyal, but we could be attacked by the Tripolitanians. I have transformed my hermitage into a fort. On seeing my battlements, I think of the fortified monasteries of the tenth century. What was thought to be gone forever has now reappeared. I have been entrusted with six

[9] CF to Marie de Bondy, April 11, 1916, in Gorrée, *Sur les traces*, 303.
[10] Ibid., August 15 and 31, 1916, 306 and 307.

boxes of cartridges and thirty Gras[11] rifles, which remind me of our youth." [12]

In his first rule, that of 1896, Brother Charles had stated: "It is forever forbidden us to carry or to own a weapon even for legitimate self-defense." But these guns were a military store, meant only for the people of Tamanrasset. He himself had no intention of touching them.

On September 5 the hermit conferred with Captain de La Roche, Second Lieutenant Constant, and Dumont, who had come to visit the now completed fort. Ouksem was there too. The captain declared himself reasonably pleased with the *bordj*, but more was needed.

"Without military manpower, which I can't supply you, you would not be able to withstand a true siege. Your Haratins could counter only an attack of ordinary marauders, not a military assault. Under these conditions, Father, I ask you to retire to Fort Moty."

"I shall not abandon these poor folk. Their lives depend on my stores of grain and dates. Famine threatens them. The first harvest, the wheat in April, was very meager. The second one, the millet ready in October, will be even worse. They cannot scatter in the mountains, unlike our settled Dag Rali, who've taken their goats and joined their nomad brothers in the Koudia. Provided they can find a well, a little milk will keep them alive."

On September 15, Charles told Marie de Bondy: "Our troops are retreating before the Senoussi. After retaking Djanet, they have evacuated it. This withdrawal before a few hundred guns is pitiful. The command has seriously erred in this matter. It is obvious that if the French retreat without even fighting, the Senoussi will advance. If the strategy is not changed, the Senoussi will be here before long." [13]

An invading force was on the move, heading from Tripolitania toward Agadez. What would be the fate of the Ahaggar, on the right flank?

In Algiers, General Moinier wanted to hear no more talk about resistance on the Tripolitanian frontier. With what troops? They were taking all his reserves to be massacred on the German front!

A little rain fell, easing the misery of the tribes. But, on September 20, the military situation in the northwest Sahara suddenly deteriorated. Three hundred Senoussi, led by a deserter who had been a corporal in the company at Tidikelt, attacked a large supply convoy en route from Fort Flatters to Fort Polignac. The enemy was driven back, but with heavy losses.

---

[11] The regulation rifle, General Gras 1874, was a light breech-loading weapon, not automatic, intended for the colonial cavalry: weight 3 kg, caliber 11 mm, range 400 m. By 1916, it was quite outdated, having been replaced thirty years earlier by the Lebel 1886.

[12] CF to General Mazel, September 1, 1916, quoted by Bazin, *Foucauld*, 445.

[13] CF to Marie de Bondy, September 15, 1916, quoted by Bazin, ibid., 446.

In Tamanrasset, the rumors of invasion were growing more detailed. News arrived that the same contingent of Senoussi, now led by Kaoucen or Sultan Ahmoud himself, was advancing on Fort Moty *with cannons*. They would be there in three days.

In spite of the pessimistic predictions of Captain de La Roche, Foucauld planned to defend himself in his *bordj*. Some Tuareg Imrad brought down from the mountains and the bravest Haratins, led by Meslar, occupied the fort, where the whole settled population of Tamanrasset took refuge, except for a few women who preferred to go hide in the mountains. Charles distributed the weapons. Would the farmers know how to use them? To resist this first challenge?

Charles sent a messenger to Moussa, who was in the southwest region with his flocks, and asked him for warriors. The *amenokal* immediately dispatched fifty men, but would they arrive in time? At best, they could cover the three hundred miles in a week. For his part, Captain de La Roche stationed runners outside of Fort Motylinski to avoid surprise and to alert Tamanrasset.

A runner from the camel corps arrived at the *bordj* on September 23 and reported to the father that Fort Moty had fallen! He could expect the enemy to arrive in Tam that very night!

Fortunately, the information was false. What had really happened? On September 18, a French patrol from Fort Moty had gone sixty miles east to Ti-n-Tarabine, to ascertain the position of the great Senoussi raiding force. The soldiers had found the residents in a state of turmoil. Six local Kel Ajjer rebels had arrived at the oasis, bearing a letter from Sultan Ahmoud to Moussa, encouraging him to join the rebellion. Learning that Moussa was not in the Ahaggar but far away on the Moroccan border, they had kidnapped three natives from Ti-n-Tarabine to act as guides. But two of them had escaped, and they told their story, spreading terror, mixing the true and the false: Sultan Ahmoud was marching on the Ahaggar with three hundred guns and a cannon. By September 24 he would be at Fort Moty, which could not hold out for a day. After that, he would take care of Tamanrasset, where the heart of the French presence resided, the marabout Charles!

Naturally the Fort Moty patrol had passed the information on to their leader, who in turn had warned Tam, without being able to verify the story. The information also fell upon the ears of ordinary marauders. At the farming center of Amsel, twelve miles south of Tamanrasset, six of the Djanet Haratins living there decided to go on the offensive and raid the fort of the marabout, whom they knew to be alone. But this operation would be risk free only if Fort Moty had already been neutralized by the Senoussi. Learning that this had not yet happened, they awaited their hour.

At Fort Moty, to which he had returned, Captain de La Roche was advised of this little Amsel plot. He decided to put it down and sent a detachment led by Sergeant Rémiot. The group first stopped at Tamanrasset on October 17 to warn Foucauld to be on the alert. That very night, Rémiot attacked Amsel. In Charles' *Carnets* appear these meaningful lines: "October 17: Rémiot, heading to Amsel arrives [in Tam] at 8 A.M. Rémiot leaves at 3 A.M. October 20: saw six men from Amsel seeking El Madani."

What happened next? Four rebels were captured and taken to Fort Moty, where Captain de La Roche had them imprisoned. The two others managed to escape. One, named Abdennebi, hid in the mountains of the Ahaggar. The other returned to Djanet. He was El Madani ag Soba. Captain de La Roche would write in his report: "There was a plot hatched against Father de Foucauld on September 21. The plot was uncovered, four of the leaders were captured and later put to death. Two others escaped." [14]

Of course, Rémiot kept Charles up to date on the operation. The father said nothing about the Amsel plot. He knew there was continuing danger, since two rebels had escaped. And one of them was El Madani, a sly Haratin Charles knew well, for at the *bordj* a few weeks earlier he had fed him and treated him for an eye ailment. Of the drama taking shape, not a word in his correspondence, and only seven words in his diary, under the date October 20: "Saw six men from Amsel seeking El Madani."

He had even striven to reassure Marie de Bondy on October 1: "Around August 24 we had a major alert, which has demonstrated the loyalty of the villagers. Instead of going over to the enemy, they grouped themselves around me and Fort Moty, ready to defend. This loyalty has been very sweet to me. These poor people could have taken refuge in the mountains, where they had nothing to fear; instead, they barricaded themselves in the fort and in my hermitage, although they knew the enemy had cannons and that bombardment was certain." [15]

The threat of famine in the mountains also encouraged them to remain: "The harvest of bechna in the Ahaggar is almost nil; rains and rising waters having damaged the *fegagir* [irrigation ditches], the gardens die of thirst", Charles wrote Laperrine October 15, 1916. "The flooding has not created as much pasture as we had expected. Insects and aphids devoured the grass as soon as it sprouted. I fear a harsh famine this winter." [16]

"I am afraid we shall have a severe famine", he said again, in a letter to Marie dated October 30, continuing: "Your gift allows me to make the necessary provisions to keep people here and in the area from *dying* of

---

[14] Quoted by Suremain, in *Bulletin des Amitiés*, no. III, 10.
[15] CF to Marie de Bondy, October 1, 1916, in Gorrée, *Sur les traces*, 308.
[16] CF to Laperrine, October 15, 1916, in *Bulletin des Amitiés*, no. 121, 19.

hunger. The spring harvest was meager; the second, in autumn, was almost nothing. Eleven years of drought. The country can endure no more." He ends with a touching detail: "The women here, who have learned to crochet, have requested that I ask you for three patterns, to fit children a year old." [17]

Early in November 1916, Charles received disturbing news from Captain Duclos, who commanded the Saharan Tidikelt forces at In Salah. In Algiers, General Moinier was about to order Major Meynier to cease all resistance on the Tripolitanian border and to evacuate the last support point, Fort Polignac, before it was overrun. Thus the Senoussi would have the way clear to enter the Ahaggar, without danger to their rear. Charles sped up the finishing of the interior of his little fort, and the work was pretty well done by November 15. Once more, a heavy threat lay over the village.

On November 16 he wrote: "How good of God to hide the future from us! What torture life would be if it were less unknown to us!" [18]

From November 18 to 21, clouds of grasshoppers descended on Tamanrasset, destroying the gardens. Sinister omen! Brother Charles wrote in his notebook: "November 24: met with Captain de La Roche. November 26: convoy with ammunition passes through. November 28: finished work on Tuareg poetry collection."

Thus ended the last *Carnet de Tamanrasset*.

December 1, 1916. 6:45 P.M.

Charles de Foucauld entered the courtyard of the desert fort and gazed at the sky, which shone with the light of millions of stars. As always, the sight produced in him a feeling of perfect happiness. He whispered:

"My Father, I put myself in your hands. I abandon myself to you, I entrust myself to you. Make of me what you will. Whatever you make of me, I thank you, I am ready for everything, I accept everything, I thank you for everything. Provided that your will be done in me, Lord, as in all your creatures, in all your children, in all those whom your heart loves, I desire nothing else. I put my soul in your hands, I give it to you, Lord, with all the love in my heart, because I love you, and because it is for me a need of love to give myself, to put myself in your hands, unreservedly. I put myself in your hands with infinite trust, for you are my Father." [19]

---

[17] CF to Marie de Bondy, in Gorrée, *Sur les traces*, 309.

[18] Quoted by Bazin, *Foucauld*, 449.

[19] Prayer by CF, known as the "prayer of abandonment", proposed by the Postulation. A slightly different version appears in "Méditations sur les saints Évangiles", in *Écrits spirituels* (Gigord, 1923), 29. See appendix 3.

The prayer led him into the office of Compline:

> Into your hands, Lord, I commend my spirit.
> My days are in your hands, save me!
> At last, all-powerful Master,
> give leave to your servant
> to go in peace, according to your promise.[20]

Not more than forty feet away, the *fellagha rezzou* spread out toward the fort. Hiding behind rocks, they advanced and soon reached an open area strewn with pebbles, which extended to the dry bed of the Tamanrasset Oued. Enormous, the walls of the fort rose in the starry sky.

For several minutes, Beuh, Kerzou, and their men looked up at the *bordj*'s ridge, the battlements that hid the walkway, and the four bastion towers at the corners. It was bitterly cold. If there was a sentry up there, he could not stay still for long, unless he was asleep. The sure instinct of the marauders could not be wrong. Those battlements were empty. Either the marabout was not on the alert, or else he was alone.

Beuh raised his hand. Very slowly, at times walking, at times crawling, the thirty-eight *fellagha* scattered and spread out silently under the half moon; then they advanced toward the fort, encircling it. They were now at the base of the enormous walls. They dropped into the deep ditch that surrounded the fort, and there, wrapped in their burnouses, rifles ready, they waited, melting into the night, completely invisible.

Then a man emerged from the tight group of kneeling camels. Standing tall, head high, heart pounding, hand trembling, he went forward out in the open and headed toward the entrance to the *bordj*. It was El Madani, the traitor.

He hesitated momentarily, about to commit a heinous crime. Perhaps, overcome by remorse, he wanted to flee? But it was too late. He felt twenty rifles trained on him.

Having gone around the low wall that hid the entrance, he raised his fist and pounded on the door three times, a long pause between each knock, as was the custom. Three knocks of destiny, which resounded ominously inside the *bordj*.

---

[20] Monastic office of Compline, brief response.

17

"Unless the Grain of Wheat Dies . . ."

Death must find us living.
—A. M. Carré

Inside, the three knocks reverberated. It was 7 P.M. Brother Charles was not surprised: he was expecting the two camel troopers from Fort Motylinski. He went into the entrance hallway, and, for form's sake, asked: "Who goes there?"

"El Boshta!"

Hearing the Arabic for mail carrier, Charles drew the bolt and opened the door halfway. For security reasons, a barrier kept the door from opening wide. No, Charles was not suspicious. Just a few hours earlier, he had written: "At the moment it seems to me that we are in no danger from Tripolitania or from the Senoussi. Our troops have received heavy reinforcements, and I hope they will thrust the enemy back beyond our borders. After September, no new alerts. The country is quite calm." [1]

Through the half-open door, he extended his hand to take the mail. Immediately an iron grip caught hold of him and tried to pull him outside. But he braced himself. Then two *fellagha* leaped out of the ditch: Mohamed ag Akada and El Ralem ag Afakou had come to the aid of El Madani, and the three men pulled Charles outside. With all his strength, he called for help, crying that the marabout was being killed:

"Marabout yemmoût!"

Three times he uttered his cry. No one responded.

They bound him, putting his hands behind his back and tying them to his ankles. Thus he was forced to kneel, as if the aggressors had wanted to accord him this last happiness, the posture of prayer. But they thought only to humiliate him and to make it easier to lift him onto a camel. Immobilized, he was thrown on the sand, between the door and the protecting wall.

---

[1] CF, personal notes, in G. Gorrée, *Sur les traces de Charles de Foucauld* (Éd. de la Plus Grande France, 1936), 314.

Lying there, he recognized El Madani and Kerzou as they led the bandits into the fort.

At the same time, two of the attackers were entering the Haratins' hamlet. El Madani had told them where to find Paul Embarek's house, which was off by itself. Guns in hand, they rushed into the hut's single, poorly lit room. Paul was there with his young wife, named Tablalt, which means rifle bullet! She had just nursed her baby. The couple was finishing a meager supper. They remained silent, terrified, convinced they were about to be murdered.

"So, Paul, you're the marabout's servant?"

"Yes."

"Why are you hiding?"

"I'm not hiding. I finish my work at six o'clock."

"Come and see for yourself what's happening in the fort."

"What is happening is God's will."

"That's enough talk, black man. Follow us."

As they were leading him away, a man from the village, Hemmedi, passed by in the distance. Surprised, he called out to them. Paul shouted: "Run! I am in the hands of the others!"

The man fled, the threats of the *fellagha* in his ears. He was going to warn the postman Lazaoui, who was staying in the village. The latter, afraid that Fort Moty had fallen, fled to the north, to go back to In Salah. The terrified Haratins shut themselves up in their houses. No one would venture out to warn Fort Motylinski. Besides, if anyone had wanted to, it would have taken him a whole day to reach the military post on foot, for it was more than thirty miles away. None of the Haratins had a mount, and at the moment there were no Tuareg, either settled or nomadic, in the area.

A few minutes later, Paul, pushed by his attackers but not tied, arrived in front of the *bordj*. It seemed as if they would kill him. But one of the men in the *rezzou*, Mohamed ben Barka, a Targui from Amsel, recognized him. He vouched for him. Embarek was merely the slave of the marabout. A slave should not be executed, any more than a domestic animal!

Under the light of the stars, Paul could make out Brother Charles, kneeling on the ground, silent, as if a stranger to what was happening, surrounded by the shouting mob. Paul tells the story: "They tore his clothes, they spit in his face. Each one of them grabbed a piece, and he rolled into the ditch with them."

They brought him back up to the door. Invectives and blows rained on the now completely powerless man, he who was only compassion and love. Then came the specific questions. "Where is the caravan you were counting on? Where are the soldiers who are supposed to rescue you? Speak, stupid!"

Charles remained silent, staring straight ahead. His lips moved gently. He was praying. He knew that *the hour had come*. "To be as small and poor as was Jesus. Silently, secretly, obscurely, like him. Passing unknown on the earth, like a traveler in the night, disarmed and silent before injustice, like him, the Divine Lamb, I shall endure being shorn and sacrificed without resisting, without speaking, and *the hour come*, I shall imitate him in his way of the Cross and his death." [2]

At a sign from the aggressors, Paul squatted down near the father, to the left of the door. He rolled his eyes in alarm. Shouts from inside could be heard, shouts of joy, savage yells. The pillaging of the *bordj* had begun. The two aggressors who had brought Paul were in a hurry to join the others. They entrusted their prisoners to a very young Targui, a fifteen-year-old Kel Ajjer named Sermi ag Thora, who positioned himself in front of them, his rifle pointed, his eye menacing, but not very sure of himself.

Fellagha came out of the fort loaded with booty: sacks of wheat, cases of cartridges, guns. They loaded the camels, which they had brought up to the door.

The bandits seemed disappointed. Of course, the arms, the ammunition, the food were a blessing from Allah. But where was the marabout's *treasure*, the gold that had been promised them? Furious, they broke everything inside that was not going with them. Books, precious manuscripts were thrown on the floor and trampled. Unbelievable to think of all those thousands of sheets flying about, the pages from the volumes of the dictionary and the collected poetry, all the work Brother Charles had patiently accumulated to make the Tuareg people live again!

Paul heard them say: "If we had found Shikat here, we would have given him what he deserves. We would have turned him into dog food!" [3]

Those not inside were calling the marabout to account. They insulted him. He remained silent, looking at them without hatred. "The danger is in us and not in our enemies. Our enemies can only cause us to be victorious."

They urged him to abjure: "Say the formula! The *shahada*!"

That was the rule. Anyone condemned to death, Christian or pagan, was called upon to say the *shahada*, that is, to renounce his own God and submit to Allah. Paying them no heed, Brother Charles continued his dialogue with Christ. "To elevate our souls, can we imagine any means more tender than the cross, through which each hour is a declaration of love, a proof of pure love in the night?" [4]

[2] *Carnets de Beni-Abbès* (Nouvelle Cité, 1993), June 7, 1904.
[3] Chikat, from the Dag Rali tribe, was a good friend of Charles and was the father of young Ouksem, Charles' guest in France.
[4] CF to Massignon, October 30, 1909.

To frighten him, they threatened him with death. Death? At last! He *knew* he was going to die. They would hear from him only these two words: "*Bâghi n'moût!* It is the hour of my death!"[5]

He closed his eyes. At last, the long-desired moment of joining the Beloved had arrived! "Let us endure all the insults, the blows, the wounds, death, by praying for those who hate us."[6] "Let us embrace suffering, with Jesus as an example, the worst opprobrium and death itself, a bloody death if God so wills, with no other motive and no other purpose than to declare to Jesus that we love him."[7]

He recalled the words he had written on Pentecost 1897, in Nazareth: "Think that you are to die a martyr, stripped of everything, stretched out on the ground, naked, unrecognizable, covered with blood and wounds, violently and painfully killed, and desire that it be today!"[8] And that desire filled him with joy, since "obedience is the consummation of love".

Some of the *fellagha* came out of the *bordj*. In spite of finding no treasure, they were reasonably content. The attack had succeeded, the marabout was a prisoner, and they would get a goodly ransom for him. They congratulated the traitor El Madani, promising him a life of delights in paradise. But it was primarily his pay he was waiting for. They then surrounded Brother Charles and pressed him with questions again.

"Are there soldiers in the country around here?"

"Where are the Fort Moty people?"

"Where is Moussa? In the Aïr or in the Adrar? Speak, stupid!"

Charles remained silent. They put the same questions to Paul, who, convinced they were going to kill him, remained silent too, terrorized.

A Haratin on his way back to the village was walking in the dry bed of the wadi. They grabbed him, roughed him up. He shook with fear.

---

[5] Paul Embarek's eyewitness account, as reported by Lieutenant Vella. This translation and the other one ("I desire death") have been disputed, Paul's accounts at times contradicting each other. Paul first stated that while he was present the marabout said nothing. In 1921 and 1927, he added that *after* the death of Foucauld he had heard the attackers bring up the *chahada*, the formula of abjuration; but in what context? Remarks among themselves to ascertain what to do with the corpse of an "infidel"? It is clear that after his death, the killers considered him a *kaffir* (unbeliever), and they took Paul for an infidel also. It appears that Bishop Nouet went too far in his 1929 interpretation of the marabout's shout as reported by the killers. It was not "I want to die" but rather "The marabout is going to die!", meaning "Come, Lord, to my aid!" Some have also suggested that perhaps Charles was killed because he refused to recant, making him a martyr in the canonical sense in which the Church understands that term. But, as far as we know, nothing supports this suggestion, which only the canonical inquiry is likely to shed light on.

[6] CF, "Méditations sur les saints Évangiles", in *Oeuvres spirituelles* (Nouvelle Cité, 1974–1997), 295ᵉ.

[7] Ibid., 251ᵉ.

[8] CF, "Nazareth", in *Oeuvres spirituelles*, June 6, 1897.

"Are there soldiers in the village?

"Yes, there are two native troopers from Fort Moty."

"Their names?"

"Bou Aïcha and Bou Djema."

"Why are they in Tam?"

"I don't know. They came this morning on business. They are supposed to leave Tam tonight for Fort Moty. Maybe they've left already."

Beuh heard. He was getting nervous.

"Keep watch", he told the sentinels. "And we must not hang around here."

The men objected. They wanted to eat and drink. The animals also had to drink, and it would take some time to draw water from the well.

They went inside to finish pillaging. They stuffed themselves with food, and they found the bottles of sacramental wine; there was no stopping them now.

Outside, under the indifferent stars, Charles and Paul were alone, in front of Sermi ag Thora, the young Targui with the cruel look.

The seemingly calm atmosphere filled Charles with joy. He knew that he was going to die and wanted to take advantage of the unexpected delay to prepare himself for the end. Nothing going on in the fort or around it concerned him any longer, for he was already beyond this world. A tremendous peace came over him. His prayers were finally answered. He was going to die a martyr! His life was a failure, but had he not, in all things, identified with the Beloved?

"When the grain of wheat that falls into the ground does not die, it is alone. But if it dies, it bears much fruit. I am not dead, so I am alone! Pray for my conversion, so that, dying, I may bear fruit." [9]

"O Jesus, you who call us so forcefully to suffering, give me the faith to shape my life to that suffering, a faith that lets me die through penance, through suffering, and, if it is your will, through martyrdom, thus conforming myself to you." [10]

Suddenly, a shout echoed in the night, coming from the sentinels whom Beuh had placed in the area around the fort.

"The Arabs are here!"

As expected, the two native soldiers were stopping by to visit the father before they headed back to Fort Motylinski. Coming from the village, they approached slowly on their swaying camels, unconscious of the danger of death awaiting them. For not one Haratin had had the courage or the opportunity to warn them.

[9] CF to Suzanne Perret, December 15, 1904, in Gorrée, Sur les traces, 321.
[10] CF, "Méditations sur les saints Évangiles", 182.

A silent gesture from Beuh. Ten shots rang out in the night. Bou Aïcha, killed instantly, fell heavily to the ground. Bou Djema was unharmed. He tried to escape, but his camel was hit before it had gone fifty feet. Once on the ground, the man was killed, riddled with bullets and immediately stripped of his weapons and clothes.

Amid the rain of fire, nobody had noticed that the drama was over: Charles de Foucauld was dead!

Paul Embarek's account: "Seeing that the two camel troopers were going to be murdered, the marabout made an instinctive movement to warn them. There was a sharp burst of rifle fire. The Targui who was near him brought the mouth of his rifle near his head and pulled the trigger; the bullet, on a downward path, struck him under the ear. The marabout supported himself with his right hand. He neither moved nor cried out. I did not think he was wounded. It was only a few minutes later that I saw the blood flowing. His body slid down slowly, and he fell on his side. He was dead." [11]

The bullet from Sermi ag Thora's rifle entered below the right ear; it exited through the left eye. The manner of this sudden death could be regarded as symbolic. It is through the ear that Viscount Charles de Foucauld had received the word of God that converted him. It is through the eye that Brother Charles of Jesus entered into eternity by receiving the uncreated light.

"The light! In the clear light of faith, I can make out a thousand new objects of which I formerly knew nothing. Without faith I would still be in the dark, I would be walking in the night, my foot striking a thousand obstacles. Now, faith illuminates those shadows like a blazing sun. With faith the road appears bathed in light and the goal of our journey shines at night in the distance like a great city whose dazzling outer wall sits atop a high mountain." [12]

On exiting the skull, the bullet penetrated the wall of the fort, to the left of the entrance. For many years, the hole would remain visible, until finally the fervent hands of pilgrims had removed every trace of it.

When they saw the body, the bandits realized they had failed. They would not be taking back to Agadez a living, humiliated marabout to serve as a hostage in the political plots of the Senoussi. He had escaped from them. He had entered into the light: "That moment in life: entering into the light, passing from a winter day to a day as brilliant as seven days!" [13]

---

[11] Paul Embarek's account, in R. Bazin, *Charles de Foucauld* (Plon, 1921), 455, and his account of April 19, 1927, included in the proceedings of the judge ordinary, archives of the Postulation.

[12] CF, "Méditations sur les saints Évangiles", 185.

[13] Ibid., 186.

After a few minutes of confusion, they conferred.

"What are we going to do with the body?"

"Let's take it away and hide it. The *roumis* will think we're holding him hostage. There are no witnesses besides Paul."

"What about the other black? And the village? Instead, let's tie the marabout's body to the tree by the wadi near the houses. The dogs will devour it. And let's kill Paul, that black kaffir!"

Just as they were about to execute him, a group of Haratins, probably rallied by Paul's wife, loomed up in the night and begged the aggressors to spare his life, declaring that he had always been a good Muslim. The proof? He had never allowed the marabout to baptize him!

And so, they freed Paul, who never got over having his life saved.

The discussion about the marabout's remains came to a quick end. The majority did not care. Some wanted to take off as quickly as possible with their loot; others wanted to keep celebrating, then wait for daylight to finish pillaging the *bordj*, which was hard to do at night. Perhaps there was some money hidden away.

Beuh made the decision: "Enjoy yourselves! And let each man guard his share of the loot."

Since they had found no meat in the father's stock of food, they went to butcher Bou Aïcha's dead camel, and they cooked it in the courtyard, over a fire made with pieces of Charles' miserable furniture.

They requisitioned the Haratins to draw buckets from the well, water the camels, and bring hay.

Then the *fellagha* spent the night eating and drinking, finally dozing off as a few sentinels stood watch.

Day dawned over Tamanrasset. The sleepers rose and resumed their discussion about what to do with the body. They could not agree, so they left it, naked and bloody, in front of the fort's door

As soon as it was light enough, they continued their systematic pillaging of the *bordj*, but without finding the hoped-for treasure. They loaded up the camels. Nothing they considered valuable was forgotten: canned goods, a few ordinary tools and kitchen utensils, candles, the needles and thread meant for the nomad women, vegetable seeds, some cretonne fabric for making clothes.

Suddenly a cry echoed outside: "On alert!"

They rushed for their weapons. There was a soldier riding a camel. An army man, one of those execrated Arabs from Fort Motylinski, Kouider ben Lakhal, a desert courier. He had come from Fort Moty, carrying the garrison's mail to be posted from In Salah.

He did not suspect anything as yet. All the same, the type of dromedaries outside the *bordj* should have made him wary. The salt caravans resting at the watering place were usually made up of pack camels.

After grabbing their guns, the *fellagha* took up positions in the ditches of the *bordj*. As soon as the camel soldier was within shooting range, they opened fire. But he was still too far away, and they missed. The man turned his mount around and tried to flee. He was going to succeed, alerting Fort Moty!

No. Hit in the hindquarters, the camel let out a heartrending bleat, stopped, wavered, and knelt. Kouider loaded his rifle. But before he could dismount, he was surrounded by a hateful, shouting mob, who fired at his feet and arms. He begged them to spare him, in the name of Allah. A bullet in the head killed him instantly.

The bandits removed his clothes and took them, along with his gear and weapons. They scattered the letters they found in the cloth bag stamped "French Postal Service". Then they went back to the fort, conferred, and, holding their weapons, encircled the village, ordering the terrified Haratins to gather outside. A collective massacre seemed to be in the works.

Paul Embarek's account: "They assembled us on the other side of the fig grove and said: 'The soldier who came this morning, bury him in the Muslim cemetery, since he recited the formula. The others, don't bury them. We had planned to take you with us to Tarhaouhaout to help us (to take possession of Fort Motylinski). But for now, call upon Allah to help us, and then go back to work in your fields. We shall soon return.' The Haratins (relieved) were in a joyful state. They said to each other: 'The French are finished. Imam El Mahdi has come!' " [14]

The sun was now high in the sky. After threatening the Haratins with death if they gave the alarm, the *rezzou* went off into the desert toward Debnat, west of Fort Motylinski.

When Tamanrasset had returned to its customary silence, Paul and the blacks fearfully made their way to the *bordj* and found the now rigid corpse of Charles de Foucauld.

Without untying him, they buried him southeast of the *bordj*, just a few feet from the door, in a ditch they filled with sand; they buried the three Muslim soldiers in the same spot.[15] Remembering that Christians were usually buried in coffins, before they covered the grave, they put around the body some boards from packing crates, a few rocks, and pages from his journal. Then Paul walled up the door of the fort to prevent more pillaging and to preserve the precious manuscripts.

In spite of Paul's version of events, it seems doubtful that the Haratins, whom Brother Charles had so often kept from starving, would have willingly come to terms with the aggressors. After salvaging the Fort Motylinski

[14] Paul Embarek's account, April 19, 1927, proceedings of the Judge Ordinary.
[15] Another account says "sixty feet away, in holes where the clay was dug".

mail, Saïd ben Mesaoud, the village chief, ordered his brother Hameyed and Paul Embarek to start for the military post at nightfall to give the alarm. They would reach the fort on Sunday December 3 at 11 A.M. As for the postman, Lazaoui, he would not reach In Salah to give the alarm until December 8.[16]

One can imagine the turmoil in the little garrison. Captain de La Roche immediately mobilized some of his men (Sergeant Rémiot, a soldier named Dumont, and some Muslim camel troopers) to try to overtake the *rezzou*. After a long search, they caught up with it on December 17, bringing down several men. The others, including Charles de Foucauld's killer and the traitor El Madani, managed to escape. In an abandoned tent, the soldiers found the sandals and a few other things that had belonged to the hermit.

Next, the column headed to Tamanrasset, finally arriving December 21, deeply upset. The captain went first to look at the grave; he set up a cross on the sand over the bodies, gave the dead military honors, but disturbed nothing. Then he went inside the fort, after breaking open the sealed door.

The camel troopers viewed the pillaged *bordj*, the books and writings that lay scattered but unharmed, the notebook on whose flyleaf Charles had written "Live as if I were to die a martyr today", the three letters of December 1, 1916, addressed to Marie de Bondy, Marie de Blic, and Massignon, all sealed and stamped. Spread over the ground were thousands of sheets from the dictionary and the poetry collection. La Roche, devout, picked up the hermit's rosary and the stations of the cross drawn by his own hand. He found in the sand the half-moon of the monstrance containing the consecrated Host from the tabernacle, thrown on the floor by the attackers. With infinite respect Captain de La Roche would take it to Fort Motylinski and entrust it to Sergeant P. d'E., a one-time seminarian, who would then receive Communion.

Charles de Foucauld's last correspondence was mailed. After hearing of the hermit's death, Louis Massignon received his letter on January 27, 1917, while in a trench on the French front. As if rising above himself, with no fear of enemy bullets that might hit him, he stood on the parapet of the snowy trench and shouted, gripped by a holy joy: "Foucauld killed in the Sahara! He has found the passage; he has arrived!" Then, falling back into the trench, he continued: "Through a bizarre exchange, he is killed and I

[16] The attack on the *bordj* and the death of C. de Foucauld have been reconstructed here from the accounts of Paul Embarek, namely, that of December 3, 1916, given to Captain de La Roche, and that of September 1, 1917, given to Captain Depommier; also from what Lieutenant Proust told René Bazin in March 1921 (in Bazin, *Foucauld*, 454, and Gorrée, *Sur les traces*, 315); and lastly, from P. Embarek's statement of February 19, 1927, appearing in "Proceedings of the Judge Ordinary for the Region of Ghardaïa", in *Bulletin des Amitiés*, no. 108, 4–7. With invaluable commentaries supplied us by M. de Suremain and A. Chatelard.

protected."[17] Later, he would add, "He died as the guest, hostage, and ransom of the Ahaggar Muslim."[18]

Weeping, Marie de Bondy opened her letter and read, "How true it is, we shall never love enough!"[19]

Learning of his death, Moussa, who felt that he was indirectly to blame, grieved deeply. He wrote to Marie de Blic on December 13, 1916:

> May the one God be praised!
>
> To Her Ladyship, our friend Marie, sister of Charles our marabout, whom the traitors and deceivers, the people of Ajjer, have murdered. From Tebeul Moussa ag Amastane, *amenokal* of the Ahaggar. May she be kept safe from harm, the Marie herein addressed!
>
> As soon as I learned of the death of our friend, your brother Charles, my eyes were shut. All is darkness for me. I have wept and I have shed many tears and I am in deep mourning. His death has brought me much sorrow. I myself am far from the place where the treacherous thieves and deceivers killed him. They killed him in the Ahaggar, and I myself am in the Adrar. But if God so wishes, we shall kill them, the people who have killed the marabout, until our vengeance is done.
>
> To your daughters, your husband, and your friends, say: "Charles the marabout has not died for you alone, he has also died for us all." May God grant him mercy, and may we meet with him in paradise!
>
> The 20 of Safar 1335, Moussa ag Amastane, *amenokal*.[20]

A year later, December 9, 1917, General Laperrine came to Tamanrasset. He felt he could not follow to the letter Charles de Foucauld's wish to "be buried in the very spot where I shall die", for the ditch would fill with water at the first rain. On December 15 he had the body exhumed, and it was laid to rest in higher ground, some six hundred feet to the west of the *bordj*.

He wrote Marie de Blic: "Your brother was as if mummified, and he could still be recognized. The transfer of his remains has been a most emotional experience."[21]

Writing to Father Villard, he supplied more details: "The bullet that entered behind the right ear exited through the left eye. He was buried in the position in which he was when killed: on his knees, his elbows fastened behind his back. We have had to bury him in that position so as not to break his limbs. We simply wrapped him in a shroud."[22]

Beside him, all that remained of the bodies of three camel troopers were bits of bone. When Laperrine showed his astonishment, one of his native

[17] L. Massignon, *Parole donnée* (Seuil, 1983), 69.
[18] L. Massignon, *Lettre à la Badaliya* (1947), 7.
[19] See the full text of this letter, above, p. 141.
[20] Quoted by M. Carrouges, *Charles de Foucauld, explorateur mystique* (Cerf, 1954), 285.
[21] Laperrine to Marie de Blic, December 1917, in Bazin, *Foucauld*, 469.
[22] Laperrine to Father Villard, December 15, 1917, in ibid.

soldiers, a devout Muslim, said: "It is not surprising, General, he was a great marabout." [23]

So ended the life of the hermit of the Sahara. But was it truly over? On February 24, 1903, he had written to his sister, in his mad desire to identify with Christ: "It is at the hour of his supreme self-annihilation, the hour of his death, that Jesus has done the most good, that he has saved the world." [24]

In 1933, the adventure issuing from the thought of Father de Foucauld began. It continues.

What happened to the murderers? In February 1918, during a French attack against dissidents in which seven men were killed, Second Lieutenant Béjot, from the Agouraï post, came across some objects that had belonged to Father de Foucauld. In 1922, near Ghat, in Tripolitania, a military officer was at the souk and recognized the Targui Sermi ag Thora, arresting him. Taken to the military post at Djanet, the murderer of Charles de Foucauld managed to escape. They pursued him. He was slain after the customary warnings were issued.

The traitor El Madani had better luck. On June 26, 1944, he appeared, as a witness only, before Major Florimont, head of the Ajjer annex, who had reopened the inquiry into the death of the hermit. Although El Madani confessed, he benefited from the statute of limitations and was freed.

[23] Quoted by Bazin, in ibid., 470.
[24] CF to Marie de Blic, February 24, 1903, *Anthologie* (Seuil, 1958), 48.

Afterword

Brother Charles was deeply shaken by a conversation Laperrine reported to him. The hermit had saved the children of a Tuareg woman from starvation. She was wildly grateful, and one day she expressed her feelings to the commander of the Oases: "It is terrible to think that such a good man will go to hell after he dies because he is not a Muslim. So we are praying for his conversion to Islam."

These remarks gave Foucauld a strong lesson in the tolerance that is seen in his last writings. Moreover, around 1908 he began to banish from his mind all temptation toward totalitarianism of the "outside the Church, no salvation" sort. He wrote, "I am here, not to convert, but to try to understand. God will welcome in heaven those who were good and upright, without their needing to be Roman Catholic."[1] From then on, his "mission" was to "look upon every human being as a beloved brother", and he added, "We must do away with the spirit of militancy."[2]

Loyal to this principle, he died as he lived: quietly, neither a hero nor a martyr, "murdered out of confusion", writes J.-F. Six,[3] by some small-time thieves come to rob him. And because of that, neither his country nor his Church nor any religious order can take up his death—so banal, so ordinary—to make of him a hero with his name engraved on a stele. No "field of honor" for the man who so boldly wrote: "Honor, let's leave that for those who desire it . . ."

Even today, his devotion puts some off. We have to go beyond the clichés of pretty religious statues to reach the pure jewel of evangelical simplicity that glowed in his heart. "He is a Saint Francis of Assisi for our time."[4] His great merit is that, having found through divine grace the secret of happiness (the contemplation of the living God), he deliberately renounced that happiness to serve his fellowman and lead him to that same love. In doing so, he believed in a model, Christ, and in a book, the Gospel.

After his conversion, once he had given up the idea of the buried contemplative life, he could have become a classic missionary, one of those

[1] Quoted by L. Lehureau, *Au Sahara avec le père de Foucauld* (Algiers: Baconnier, 1944), 115.

[2] CF to J. Hours, January 9, 1912.

[3] J.-F. Six, *L'Aventure de l'amour de Dieu* (Seuil, 1993), 325.

[4] Ibid.

admirable White Fathers he knew in Africa. But such was not his vocation. Determined to follow to the letter the life of Christ, he went to live among the poorest and dared to gamble on converting them through nothing more than the example of his hidden life and the disinterested love he showed them. "The sanctification of the peoples of this region is in my hands. They will be saved if I become a holy person", he noted in the resolutions he made upon arriving in Beni Abbès. His life was made up of little kindnesses, subtly showing the love that the most ordinary creatures inspired in him, "seeing that no soul was wounded, no matter how slightly" (Massignon).

But why the desert then? He was drawn to it, fascinated, after his service in Algeria and his exploration of southern Morocco. By its nature the desert is the place where the spirit feels closest to its Creator: "I will lead her into the wilderness: and I will speak to her heart" (Hos 2:14b). Also perhaps because he felt himself, wished himself, "small". He had chosen the desert and the humble Haratin village as the perfect laboratory for the experiment in the gift of love that he wished to try and to which his particular vocation had called him. Far from the world's major ideologies and the Vatican's strategies, he humbly put into practice in the here and now the evangelical life, the hidden life of Jesus in Nazareth, instead of being satisfied with proclaiming its principles. He knew that time was needed before men could change, before they would become converted. "It will take centuries", he admitted without pessimism, knowing that for God time does not exist.

René Bazin tells us, "He has shown the way. He has been the monk without a monastery, the master without a disciple, the penitent who sustained in solitude the hope for a time he was not to see." [5]

Thus he is more than a founder. "He is the initiator of a whole missionary and spiritual movement" (H. Didier). He invented a monasticism without cloister. He was successful at contemplation and apostolic action; he managed to fit in to the human condition—in its most ordinary aspects, always, and at times in its most suffering—all the while preserving that part of the inner life turned toward God, which is the sole grandeur of the human condition. He showed that one can be alone with God and at the same time be committed to man. He called for humility and poverty in the priest and equality between the choir monk and the lay monk. He showed that it is possible to preach silently, that the true apostolate is that of example, coming before that of speech. He prepared a place for laymen in evangelization.

His life was a perpetual tearing away. He gave up a beloved family, and it

---

[5] R. Bazin, *Charles de Foucauld* (Plon, 1921), 472.

must not be forgotten how much they did for him. Though a hermit, he was also to welcome visitors, feed them, care for them. Though a priest, he wanted to remain as humble as a lay brother. Though a cloistered monk, he was constantly leaving the walls behind, in the name of charity, to travel. Though an intellectual, he worked with his hands. Though an aristocrat, he effaced himself to the point of becoming the servant for a convent of humble nuns; later, in the desert, he served slaves and soldiers. Although he loved simplicity, he bravely faced theological studies in Rome. He gave up saying Mass to go into the desert alone. *He let Jesus do with him what he would.*

Initially concerned about literary fame, he effaced himself to the point of letting his writings appear under the name of another (Motylinski). Having failed while he lived, he joyfully left for those who wish to follow his path the tangible benefits of what he did. Above all, "his faith is astounding" (Six).

Being a universal brother, he realized the ideal of Thérèse de Lisieux, "To love is to give all and to give oneself", by a radical means, following in the footsteps of Jesus. By his extreme example, he encouraged a new interest in the solitary life of the hermit. René Voillaume reminds us that, after Charles died, "Groups of all kinds have found strength and life in his spirituality. Laymen, secular priests, monks, and nuns have found a renewal of their vocation through contact with this soul so nobly faithful to the Scriptures." [6]

As a true contemplative, at the same time totally committed to others, particularly those most suffering; so near to God; so close to the poor—he has provided an example of faithfulness, even unto martyrdom.

---

[6] E. Voillaume, in the preface to G. Gorrée, *Charles de Foucauld* (Chalet, 1957). (See Appendix 1 on the fraternities.)

Appendices

Charles de Foucauld is a man who never stops being born.
He will be seen in the future
as one of the most truly spiritual Frenchmen of this century
and probably as a saint.

—Jean Guitton
of the Académie Française
Portraits et circonstances.

1. Charles de Foucauld's Spiritual Family

As we have seen in this book, the thinking of Foucauld the founder, which began in the Cistercian house at Cheiklé in 1896, continued to evolve while adjusting to practical realities. The 1896 plan pushed asceticism to limits beyond ordinary human nature. It was suitable only for hermits such as those who lived in the deserts of Syria and Egypt back in the sixth century. Father Huvelin firmly opposed such excesses, so foreign to traditional monastic life.

The 1899 plan, with its slight modifications, was no less unworkable, "conceived for who knows what society of angels" (Barrat).

With no success in recruiting disciples—the living conditions at Tamanrasset being so unusual—Foucauld gave up on strict obedience to his prescripts but kept the spirit of his rule. He explains in a diary entry, July 22, 1905: "Follow the regulations without making adherence a strict duty. The objective is the life of Nazareth in its breadth and simplicity. Your life of Nazareth can be led anywhere: lead it in the place where it is most beneficial to your fellowman."

Foucauld always remained firm as to the basic principles. He wrote to Father Antonin on May 13, 1911: "Large monasteries assume a worldly importance inimical to humility and abjection."

On his own among the inhabitants of the village, he agreed to do "apostolic work" in their service. Charity was his law.

In the same vein, he turned his concerns toward laymen, the Christians of France, to increase their awareness of the need to convert populations not reached by the gospel. He wrote: "God will never allow all those who love him to enter the religious life. He will give some of them the mission of living in the sanctity of marriage, in the midst of society, providing an example of virtue and carrying on an apostolate that priests cannot, bringing the light of Christianity into circles the priest enters rarely or not at all." [1]

That is why, starting in 1909, he had envisioned an association, the Union of Brothers and Sisters of the Sacred Heart, which Bishop Livinhac, superior general of the White Fathers, would characterize as a "great and holy enterprise". At Charles' death, this fragile structure would have only forty-nine members, among them Louis Massignon, who in 1928 published the Directory for the group.

But what can be said about those devoted to the religious life, "little brothers" and "little sisters" wishing to revive the rule of 1899?

Here again, Foucauld proved revolutionary in his concept of monachism. While respecting the traditional prescripts of the priesthood and monasticism (poverty, chastity, obedience), for his little brothers and sisters he asked the relinquishing of the then-practiced separation between choir monks and lay monks. He also rejected the idea of collective community property, which created such a feeling of security. He offered a new form of apostolate, one of example, extreme poverty, and holiness, rather than one of preaching (although he never criticized priests and monks who did preach). In the face of a Church sometimes pompous and triumphalist, he offered a humble clerical model based on the true evangelical values of love-charity, which gives all.

Which leads to an obligation to work with the hands and take on the work of the poorest class in the chosen country. In this, Foucauld is the precursor of the worker priests and the working missionary nuns. He destroys the traditional image of the contemplative monk or nun separated from the world and that of the priest as bureaucrat of the faith. The member of an order, priest or not, is envisioned by Foucauld as first of all the universal brother immersed in the mass of the poor, and poor himself. This ideal in no way implies criticism of traditional monks and priests. It is a different vocation, complementary, the need for which Foucauld sensed in his world in evolution, which heralded the Third World of the poor and the outcast.

---

[1] CF to Massignon, January 1, 1914.

This change in role brings with it a risk, of which Foucauld himself was the victim: living with the poor and doing the same work they do, there is the danger of being overwhelmed by material obligations. It is a choice, meant for the strong who are called upon to assume it, the sought-after ideal being to find God and contemplate him amid a mass of often hostile unbelievers, while at the same time doing difficult, humble, and servile work.

The First Fraternities

When Charles de Foucauld died in 1916, only one of his projects had materialized: the Association (Union). It brought together priests, monks and nuns, and laymen.

In 1917, with the help of Louis Massignon, who published some excerpts from the *Directoire*, the Association expanded, approved by the Church. It published a monthly newsletter. In 1921 René Bazin's biography, requested by Massignon, was published by Plon, and its great success led to the creation of the "legend of Father de Foucauld". Today the book gives off a slightly musty odor of what appears to us colonialism and nationalism, but it reflects the taste of the time and the aftermath of the great 1918 military victory.

In spite of a certain verbosity, this remarkable book moved countless readers, among them a seminarian of the great seminary at Issy-les-Moulineaux, René Voillaume, who imparted his enthusiasm to some of his fellow seminarians, with the encouragement of Bishop Weber, their superior.

In 1923, René Bazin published *Écrits spirituels*, an anthology of Foucauld's meditations and excerpts from his notebooks. The complete text of the *Directoire* was published in 1928. The 1920s also saw the appearance of the first disciple-hermits: Father Henrion in southern Tunisia and Father Peyriguère in southern Morocco.

In 1933 the first community was created, the Petits Frères du Sacré-Coeur, in El Abiodh Sidi Sheikh, in the Sahara (South Oranais). The group formed around René Voillaume included Georges Gorrée (who has furnished us with much unpublished material) and other "brothers of solitude". The same year saw the formation of the Petites Soeurs du Sacré-Coeur (in white) in Montpellier. In 1936 Sister Magdeleine founded the non-cloistered Petites Soeurs de Jésus (in blue) in Algeria and, later, in Tubet (Provence). Many other religious and lay fraternities followed.

In 1956 René Voillaume founded in the Aix-en-Provence diocese the Petits Frères de l'Évangile, then, in 1963, the Petites Soeurs. He sums up his rich experience by saying: "We are almost astonished at having been led so far by a man who taught us no spiritual doctrine or bequeathed us any special tasks to carry out other than to adore the Blessed Sacrament and to take the gospel seriously in our daily life. It is precisely this silence in speech and this severity that fulfill our expectations. For each of us, Brother Charles is a witness who does not let us rest and who unceasingly urges us to take seriously the demands of the gospel." [2]

The fraternities born from the thinking of Charles de Foucauld are flourishing in the world today. This is indeed the wheat grown tall, sprouting from a seed buried in the Saharan sand in 1916. To give just one example, when Sister Magdeleine died in 1991, her foundation had fourteen hundred members of sixty nationalities.

1. Congregations and Associations connected with Charles de Foucauld (as of June 30, 1995, listed in the order in which they were created, the figure in parentheses indicating the number of countries with foundations).[3]

— 1933 in Montmartre and El Abiodh Sidi Sheikh (Algeria): Petits Frères de Jésus (46). Founded by René Voillaume.
— 1933 in Montpellier. Petites Soeurs du Sacré-Coeur (8). Founded by Sister Magdeleine.
— 1950 in Belgium and France. Lay fraternities, in 1955 consolidated into the association known as the Fraternité Séculière Charles de Jésus (29).
— 1951 in Tubet (Bouches-du-Rhône). Priestly fraternity, Jesus Caritas (51).
— 1952 in Ars (Ain). Sisterhood, Jesus Caritas (23).
— 1955 in Beni Abbès. Sodalité Charles de Foucauld (52). Founded by Louis Massignon.
— 1956 in Sambuc (Bouches-du-Rhône). Petits Frères de l'Évangile (20).
— 1963 in Santa-María (Venezuela). Petites Soeurs de l'Évangile (10).
— 1966 in Gand (Belgium). Petites Soeurs de Nazareth (6).
— 1968 in Montserrat (Spain). Comunidad de Jesús.
— 1969 in Foligno (Italy). Communità Jesus Caritas.
— 1976 in Haiti. Petits Frères de l'Incarnation.
— 1977 in Bangui (Central African Republic). Petites Soeurs du Coeur de Jésus.
— 1980 in Quebec. Petits Frères de la Croix (2).

[2] Preface to J.-F. Six's book *Itinéraire spirituel de Charles de Foucauld* (Seuil, 1958), 8.
[3] According to Father Pierre Moitel, in *Jesus Caritas*.

— 1985 in Haiti. Petites Soeurs de l'Incarnation.
— 1991 in Nay (Pyrénées-Atlantiques). Fraternité C. de Foucauld (22).

Altogether, eleven religious congregations and seven associations, or eighteen families (339 fraternities, counting all the branches) consolidated since 1955 under the label Association Générale des Fraternités du Frère Charles de Foucauld.

There is an international quarterly sponsored by the eighteen families: *Jesus Caritas.*

2. Religious Congregations (in 1997),

Paris and the surrounding area
—Petites Soeurs du Sacré-Coeur, 38, rue Albert-Thomas, 10ᵉ.
—Petites Soeurs de l'Évangile, 23, rue Villot, 93120 La Courneuve.
—Petites Soeurs de Nazareth, 34, rue Doudeauville, 18ᵉ.
—Petits Frères de Jésus, 20, rue Pierre-Leroux, 7ᵉ.

In the provinces
—Petites Soeurs de Jésus (motherhouse), Le Tubet, 13090 Aix-en-Provence.

Outside France
—Comunità Jesus Caritas, Foligno (Italy).
—Comunidad de Jesús, Barcelona (Spain).
—Petits Frères de l'Évangile, rue de Robiana, 6, 1013 Brussels.
—Picole Sorelle di Gesù (headquarters), Via di Aque Salvie 2, Tre Fontane, 00142 Rome.
—Petits Frères de la Croix, 4880 Lionel-Groulx, Saint-Augustin de Desmaures, Quebec, Canada.
—Petits Frères de la Croix, 125, Sentier de la Sainte-Montagne, Sainte-Agnès-de-Charlevoix, Quebec, Canada
—Petits Frères et Petites Soeurs de l'Incarnation, Haiti.
—Petites Soeurs du Coeur de Jésus, Central African Republic.

And so forth, a number of congregations creating fraternities in various parts of the world.

3. Associations.
—Jesus Caritas (fraternity of priests). Publishes the review *Jesus Caritas,* 44, Cité de Fleurs 75017 Paris.
—Jesus Caritas (fraternity for unmarried laymen).
—Fraternité Séculière Charles de Jésus.

—Sodalité Charles de Foucauld, 127, rue Notre-Dame-des-Champs 75006 Paris (Coordinator, Father J.-F. Six).
—Groupe Charles de Foucauld, "Barre", 47240 Bon-Encontre.

4. Nondenominational Association
—Amitiés Charles de Foucauld, 7, rue Vauquelin 75005 Paris (to make Charles de Foucauld better known and to support the cause of beatification). Publishes a quarterly newsletter, *Les Amitiés Charles de Foucauld*. Director, Father Pierre Sourisseau.

2. Chronology

1858	September 15. Birth of Charles de Foucauld, Strasbourg.
1859	*War against Austria. Victory of Solferino. Darwin publishes* Origin of Species.
1860	*Unification of Italy. Nice and Savoy go to France. U.S. Civil War.*
1864	Death of his mother, followed by that of his father. Charles is taken in by his grandparents, the Morlets. *Pius IX condemns Modernism.*
1867	*Marx publishes* Das Kapital. *Birth of Germany (Kaiser Wilhelm I and Bismarck).*
1869	*Suez Canal opens.*
1870	*End of the pope's temporal power.*
1870–1871	*Franco-Prussian War. Defeat of France. End of the Empire. Occupation. Loss of Alsace-Lorraine. The Third Republic.*
1871	Flight of the Morlets and the Foucaulds to Nancy.
1871–1874	At the lycée in Nancy.
1873	*The great pilgrimages. Building of Sacré-Coeur in Montmartre. Invention of the typewriter.*
1874–1875	Charles studies with the Jesuits in Paris. Loses his faith.
1875	*Verlaine converted: "Dear God, you have wounded me with love!"*
1876	*Bell invents the telephone.*
1876–1878	Charles is a cadet at Saint-Cyr.
1877	*Invention of the phonograph and the electric lamp.*
1878	Death of his guardian, Colonel de Morlet.
1878–1879	At the cavalry school in Saumur.
1879	*Conquest of the Sahara begins.*
1879–1880	Second lieutenant in the Fourth Hussars, Pont-à-Mousson.

1880	Stationed at Sétif (Algeria).
1880	*Decree against teaching by religious communities. Establishment of free and compulsory public schooling on the primary level.*
1881	*Rebellion of Bou Amama in the South Oranais. Flatters mission destroyed. Tunisia is occupied and becomes a French protectorate.*
1881	Charles, put on leave for disobedience, retreats to Évian. Reinstated at his request, fights in Algeria with African Fourth Infantry.
1882	Resigns from army to explore Morocco.
1883–1884	Exploration of Morocco.
1885	*Rabies vaccine (Pasteur).*
1885	Charles in Algiers. Becomes interested in the Sahara.
1886	*Freud begins practicing psychoanalysis in Vienna.*
1886	Foucauld moves into a Paris apartment, 50 rue de Miromesnil. Conversion in the Saint-Augustin Church (October 29 or 30).
1888–1889	Pilgrimage to the Holy Land. Retreats at Solesmes, Soligny, and Notre-Dame-des-Neiges. Publishes *Reconnaissance au Maroc.*
1890	*Catholics rally to the Third Republic at the urging of Leo XIII and Bishop Lavigerie.*
1890	Charles a novice at Notre-Dame-des-Neiges (Brother Albéric).
1890	Novice at the Trappist monastery in Cheiklé (Akbès, Syria).
1892	Provisional Cistercian vows. Turning over of all his worldly goods to his sister.
1893	*First gasoline-powered vehicle (Albert Dion).*
1893	Thinks for the first time of founding a monastic community.
1894	*Hersing discovers the plague bacillus.*
1895	*Discovery of radioactivity. First motion picture.*
1896	First rule of the Little Brothers of Jesus.
1896	Theological studies in Rome.

1897   *Branly and Marconi invent the wireless.*

1897   The Cistercians release Foucauld from his vows. Second trip
            to the Holy Land. Servant for the Poor Clares of Nazareth.

1898   *The Dreyfus Affair divides France.*

1898   *Écrits spirituels.* Stay with the Poor Clares of Jerusalem. Mother
            Élisabeth invites him to become their chaplain.

1899   *Metro opens in Paris.*

1899   Rule of the Hermits of the Sacred Heart. Constitution of the
            Little Brothers of Jesus.

1900   Plan to purchase land for a community on the Mount of
            Beatitudes. Rome. Return to France. Preparation for priest-
            hood at Notre-Dame-des-Neiges. *Planck: quantum theory.*

1901   Ordained priest of the diocese of Viviers. *Passage of laws expel-
            ling religious communities.*

1901   October 29. Begins life in Beni Abbès.

1902   Foucauld fights against slavery. The army subdues the Tuareg
            (Battle of Tit). Laperrine pacifies the Sahara.

1903   Rebellion in southern Morocco, *rezzous.* Charles goes to the
            wounded in Taghit. Meets Laperrine. *Russo-Japanese War. First
            flight: Wright brothers.*

1904   First pacification tour with Laperrine. Translation of the Gos-
            pels into Tamasheq. *Pius X opposes Modernism.*

1905   *Méditations sur les Évangiles.* Second pacification tour. Takes up
            residence in Tamanrasset, August 11. *Laws on the sepa-
            ration of Church and state. Einstein's theory of relativity. Mendel's
            genetics.*

1906   *French protectorate in Morocco, which is pacified by Lyautey.* Charles
            in Beni Abbès. Meets Lyautey. Fails in search for a companion
            (Brother Michel).

1907   In Salah. Establishment of a small hermitage. Death of Moty-
            linksi. Visit to the Iforas with Dinaux.

1908   In Tamanrasset, ill. The pope authorizes him to say Mass with-
            out a server. He discovers Assekrem. Laperrine builds Fort
            Motylinski. Completes the anthology of Tuareg poetry.

1909   Stay in France. Foucauld invites Louis Massignon to Taman-rasset. Accompanies Laperrine on tour. Assekrem. *Beatification of Joan of Arc.*

1910   Accompanies Laperrine on tour. Building of hermitage at Assekrem, 8950 feet. Moussa sees France. Laperrine leaves. Father Huvelin and Bishop Guérin die. *French Algeria has a population of 760,000 European colonists and 4,700,000 Muslims and Jews.*

1911   Stay in France. Failure to find companions. Famine in Tamanrasset. *Italy annexes Turkish Tripolitania. Franco-German Agadir crisis.*

1912   *The Turks declare holy war. Conquest of Morocco by Gouraud, Lyautey, and Mangin.*

1913   Stay in France with young Ouksem. Massignon gives up.

1914   *War in Europe. Battle of the Marne.* Foucauld ill (scurvy and fevers). *The French colonies: 6,200,000 square miles; 48,000,000 inhabitants (600,000 soldiers for France). Panama Canal opens.*

1915   Desert battles around Djanet and Moroccan *rezzous* to the southwest. Charles builds his Tamanrasset fort to protect the population against pillagers. *Battle of the Dardanelles.*

1916   *Battles of Verdun, Jutland, and the Somme. Lyautey appointed minister of war.* Fighting in the Sahara for Djanet. Foucauld moves into the fort.

1916   December 1, Foucauld murdered by a Senoussi *rezzou* at the gate of his fort.

1917–1918   Recalled to the Sahara, Laperrine restores order, with Moussa.

1917   December 15, Laperinne has Foucauld's body exhumed. Later he will be buried in El Golea, his heart staying in Tamanrasset.

1919   With approval from Bishop Amette, the cardinal of Paris, the Union des Frères et Soeurs du Sacré-Coeur becomes the Association Foucauld, at the instigation of Louis Massignon, teacher at the Collège de France. Massignon plays decisive role in preserving Foucauld's memory.

1920   Death of Laperinne, death of Moussa.

1921   Appearance of René Bazin's *Charles de Foucauld*, published by Plon. Admiral Malcor and Father Henrion, on becoming priests, adopt the habit of Charles de Foucauld.

1920–1930   Creation of several brotherhoods inspired by Father de Foucauld.

1922   His murderer is executed. Death of Marie de Blic.

1926   Near Ghardaïa and in southern Morocco Fathers de Chatouville and Peyriguère adopt the life of Foucauld.

1927   Cause of beatification begins.

1928   Massignon publishes Foucauld's *Directoire* (regulations of the Association).

1934   Death of Marie de Bondy.

1967   On March 26, Paul VI holds Foucauld up as an example, "the universal brother, model of charity".

1983   On September 12, John Paul II holds him up as an example because of "the holiness of his daily life".

2001   On April 24, John Paul II declares him venerable.

2005   On November 13, Benedict XVI declares him blessed.

2020   On May 27, Francis I clears the way for his canonization.

2021   On May 26, Charles de Foucauld is canonized by Francis I.

3. Father de Foucauld's Prayer

My Father,
I abandon myself to you.
Make of me what you will.

Whatever you make of me,
I thank you.
I am ready for everything
I accept everything.

Provided that your will be done in me,
In all your creatures,
I desire nothing else, Lord.

I put my soul in your hands,
I give it to you, Lord,
With all the love in my heart,
Because I love you,
And because it is for me a need of love
To give myself,
To put myself in your hands unreservedly,
With infinite trust.

For you are my Father.[1]

---

[1] "Méditations sur l'Évangile", in *Écrits spirituels*, 29. Also see page 312, above.

Bibliography

Works of Charles de Foucauld

With the exception of *Reconnaissance au Maroc*, Foucauld had asked that nothing be published under his name, a wish inspired by humility. He was referring only to his linguistic works; he had never envisioned the publication of his spiritual writings. His beneficiaries have believed that this proscription should be ignored, and, because of that, his extensive writings (more than ten thousand pages) have not been scattered and consigned to oblivion. The beneficiary of his spiritual writings is the Société des Pères blancs (the White Fathers, missionaries in Africa), whom Foucauld had designated as heir; the order has entrusted these works and the responsibility for their diffusion to the Association Charles de Jésus, which has led to numerous editions, listed in detail below. Publishers include Plon, Arthaud, la Colombe, de Gigord, Desclée, le Seuil, and Nouvelle Cité. Other materials, unpublished, are in the hands of the Association Charles de Foucauld and the Postulation for beatification, which is the ultimate possessor of the mansucripts.

Letters are, of course, the property of the recipients, who have transmitted them to a number of editors. Some correspondence remains unpublished.

1. Secular Works

Reconnaissance au Maroc. Challamel, 1888. Éditions d'Aujourdhui, 1985.
Carnet de Beni-Abbès, 1902–1905. Nouvelle Cité, 1993.
Carnets de Tamanrasset, 1905–1916. Nouvelle Cité, 1986.
Poésies touarègues. Leroux, 1925.
Textes touareg en prose. Édisud, 1984.
Dictionnaire touareg-français. Algiers: A. Basset, 1918–1920.
Grammaire touarègue. Algiers: A. Basset, 1918–1920.
Dictionnaire abrégé. Algiers: A. Basset, 1918–1920.

2. Spiritual Works

Statuts de l'Association des frères et soeurs du Sacré-Coeur de Jésus. Algiers, 1909.
Écrits spirituels de Charles de Foucauld. Introduction by R. Bazin. Gigord, 1923:
——. "Méditations sur les saints Évangiles" (1896).
——. "Retraite à Nazareth" (1897).

———. "Huit jours à Éphrem" (1898).

———. "Retraites à Beni-Abbès" (1902–1904).

———. "Correspondance diverse".

Directoire de l'Association des frères et soeurs de Jésus. Introduction by L. Massignon. Paris, 1928. *Règlement et directoire*. Nouvelle Cité, 1995.

L'Évangile présenté aux pauvres du Sahara. Bulletin of the Association C. de Foucauld, 1930. Arthaud, 1938.

Notre Modèle (or *Le Modèle unique*). Introduction by L. Massignon. Cairo, 1917. Publiroc, 1935.

Nouveaux écrits spirituels. Introduction by P. Coudray with a letter from Paul Claudel to Pius XII. Plon, 1950:

———. "Lecture des saints Évangiles, selon S. Matthieu".

———. "Considérations sur les fêtes de l'année".

———. "Méditations sur les saints Évangiles".

———. "Correspondance diverse".

Méditations sur le Pater. Bénédictines de Meudon, 1952.

Pensées et maximes. La Colombe, 1953.

Miscellanous writings. Introduction by Gorrée in *C. de Foucauld intime*, 1952; and by Barrat in *Charles de Foucauld et la fraternité*, 1955. Includes dates, vows, promises, resolutions.

Anthologie des oeuvres spirituelles de Charles de Foucauld. Collected and introduced by Denise Barrat. Seuil, 1958. Meditations, feast days, 1901–1906 diary, monastic foundations and rules, notes and retreats, slavery, letters.

Contemplation. Beauchesne, 1969. Meditations on prayer, faith, and the Gospels.

Oeuvres spirituelles de Charles de Foucauld. 16 vol. Introduction by Msgr. Jacqueline. 131, rue Castagnary, Paris: Nouvelle Cité, 1974–1997:

———. *Méditations sur l'Ancien Testament* (1896). *Sur les psaumes et les prophètes* (1897). *Extraits de l'Écriture. Petites notes sur la Bible. Méditation sur le Pater*.

———. *Méditations sur les passages des saintes Évangiles relatifs à quinze vertus* (1897–1898).

———. *Méditations sur l'imitation de N.-S., l'amour du prochain, la pauvreté et l'abjection* (1897-1898). *Essai pour tenir compagnie à N.-S. Jésus*.

———. *Considération sur les fêtes de l'année*. 1987.

———. *La Dernière Place*. 1974. Retreat in the Holy Land.

———. *Le Voyageur dans la nuit*. 1979. Spiritual notes, 1916, and letters to Father Huvelin.

———. *Carnet de Beni-Abbès, 1902–1905*.

———. *Carnets de Tamanrasset, 1905–1916*.

———. *Lettres à un ami de lycée*. 1982. Correspondence with G. Tourdes, 1874–1915.

——. *L'Esprit de Jésus*. Meditations on the Gospels, 1898–1915.
——. *Crier l'Évangile*. Retreat at Ephraim in the Holy Land in 1898. Choice made in Nazareth, 1900.
——. *Seul avec Dieu*. Retreat at Notre-Dame-des-Neiges, 1900–1901. Retreats in the Sahara, 1902 to 1905 and 1909.

3. Letters

À Henri de Castries. Nouvelle Revue des jeunes, 1931. Grasset, 1938.
À mère Saint-Michel, abbesse des clarisses de Nazareth. Éd. Saint-Paul, 1946.
À Mgr. Caron. Bonne Presse, 1947.
Lettres inédites du général Laperrine. La Colombe, 1955.
À l'abbé Huvelin. Introduction by J.-F. Six. DDB, 1957.
Lettres et carnets. Le Seuil, 1966.
À Marie de Bondy. DDB, 1966.
Lettres à mes frères de la Trappe. Cerf, 1969.
Lettres à un ami de lycée. Nouvelle Cité, 1982. Correspondence with G. Tourdes, 1874–1915.
L'Aventure de l'amour de Dieu, quatre-vingt lettres de Foucauld à L. Massignon. Introduction by Father Six. Seuil, 1993.
Cette Chère dernière place. Introduction by P. Sourisseau and A. Robert. Cerf, 1991. Miscellaneous letters, mostly dealing with Trappist matters.

In addition, in a number of the early biographies there appear unpublished letters, and many of these have also been used by later writers. In Bazin, 1921, and Pottier (*Vocation saharienne*), letters to Maunoir, Dinaux, Lacroix, Lyautey, Nieger, Regnault, and Duveyrier; Castillon de Perron, 1982, to Marie de Bondy; Gorrée (*Traces*, mostly Marie de Bondy and Marie de Blic); Gorrée (*Amitiés sahariennes*), mostly to military officers Laperrine, Sigoney, and Duclos.

Similarly, many unpublished letters have appeared in journals. In *Cahiers Charles de Foucauld*, correspondence with Dom Martin, Bishop Guérin and the White Fathers, J. Hours; in *L'Appel du Hoggar*, to Fathers Jérôme, Antonin, and Augustin, and to S. Perret.

Books about Charles de Foucauld

André, Marie. *L'Ermite du désert, Charles de Foucauld*. Apostolat de la prière, 1937.
——. *Charles de Foucauld*. Casterman, 1954.

Barrat, Denise, and Robert Barrat. *Charles de Foucauld et la fraternité*. Seuil, 1958.

Bauchard, R. *Le Père de Foucauld et le marquis de Morès à l'école de cavalerie de Saumur*. Saumur, 1947.

Bazin, René. *Charles de Foucauld*. Plon, 1921.

Béjot, Lieutenant. *Au Sahara, l'assassinat du père du Foucauld*. Aubanel, 1929.

Bernard, Augustin. *Un Saint français, le père de Foucauld*. Plon, 1917. The first biography.

Blanchet, A. *Message et spiritualité du père de Foucauld*. Gigord, 1951.

Boissieu, De. *Le Père Charles de Foucauld, étude d'une conversion*. Perrin, 1945.

Bodley, R. V. C. *Le Désert était son chemin*, Laffont, 1955.

Borel, J. *Le Hoggar, sur les pas de Charles de Foucauld*. Claire Vie.

Boucher. *La Vie héroïque de Charles de Foucald*. Bloud et Gay, 1931.

Carrouges, Michel. *Charles de Foucauld, explorateur mystique*. Cerf, 1954.

———. *Charles de Foucauld devant l'Afrique du Nord*. Cerf, 1961.

———. *Le Père de Foucauld et les fraternités d'aujourd'hui*. Centurion, 1963.

Castillon du Perron, Marguerite. *Charles de Foucauld*. Grasset, 1982.

Charbonneau. *La Destinée paradoxale de Charles de Foucauld*. Paris, 1958.

Chauleur, Sylvestre. *Charles de Foucauld et mère Saint-Michel*. Éd. Saint-Paul, 1946.

Coudray. *Charles de Foucauld*. Chaix, 1949.

Cristiani. *Pèlerin de l'absolu*. Mediapol, 1972.

Crozier, A. *Un Apôtre du Sahara*. Saint-Paul, 1914.

Dalle, S. *Le Père de Foucauld*. Champrosay, 1942.

Debouté, Eugénie. *Charles de Foucauld, le frère universel*. Mediapol, 1991.

Deloncle, P. *Charles de Foucauld le prédéstiné*. Rebout, 1946.

Dermine, J. *La Vie spirituelle du père de Foucauld*. Desclée, 1934.

Didier, Hugues. *Petite Vie de Charles de Foucauld*. DDB, 1993.

Doncoeur, P. *À la suite du père de Foucauld*. Paris, 1942.

Duchène. *Le Père Charles de Jésus*. Algiers, 1918.

Du Jeu, S. *Vie extraordinaire de Charles de Foucauld*. Toulouse, 1930.

Duparc. *Le Père de Foucauld, apôtre des sables*. Dardelet, 1942.

Francheschi, G. *Charles de Foucauld*. Buenos Aires, 1950.

Gallieni, H. R. *L'Ermite du désert*. Klotz, 1933.

Ganne, Gilbert. *Tamanrasset ou le désert fertile*. SOS, 1975.

Gautier, E. F. *Figures de conquêtes coloniales*. Payot, 1931.

———. *Laperrine et le père de Foucauld*, Payot, 1931.

Gorrée, G. *Sur les traces de Charles de Foucauld*. Éd. de la Plus Grande France, 1936.

———. *Au service du Maroc, Charles de Foucauld*. Grasset, 1938.

———. *Les Amitiés sahariennes du père de Foucauld*. Arthaud, 1946.

———. *Charles de Foucauld intime.* La Colombe, 1952.

———. *Charles de Foucauld.* Chalet, 1957. Commemorative volume for centennial of Foucauld's birth.

Guillon, Charles. *La Vie heroïque du père de Foucauld.* Paris, 1933.

Hérisson, Robert. *Avec le père de Foucauld et le général de Laperrine.* Plon, 1937.

Jauffrès. *Un Moderne Père du désert, Charles de Foucauld.* Annonay, 1917.

Jifé. *Charles de Foucauld.* Dupuis, 1959. Comic book.

Joergensen, J. *Charles de Foucauld.* Beauchesne, 1941.

Julia. *Charles de Foucauld, le moine sans clôture.* Bonne Presse, 1948.

Lacharrière, J.-L. de. *Au Maroc en suivant Charles de Foucauld.* Sté. d'Éditions géographiques, 1932.

Lefranc. *Vie du père de Foucauld.* Albin Michel, 1948.

Lehureau, Léon. *Au Sahara avec le père de Foucauld.* Algiers: Baconnier, 1944.

Lepetit, Charles. *Plus loin sur la piste.* Cerf, 1981.

Lesourd, Paul. *La Vraie Figure du père de Foucauld.* Flammarion, 1933.

Lyautey, Pierre. *Charles de Foucauld.* Éd. Universitaires, 1966.

Marchon, B. *Charles de Foucauld.* Centurion, 1985.

Mauger, P. *Le Père de Foucauld à N.-D.-des-Neiges.* Lyon, 1946.

Merad, Ali. *Charles de Foucauld et l'Islam.* Chalet, 1967.

Nord, Pierre. *Charles de Foucauld: Français d'Afrique.* Fayard, 1957.

Pichon, Charles. *Charles de Foucauld.* Éd. de la Nouvelle France, 1946.

Poirier, L. *Charles de Foucauld et l'appel du silence.* Mame, 1936.

———. *Charles de Foucauld au Maroc.* Mame, 1948.

Pottier, R. *La Vocation saharienne du père de Foucauld.* Plon, 1939.

———. *Charles de Foucauld et Marie de Magdala.* Sorlet, 1942.

———. *Charles de Foucauld le prédéstiné.* Sorlet, 1944.

Quesnel, Roger. *Charles de Foucauld, les étapes d'une recherche.* Mame, 1966.

Renard, E. *Le Père de Foucauld.* Spes, 1932.

Robert, C. M. *L'Ermite du Hoggar.* Baconnier, 1938.

Schneider. *Le Petit Pauvre dans ses ermitages.* Grasset, 1930.

Segonzac, R. de. *Le Père de Foucauld.* Éd. du Panorama, 1933.

Six, J.-F. *Itinéraire spirituel de Charles de Foucauld.* Seuil, 1958.

———. *Vie de Charles de Foucauld.* Seuil, 1962.

———. *Charles de Foucauld aujourd'hui.* Seuil, 1966.

———. *L'Aventure de l'amour de Dieu.* Seuil, 1993. About Foucauld and Massignon.

Vandewalle. *Charles de Foucauld.* Fleurus, 1984. Comic book.

Vaussard, M.-M. *Charles de Foucauld, maître de la vie intérieure.* Cerf, 1933.

Vignau, J. *Frère Charles ou la vie héroïque de Charles de Foucauld.* Albin Michel, 1943.

Vignon. *Charles de Foucauld.* Fleurus, 1953.

Ville, L. *L'Ermite de Beni-Abbès.* Tolra, 1929.
Voillaume, R. *Charles de Foucauld.* Chalet 1970.

Anonymous Works

Benedictine at la Pierre-qui-Vire. *Spiritualité du désert, le père de Foucauld.*
Saint-Paul, 1946.
Franciscan Missionaries of Mary. *Le Père de Foucauld.* Vanves, 1931.

Theses

Durand, Bénédicte. "Charles de Foucauld géographe." Master's thesis in
geography, Paris, Sorbonne, 1991.
Kergoat, Louis. "Charles de Foucauld et l'Islam." Doctoral dissertation, Paris,
Sorbonne.
Ledoux, Richard. "L'Apostolat du père de Foucauld au Sahara." Montreal,
1987.

Audiovisual

Chatelard, A. *Charles de Foucauld.* 14380 Saint-Sever: Atelier du Carmel.
Audio montage.
Delaborde, J. *Charles de Foucauld.* 1987. Audiovisual montage.
Poirier, Léon. *l'Appel du silence.* 1936. Film. Television version for French
channel TF1 and videocassette, Paris, 45 *bis*, rue de la Glacière: Voir et
dire, 1996. Poirier's book with the same title was published in 1936 by
Mame.

Journals Devoted to Foucauld

L'Appel du Hoggar. Bulletin of the organization Amitiés Foucauld l'Africain.
Bul. trimestriel des Amitiés Charles de Foucauld. Bulletin of the Association
Charles de Foucauld. Since 1965.
Cahiers Charles de Foucauld.
Jesus Caritas. Quarterly of the Message de C. de Foucauld association and
the fraternity. Since 1954.

Miscellaneous

Bernard-Marie, frère. *Le Père Crozier, l'ami stigmatisé du père de Foucauld.*
Chalet, 1988.
Blanguermont, Claude. *Le Hoggar.* Arthaud, 1984.

Gilbert-Lafon. *Écho des entretiens de l'abbé Huvelin*. Roblot, 1917.

Gorrée, G., and M. Thiout. *Laperrine, la plus belle amitié du père de Foucauld.* Arthaud, 1946.

Huvelin, Henri. *Quelques directeurs d'âmes au XVIIᵉ siècle*. Lecoffre, 1925.

———. *L'Amour de Notre-Seigneur*. Lecoffre, 1925.

Lafon, Michel. *Vivre Nazareth aujourd'hui, la famille spirituelle de Charles de Foucauld*. Fayard, 1984.

———. *Le Père Périguère, disciple de Charles de Foucauld*. Fayard, 1993.

———. *Prier quinze jours avec Charles de Foucauld*. Nouvelle Cité, 1996.

Lefebvre, M. T. *L'Abbé Huvelin*. Lethielleux, 1956.

Lyautey, Louis. *Paroles d'action*. Colin, 1927.

———. *Chevauchées impériales*. Spes, 1939.

Magdeleine de Jésus. *Du Sahara au monde entier*. Nouvelle Cité, 1981. The author is the founder of the Petites Soeurs de Jésus.

Massignon, Louis. *Parole donnée*. Seuil, 1983. Massignon's collected writings.

———. *Correspondance Claudel-Massignon 1908–1914*. Desclée, 1973.

Portier, L. *Un Précurseur, l'abbé Huvelin*. Paris, 1979.

Pottier, R. *Un Prince saharien méconnu, Henri Duveyrier*. Plon, 1938.

Sanson, C. *l'Union apostolique du Père Crozier et du Père de Foucauld*. Paris, 1984.

Vermale, Paul. *Au Sahara*. Larose, 1926.

Voillaume, R. *Lettres aux fraternités, À la suite de Jésus, Au coeur des masses, les fraternités*, etc. Cerf. Works by the founder of the Petits frères de Jésus.

Index

Information about Charles de Foucauld has been arranged under four main entries: Foucauld, Charles de (child); Foucauld, Charles de (explorer and officer); Foucauld, Charles de (monk); and Foucauld, Charles de (priest and hermit).

on Charles' health and mission, 93,
  260–61, 266, 267–68
and colonization of Africa, 207, 209–
  12, 250–51, 266, 279, 288–89, 290
at fall of Fort Djanet, 39–40
and pacification tours, 68, 210–22, 228,
  274
Latouche, Adolphe de, 62 n. 30
Latouche, Amélie de. *See* Morlet, Amélie
  de (step-grandmother of Charles)
Latouche, Georges de (cousin of
  Charles), 27, 72
  as conservator for Charles, 62–63, 62
    n. 30, 70
  on explorations of Charles, 66–68, 67
    n. 1, 70, 79–80, 82, 91
Lau, Bishop, 237 n. 29
Laurain, Father, 272–73
Lehureau, Captain (commander of
  Southern Territories), 284–85
Leo XIII, 128, 175
Lettres persanes (Montesquieu), 36
Life of Jesus (Renan), 30
Little Brothers of Foucauld, 287 n. 10
Little Brothers of the Heart of Jesus,
  176
  companions,
    awaiting, 197–201, 208, 220, 264
    first companions, 250–54, 254 n. 16,
      255, 331
    Massignon, 93, 118, 269–71, 275–76,
      280–81
    recruitment of, 190, 220, 236–37,
      247
  conversion by love, 264–69, 267 n. 7,
    276–77
  founding,
    approval by Vatican, 272–73
    permission, 173–75, 178–79, 198–
      201
  lay association,
    establishment, 295, 296–97, 297
      nn. 39–41
    formation, 268, 269, 272–73, 284
  mission of, 171–73, 264, 268, 325
  rules, 187 n. 5
    early ideas, 130–35, 137–39, 162–
      68
    modified, 236–37, 309
    and structure, 255, 281

spiritual family, 329–31
  congregations and associations, 332–
    34
  first fraternities, 331–32
Littré, Maximilien, 30, 99, 99 n. 23
Livinhac, Bishop (superior general of
  White Fathers), 183, 192–93, 330
Loti, Pierre, 36
Louis IX, Saint (king of France), 22
Louis Philippe (king of France), 95
  n. 12
Lyautey, General (resident general of
  Morocco), 59, 60, 225–26
  on holiness of Charles, 226–27, 250–
    51
  policies of, 226, 265, 291, 296, 298

MacCarthy, Oscar (explorer), 74–75
  rapport with Charles, 68–70, 83, 84
Magdeleine, Sister (founder of Little
  Sisters), 331, 332
marabout,
  defined, 39 n. 37
Mardochée Abi Serour,
  character of, 70, 72, 75, 76
  in Moroccan exploration, 70–81, 81
    n. 15
Marie-Ange de Saint-Michel, Mother
  (abbess of Poor Clares), 152–53, 160–
    62
Marthoud, Dom Polycarpe (founder of
  Notre-Dame-des-Neiges), 113, 115,
    123
  on asceticism and holiness, 124, 125–
    28
  on Charles' founding new order, 132–
    35
Martin, Dom (abbot of Notre-Dame-
  des-Neiges), 116, 119
  on holiness of Charles, 117, 179, 199–
    200
  and ordination of Charles, 173–74, 175,
    176
martyrdom and death, desire for, 127–28,
  135, 167, 176
  changes in, 299
  on day of Charles' death, 317, 317
    n. 5
  in depression over uselessness, 252,
    258–60